PRAISE

for *Home Ground*

"*Home Ground* is a treasure house of a book, chocked with gems of the American vernacular. To learn these terms for features of the landscape is like putting on a new pair of glasses—the land comes more vividly into focus. But to call this a reference work is to shortchange it—the entries are written by some of our best writers, and the result is an unexpected page turner."
— **Michael Pollan**

"A way of reclaiming the language that gives definition to landscape from the denatured terms of modern public discourse. It celebrates specificity."
— *New York Times*

"The most exquisite kind of wisdom . . . Fabulously well-executed, a gift in every sense of the word."
— *Chicago Tribune*

"A keeper for anyone who is curious about words for physical spaces and places."
— *Minneapolis Star Tribune*

"A fascinating work in landscape etymology."
— *Washington Post*

"Dazzling. . . . An e
like an act of patr
— *Memphis*

HOME GROUND

Trinity University Press would like to thank
the many people who dedicated their intelligence,
imagination, and talents to making *Home Ground* a reality.

We also wish to express our deep gratitude to
the following individuals and organizations
for generously supporting the project.

ANONYMOUS

JOHN AND SUSAN BRENNAN

THE FAMILY ADVISORY BOARD
OF THE COMPTON FOUNDATION

THE KENDEDA FUND

NATIVE SONS NURSERY, INC.,
ARROYO GRANDE, CALIFORNIA

HOME GROUND

A Guide to the American Landscape

BARRY LOPEZ AND
DEBRA GWARTNEY, EDITORS

TRINITY UNIVERSITY PRESS
SAN ANTONIO

Published by Trinity University Press
San Antonio, Texas 78212

Cover design by Rebecca Lown
Book design by BookMatters, Berkeley
Jacket illustration: Mountain Waterfall,
©iStockphoto.com/Tony Link Design

ISBN 978-1-59534-175-4 paper
ISBN 978-1-59534-088-7 ebook

CIP data on file at the Library of Congress.

23 22 21 / 5 4

Contributing Editors
WILLIAM L. GRAF
KEVIN BLAKE

Advisory Editor
KATHLEEN C. PARKER

———————————

Advisory Board
KENNETH I. HELPHAND
MARY HUFFORD
ENRIQUE LAMADRID
IAN STIRLING
ISABEL STIRLING
BARRE TOELKEN
LUIS VERANO

Researchers
LORRIE NELSON   JULIE POLHEMUS

———————————

BARRY ANCELET   IVY MILLER
EMMA HARDESTY   RICHARD NELSON
RYAN HEDIGER   LAURET SAVOY
LAWRENCE KAPLAN   ROGER WELSCH
KATE WESTHAVER

*The writers wish to express their
gratitude to the many writers and informants
who aided their research.*

WRITERS

AND THEIR HOME GROUNDS

JEFFERY RENARD ALLEN
Chicago, and now New York City

KIM BARNES
Clearwater Country in Idaho—its mountains,
its rivers, and all of its feeding streams

CONGER BEASLEY, JR.
Wah-to-yah ("Breasts of the World") or Spanish Peaks, Colorado

FRANKLIN BURROUGHS
Bowdoinham, Maine

LAN SAMANTHA CHANG
Iowa City, Iowa

MICHAEL COLLIER
My birthplace, Phoenix, Arizona

ELIZABETH COX
Chattanooga, Tennessee

JOHN DANIEL
Upper Long Tom River, inland Coast Range foothills, Oregon

JAN DEBLIEU
The Outer Banks, North Carolina

WILLIAM DEBUYS
Sangre de Cristo Mountains, New Mexico

GRETEL EHRLICH
Wyoming and the central coast of California

CHARLES FRAZIER
The Southern Appalachians

PAMELA FRIERSON
Volcano country of Hawai'i Island

PATRICIA HAMPL
The North Shore of Lake Superior

ROBERT HASS
*The San Francisco Bay Area, where I was born
and grew up and where I now live*

EMILY HIESTAND
*Coastal Massachusetts—from Cape Ann to the
Boston Basin—and the American South*

LINDA HOGAN
*I relate to Oklahoma strongly, but love my little valley where I live
with my horses in Idledale, Colorado, near the Red Rocks Park*

STEPHEN GRAHAM JONES
*West Texas. More specifically: the Permian Basin. More specific:
a place called Greenwood, about fifteen miles east of Midland.*

JOHN KEEBLE
The Interior West. We live in rural eastern Washington.

BARBARA KINGSOLVER
The terminus of Walker Ridge, Holston River watershed, Virginia

WILLIAM KITTREDGE
*Missoula County, Montana, where I've lived for over thirty
years, and Lake County, Oregon, where I grew up*

JON KRAKAUER
Boulder County, Colorado

GRETCHEN LEGLER
*The little eighty-acre parcel I share with my
partner, Ruth, in the woods near Jay, Maine*

ARTURO LONGORIA
The Texas brushlands, Zapata County and Starr County, Texas

BILL MCKIBBEN
The mountains on either side of Lake Champlain

ELLEN MELOY
The canyons of the lower San Juan River, Utah

ROBERT MORGAN
Southern Appalachians of western North Carolina, though I have lived in the Finger Lakes region of upstate New York for thirty-five years, and in many ways that seems like home also

SUSAN BRIND MORROW
New York State

ANTONYA NELSON
Route 66

ROBERT MICHAEL PYLE
Gray's River, Wahkiakum County, Washington

PATTIANN ROGERS
A mile east of Wildcat Point, the site of Kit Carson's last campfire, Colorado

SCOTT RUSSELL SANDERS
Monroe County, Indiana

EVA SAULITIS
Prince William Sound, Alaska

DONNA SEAMAN
The beautiful Hudson Valley in New York State. My true place is Poughkeepsie.

CAROLYN SERVID
Sitka, Alaska

KIM STAFFORD
Columbia River watershed

MARY SWANDER
Kalona, Iowa

ARTHUR SZE
Santa Fe, New Mexico

MIKE TIDWELL
Takoma Park, Maryland

LUIS ALBERTO URREA
*My heart's home ground is the Front Range of the
Rocky Mountains from border to border*

LUIS VERANO
The South Hills, Eugene, Oregon

D. J. WALDIE
*Lakewood, a working-class suburb of Long Beach, California,
where I still live in the house my parents bought in 1946*

JOY WILLIAMS
Cascabel, Arizona, and the Ducktrap River, Maine

TERRY TEMPEST WILLIAMS
The Colorado Plateau

LARRY WOIWODE
Southwestern North Dakota

CONTENTS

INTRODUCTION

BY BARRY LOPEZ

SOME YEARS AGO I WALKED INTO THE OFFICE OF A MAN
named Jim Kari, at the time the director of the Native
Language Center at the University of Alaska, and was
brought up short by a striking contrast posted on his wall.
Arranged side by side above his desk were a pair of identical United States Geological Survey maps showing the
topography of a section of south-central Alaska's Susitna
Valley. The map on the left bristled with more than a
hundred colored pushpins, each bearing a tiny paper flag
with a Deni'ina place-name on it, the Athabaskan language spoken by the indigenous people still living there.
Fewer than a dozen names appeared in English on the
right, neatly printed on the quadrangle as an official part
of the map.

Mr. Kari's point, that a region hardly known to its relatively new landlords is, in fact, minutely and extensively
known to its long-term residents, dramatizes a truism
about belonging, about intimacy with a place. The deeper
point made on me by Mr. Kari's maps that morning is
that the English words on them were arbitrarily chosen,
little more than points of orientation. The Deni'ina words,
which Mr. Kari had gathered during his years of hiking
the Susitna River drainage and interviewing resident
people, had grown up over many centuries, out of the
natural convergence of human culture with a particular
place.

Mr. Kari's declaration, about arbitrary imposition and
real authority, given a much larger frame of reference,

amounts to an observation about modern loss and belonging which many of us can identify with. Some of us in the United States can trace our family lines back many generations to, say, the Green Mountains of western Vermont, the urban hills of the San Francisco peninsula, or the sandhills of western Nebraska; to small towns along the Mississippi River or a red-earth farm in Alabama. Many of us have come from ranching, farming, or logging families, and might have listened with a measure of envy while a grandparent spoke of these places of origin, using a language so suited to the place being described it fit against it like another kind of air. A language capable of conveying the most evanescent of the place's characteristics.

Today, the majority of us raise our families, go to school, find employment, and locate much of our inspiration in urban areas. The land beyond our towns, for many, has become a generalized landscape of hills and valleys, of beaches, rivers, and monotonous deserts. Almost against our wills the countrysides of our parents' and grandparents' generations—the Salinas Valley we might have once pictured reading John Steinbeck, images of Sarah Orne Jewett's Maine or the barefoot country of Eudora Welty's stories, of Willa Cather's Nebraska and New Mexico—almost without our knowing it, the particulars of these landscapes have slipped away from us. Asked, we might still conjure them, but we probably could no longer still name the elements that make them vivid in our memories.

It has become a commonplace observation about American culture that we are a people groping for a renewed sense of place and community, that we want to be more meaningfully committed, less isolated. Many of us have come to wonder whether modern American life, with its accelerated daily demands and its polarizing choices, isn't indirectly undermining something foundational, something essential to our lives. We joke that one shopping mall looks just like another, that a housing development on the outskirts of Denver feels no different to us than a housing development outside Kansas City, but we are not always amused by such observations. No more than we are amused when someone from the rural countryside implies that his life is spiritually richer than ours because the place we've chosen to live is Park Slope in Brooklyn or the South Side of Chicago.

What many of us are hopeful of now, it seems, is being able to gain—or regain—a sense of allegiance with our chosen places, and along with that a sense of affirmation with our neighbors that the place we've chosen is beautiful, subtle, profound, worthy of our lives.

It is with these thoughts, about the importance of belonging, of knowing the comfort that a feeling of intimate association with a place can bring, that we began work on *Home Ground*. We wanted to recall and to explore a language more widespread today than most of us imagine, because we believed an acquaintance with it, using it to say more clearly and precisely what we mean, would bring us a certain kind of relief. It would draw us closer to the landscapes upon which we originally and hopefully founded our democratic arrangement for governing ourselves, our systems of social organization, and our enterprise in economics. If we could speak more accurately, more evocatively, more familiarly about the physical places we occupy, perhaps we could speak more penetratingly, more insightfully, more compassionately about the flaws in these various systems which, we regularly assert, we wish to address and make better.

AS A BOY GROWING UP IN THE SAN FERNANDO VALLEY OF southern California, I found solace in the way big winds blew through groves of eucalyptus trees in this—back then—agricultural region. The animated rustling that enlivened those trees. I found inspiration in the stark barrenness of the Mojave Desert, in the way storm surf exploded on the coastal beaches, and in the splendor of Hoover (at the time, Boulder) Dam. Later, an adolescent in the Murray Hill section of Manhattan in the late 1950s, I became familiar with a landscape altogether different from this one. I was sent to camp that first summer on Long Island's South Fork. Before this, I thought only rivers forked. My family bought a second home "at the shore," in Bay Head, New Jersey—it wasn't called "the coast" here. We made family trips to New Hampshire, where there was such a thing as a monadnock; and out on Staten Island, I learned, they called some of the sloughs and creeks kills. I remember speculating then with my younger brother about the formerly enigmatic Peekskill, New York, whether it wasn't named for the kill on which Mr. Peek had his farm.

My prep school friends on 83rd Street in Manhattan described the Pine Barrens of New Jersey contemptuously as a cultural and geographic extension of Appalachia, accurate on neither count; and they described the Finger Lakes of western New York as a romantic locale, a place you might want to honeymoon. The image of a "finger" lake preoccupied me for a while as a twelve-year-old. Were there five of them in parallel? Did something like a palm connect them all?

My roommate in college felt the same compulsion I did to travel and to see the physical world. On any given weekend we might drive as much as a thousand miles to get to the Straits of Mackinac in northern Michigan, or see the woody draws and prehistoric ceremonial mounds of eastern Iowa, the bayous and playrees of Mississippi, and the bluegrass hills of central Kentucky. Was there a season, we'd wonder, when they were bluest?

Driving the country wasn't the obsession for us; it was seeing how these varied landscapes followed up on one another, from one side of the continent to the other. Through my late teens and early twenties especially, but down to the present, too, I'd drive whatever distance was needed to actually come up on, for example, the Painted Hills of eastern Oregon. Or to watch light shimmer on windswept sawgrass prairies in central Florida. Everywhere I went, state promotional materials touted their home ground as "the land of contrasts." Some had more contrast than others, of course, and in a few, like North Dakota, the contrast was subtle. The country as a whole, however, had contrast enough—in its lava fields, alpine tundra, canyons, and barrier islands—to defeat a lifetime of looking. Further, many of these landforms, depending on where you went or whom you asked, were called—the very same landforms—by different and occasionally quite local names. In that lifetime, you might never get it all straight.

It had come to me as a fourteen-year-old reading *Moby-Dick*, a moral drama set in an intensely physical place, that this seemingly unfettered, nearly unmeasureable American landscape I had become acquainted with (Colorado's fourteeners, Appalachia's Carolina bays, Manhattan's tidal races, a complex landscape, robust with suggestions of freedom, power, and purity) it came to me that this particular landscape had distinctively stamped the long line of American literature, starting with Cooper and Hawthorne and coming up through Twain, Cather, and Steinbeck, through Stegner, Mary Oliver, and Peter Matthiessen, through Wendell Berry and Gary Snyder. In fact, it is striking the degree to which the work of so many American writers is informed by sentences of wonder, meditation, and confoundment, of intimacy, alienation, and homage, inspired by the features—plowed land, deep woods, mountain streams—of American landscapes. In *Inheritance of Night*, William Styron writes: "You look out once more at the late summer landscape and the low sorrowful beauty of the tideland streams, turgid and involute and secret and winding through marshes full of small, darting, frightened noises and glistening and dead silent at noon except for a whistle, far off, and a distant rumble on the rails."

Whatever their styles and emphases, many American poets and novelists have recognized that something emotive abides in the land, and that it can be recognized and evoked even if it cannot be thoroughly plumbed. It is inaccessible to the analytic researcher, invisible to the ironist. To hear the unembodied call of a place, that numinous voice, one has to wait for it to speak through the harmony of its features—the soughing of the wind across it, its upward reach against a clear night sky, its fragrance after a rain. One must wait for the moment when the thing—the hill, the tarn, the lunette, the kiss tank, the caliche flat, the bajada—ceases to be a thing and becomes something that knows we are there.

IN MY EARLY TWENTIES I CAME UPON ERWIN RAISZ'S hand-drawn maps of the continental United States, done while he was teaching at Harvard in the 1930s and 40s, a kind of cartography that bordered on fine art. His creations are distinguished by a level of detail that is almost bewildering, by an absence of roads, and by a variety of typefaces (including his own hand-printed letters) that tend to disappear into the maps' shaded contours, enhancing the sense that you're looking at a document in which the authority of the place, the physical eminence of it, overwhelms all else. The one I have in hand now, drawn in 1941, was issued in a revised edition in 1965, a few years before I purchased it. It's called *Landforms of the Northwestern States* and includes Washington, Oregon, Idaho, and the mountains of western Montana. It measures about three feet by two. Its white paper is soiled from handling and worn through at its creases from refolding. These flaws, however, only intensify for me a sense that Raisz's depiction is of a fabled land, a place that, like a palimpsest, lies invisible beneath all the commercial roadmaps I've used over the years.

It would take hours, and something akin to insatiable curiosity, for someone to pore over each of the map's revealing nib strokes. (Some of its features—the drainage of the Wounded Doe River in Idaho, or Mission Bottom, situated below the Eola Hills in western Oregon—are best brought to life with a magnifying glass and, overall, the task of full comprehension is nearly impossible without some sort of imposed grid, to keep one from getting lost in the pen-and-ink work.) The map suggests a novel, though it has neither narrator nor time line. Start your examination anywhere and you are soon impressed by how neatly all the pieces come together, the almost eerie continuity of it all. Raisz's approach to landscape here is of a fit with J. B. Jackson's writing about America's vernacular landscape. Raisz illustrated and Jackson, a cultural geographer in New Mexico, wrote with affection for the unpretentious.

Raisz employs two sorts of language on his Northwest map, colloquial and formal. In an unnamed valley east of Poker Jim Ridge in central Oregon, he uses the generalized descriptive "rolling sagebrush land, low relief." In eastern Washington, he labels an immensity of thousands of square miles "Channeled Scablands," a technical term geographers use to describe a singular landform, one created over several centuries at the end of the last ice age, when a glacial lake the size of Lake Huron repeatedly formed in Montana only to burst its western ice dams and roar again across southeastern Washington, creating a scoured landscape and deepening a gorge in the Cascade Mountains through which the Columbia still flows to the Pacific.

Raisz's language pulls one as deeply into his maps as his graphics, which seem such a mysterious form of storytelling. There is no end to the allure of the names he placed on this particular map—the Horse Heaven Hills,

Disgrace Creek, Craters of the Moon. Each is a unique place though, not a generic entity. Looking to other Raisz maps, I would wonder what a "scalded flat" might be, or a "pimple mound." And what about a "pencil bluff," an "eyebrow hill"? Some of these expressions I couldn't find in any book I consulted, though people somewhere probably used these words every day to designate a feature that oriented them in space, like "hole," "basin," "fork," or "meadow." This was a fundamental language. Something or other had a hole in it, or it split apart like the tines of a fork, or it looked like somebody's eyebrow. Like Jim Kari's Deni'ina map, the language on Raisz's maps radiates a sense of belonging.

Raisz's maps lack the high resolution, scale, color, and specificity of modern U.S. Geological Survey quadrangles, but they are intimate and neighborly where the latter are cool and analytic. They are in harmony with the unprecedented views humans first experienced in the initial decades of the Age of Flight, when pilots navigated by looking at the ground below, when they became the first of us to take in entire creek drainages at a glance, when, like Beryl Markham and St-Exupéry, they were dazzled by the scope of what they could see, by the detail in it, not yet obscured by speed, greater altitude, and fouled air.

The maps, then, I began studying as a child, the country I started driving through as a young man—a maze of winding, unpaved roads in the Smoky Mountains, the redrock canyon country of the Colorado Plateau, the farmlands of the San Joaquin Valley, with their windbreaks of lombardy poplars—and, finally, the local speech that might be overheard in rural cafés or elicited by a traveler seeking directions: all this combined to prompt questions about what, in the end, one could really know about the larger home land. What was the difference between a clove and a hollow to West Virginians? How many types of flats were there in the West—creosote flats, gumbo flats, antelope flats, tidal flats? Would trying to sidle through terrain vague (the narrow space between two city buildings) tell you something about the stark nature of a city, in the same way squeezing through a slot canyon in Utah would be revealing about the Colorado Plateau? And what *was* a ronde (as in Grande Ronde, Oregon), a yazoo (Yazoo, Mississippi), a vega (Las Vegas, Nevada)?

One windy day after a week of rain I was driving east across the Llano Estacado in panhandle Texas with a local man. He said, "Look yonder at them white caps in the bar ditch," and I caught a sense of the open ocean on the Staked Plain of Francisco Vásquez de Coronado. When I traveled to eastern Washington late one summer to see for the first time the unbroken expanse of wheat growing on low, rolling land there, a stretch of loess hills local people call the Palouse, it seemed an erotic landscape to me. What would a child's erotic landscape be?

DURING A LONG PERIOD OF FIELD RESEARCH THAT brought me into regular contact with wild animals on their remote home grounds, and after decades of living in a place where wild animals from deer mice and dusky shrews to Roosevelt elk and black bear are common, I've wondered what they see that we miss. Or what we so frequently miss because we are impatient and cursory. The human eye is sensitive to a narrow range of electromagnetic energy; and we're predisposed to divide the whole of a landscape into objects of a certain size and limit—a gulch, a woodlot, a pond. Much that would be arresting to an animal's eye is not apparent to us. How is the land we see divided and composed according to the way we see? What draws our attention?

It's hard to see deeply into a landscape that, at first glance, appears to be without distinction—the mixed woods monotony of a New England hillside, for example. After a patient and close look, however, one might nevertheless be able to pick out clusters of the same species of tree emerging from that visual chaos. Logic suggests some quality of the soil favors the presence of this species over others in that particular place—a trace mineral or marginally better drainage. It's just these slight variations in the chemistry and texture of the soil, in fact, that give a particular stretch of woods its distinctive regional look, that allow someone to say with authority, "That's a Berkshire hillside."

The subtly discontinuous nature of a hillside forest or a prairie grassland is often due to the presence of a catena. When bedrock begins to disintegrate—an early stage in the development of soils—its homogenous raw materials are affected differently by such things as drainage patterns, contours, and the degree of the slope on which they rest. The debris produced within a limited area by a parent rock eventually becomes a closely associated set of soils, each one taking on an individual identity as it matures. A trained eye infers the existence of such a catena—a drift of adjacent sibling soils—from the color, general health, and spacing of different species of trees and grasses across a hillside.

Many landscape features that initially seem identical in our eyes to landforms we've seen elsewhere turn out, on close examination, to be unique to a place. In part this accounts for the large number of differing regional terms used for similar landforms, many of which have never been written down. And it helps explain why a creek in Wyoming is not the same thing as a creek in Maine, and why there is such a large family of dunes, from medanos to lunettes. If you are hiking in northwestern New Mexico, someone local might guide you through a tsegi. *Tse* is the Navajo word for rock, and *tsegi* the generic term for canyon. Similarly, an Iñupiaq hunter in Alaska might guide you through a landscape of *piŋut* (pingos) on the coastal plain or *nunatat* (nunataks) in the Brooks Range, Iñupiaq terms familiar in their anglicized form to many Alaskans. While some regional non-English terms have come into widespread use—bayou (Choctaw), esker (Gaelic), arête (French), cripple (Dutch), playa (Spanish)—other regionalisms such as delmarva bay and sassat remain opaque to an outsider. How a particular culture or subculture divides and names the features of its homescape, and the way it perceives how one thing grades into another—when exactly a draw becomes a gulch or a tarn a lake—is in the end peculiar to that culture. Thus, it's hard to be certain about what someone else's word for something might be. Or even what that word might mean.

In "Descriptive Topographic Terms of Spanish America," an article that appeared in the September 1896 issue of *National Geographic*, Robert T. Long laments a lack of English-language descriptive terms for land features in the Southwest, offering his praise for the far greater range of Spanish terms with which he had become familiar. In *How the Canyon Became Grand*, Stephen Pyne traces the evolution of the notion of a "grand" canyon on the Colorado River, starting with the first Spanish perception of it as no more than a huge, inconvenient ditch, thwarting the advance of explorers not at all familiar with a *cañón* on this scale. In *All the Pretty Horses*, Cormac McCarthy's riveting evocation of the west Texas borderland through which he has his protagonists moving is so strong it nearly eclipses the presence of the two riders. In each of these three works, one is aware of the intensity of the author's connection to a particular region, and of the great array of terms we use to locate ourselves in such potentially effacing landscapes. We employ domestic animals (hogback ridge), domestic equipment (kettle moraine), food (basket-of-eggs relief), furniture (looking-glass prairie), clothing (the aprons of a bajada), and, extensively, ourselves: a neck of land, an arm of the sea, rock nipples, the toe of a slope, the mouth of a river, a finger drift, the shoulder of a road. We do this intentionally, to make what is separate from us a part of where we are. We put a geometry to the land—backcountry, front range, high desert—and pick out patterns in it: pool and riffle, swale and rise, basin and range. We make it remote (north forty), vivid (bird-foot delta), and humorous (detroit riprap).

It is a language that keeps us from slipping off into abstract space.

THE POCKINGS MOUNTAIN SHEEP LEAVE BEHIND WHEN they nose snow aside to get at buried grass are called feeding craters. When a rainbow trout strikes a mayfly on the placid surface of a creek, the departing ripples mark a fish strike. These things are too ephemeral to be taken for landforms or waterforms. For the scorched earth that forest fires leave behind, however, we have a word: brûlé. When a meandering river cuts through a point bar and leaves behind a meander scar, and the scar fills with water, we call it an oxbow lake. We try to slow and steady the temporal and spatial scales of the Earth's dynamic surface, to have it conform more closely with our own scale of living and understanding.

The language we employ to say what we're looking at or to recall what we've seen, for many English speakers, is now collapsing toward an attenuated list of almost nondescript words—valley, lake, mountain. Used along with "like a," these words now stand in for glade, tank, and escarpment. Most of us today are more aware of brown lands than wetlands, the former an expanding urban habitat, the latter a shrinking natural one. Fewer of the people who once made up the country's farming cultures are now around to explain what an envelope field is. The old-time loggers have taken the cowfaced slopes with them into retirement. And the jackass miners of the Mojave are no longer around to tell us how an adit differs from an aven. At a time when the country's landscapes are increasingly treated as commodities, subjected to a debate over their relative and intrinsic worth, and when city planners, land conservators, real estate developers, and indigenous title holders square off every day over the fate of one place or another, this can't be good.

ONCE, ON THE UPPER BORO RIVER IN BOTSWANA, traveling in dugout canoes with local tribesmen, I went ashore with ten or twelve others to rest in the shade of acacia trees during the heat of the day. The men conversed quietly in Tswana. The sound of the language was so beautiful in my ear I turned on a portable tape recorder so I could listen to it again in the years ahead, or maybe play it one day for Aranda people in Australia, whose language I also like to hear, the run of it, mellifluous, like birdsong.

We have a shapely language, American English. A polyglot speech, grown up from a score of European, African, and Asian immigrant tongues, and complexly veined with hundreds of expressions native to the places we now occupy—Uto-Aztecan, Eyak-Athabaskan, Iroquoian, Muskogean, Caddoan, and Salishan. We have named the things we've picked out on the land, and we've held on to the names to make ourselves abiding and real, to enable us to resist the appeal of make-believe lands, hawked daily as anodynes by opportunists, whose many schemes for wealth hinge on our loss of memory, the anxiety of our alienation, our hunger after substance.

IN THE PAGES THAT FOLLOW, A COMMUNITY OF WRITERS has set down definitions for landscape terms and terms for the forms that water takes, each according to his or her own sense of what's right, what's important to know. The definitions have been reviewed for accuracy by professional geographers, but the writers' intent was not to be exhaustive, let alone definitive. In concert with each other, they wanted to suggest the breadth and depth of a language many of us still seek to use purposefully every day. Their intent was to celebrate and inform, and to point us toward the great body of work which they perused in their research and which, along with a life experience of their own, they brought into play to craft what they had to say.

It was my privilege, and that of Debra Gwartney, the managing editor, to have worked to bring their conception to these pages.

BARRY LOPEZ
McKenzie River, Oregon

HOME GROUND

ʻaʻā

While highly fluid pāhoehoe lava can flow like a river,
with no more than a slight metallic hiss, rubblelike ʻaʻā
lava moves with a sound like crockery breaking. Much
Hawaiian volcanic terrain is streaked with both kinds
of congealed lava. It is hard to imagine that shiny, ropy
pāhoehoe could come from the same source as the dull,
jagged clinkers of an ʻaʻā flow, but lava may emerge from
a vent as ʻaʻā rather than pāhoehoe if it has undergone a
vigorous stirring during the eruption. The transformation can also occur on the surface as pāhoehoe plunges
down a steep slope, becoming more viscous from loss
of gas. Hawaiians have long summed up the unforgiving
nature of ʻaʻā in sayings such as *He ʻaʻā ko ka hale*, which
means "Only lava rocks [ʻaʻā] will be found in [that]
house," suggesting an incident of domestic calamity.
And yet ʻaʻā fields have traditionally been used to grow
sweet potato: Hawaiian farmers constructed trails across
them made of smooth stepping stones, piled compost in
the rubble, and planted seeds.   PAMELA FRIERSON

abutment

Often used in architecture to indicate the support pressure
formed to sustain an arch or span by another force such as
a pier or wall, and in dentistry to refer to the immediately
adjacent teeth supporting a dental bridge, abutment is
rooted in the French *abut*, which suggests a limit or the
place where ends meet. In *Suttree*, Cormac McCarthy
writes: "As he came about the abutment and entered the
gloom beneath the bridge three boys darted out the far
side and clambered over the rocks and disappeared in the
woods by the river." A bridge abutment, or the abutment
of a dam, is the connection between the metal or cement
structure and the river's bank. There is the sense as well
that natural formations—rock arches and natural bridges,
for instance—form such a junction with their supporting

sidewalls. In *Walden*, Henry David Thoreau writes: "Once it chanced that I stood in the very abutment of a rainbow's arch, which filled the lower stratum of the atmosphere, tingeing the grass and leaves around, and dazzling me as if I looked through colored crystal."   PATRICIA HAMPL

accordant landscape

Synonyms for the adjective accordant include consonant, agreeing, harmonious, corresponding, so it comes as no surprise that an accordant landscape contains two or more matching or congruent topographical features. Streams, folds, or summits, for instance, that occur at approximately the same elevation or have a similar orientation create accordant landscapes. Such uniform terrain can seem peaceful or monotonous, depending on your state of mind.   DONNA SEAMAN

acequia

Acequias, or irrigation ditches, are found throughout the American Southwest. The word comes from the Arabic *al-sāqiya*, which means "water conduit" (not necessarily for irrigation). The Moors, who occupied Spain for nearly 800 years, until 1492, were deeply versed in survival techniques from the North African deserts and introduced methods for water management to the Iberian Peninsula. In the sixteenth century, Spanish colonists to the arid Southwest brought with them a sophisticated understanding of irrigation systems, which in some areas merged with equally elaborate systems devised by pre-Columbian cultures, such as the Hohokam of central Arizona. Settlements throughout the Southwest benefited from this knowledge. Water from a primary source, such as a river, was diverted into an *acequia madre* (mother ditch), which usually ran along the uphill edge of a string of meadows and fields. The course of the acequia was interrupted by

numerous gates or *presitas*, which divided the water into
smaller ditches called *regaderas* that radiated through
the fields like capillaries from an artery—a notion that
the Spanish terminology incorporates. "You had to
admire those first settlers," writes William deBuys in
his book *River of Traps*. "Without benefit of transits or
levels they laid the ditch out so that the water neither
charged nor pooled. They eased it along, although
the land was not easy, transforming the valley into a
garden." CONGER BEASLEY, JR.

acre

The distant, Indo-European root of the word acre did not
mean the measure of a place. It meant movement, specifically the movement of flocks driven over open ground.
As the word evolved, it came to indicate any untended
land. Finally, an acre became the abstract measure laid
over that land to commodify it. The evolution of acre
from open commons to private property took at least a
thousand years, but by the twelfth century an English
acre was a unit of land that a man and a yoke of oxen
could plow in a day. This was later fixed by custom and
statute in the United States as a square of land 208.7 feet
by 208.7 feet (43,560 square feet or 4,840 square yards).
For easier estimation, an acre is about the same area as an
American football field, excluding the end zones. In the
West's short-lived cattle economy of the open range
in the mid–nineteenth century, acres of land hardly
mattered, there were so many of them. Acres weren't for
measuring but for bragging. D.J. WALDIE

acre-foot

In a landscape where porcupines lead undisturbed lives,
every attentive resident knows how far you mean when
you say something is "two porcupines away"—it's twice
the breadth of what one has come to know as a single

porcupine range. Similarly, we learn to quickly locate a feature on the horizon if someone says, "It's a thumbnail to the left of the highest peak there." Folk measurements like these—or the stone's throw, the day's ride, or the pace—though not precise, are accurate. The acre-foot joins together two once imprecise folk measurements to create a term that, apparently, leaves nothing to interpretation. It's exactly 43,560 cubic feet of water—a single acre, one foot deep. Given the behavior of water, however, such precision is rarely dead accurate, which accounts for the enduring wisdom behind the use of folk measurements.   BARRY LOPEZ

---

aguaje

The word aguaje, as well as aguada, comes from the Span-ish word *agua*, meaning "water." In the American South-west and northern Mexico a water hole or water lot—a pond or trough for cattle—is called an aguaje. The word aguada is more commonly used in Honduras and other Central American countries, where it denotes essentially the same thing: a place to give cattle water. In Venezuela a small stream is called an aguaje.   ARTURO LONGORIA

---

ahupua‘a

The most important unit in the ancient Hawaiian system of land division was the ahupua‘a, a pie-shaped wedge running from a high point on the island to the coast and some distance out to sea. Since Hawaiian islands tend to have rain-carved valleys originating at central mountains and opening out toward the coast, an ahupua‘a often roughly followed the contours of watersheds. The coastal boundaries were marked by an *ahu*, a heap of piled stones supporting a carved wooden image of a *pua‘a*, or pig—symbol of the tribute paid annually to the paramount chief of the island by the lesser chiefs in charge of each ahupua‘a. The commoners within an ahupua‘a, living in extended families, held tenancy to small landholdings called *'ili*. The ahupua'a provided the resources to sustain a community: access to upland forests for timber, lowlands for growing crops, and fishing and gathering along a stretch of coast. This traditional system ended in 1848 when Kamehameha III was persuaded by foreigners to institute the Great Mahele (division), which allowed land to be bought and sold. In modern times ahupua'a holds both the traditional meaning and a broader one of environmentally responsible land use.   PAMELA FRIERSON

aimless drainage

A stream or river with an aimless drainage pattern wanders or meanders, it seems, at random across a plain, the flow resembling large, loopy script written on the land. Such meandering waterways—also known as deranged drainages—tend to form in either recently glaciated terrain, where no clear slope funnels water toward the sea, or in the collapsed limestone rubble of karst topography. Good examples of aimless drainages can be found in the glacier-scoured landscapes of Quebec Province.   JAN DEBLIEU

ait

An ait, or eyot as it is sometimes spelled, is a small island, especially one found in a river, but also in a lake. Ait is, in fact, derived from the Old English word for small island. In Mary Clearman Blew's *All But the Waltz: A Memoir of Five Generations in the Life of a Montana Family*, the author remembers going with her grandmother and a friend to rescue a sow and her piglets caught in the middle of the rain-swollen Judith River: "On a bare ait at midcurrent, completely surrounded and only inches above that muddy roiling water, huddle the pigs." Although the term is seldom heard in modern times, ait-land has a particularly pleasing aural kinship to its synonym island, despite the fact that the two do not share a common derivation. KIM BARNES

alcove

In its most common geologic application, alcove refers to a recess or niche in a cave or in the walls of complexly formed canyonland. This is one of many such terms with its origins in architectural expression. In a cave, an alcove may have the appearance of vaulting, as might alcoves in churches and cathedrals, and typically it would be adjacent to a wider chamber and likely permit no passage except back into that chamber where the principal action ensues. In canyonlands, an alcove may appear as a simple opening in a rock wall, adjacent to the ground or, higher up, to the open air, perhaps providing shelter from the elements, or a respite otherwise. The like can be seen in Canyon de Chelly and Alcove Canyon in Arizona, in Utah's Alcove Canyon, and at Alcove Mountain in the Flathead region of Montana. In a May 31, 1805, journal entry, Meriwether Lewis noted the sculpted, light-colored rock along the upper Missouri and, while reflecting the inclination of many other observers of the era to form their solace by envisioning landscape as evidence of God's handiwork, waxed rhetorical: "We see the remains of or ruins of eligant buildings; some collumns standing and almost entire with their pedestals and capitals . . . nitches and alcoves of various forms and sizes are seen at different heights as we pass . . . so perfect indeed are those walls that I should have thought that nature had attempted here to rival the human art of masonry had I not recollected that she had first begun her work." A less common application of the term is to fingers of still water that parallel a river and connect to it. These provide refuge for aquatic creatures, in this case from the turmoil of quicker currents in the prime chamber of their existence. Fish—salmon, trout, shiner, and sucker, among other species—seek out the rich supply of food here, especially during the scouring of high runoff periods. The relative quiet of such alcoves may also be favored by fish as breeding and rearing regions. The term extends to niches in the walls of oceanic environments as well, where creatures—sometimes mythical in their aspect—abide in the yet deeper dark.   JOHN KEEBLE

alluvial fan

Alluvium is the sediment deposited by the flow of a river, so an alluvial fan is the mass of sediment, sand and gravel, silt and clay, deposited in a fanlike shape by the flow of a mountain stream or river when it has left a confined channel and opened onto a broad plain. Alluvial fans occur in humid as well as arid and semiarid land-scapes, although the most prominent ones are in deserts. A series of fans, formed by parallel streams flowing out of a range of mountains, sometimes forms a continuous and overlapping apron of sediment which is called a bajada or alluvial apron. Norman Hinds notes an instance in his *Evolution of the California Landscape*: "Because of the height of the ranges around Death Valley and their consequently steep slopes, a host of valleys has been eroded into them and the streams have carried quantities of debris into the basin forming alluvial fans and aprons." ROBERT HASS

anchor ice

Anchor ice forms in freshwater like a second skin over the frozen bottoms of chilled rivers and streams. Cold bottom water slows and then pools behind stones, initiating its formation. Eventually, the spread of ice may bind rocks, plants, invertebrates, and other organisms together in sheets, pinning them to the streambed. In a similar fashion, anchor ice may coat submerged struc-tures or objects—pier footings and boat anchors—in cold, motionless water. Anchor ice also forms on the floors of polar seas, where it is known as *anaġlu* to Iñupiaq Eskimos. When the mass of this type of anchor ice is sufficient, it will suddenly break loose in jagged fragments and rise to the surface. (Exuding its salts diminishes the specific gravity of sea ice; when a section of it grows large enough for the force pushing it toward the surface to overcome the strength of its anchor hold, it rises.) In like fashion, when strong currents or storms churn the upper layers of water, the agitation might cause spears and blocks of anchor ice, with their load of embedded seaweed, abrasive sand, rocks, and shells, to break free. Such unexpected surfacing of huge ice chunks can upend, puncture, or damage a small boat. Other names include depth, underwater, and lappered ice.   EVA SAULITIS

angle of repose

Nearly self-explanatory, the oxymoronic-seeming term angle of repose designates the maximum angle at which a slope of loose material (such as soil or sand) remains stable. It is the point at which gravity challenges friction, the tense moment before one succumbs to the other. Particulate solids, poured onto a horizontal surface, will form a conical pile; the resulting slope—which depends on particle size, with larger particles supporting steeper slopes—is known as the angle of repose. It's a term begging to be made metaphorical for human relations, as Wallace Stegner demonstrates in his Pulitzer Prize–winning novel by the same name. In the book, the fraught connection of the present to the past, one generation to the next, replicates the peculiar tension between friction and gravity, between hanging on and falling apart. "You were too alert to the figurative possibilities of words not to see the phrase as descriptive of human as well as detrital rest," Stegner writes. "As you said, it was too good for mere dirt; you tried to apply it to your own wandering and uneasy life. It is the angle I am aiming for myself, and I don't mean the rigid angle at which I rest in this chair." ANTONYA NELSON

angostura

A narrow way: the narrows. A tight squeeze. The term angostura relates to the narrowest of mountain ravines or trails. (The harrowing scene in Cormac McCarthy's *Blood Meridian* where two mule trains meet—one going down a mountain and the other climbing—and one mule train is forced to plunge off the cliff in eerie silence, is a classic portrait of an encounter at an angostura. Anyone who has ridden a long-distance bus in Mexico, moreover, will never forget passing on a narrow curve at midnight.) In the water, an angostura could be a particularly tight stretch of river—expect whitewater there. One *could* extend it to the sea, since an angostura might be defined loosely as a strait, as in the Straits of Juan de Fuca—a reasonably tight stretch. However, the proper word in Spanish for this is *estrecho.* You know what they say about the Road to Heaven: *El camino al infierno es ancho, pero el camino al cielo es una angostura.* LUIS ALBERTO URREA

anse

Many of the earliest maps of the Great Lakes, drawn by French explorers and trappers, feature the oft-repeated word anse, French for inlet or bay. Such markers promised welcoming shelter for fledgling coastal settlements, many of which still bear the name. L'Anse, Michigan, a lumber community in Baraga County, is located on L'Anse Bay, an embayment of the larger Keweenaw Bay, part of Lake Superior. French-influenced maritime regions also bear the name, like the old sealing town of L'Anse-au-Loup—"wolf cove"—on the Labrador Coast of Newfoundland. On the island of Newfoundland, L'Anse aux Meadows marks the site of the first

European settlement in the Americas, founded about
A.D. 1000.   MIKE TIDWELL

antidune

Although it sounds endemic to the ocean shore, an
antidune is a feature of shallow, swift-running rivers
and creeks, an ephemeral ripple of sand that migrates
upstream against the water's flow. First a wave appears
on the surface while bottom currents dig out a tiny
furrow in the streambed; then the water slows slightly as
it climbs out of this dip, dropping some of the sediment
it carries. Over a few hours a long, low hump begins to
build on the streambed, perpendicular to the current.
This pattern continues: Water climbs the tiny dune
and slows, dropping sand, then rushes down the other
side, eroding the downstream face. The ripple moves
upstream, often quite rapidly. On the surface a wave
of water continues to stand, a reflection of the wave of
sand below. An antidune may travel several feet over
the course of a day, or after a short time it may simply
dissolve.   JAN DEBLIEU

aquifer

Water, the treasure of Earth, covers two-thirds of the
planet. Some is visible, but much lies beneath the surface,
hidden waters traveling through sand, rock, and gravel.
These hidden seas are created in part when rain and
snow trickle downward. Sometimes rivers dive deep and
enter holds of water beneath even parched ground. These
stores of water are called aquifers. The Ogallala Aquifer
is the largest on the continent, reaching from the plains
of South Dakota to Texas. The aquifer is declining by
an average of 1.74 feet a year—over one million acre-
feet—so excessive is the demand for agricultural and
domestic purposes. In places in this region the land is
actually collapsing. Native American people of several

tribal traditions have long said that prairie dogs "call the rain." Like all Earth's waters, aquifers rise and fall with the moon, and as it turns out, this slow, strong pumping in the aquifers beneath prairie dog towns is what draws rainwater into those aquifers, replenishing them. Where prairie dog holes have ceased to exist, due to land development that has destroyed their habitat and the slaughter of prairie dogs for sport, the soil has become so hard rain can no longer reach the aquifer. The rain in fact has disappeared.   LINDA HOGAN

arch

Millions of years of Earth time and Earth water create a natural arch, rib bone of Earth—red sandstone, pale limestone, dark basalt—by flaking small pieces of rock off a slender wall until a hole finally forms. Water, the agent of erosion, dissolves the rock and gathers in its small cracks and fractures, freezing and expanding, loosening rock grains sometimes too small to see. Arches are Earth clean to the bone. A person walking through one walks through Time. Land arches are most common in the Southwest, particularly in the Utah canyonlands and the Four Corners area. Sea arches occur in coastal bluffs, where it's the constant pounding of ocean waves that wears a hole through a promontory wall. Natural bridges are a type of arch, but they are created in a different way. Instead of rainwater and snowmelt, it's the current of a stream or river that eventually cuts a hole in the rock. A century ago it was believed that, along with water, wind was a major force in the erosion of arches and natural bridges, but—strange as it may sound—wind plays no role.   LINDA HOGAN

archipelago

The word is drawn from the medieval Italian *archi*, meaning "chief" or "principal," and *pelagus*, Greek for

gulf, pool, or pond, and perhaps influenced, if not cor-
rupted by medieval Italian nomenclature for the Aegean
Sea—*egeopelagus*. But hardly a pool or a pond, that archipelago is a formidable stretch of water with which Italian
seafarers were, no doubt, familiar. They might well have
known it as the medium for Odysseus' return to Ithaca—
long delayed by misfortune and enlarged by mythical
island encounters. Archipelago is now somewhat loosely
applied to either or both a body of sea that contains multiple islands and to the islands themselves. Archipelagoes
are often—but not always—in proximity to a mainland,
as with the Arctic islands, Alexander Archipelago, and
Florida Keys. Because of the complexity of currents
about the islands, the varying sizes and upper elevations
of the islands, and commonly the abundance of shallows,
bays, inlets, and estuaries along the coastlines, the islands
in general function as rich nutrient sources and as nesting and resting places for migratory waterfowl, among
other creatures. Archipelagoes typically have diverse floral and faunal activity and complex, sometimes unusual,
biological interfacings. Seen from the air, archipelagoes
invite contemplation of Mandelbrot's fractals, amplify-
ing into ever-greater detail. The term has long inspired
fantastical and metaphorical applications, as in Herman
Melville's *Encantadas*: "for the most part an archipelago of
aridities, without inhabitant, history, or hope of either in
all time to come." JOHN KEEBLE

arenal

A large sandy area, specifically a place too sandy for
planting but not sandy enough to produce dunes. The
word is occasionally used to designate a place where
quicksand is found, but the proper expression here is
arena movediza, literally "movable sand." Arenal is from
arena, Spanish for sand, though in English that word is
commonly used to designate a field set aside for athletic

competition. The connection lies with the Roman practice of using sand (*harena* in Latin) in amphitheaters such as the Colosseum, primarily to soak up blood. The sandy surface in a modern bull ring limits the bull's ability to turn or to surge quickly, and heightens the impression of force and action when it flies up from the bull's hooves. Only incidentally does it soak up blood.   LUIS VERANO

arête

Derived from the French word for fish bone or spine, an arête is a knife-edged ridge on a mountain formed by the glacial erosion of two or more surrounding cirques, marking the upper limit of their headwalls. Some arêtes have slopes that drop unbroken more than a thousand feet, a sheer, dizzying fall that accounts for the feature's mystique of risk and danger. There are numerous arêtes at over twelve thousand feet in Colorado alone, such as Ellingwood Arête on Crestone Needle.   ARTHUR SZE

armor

Armor forms in a riverbed when the current flushes away silts, sands, and smaller gravels to such an extent that only heavier materials remain. These coarse gravels and stones, under the endless pushing of the water, may gradually settle into a smooth and durable surface called armor, which is capable of resisting the disturbance of powerful floods. In theory, however, no armor can last forever, for a flood mighty enough to tear it out and rearrange its component materials must inevitably come. The terrestrial equivalent of armor is desert pavement.
WILLIAM DEBUYS

armored mud ball

An armored mud ball is the compact lithic record of an ephemeral journey, whereby a mud glob gathers a crust of stones that together metamorphose into rock. Like the caddis larva forming an exoskeleton of sand—soft center, hard shell—the armored mud ball represents the preservation of a traveling ball of mud or clay, coated with sand, pebbles, or larger stones. Presumably, the pebbly coating occurred when the original mud ball was dandied by waves across a beach, or rolled along the bed of a stream, then was buried in protective strata and hardened over geologic time. A similar effect occurs with armored ice balls, where a snowball rolling off a glacial scarp gathers a rind of ice particles that protect the softer interior. Prized as oddities by geologists, armored mud balls have been found, among other places, in Japan, the South Dakota Badlands, and the Valley of the Connecticut—which holds the best-known stream-formed exemplars.   KIM STAFFORD

arroyo

The Spanish word *arroyo* means "large creek." Often steep-walled, an arroyo may be flat-bottomed sand or laden with boulders and gravel. *Arroyuelo* and *arroyito* are the diminutive forms and mean "rill" or "brook." Arroyos are ephemeral streams, carrying water only briefly during such events as spring runoff or the summer monsoons. In the American Southwest the words arroyo and wash are sometimes used interchangeably, as are arroyo seco (meaning "dry") and dry wash—though the English terms often describe shorter or abbreviated water courses stretching less than a mile and not necessarily part of a specific arroyo. In *Tongues of the Monte*, J. Frank Dobie writes: "Three hours later, while following a thickly bushed arroyito, my mozo's intermittent hiss to the mule not audible, I suddenly heard a low but harsh cry, 'Alto!'" In *Land of Clear Light*, Michael Jenkinson writes: "The summer storms often produce flash floods that fill arroyos with roiling muddy water within a few seconds, a won-

drous sight to behold unless your car, camp, or person
happens to be in its path." ARTURO LONGORIA

artesian basin

A low-lying district where groundwater is confined
under pressure from surrounding layers of rock is called
an artesian basin. These basins are often found where
an aquifer (a water-bearing lens of earth) lies trapped
in a syncline, or U-shaped fold, by impermeable layers
above and below. When a well or rift breaks the surface,
the subterranean water erupts upward. Artesian springs
are usually reliable, unless the underlying aquifer is
overtaxed by wells or otherwise drained. The Brown
Palace Hotel in Denver possesses its own pure artesian
well, freeing the hotel and its guests from the city's
chlorinated water system. The late Olympia (Washington) Brewery advertised its source with the slogan "It's
the water!" and launched an advertising campaign in
the 1980s involving mythical creatures called Artesians.
The term originates in Artois, the historic French
province where such wells were first described.
ROBERT MICHAEL PYLE

atarque

There is an important atarque not far from Albuquer-
que. The word's roots come from Spanish: *atracar* is
to cram or glut; *atarquinar* is to cover in mud or slime.
Malcolm Ebright, in *Land Grants and Lawsuits in Northern
New Mexico*, defines atarque as a diversion dam for an
irrigation ditch, but it is just as often used locally in
New Mexico to refer to the small reservoir behind the
dam or to the entirety of the local irrigation works. Or,
by some, casually to refer to any natural or man-made
watering hole. All of which brings us to Cibola County
in east-central New Mexico. Atarque Lake, twenty

miles south of Zuni Pueblo, is surrounded today by an old lake bed; as it receded over the millennia the lake did indeed slime the landscape. Atarque Lake feeds the Atarque aquifer, which includes, twenty miles farther south, Zuni Salt Lake, one of the Zuni people's holiest female deities. Phoenix, Arizona, tried to take water from the Atarque aquifer for a major coal-related project, but the Zuni wrestled the city to a draw and saved what's left of the aquifer's water. An interesting trivia note: the far southeastern end of the old lake is the home of the Very Large Array Deep-Space radio antenna project.

LUIS ALBERTO URREA

atoll

An atoll is a midocean coral reef, roughly circular in shape or sometimes open-ended like a horseshoe, that encloses a lagoon. An atoll—the term originates in the Maldive Islands—may be many miles in circumference and may be surmounted by or, more rarely, surround low sand and coral islets. Before he had ever seen an atoll, Charles Darwin, while aboard the *Beagle*, relied on ship captains' charts and descriptions of oceanic islands to come up with a beautifully simple theory of atoll formation. Whereas volcanic islands wear down and subside after eruptions cease, Darwin surmised that their fringing coral reefs continue to grow. These reefs will remain, he argued, if their upward growth can keep pace with islands' subsidence and if sediments accumulate on or within them to form sand and coral islets. (It wasn't until the U.S. Navy drilled more than a mile deep in the coral formation on Eniwetok Atoll in the Marshall Islands in 1952, reaching the atoll's submerged basalt foundation in preparing for the world's first hydrogen bomb test, that Darwin was proved right.) Kure Atoll in the Hawaiian archipelago is the northernmost atoll in the world. It lies close to what is called the Darwin

Point—the latitude at which coral growth can no longer keep up with an island's sinking under its own weight. PAMELA FRIERSON

avalanche chute

An avalanche chute is a natural channel down a steep mountain slope, the path followed by an avalanche's tumultuous racing snow and debris. David Lavender captures the feeling of the tumult in *One Man's West*: "Down the slope we'd just quit pounded the avalanche. A cloud of powdered snow rose hundreds of feet above it. Through the reverberations we could hear the air popping like a giant whip as it rushed in to fill the vacuum left by the slide. A wall of air surged ahead, booming like thunder from cliff to cliff." A chute is initially scraped raw by the force and speed of an avalanche; whatever disturbed soils might remain, however, are prime for new vegetation, making avalanche chutes a preferred habitat for grizzly bears, which forage on the fresh sedges, forbs, and grasses. An avalanche chute that descends through a forested hillside creates with that opening a useful edge for wildlife such as deer, as it allows them either to graze in the open or move back into the protection of the trees. Songbirds are also known to take advantage of these mountainside clearings adjacent to their normal forest canopy habitat. CAROLYN SERVID

back bay

In that the word back typically refers to a feature seen as "behind" some other feature, it follows that Back Bay is the region behind the city of Boston, which faces the ocean. Boston's Back Bay is not a natural feature but was formed by the construction of a long milldam in 1814. The intent of Massachusetts legislators when they ordered the building of the dam was to stop the flow of water to 430 acres of tidal flats near the Charles River and reroute the water to hydropower plants. The result of this construction was an enormous, boggy swamp, which the city began to fill in 1857. Some of the city's most notable landmarks, including Trinity Church, were built on the earth fill of Back Bay. Another Back Bay, located on the coast southeast of Norfolk, Virginia, includes a watershed that covers 104 square miles and contains 40 square miles of surface water, the average depth of which is four feet. Here the Back Bay National Wildlife Refuge, more than 8,000 acres in size, was established in 1938 as a refugia and breeding area for migratory birds.

LAN SAMANTHA CHANG

backcountry

Backcountry, typically defined as "any remote or undeveloped area," is called in some regions backwoods, boondocks, or hinterland. Poverty tends to be a common denominator for the people who live there. Backcountry people have existed on the edge of American civilization since colonial times, when their economy was based on the trade of goods among families living in settlements that lay within and just beyond the Appalachian Mountains and its subranges, including upstate New York, central and western Pennsylvania, the Kentucky and Ohio River valleys, as well as territory in Virginia and the Carolina highlands. At that time the Appalachian backcountry was often referred to as the "settled region of the frontier." During the Great Awakening of the 1750s, however, the majority of backcountry people isolated themselves to some degree by converting to the Baptist faith. As the numbers of backcountry settlers grew, conflicts arose around property ownership. Rivalries burst into violence until the time of the American Revolution, a war that tended to bind backcountry people even more closely together, as most of them were of Irish or Scottish descent. Herman Melville hinted at the strong and strange community bonds when he wrote in *Moby-Dick*, "What says the Cannibal? As I live he's comparing notes; looking at his thigh bone; thinks the sun is in the thigh, or in the calf, or in the bowels, I suppose, as the old women talk Surgeon's Astronomy in the back country." Though the region's inhabitants were once derisively labeled "hillbillies," backcountry life is now considered a uniquely American experience that began to define the values of the American character.   ELIZABETH COX

back forty

At one time, the term back forty represented the land of least monetary value on a piece of property—the section farthest from the house or road, the piece least desirable and last developed, the forty acres Andrew Johnson had in mind when he refused to give freed slaves "forty acres and a mule." It is property previously untilled and unlimed, the hardest to cultivate. The term originated from the rectangular survey method devised by Thomas Jefferson and used by the federal government, wherein a section was one square mile, or 640 acres. A sixteenth of a section was—and still is—forty acres. In current parlance, back forty designates the cast-off or forgotten terrain that nonetheless deserves the same protection and consideration as more obviously valuable conservation projects. For instance, the Environmental Defense Network's "Progress from the Back Forty" project promotes stewardship of the often-neglected portions of private land. ANTONYA NELSON

backland

The word backland commonly refers to an area remote from centers of population, and is interchangeable with hinterland or backcountry. In farming regions backland is the acreage far from the road or farmhouse. In parts of the Deep South the word has a special sense, referring to the zone of a floodplain separated from the river by a natural levee (a barrier of soil deposited over the centuries by the swollen river) and therefore sheltered from flooding. Backland in the Deep South is useful for cultivation, especially in dry years and for crops such as corn that thrive in moist soil near a river. Farther back from the levee, but still on the floodplain, is low ground known, particularly in reference to the Mississippi River, as back swamp. It is interesting that while we often hear the word backland, we rarely hear someone talk about front land, suggesting that land in the foreground doesn't need an adjective. The distinction is almost always with land lying farther away, beyond. Where we live, where we stand, the foreground, is just land; it is the place beyond that is backward. John McPhee alludes to the social prejudice in *The Pine Barrens,* writing: "A surprising number of people in New Jersey today seem to think that the Pine Barrens are dark backlands inhabited by hostile and semi-literate people who would as soon shoot an outsider as look at him." ROBERT MORGAN

backwall

The steep slope at the back of a glacial cirque, which is subject to intense physical weathering, is called the backwall or sometimes the headwall. Because alpine glaciers typically form on the north side of a ridge, and therefore outside the reach of direct sunlight, the steep backwall casts an especially long shadow on the cirque floor. This keeps snow on the floor longer; the wet ground then erodes and deepens the cirque.   JEFFERY RENARD ALLEN

backwater

The words back and water have been used and recorded together since medieval times, and are so familiar they have long been understood as metaphoric for a small town, a place far from the centers of population, culture, and commerce. In geological or geographical terms, backwater means water held behind a dam or other barrier. Backwater is the still or slow water of a stream spread by an obstacle, such as a rock. It is also water at the edge of a river pool held back by the force of the mainstream current, often drifting slowly upstream in an eddy littered with foam and floating debris. Along the coast, backwater can refer to connected lagoons. And in Mississippi River parlance of the nineteenth century, the word meant the swell thrown back by the paddles of a steamboat, as well as the eddies the steamboat pilot sought out to help push his craft upriver.   ROBERT MORGAN

badlands

Badlands are regions dissected into steep hills and deep gullies by the action of wind, rain, and flash floods. The name was originally applied to a semiarid area in South Dakota east of the Black Hills, called *les mauvaises terres à traverser* by the French because it was so difficult to cross; the term is now generally applied to similar lands throughout the continent. In *All the Strange Hours*, Loren Eiseley writes: "I will never forget my first day of registration at the University of Pennsylvania. I had come directly from the Mauvaises terres, the Tertiary

badlands of western Nebraska, into a great city of banging, jangling trolleys, out of a silence as dreadful as that
of the moon." The friable topography of the Badlands,
composed primarily of shales, clays, and sandstones, has
been sculpted into a maze of barren ravines and tunnels, and grassy-topped tables. (The sparse vegetation is
deceptive; while puny on the slopes, it can be comparatively lush on the flat tops.) The average slope angle in
the heart of this desiccated world often exceeds thirty-
five degrees—steep enough to drive rain from seasonal
summer thunderstorms downhill with scouring force,
leaving the sides of the tables looking barren and peeled.
The Lakota Sioux name for the Dakota Badlands is *Mako
Sica*, meaning "eroded land," a region they were wary
of. During the Ghost Dance conflicts of the late 1800s,
diehard Lakota warriors assembled on remote tables in
the depths of the Badlands, out of sight of white authorities who feared the dancing would foment an outbreak of
violence. CONGER BEASLEY, JR.

bajada

The word bajada means "slope" in Spanish and is taken
from the verb *bajar*, to descend. A bajada comprises a
sequence of alluvial fans spreading into a desert valley
at a shallow angle from a series of steep side canyons. In
the Cabeza Prieta National Wildlife Refuge, a remote
part of the Sonoran Desert west of Tucson, Arizona,
each alluvial fan suggests the flaring pleats of a starched
apron. The overall convexity of each apron, together
with the pattern of their abutment, gives the long bajada
its characteristic undulating surface, which may run
for miles around the base of a mountain. Craig Childs,
writing about these outwash plains of flash flood–borne
debris in *The Secret Knowledge of Water*, notes that this
deceptively still landscape is "not idle," that the moun-

tains are "bitterly seared. Rising a couple of thousand feet off the floor [of a Cabeza Prieta valley], they are offset by swaths of bulged, rolling desert bajadas that take days to cross." TERRY TEMPEST WILLIAMS

bald

Interspersed among the forested high ridgelines of the southern Appalachians are about ninety mystifying clearings, known locally as balds. These patches predate European settlement, and the explanations for their presence range from lightning fires to grazing by mammoths. Some of the patches are grassy balds; others, sometimes called slicks, are filled with laurels, rhododendrons, and other members of the heath family. (Gregory Bald, at nearly 5,000 feet in the Smokies, boasts twenty-one varieties of azalea.) Many of the balds are located in Great Smoky Mountains National Park; since cattle grazing is prohibited within its boundaries, managers now use weed-eaters and sickle-bar mowers to keep encroaching trees at bay. BILL MCKIBBEN

ballena

In the arid basin-and-range country of the southwestern United States and Mexico, cloudbursts send torrents of runoff down ravines cut into the flanks of sparsely vegetated mountains. The flash floods may deposit enormous quantities of sand, gravel, and mud at the mouth of a given ravine, where the sediments fan out across the basin floor and are compressed over time into a gently sloping carapace of conglomerate rock. Flowing water may subsequently carve deep, parallel grooves into the alluvial fan until all that remains of it is an array of elongated humps. These remnant conglomerate humps, which resemble the backs of immense whales breaching in unison, are known colloquially as ballenas—Spanish for whales. JON KRAKAUER

bally

Wintun Indians, who live in north-central California, have several principal groups speaking related dialects, so variations in the spelling of this term are common. *Bally*, *bolly*, or *bolla* means "high peak" in Wintun, while *yola* or *yallo* means "snow" or "snow-covered." In the Mendocino National Forest, the Yolla Bolly Wilderness takes its name from Wintun and means the wilderness with "snow-covered peaks."   ARTHUR SZE

banco

A broad term in use predominately in Texas, banco, like its English cognate bank, refers to just about anything heaped, pushed, or fallen into some kind of slope or incline. Examples would be *banco de arena* (sand bank), *banco de nieve* (snow bank), and, of course, the bank of a river, whether it's bermed up or not. But then banco covers more than bank. In the Gulf of Mexico, you'll find coral reefs (*bancos de coral*) with names like Banco Nuevo and Banco Inglés. Yet another use is along the Rio Grande in Texas, where banco means those banks that America and Mexico were always swapping back and forth before the Rio Grande was tamed with dams and treaties. The Socorro Mission (La Purísima) in El Paso sits on one such banco. An 1829 flood changed the river's course not just from north of the mission to south of it, but far enough south that you can't even see the river from the mission anymore. So in places like that, though it doesn't feel like you're standing on the bank of a river at all, you are nevertheless on a banco.   STEPHEN GRAHAM JONES

bank

The high ground abutting a waterway, lake, arterial, or other agent of transport is called a bank, as in streambank or roadbank. Material may also be stacked, blown, or plowed and said to be banked, as in snowbank. Bank slope varies, from the angle of repose (around 35 degrees) on a loose, established bank to a much steeper incline, as when firm material is scooped out abruptly by a flood. When the cut exceeds 90 degrees, a bank becomes an overhang. Left and right banks are so called with respect to downstream direction. The term also refers to a bank of vegetation growing on a soil slope, as Darwin described in the graceful penultimate paragraph of *The Origin of Species*: "It is interesting to contemplate a tangled bank... and to reflect that these elaborately constructed forms... have all been produced by laws acting around us." Bank also refers to a submerged plateau shelf, or shoal, relatively shallow but navigable, such as the once famously productive Grand Banks off Newfoundland.   ROBERT MICHAEL PYLE

bar

In navigation, a bar is a shoaling—a shallowing—of water caused by any landform, from coral reef or barrier island to a ridge of sand. On rivers, the culprit is usually a sandbar. While making life difficult for river pilots, as Mark Twain recounts in *Life on the Mississippi*, sandbars also create pockets of calmer backwater where algae, invertebrates, and fish can flourish. Since water moves more slowly inside a curve or meander than on the outside, it tends to drop suspended sand and gravel there, creating a meander bar or point bar. A separation bar curls outward from the shore in the direction of the current, while a reattachment bar curls back against the current, a shape formed by eddies just downstream from a constriction, such as a narrows. A sandbank across the entrance to a harbor or bay is a bay-mouth bar, which sometimes takes the shape of a crescent moon. Then it is known as a lunate bar. In *Adirondack Explorations*, Verplanck Colvin gives us a sense of a purely terrestrial bar: "It was evening when the deep valley widened, and the mountains, parting to right and left, made space for a small plateau or upland prairie—a *bar*, in mountain parlance—then, circling and closing in darkly and gloomily, seemed to forbid further progress." SCOTT RUSSELL SANDERS

B

baraboo

The origin of the word baraboo is uncertain. Some sources say the name comes from the French *rivière à la barbeau* or "sturgeon river," an early description of what is now called the Baraboo River, which flows through south-central Wisconsin. Alternatively, the term may have come from Baribeau, the surname of two French brothers who owned a mill at the confluence of the Baraboo and Wisconsin Rivers, or from Baribault, the name of a French trapper who had a trading post at the mouth of the river. The oval ring of hills through which the river runs also took the name Baraboo. These hills, which rise as much as 500 feet above the surrounding terrain, are made of ancient sandstone that under heat and pressure metamorphosed in the Precambrian era into extremely durable pinkish-purple quartzite—Baraboo Quartzite. The rock was subsequently covered by softer strata, which eventually were worn away by wind, water, and glacial ice, leaving the quartzite islands to stand together in early Cambrian seas—today's Baraboo Hills. Baraboo at one point crept into geographic glossaries as a generic label for clustered hills, but this use is now regarded as antiquated and imprecise. GRETCHEN LEGLER

barbed drainage

Visualize an expressway. Its entrance ramps point in the direction of the traffic flow, so that traffic merges smoothly with it. That is also how tributaries normally

29

enter rivers—angling downstream, their current merging smoothly with the river's. If the flow of traffic were reversed, cars would need to almost reverse direction to enter the expressway from an on-ramp. That is analogous to what happens in a barbed drainage, a peculiar drainage pattern that results from stream piracy. Given the right conditions of soil and slope, a river erodes upstream, its bed cutting ever more deeply into the slope it descends. Eventually, it cuts across the height of land and into the headwaters of the opposite slope. It then siphons off those headwaters, because its channel lies below. Thus westward-oriented tributaries now enter a channel that flows eastward, or vice versa. Represented schematically, the "captured" tributaries look like the barbs on a porcupine quill.   FRANKLIN BURROUGHS

barchan dune

Dunes form wherever there is enough sand and propelling wind, as well as an absence of vegetation, and they acquire one of several characteristic shapes, depending on the velocity and direction of the wind. A barchan, or barkhan, dune is a crescent-shaped sand dune formed in places where the direction of the wind is fairly constant. The windward or stoss slope of the dune is gradual, the leeward side, or slip face, is steep, and the crest slightly horned. Dunes travel as individuals or in groups of varying size, like ocean waves. Here is Edward Abbey in "Desert Images" from *The Serpents of Paradise*: "Seen from the bird's point of view, most . . . desert sand dunes have a crescent shape, like the new moon. The horns of the crescent point downwind, with the slip face on the inside of the curve. This type of dune is called a barchan—a Russian term." According to the *Oxford English Dictionary*, the term is originally Kazakh, that is, Turkic. In the Great Sand Dunes National Park in southern Colorado there are waves of barchan dunes set against the Sangre de Cristo Mountains.   ROBERT HASS

bar ditch

A bar ditch is a gradual, often grassy dip running along the shoulder of the road, into which road water can drain. While the term is a corruption of both barrow ditch and borrow ditch and shares characteristics with both, a bar ditch is more recent than either, as it came into use more or less with graded roads, which, without proper drainage, can get slick. In common usage, however, whether there's a functional drainage ditch or not, just about any space between the road and a fence is a bar ditch, as Elmer Kelton writes in *The Time It Never Rained*: "Charlie let the pickup come to an easy stop on an area where the bar ditch was shallow and almost flat." One thing to watch out for in a bar ditch, aside from vehicle clearance, is rattlesnakes. They like to stay close to the warm asphalt. The men who mow the ditches say that's where the big ones are. And though some will suggest that the "bar" in bar ditch comes from its function of "barring" cattle from getting into the roadway, all the dip does in relation to cattle—if anything—is make them have to lunge up the short incline for a couple of steps, which leaves them clambering onto the blacktop for footing and probably strands them in more headlights than not.   STEPHEN GRAHAM JONES

bar finger

Bar fingers are elongated lenses of sand or sediment lying beneath the distributary channels of bird-foot river deltas. As Andrew Goudie explains in *The Nature of the Environment*: "If a river branches where it enters the sea to form distributaries, the distributaries will build outwards as long sand fingers, called bar-finger sands; whereas the finer muds and silts get washed into the still water between the distributaries, so that they gradually fill up with mud and swamp deposits." Such a delta takes the shape of a heron's foot—narrow, splayed toes, each consisting of a river channel banked on either side by marshland. The underlying bar fingers enjoy other anatomical associations as well. A bar finger can be lingulate (tongue-shaped), and their sands are often characterized as being coarser upstream at the "bar head" and finer downstream at the "bar tail." MIKE TIDWELL

barranca

The word *barranca* (or *barranco*) is Spanish for cliff or precipice and is used in the Southwest and Mexico when referring specifically to the cut or steep bank made by water erosion along the edges of streams, arroyos, or rivers. Barranca is used as well when referring to the steep side of a gorge or cañón. Terms such as *barranca mesa* (*mesa* means "table"), which one might hear around Los Alamos, New Mexico, refer to the ground directly above the barranca—that area of level land that is yet to be eroded. In *The Iron Heel,* Jack London writes: "A quarter of a mile from Glen Ellen, after the second bridge is passed, to the right will be noticed a barranca that runs like a scar across the rolling land toward a group of wooded knolls." ARTURO LONGORIA

barrens

Open, desolate landscapes of bare rock and sparse vegetation—the Burren of Ireland or the tundra plains of northern Canada—are the sorts of places that live up to the bleak image the word barrens conjures in the mind. But in the eastern United States and parts of the Midwest, the term is more relative. Settlers often called a piece of land a barrens simply to contrast it with neighboring areas of greater potential for agricultural or timber production. Barrens' soils are usually sandy or rocky, low in nutrients, and lacking the ability to hold water. Such poor land grows thin forests, stunted and shrubby. The predominant tree tends to lend its name to the place: for example, pine barrens, oak barrens, cedar barrens. The most widely known example of this plant community in North America is, surely, the New Jersey Pine Barrens. CHARLES FRAZIER

barrier beach

A narrow ridge of offshore sand rising just above high-tide level, running parallel with the coast but separated from it by a lagoon, is called a barrier beach. (The term is frequently, though incorrectly, used as a synonym for barrier island, a larger and more complex coastal barrier, of which sand makes up a relatively small portion.) The more nearly spherical a grain of sand, the older it is, according to writer Annie Dillard, who also points out in her book *For the Time Being* that little or no sand lies beneath the deep oceans. Gustave Flaubert was somewhat obsessed with the movement, ubiquitousness, and all-conquering nature of sand. In all his works it possesses great significance. JOY WILLIAMS

barrier island

Although barrier islands make up only ten to fifteen percent of the world's shorelines, they are the most common coastal landforms on the East and Gulf coasts of the United States. Most are long and linear and associated with major embayments, but some—such as the Sea Island chain of Georgia and South Carolina—are shorter and squarer in shape. The Outer Banks of North Carolina illustrate a wealth of barrier island features— spits, beaches, marshes, lagoons, and inlets—and others, such as Texas's Padre Island, are well-known refuges for resident and migratory birds. The most dynamic of all coastal systems, barrier islands constantly shift at the

whim of wind and wave, in time actually rolling over
upon themselves.   JOY WILLIAMS

basin

A basin is a large hollow or depression in the earth,
either erosional or structural in origin; it is also a
region that is drained by a river and its tributaries. The
Mississippi River and its tributaries drain a basin that
covers approximately two-fifths of the coterminous
United States. The term basin also applies to an area
of inland drainage where rivers unable to reach the sea
either flow into lakes or evaporate in playas. The Great
Basin, centered in western Utah and Nevada, is a prime
example. A cold desert in the Basin and Range province,
the Great Basin encompasses Death Valley, nuclear bomb
test sites, and Yucca Mountain, a proposed nuclear-waste
storage site. In his book *Basin and Range*, John McPhee
describes the Great Basin as "an ocean of loose sediment
with these mountain ranges standing in it as if they were
members of a fleet without precedent." The term is also
widely used for many of the land's bowl-shaped features,
such as a ski basin in a single mountain. In her poem
"The Matrix," Amy Lowell writes: "Brown lily-pads lie
heavy and supine/Within a granite basin, under one/
The bronze-gold glimmer of a carp; and I/Reach out my
hand and pluck a nectarine."   DONNA SEAMAN

basin and range

The extension or stretching of the Earth's crust normally
results in downfaulted valleys, or grabens, and upfaulted
mountains, or horsts. North America's huge geological
province of north-south–oriented mountains and valleys
created in this way is known as basin and range country
(roughly 400,000 square miles) and runs between northern Mexico and southeastern Oregon, and the Sierra

Nevada of California and the Wasatch Mountains of Utah. It includes parts of all the major North American deserts—the Great Basin, Mojave, Sonoran, and Chihuahuan. Death Valley, on the Nevada-California border, reaches a maximum of 282 feet below sea level, while the Panamint Mountains just to the west rise to some 11,000 feet in elevation. At the foot of such snowy ranges as the Ruby Mountains in Nevada and Steens Mountain in Oregon, peat-bog marshes form despite the aridity of the basins, providing havens for migrating waterfowl. Runoff from Steens Mountain flows through glacial valleys to the Malheur National Wildlife Refuge and drains into a series of alkaline playas where the waters evaporate.   WILLIAM KITTREDGE

basket-of-eggs relief

An area of closely spaced drumlins separated by small marshy areas is called basket-of-eggs relief because, from a distance, the drumlins—low, smooth, oval hills formed by glacial movement—resemble eggs gathered in a basket.   PATTIANN ROGERS

batture

The term batture, recorded in English as early as the mid–nineteenth century, is French and in the lower Mississippi River basin most often refers to the elevated riverbed between levees. It is well known that the streets of New Orleans, for example, lie lower than the surface of the Mississippi. Only the levees, when they hold, prevent the river within the batture from flooding the city and surrounding countryside. Batture is also used in Louisiana to denote solid ground between low water on a river and parallel levees, and less often refers to a seabed raised, by floor shifting and deposits, above the surface of the water.   ROBERT MORGAN

bay

A bay is a smaller body of water extending off a larger
one (usually an ocean or lake) and forming an indentation in the shoreline. Bays usually develop when the
water level of a sea or lake rises above and submerges
a portion of the shore. Virginia and Maryland's Chesapeake Bay was created 10,000 years ago when the melting
of Earth's enormous glaciers caused the Atlantic Ocean
to rise. When protected from the full brunt of the ocean's
pounding waves, bay waters become havens for marine
life. In Ohio, Arkansas, and along the Mississippi River, a
bay is a tract of prairie or open land partially surrounded
by woods. A Carolina bay is a low, marshy area where
bay trees (laurels) thrive. In Florida and other southern
Atlantic states, a bay is synonymous with a slough,
wetland, or watergrass meadow.   DONNA SEAMAN

bayhead

The water in a bay always opens into a larger body of
water, such as a lake or ocean, at a nondescript point.
The opposite end of the bay—that is, the portion that
thrusts farthest into land—is known as the bayhead. The
term is curious, in that bays are never said to have feet or
tails, only heads. Along the coastal plain of the Southeast,
the term takes on a different meaning altogether. There,
bayhead refers to an area of swampy vegetation either
at the inland edge of a bay water or at the headwaters of
a stream. In the latter case, it is named not for the body
of water into which its moisture flows, but for the thick,
evergreen vegetation to which it plays host—red bay,
sweet bay, loblolly bay.   JAN DEBLIEU

bayou

Bayou is a word that sounds French but is in fact of
Choctaw origin, deriving from *bayuk*, meaning "small
stream." In recorded usage since 1818, bayou most com-

monly refers to marshy offshoots and overflowings of lakes and rivers in the delta of Louisiana and the Gulf area. In a region of mostly swamps and marshy prairies, the bayous are spaces of open water, sluggish or stagnant, often the abandoned channels of the river delta cut off into oxbow lakes in the river's variorum history of trial and evolution. Bayou can also refer to a secondary channel, away from the mainstream, where the current is slower and the volume smaller. Sometimes a tributary is referred to as a bayou, as is any sluggish stream. The word can be said to refer to any slow water in a marshy area, if not dead water perhaps sleeping water, or dreaming water.   ROBERT MORGAN

beach cusp

Beach cusps are the individual crescent arcs in a sequence of linked sandbars at the edge of a beach addressed by waves from two directions. An indentation in sand expressing the fanning force of water. Like other sand features such as shoals or spits, the ephemeral beach cusp represents a visible expression of the less visible. At the ocean's edge, a series of broad, hidden vectors based in prevailing winds, ocean currents, and long swells localized as waves are all expressed in a language available to human perception—a series of rhythmic shapes in beach sand, where water's deft knife scallops the coast.
KIM STAFFORD

beaded drainage

Beaded drainages are features of thermokarst (pitted, hummocky landscapes formed by melting permafrost). Necklace-like arrangements of button-shaped pools joined by short channels, these drainages form on ground underlain by vertical ice wedges. Such ice wedges develop in Arctic regions when the ground contracts and splits, allowing water to enter the rifts and freeze. Over these, streams carve narrow, deep channels through turf and peat to the sediment underneath. At intersections of melting ice wedges, pools form. When encountering smaller pools, a traveler or animal might wade or hop across. Larger ponds can be ten feet deep and eighty feet wide. Beaded drainages decorate silt lowlands of the western Canadian Arctic and northern Alaska, often in the company of pingos and thaw lakes.   EVA SAULITIS

beaver dam

Beavers—famously industrious aquatic rodents who eat the bark of maple, linden, birch, and poplar trees—live gregariously in colonies that thrived for centuries before the animals' habitats were radically altered by human-kind. Master builders, beavers protect the entrance to their burrows in the banks of streams, and create food storage areas by constructing remarkably sturdy dams out of trees they cut down, some as wide as eighteen inches in diameter—great, tangled, well-anchored, slop-ing heaps that hold back large ponds, where they then erect impregnable lodges. Beaver dams and ponds can help prevent spring floods, and they preserve water dur-ing dry spells. Systematically hunted for their fur (beaver skins once served as currency in northern North Amer-ica), beavers were vanquished from most areas but are now being reintroduced in the Northeast. Oregon, where the animal was hunted to near extinction, has retained its nickname, the Beaver State.   DONNA SEAMAN

beaver meadow

The beaver meadow is considered by many to be the most valuable of all meadow types. Where waterways—creeks, streams, or rivers—are blocked or slowed by beaver structures, a creeping wetland is created. In addition to the myriad species that thrive in such a locale, the wetlands act as enormous biological filters.

Beaver-created wetlands not only cleanse the water, but in detaining it permit the percolation of that water to the layer that holds groundwater. When a given dam is abandoned—the beaver having eaten their way through the softwood trees (aspen, cottonwood, willow) and moved on—the land will quickly revert to forest, but with a revitalized soil base. Such is the case with western New York's Beaver Meadow Creek Park, as well as Beaver Meadow Falls near Lake Placid in the Adirondacks. The value of a beaver-created meadow was recognized by explorer Antonio Armijo in 1829. When he came upon a rich mosaic of springs, mesquite, and grass meadows as well as an abundant population of beaver in what is now southern Nevada, he named the place "Las Vegas," meaning "the meadows"—beaver meadows in this case. At that time millions of beaver populated the continental United States. In fact, they are second only to humans in terms of the role they've played in shaping the American landscape. ANTONYA NELSON

beaver slide

The path made by beaver lurching between home waters and the trees they skin for food is called a beaver slide. When cross-country travelers slog through willow thickets or alder bogs, they may find a few steps of easy going at this slick open run where beaver have pulled their woody plunder toward the pond. Before the settlement era in the West, fur trappers followed the beaver sign of dams, whittled trees, and beaver-slide boulevards through the tangle as deep into the mountains as those plush webfoots pioneered. After settlement, western ranchers invented a tall comb of pine poles, a ramp up which they slid loose hay, which then fell to form a haystack. They called this implement, big as a house, a beaver slide. We also use the phrase beaver slide to name ridges, cliffs, and basins throughout the West when they have the scooped-out look of the beaver's work. One Beaver Slide is a basin in Montana's Big Horn County, another a cliff near Meeteetse, Wyoming.   KIM STAFFORD

bedrock

Of all the terms used to describe features of the land, this one—bedrock—is most often called up in literature and religion as a metaphor for steadfast dependability, comfort, and security. It's a true enough allusion: the rock that lies hidden deep beneath layers of topsoil and subsoil can be relied upon not to change its composition. It does not weather or shift in response to the capricious atmospheric forces that constantly rearrange the more superficial elements of the landscape. Although any sense of the Earth as unchanging is ultimately an illusion (the very continents are moving, in fact, at a rate of an inch or more per year), from the perspective of a human lifetime the bedrock may be counted on not to change perceptibly. It seems to lie immutable beneath our feet and serves as a foundation and parent material to the land, both structurally and chemically, since its mineral composition, permeability, and other characteristics may greatly influence the layer that forms above it.   BARBARA KINGSOLVER

beheaded stream

A captured stream is regarded as "beheaded" when its headwaters are taken over by its captor stream, which at some point broke through the physical division between the two—a natural occurrence in the ongoing dynamic process of a drainage system. The aggressor literally chops off the headwater and diverts the captured stream into its own flow, an act of stream piracy. Some misfit, or underfit, streams begin this way. Without the runoff from its headwaters, such a stream becomes too small to cut through its own valley. GRETEL EHRLICH

belt

The term belt suggests a region with a distinctive cultural characteristic. Thus: Bible Belt—that area of the South and southern Midwest noted for Christian fundamentalism. Black Belt—often used to refer to a region of rich farmland in the South, but at the turn of the twentieth century African American leader Booker T. Washington popularized the term to distinguish areas in the Deep South where the majority of black Americans resided. (When many African Americans were fleeing to the North to escape the injustices of southern racism and legalized segregation, Washington believed they should remain in the South and construct a separate black nation.) Farm Belt—once called the "breadbasket of the nation," a vast area of deep, fertile soil spread over parts of fourteen states, mostly in the Midwest, stretching as far north as Minnesota and as far west as the Dakotas, that remains the agricultural center of the United States. Iron Belt—an area generally identified with northern Minnesota and Wisconsin and Michigan's upper peninsula, which between 1855 and 1900 replaced the East as the nation's center for the mining of iron ore and the manufacturing of steel after rich iron ore deposits were discovered in the Lake Superior region and neighboring areas. JEFFERY RENARD ALLEN

bench

A terrace, shelf, or platform—usually narrow and relatively level, and backed by a steep grade—that breaks the continuous line of a slope is called a bench. Benches often mark former shorelines, and wave-cut terraces in the flanks of the Wasatch Mountains east of Salt Lake City, Utah, provide a dramatic example of this type of formation. Here, the liquid hand of ancient Lake Bonneville, the huge Pleistocene body of water of which Great Salt Lake is a remnant, has been at work. This staircase of distinct platforms tells the story of long pauses in Lake Bonneville's episodic fluctuations. Brewster Ghiselin deftly captures the respite a mountain bench offers a climber when he writes: "We easily turned from the path, / To the dusk of the bench and the poorwills, / Having no time to gain / Or lose, being paid by the moment." The benches of the northern California coast at Big Sur and near Bodega Bay were formed as the continent was successively uplifted by tectonic forces, elevating these benches above the waves that created them. A length of floodplain parallel to and stretching away from a riverbank is also called a bench, as is each surface of worked ground in the sequence of steps rising up the side of an open-pit mine. In Idaho and other parts of the West, a bench is also any flat surface that provides working access to a mine and, often, any of a series of broad terraces adjacent to a large river, as indicated in "We topped the rise above the river and saw cattle grazing the bench."   TERRY TEMPEST WILLIAMS

bend

The curved part of a stream or river is called a bend. The Rio Grande, marking the border between Texas and Mexico and defining the 118 miles of the southern border of Big Bend National Park, abruptly changes its southeasterly flow to the northeast and forms the amazing "big bend." "Big," of course. It's Texas. Not just canyon rivers but alluvial rivers such as the Mississippi also have bends. A river moving through a 180-degree turn creates a horseshoe bend. Vicksburg, Mississippi, site of a famous Civil War battle, was once located on such a bend. And the Colorado River forms a horseshoe bend as it makes a

wide sweep around an enormous sandstone escarpment
in the stark canyonlands near Lake Powell, south of Page,
Arizona. In *My First Summer in the Sierra*, John Muir wrote
of attempting to force sheep across a stream: "They
were driven into a horseshoe bend and fairly crowded
off the bank. They seemed willing to suffer death rather
than risk getting wet." A clever use of a horseshoe
bend.   PATTIANN ROGERS

bergschrund

A bergschrund is a gaping ice crevasse created when
a valley glacier begins to move out of the mountain
cirque basin where it was born. The ice mass set in
motion produces the cavernous bergschrund when,
flowing downstream, it breaks away from the stationary
ice that remains frozen to the cirque's rock headwall.
Bergschrunds can extend all the way across the head of
glacier and may be as deep as 300 feet, posing significant
obstacles and hazards for mountain climbers trying to
ascend or descend the rock and snow slopes that rise
above these yawning icy chasms. Mountaineering stories
note bergschrunds on many peaks in the American
West, including the Tyndall Glacier bergschrund in
Rocky Mountain National Park, the Winthrop Glacier
bergschrund on Mount Rainier, and the Middle Teton
Glacier bergschrund in Wyoming.   CAROLYN SERVID

berm

A ridge of sand, rock, and other debris can be found
running along the back of most beaches. This berm—the
term can also include the flat behind the ridge—marks
the spot reached by the swash of water from the highest
wave of the worst storm; it will stand witness until some
higher wave eventually scours farther up the shore. A
series of smaller berms mark successively lower high-
water marks, right down to the line of seaweed along

yesterday's high tide line—each more ephemeral than the last. The term has slowly acquired more meanings: in the nineteenth century, it was the bank of a canal opposite the towpath; in our time, it is the raised shoulder at the side of a road.　BILL MCKIBBEN

bight

A bight is a long gradual bend or gentle indentation in the shoreline of an open coast or bay. The bight region in New York is a great expanse of shallow ocean between Long Island and the New Jersey coast. In "The Bight," poet Elizabeth Bishop describes the busy scene along a bight: sponge boats "bristling with jackstraw gaffs and hooks"; pelicans diving, hitting the water hard, flying off "with humorous elbowings"; a dredge at work; shark tails hung to dry; broken boats piled up—and at low tide, "how sheer the water is." Totem Bight State Historical Park, located along the curving shoreline of Revillagigedo Island, Alaska, contains a model native village with an authentically constructed clan house and fourteen totem poles replicating those of the Tlingit and Haida peoples. Originally a fish camp of these native peoples, the site was once called Mud Bight.　PATTIANN ROGERS

biscuit board

A biscuit board landscape is a rolling upland on a glacial plain on the sides of which is a series of hollowed-out cirques that appear as if a biscuit cutter has taken a bite out of them. In the southern Andes of Patagonia, where glaciers have carved out cirques, biscuit board topography is common. Closer to home, the grooved, eroded upland around Mount Lyell, the highest peak in Yosemite National Park, is described as biscuit board, as are the uplands surrounding the Wind River Mountains in Wyoming and the crest of the Colorado Front Range. GRETEL EHRLICH

blackland

B

Any area of heavy, sticky soil, blackland gets its dark color from high concentrations of organic material. The claylike consistency for which it's better known is due to the mineral montmorillonite, which permeates the soil. While difficult to farm—montmorillonite tends to swell when wet, crack when dry—blackland often has high yields simply because the soil is so fertile. One example of blackland is the Black Belt of Mississippi and Alabama. Another, larger example is the Texas Blackland Prairie. Also called Cornucopia and the Black Waxy, the Texas Blackland Prairie extends in a narrow channel from San Antonio to above Dallas, covering forty-five counties. Though the Kadohadacho and Hasinai Caddo subsistence-farmed there for generations—growing beans, pumpkins, and corn—white settlers, more interested in surplus farming, were only able to take advantage of the richness of the soil once they'd learned to adapt the moldboard plow. (Originally designed to shed mud and thus keep the plow from gumming up, the moldboard was no match for blackland soils.) Another trick the white settlers picked up was applying soapstone to their wagon wheels and plowshares so the mud wouldn't stick so much. A third, less effective but more entertaining method of staying out of the mud—at least for a few reckless steps—was walking on stilts. STEPHEN GRAHAM JONES

black sand country

Talk among prospectors in the most lively days of the gold rush in the American Southwest often turned to the topic of black sand, for miners believed that the dark mineral on a riverbank or shore was a telltale sign of nearby gold. But they were a bit off in that assumption: iron-rich and heavy black sand does remain in streambeds and beaches while other minerals are swept away by water, and gold—also heavy—stays put while lighter materials are washed off; but the presence of one doesn't necessarily signal the presence of the other. Though not as valuable as gold strikes, black sand regions hold their own kind of fascination. For instance, the beach at Fort Funston in the Golden Gate National Recreation Area is the ideal place to try a magnet experiment: the dark-colored minerals there (magnetite) will cling to the ends of a magnet that is dipped into the sand. And many visitors flock to Hawai'i to watch black sand forming along the coastal fringes of the island's active volcanoes. When lava from Hawai'i's Mauna Loa, for example, comes down headlong, like a curtain, into the cold ocean water, some of it instantly "freezes," reforming itself into shards of black glass. Erosion of the underlying mafic (dark) basalts by wave action produces the sand, rich in iron and magnesium, that is characteristic of Hawai'i's black beaches.   ELIZABETH COX

blaze

Blaze, meaning a white patch on a horse's forehead, was applied by English colonists to the marking of a forest route by periodically axing off a piece of tree bark to expose a portion of lighter-colored wood. The Native Americans they learned from blazed lightly with tomahawks when pursuing wounded prey, to code the way back. For Euro-Americans the word came to signify both the marking and the making of a path, road, or survey line, and the fact or fancy of "blazing a trail" took on mythic status with the westward expansion. Many hiking trails still bear blazes, made in the traditional fashion or applied as small metal plates instead, usually superfluous in summer but useful to ski-trekkers when snow has buried the trail. There may be woodsmen in some hinterlands of the continent who still of necessity blaze trees, but the last blazers are chiefly foresters who use spray paint and plastic ribbons to mark timber sales. For the rest of us, as we blaze into our future, the term has ascended to pure metaphor.   JOHN DANIEL

blind creek

To most eyes a dry creek is a place where a creek once flowed and after a rain will likely flow again. Such a waterway is an ephemeral creek, technically. But by another way of seeing, some such creeks never entirely disappear. A ghost, if you will, holds the creek's place, moving slowly in darkness below the dry, sun-baked surface. In the mind of a local resident finely attuned to such things, you've come upon the invisible but real when you stand above a blind creek. Dig, and the water will come to light, like the blind floor revealed when the carpenter's floor is taken up.   BARRY LOPEZ

blowdown

In forests damaged by high wind, the resulting tree debris is called blowdown. In the summer of 1999, for instance, violent storms laid waste to 400,000 acres of forest in northern Minnesota's Superior National Forest. In May 1980, the blast from Mount St. Helens in Washington State's Cascade Mountains "mowed trees down like blades of grass," according to one scientist who studied the volcano; in the end, more than four million board feet of timber dropped to the ground. Consisting of formerly living organisms, this blown down material—utterly natural—has at times instantly become fodder for deeply divisive controversy. To the U.S. Forest Service, blowdown represents potential fuel for catastrophic fire. To the timber industry, its quick collection equals salvage revenue. To environmentalists, tampering with the downed trees symbolizes the government's wish to manipulate rather than protect wilderness. One of the sticky issues surrounding blowdown is that the dried and rotting timber becomes forest duff, which in turn is part of the fuel that burns in a forest fire. Most scientists consider such burns an integral part of the forest system, regenerating plants and increasing light levels to allow young plants to survive, but the timber industry and those who live in heavily timbered areas are more invested in preventing fire—which leads inevitably to a quagmire about how to best take care of the toppled trees. ANTONYA NELSON

blowhole

A resemblance to the jet of compressed air and water vapor expelled by whales may explain the geological terms blowhole and the more geyserlike spouting horn. Along sea cliffs where rock is prone to developing fissures, blowholes—narrow openings to the surface—may develop when the force of waves compresses air within clefts or sea caves. Along the coasts of volcanic islands, such as those that comprise Hawai'i, lava tubes sometimes supply the seaward openings, with air and salt water jetting from a portion of collapsed roof. Strong wave action can push spray out through such openings in an explosive plume like a geyser: Spouting Horn at Lāwa'i, on the south shore of Kaua'i, can sometimes reach ninety feet. The term blowhole is also used to describe an opening through a snow bridge and into a crevasse where air movement is palpable, or a very small opening through which gas escapes on the surface of a lava flow. PAMELA FRIERSON

blowout

The term blowout denotes a depression or deflation caused by incessant or periodically strong winds sweeping soil, sand, or gravel out of a flat. These depressions often start where surface vegetation has been scarified, denuded by fire, broken by animals as in a wallow, or damaged by off-road vehicles. Rabbits' warrens precipitated blowouts in San Juan Island National Historical Park in Washington, while down the coast near Florence, Oregon, dune-buggy cuts have invited deep blowouts in Oregon Dunes National Recreation Area. Blowouts can perpetuate themselves, their edges further channeling the wind. Where dune grass or sand verbena hold some but not all the home material in place, the wind may scoop deeper and deeper around the plants, stranding their taproots like pilings at low tide. Prospectors use the term blowout to describe colored, altered rock outcrops that signify ore deposits below, while gas and oil workers use the term for wells that have burst their caps.   ROBERT MICHAEL PYLE

blue hole

Blue holes, deep depressions filled with water sometimes so intensely blue they appear bottomless, are one of the spectacular formations of karst topography: limestone bedrock sculpted by the dissolving effects of rainwater or groundwater. Though there are many North American examples, such as the Blue Hole in northwestern Ohio, most famous is the Blue Hole sixty miles off the coast of Belize, a haven for deep-water scuba divers. Located in the aquamarine shallows of Lighthouse Reef, this blue hole is a near-perfect circle more than a thousand feet across, its deep indigo water a result of its four-hundred-foot depth. Though now submerged, it formed on dry land, either as a cavern whose roof finally collapsed or as a sinkhole. Then melting glaciers at the end of the Ice Age flooded continental margins along the Atlantic coast, turning this land formation into one in the sea. The eerily pure color of a blue hole may not always signal depth: A shallow blue hole in the New Jersey Pine

Barrens sometimes called the Jersey Devil's Bathtub owes its saturated hue to the purity of strongly upwelling spring water—undoubtedly also the force that created the formation. PAMELA FRIERSON

bluff

A bluff—a high bank above a river, a headland of precipitous cliffs—is created when elements of Earth go to battle. In nearly all Earth's processes, one element is pitted against another, and the weaker is washed away, swept off, compressed. What is weakly held together breaks down easily. Bluffs come from such processes. Some bluffs were susceptible to prevailing winds, others to movements within the Earth, others to scouring ice. Some are layered up with the sand of a long-ago sea or the pebbles of a former stream or with the fossils of animals. Many bluffs come to life when water cuts down through the seams of Earth layers, creating slippage and collapse. The ocean, the ever-ongoing movement of waves against the shore, carves other bluffs, as at the edge of Puget Sound and along the California coast. Rattle-snake Mountain in Nebraska was shaped by upward sweeping winds. *Nana Wyah*, the sacred Chickasaw Bluffs in Oklahoma, were renamed after the Trail of Tears. Mount Rushmore, carved into Lakota sacred land, is a granite bluff. And Bluff is a little town on the banks of the San Juan River in Utah, ringed by its namesake landform. In *Islands in the Stream*, Hemingway writes: "The house was built on the highest part of the narrow tongue of land between the harbor and the open sea. It has lasted through three hurricanes and it was built solid as a ship. It was shaded by tall coconut palms that were bent by the trade wind and on the ocean side you could walk out of the door and down the bluff across the white sand and into the Gulf Stream." LINDA HOGAN

boathook bend

A boathook bend is a particularly sharp bend in a river, taking its name perhaps from the long wooden or aluminum pole outfitted with a steel hook or point on one end used by boaters to pick up lines that are out of reach.   PATRICIA HAMPL

bocage

When Allied troops stormed ashore in Brittany and Normandy in 1944, they encountered the irregularly shaped agricultural fields and many hedges that characterize that part of the French countryside. This bocage country challenged the movement of vehicles and equipment, which had to be brought through or around long walls of hedges growing atop steep roadside banks. The French term applies both to the hedge itself and to a landscape made up of such hedges. In North America the term refers generally to a landscape of small fields surrounded by low hedges. In parts of Louisiana, bocage is used to designate a peaceful, shade-giving place. There is a Bocage subdivision in Baton Rouge and, near New Orleans, the storied Bocage Plantation, carved from the once wild banks of the Mississippi River in order to plant fields of indigo, cotton, and sugarcane, separated by long borders of towering live oaks. The bocage country of Louisiana compares with French long lots of the same region. These irregularly shaped parcels have a narrow end fronting on a river, with the long axis of the property perpendicular to the waterway. The advantage to the French long-lot system is that many more property owners have river access.   MIKE TIDWELL

bog

A low-lying area saturated with water creates a hollow of decomposed vegetation in wet, spongy ground. This strange land is called a bog, a word that's been used since about 1450 to refer to such places. The ground sinks underfoot—collapses, sucks under. It is a netherworld dimly lit, and a rank smell hangs in the air. Yet a bog is far from dead. It supports plant life; as an ecological system, it can be described as a plant community. Cattails, rushes, sedges, and bulrushes are plants that initially creep into a lake and begin to transition that body of water into a bog. The term most often applies to wetlands that have little inflow of water through streams and are fed, instead, mainly by precipitation. What happens is that the plant material growing in the lake dies off and eventually becomes peat. When the dead and dying vegetation rises to the water level of the lake, this accumulation of peat forms a dome, which prohibits any new plants from growing. Without the inflow and outflow of water, a black skin forms, an oily and idle mire locked in a world of its own contrivance. A foot stepping in goes beneath the surface, fast like a thief. Bogs can be found throughout the United States—Web's Mill Bog, New Jersey, for instance, and Hanging Bog near Cedar Rapids, Iowa. The term bog is also often used in literature to represent the cessation of growth, or a human's stuck place. In *The Red Badge of Courage*, Stephen Crane uses a bog to express the conditions of the Civil War: "He was obliged to walk upon bog tufts and watch his feet to keep from the oily mire. . . . The youth went again into the deep thickets. The brushed branches made a noise that drowned the sounds of the cannon. He walked on, going from obscurity into promises of a greater obscurity." ELIZABETH COX

bogan

Bogan is an apparent colloquial shortening of the word pokelogan, which itself is of uncertain, but possibly Native American, origin, though it may have resulted from conflation with the more succinct bog. The term is most in use in the northeastern United States and the Canadian Maritime Provinces. A bogan is a marshy backwater, commonly narrow and tranquil, and to which is ascribed darkness, as the artist Jasper Johns writes in "New Zealand's Pre-Raphaelite Fetish": "tie-dyed and bogan-black." JOHN KEEBLE

boghole

A boghole is a soft, earthy hole in which cars, people, and animals can get stuck; it is characterized by "histic" soil—that is, organic with very little mineral matter. Bogholes are not to get out of, not easily escaped, a dead end. Hole in Bog Peatland, one well-known boghole, is located in north-central Minnesota. This raised bog, which began in a lake depression, has a history of complex formation that spans thousands of years. As the depression filled with dead plant material, peat spread over the soil ridges, creating a great heap of decomposing matter with holes that eventually became filled with quicksand. Bogholes are present wherever bogs are found, or where bogs have been. ELIZABETH COX

bogmat

A bogmat begins with submerged plants growing on a lake's floor, then moves to a second stage of development, the growth of plants whose roots stay on the bottom but whose leaves float—water lilies, for example. The proliferation of plant roots that thrive in water eventually creates a fragile surface on the water, a thin mat of vegetation over the lake. In the fourth stage of bogmat development, the sedge or fen stage, this fragile mat thickens and the assemblage of plants grows more limited in variety. As seasons pass, shrubs (cranberry, poison sumac) become part of the mat. Leaf forms change. Thick, hoary leaves suggest a lack of water, even when water is abundantly present. Finally, the surface becomes thick and oily, yet still unstable enough to swallow up a team of horses. Bogmats at this point are considered "physically wet but physiologically dry." These conditions cause a nutrient deficiency for plants, due to lack of drainage. The result: poor aeration, diminished nitrogen, increased acidity. This brings about the last stage of bogmat formation: the growth of tamarack trees, which provide shade, a new element, and of hummocks with shallow root systems. The mat thickens, the forest grows more dense, and the earth becomes, once again, firm beneath the feet. A witness to what Emily Dickinson called "truth's superb surprise."   ELIZABETH COX

bogue

A term that sounds French but is actually from Louisiana Choctaw, bogue is now used interchangeably with bayou, but originally bogue just meant a stream or waterway.   ROBERT MORGAN

boil

A boil is turbulence in a river resulting from such causes as deep holes, channel changes, or underwater obstructions. It can also be a large upheaving of moving water in a river. In *Life on the Mississippi*, Mark Twain writes of how he came to master the language of the water: "Those tumbling 'boils' show a dissolving bar and a changing channel." A sand boil is a land term that refers to sand in a low mound, produced by liquefied sand pushing up to the ground surface.   ARTHUR SZE

bolson

Bolsón is the American-Spanish version of *bolsa*, Spanish for a large purse or pouch. The image of a colossal purse is helpful in envisioning a bolson in the landscape: an extensive, saucer-shaped basin, closed at the bottom and surrounded on all sides by mountain slopes. These pouchlike depressions occur in the arid and semiarid mountainous areas of the southwestern United States and Mexico. In such desert regions, the runoff from irregular rains drains down surrounding slopes and collects in the low-lying, unvegetated area of the bolson, creating a shallow lake. The lowest area of a bolson is called the playa, and the lakes that form there are known as playa lakes. Although some playa lakes are nearly permanent, most are ephemeral; formed during the inundations of desert rain, they evaporate in dry periods, leaving behind deposits of salt and other sediments. Over time, layers of sediment accumulate, and when dry, the playa may appear as a salt flat. The bolson itself—the basin that holds the intermittent playa lakes—can be very large indeed. In the novel *A Mule for the Marquesa*, western writer Frank O'Rourke describes one bolson as "ten thousand miles of the high desert, cupped within the waterless mountains." O'Rourke may be taking slight poetic license, but maybe not: a bolson of ten thousand square miles isn't, as one scientist put it, "completely out of bounds." Some notable bolsons include the Bolsón de Mapimí, in northern Mexico; Hueco Bolson, which extends from New Mexico through El Paso into Mexico; and the Jornada del Muerto bolson, east of Las Cruces, New Mexico. Another term for bolson is playa basin. EMILY HIESTAND

boondocks

Boondocks are areas of underdeveloped backcountry woods and dense brush, also called the sticks, a term that came into use in Kentucky in the 1800s when large poplar forests were being logged. Boondocks is an American adaptation of the Tagalog word bundok, meaning "mountain." Filipinos fighting the United States for their country's independence in 1899–1902 established bases for their resistance in mountainous terrain, forcing the U.S. military to regularly patrol the boondocks. Boonies became a clipped form of the word. The term is often used pejoratively; to be labeled as coming from the boondocks is synonymous with being called backward, clumsy, ignorant. To boondock means to make love in a car: whether amid summer sounds of crickets, the rustlings of night creatures and restless grasses or a small creek, or in the cold silence of empty trees and blue shadows on snow at midnight, some people believe a secluded backroad in the boondocks provides the perfect place for this activity.   PATTIANN ROGERS

borderland

A land or district on or near the border between two countries or districts is borderland, conveying the idea of a fringe or intermediary state or region. In the Southwest, the borderland is the stretch between Mexico and the United States, and the term carries with it the idea of a mixing and confluence of cultures. It also includes the idea of disparate economic systems that produce poverty, along with cultural interactions rich in ambiguities and tensions. Chicana poet and activist Gloria Anzaldúa describes the U.S.-Mexico borderland as *"una herida abierta"*—an open wound. Borderland is thus no longer a geographical term but a geopolitical one.   ARTHUR SZE

boreal forest

South of the treeless Arctic tundra, a forest shawl wraps eleven percent of the Earth's northern terrestrial surface. This circumpolar boreal forest is white spruce–dominated, carpeted with lichens, moss, orchids, heaths, quilted with peat bogs, and cut by cold, silty rivers. In *Crossing Open Ground*, Barry Lopez describes one view of this landscape: "a backdrop of hills: open country recovering from an old fire, dark islands of spruce in an ocean of Labrador tea, lowbush cranberry, fireweed . . . each species of leaf the invention of a different green: lime, moss, forest, jade." Boreal forces shape this forest: hot summers of endless daylight; frigid, dark winters; spring floods; permafrost; cycles of insect infestation and fire that decimate vast acreages. Yet fauna thrive: red squirrel, mink, moose, bear, wolf, lynx, marten, red fox, vole, muskrat, beaver, grouse, ptarmigan, porcupine, caribou, snowshoe hare, salmon, sheefish, whitefish, northern pike. And flora: spruce, tamarack, paper birch, quaking aspen, balsam poplar, blueberry, crowberry, Labrador tea, willow, cranberry, saxifrage, prickly rose. Indigenous people, to this day, rely on an intimate knowledge of geography to subsist on these animals and plants. Some non-Natives also pursue this intimate geographic knowledge of the boreal forest. For several years, the poet John Haines homesteaded in the boreal forest south of Fairbanks, Alaska, hunting and trapping for subsistence, receiving the forest's spiritual and artistic sustenance. Of this time Haines wrote, "I am living out a dream in these woods. Old dreams of the Far North."   EVA SAULITIS

borrow pit

In the mountain West, if you "borrow" dirt from the side of the road to create a drainage ditch, you've made a borrow pit. The term probably derives from the English word *barrow*, meaning a large mound of earth or stones covering a gravesite, or tumulus. A borrow pit also refers to a hole in the earth from which dirt or gravel have been excavated for use elsewhere. In the glaciated Midwest, for example, borrow pits are found next to just about every freeway, the terrain there so flat that earth has to be borrowed to build overpasses. In an era of hand tools, dirt to build up a roadbed was borrowed from a pit and conveyed to the worksite with a wheelbarrow; thus sometimes the feature is called a barrow pit or ditch.

This is Kent Haruf near the opening of *Eventide:* "Beyond the barrow ditches the irrigated corn stood up eight feet tall, darkly green and heavy." CONGER BEASLEY, JR.

bosque

The English bosk is a small woods or thicket especially heavy with bushes or shrubbery. The word comes unchanged from the Middle English *bosk*, meaning "bush." "And with each end of thy blue bow dost crown / My bosky acres, and my unshrubb'd down," as written by William Shakespeare in *The Tempest*, act 4, scene I. Bosks were often used as hiding places by escaped slaves traveling the Underground Railroad. Those hunting for them generally failed to search these small, bush-filled woods, thinking the escapees would more likely hide in large forests. *Bosque* is Spanish for forest and is slightly different from the English term in that it refers specifically to trees. In the Southwest, the term refers to a riparian forest situated along a river. Bosque del Apache, now a national wildlife refuge located along the Rio Grande near Socorro, New Mexico, was first named by the Spanish who observed Apaches routinely camping there. Corrales Bosque Preserve, near Rio Rancho, New Mexico, provides a migratory stopover and nesting habitat for over 180 species of birds. PATTIANN ROGERS

boss

In geographical terms, a boss is a rounded rise of volcanic rock. Storm King Mountain in the Hudson Valley is a well-known American example. The word itself as a historical concept is worth noting. Boss is undoubtedly a variation on the many *p/b* sounds that denote a rise or hollow rise or a rounded thing hollowed out, such as bosom, bubble, hub, cup/cap, *caput* (head, Latin) and *kube* (head, Greek), Cybelle from Kubebe (goddess of the mountain caves); the Arabic *(q)uba,* dome, *muqabr,* tomb, and *ka'aba,* the sacred domed meteoric rock in Mecca. The boss is the *omphalos,* a word that means center, eye, or "navel boss," the rounded thing that rises up at the center of the world. The ritual circling around a raised dome-shaped structure representing the omphalos, natural or man-made (such as Mount Kailas, or the universal domed saint's tomb or *stupa*), represents one of the primal features of the human connection with landscape. It may relate to the simple animal nature of a human being: an animal with eyes in the front of the head can only fully take in an object by circling around it. Emerson wrote, "The eye is the first circle; the horizon which it forms is the second; and throughout nature this primary figure is repeated without end. It is the highest emblem in the cipher of the world." SUSAN BRIND MORROW

bottom

In common usage, bottom is of course just the low part of whatever you're talking about. In business, there's the bottom line; for Gertrude Stein, talking about people, there was the bottom nature; and when referring to landscape, there's bottomland, a term that suggests, if not an alluvial floodplain, then at least some swampy or marshy area—a wetland, drained or not. As bottomland sounds rather formal, common usage has shortened it simply to the bottoms, a term that, being plural, preserves the fact that bottomland isn't just one place, but a series of interconnected places along a creek, stream, or river. Joe R. Lansdale uses it this way in his book *The Bottoms,* set in 1930s east Texas: "Through our thin walls I could hear the crickets outside, and somewhere in the bottoms, the sound of a big bullfrog bleating." In place names, you'll find the term in both singular and plural: for every Yazoo Bottoms (Mississippi) and Cheyenne Bottoms (Kansas), there's a Foggy Bottom (Washington, D.C.) and Sugar Bottom (Iowa).   STEPHEN GRAHAM JONES

boulder garden

Whitewater rafters are very familiar with the term boulder garden: a pile of boulders, often found at the mouth of a creek as it enters a river, creating a rapid. (In local usage, such a feature might also be referred to as a rock garden.) Many times, the rapid itself is named after this defining geomorphological characteristic, as in the Boulder Garden of the lower Lehigh River in Pennsylvania. At low water, the technical difficulty of navigating such a passage can deter even the most seasoned river runner. A boulder garden is not limited to waterways, however, and can refer to a scattering of large boulders along dry ground, often left by glacial movement or by rocks being driven up from deep within the earth, as is the case with Boulder Garden in the Adirondacks and Boulder Gardens located on the southwest corner of British Columbia's Babcock Mountain. Mountain bikers must watch for such clusters, especially the smaller, hidden rocks within the boulder garden, referred to as baby heads. Domestication and appropriation of natural landscape features have resulted in man-made boulder gardens, which often feature giant rocks that have been hauled in to be displayed amid an assortment of carefully arranged plants, flowers, and trees.   KIM BARNES

boulder jam

When a rock falls off a mountain and jams in a narrow passage, that's a jammed boulder. When rocks are driven down a watercourse by a flood and pile up in such a way as to block the normal flow of water, that's a boulder jam. Boulder jams are mostly of interest only to kayakers and other creek travelers who come upon them suddenly. Exasperated hikers find the jammed boulder a nuisance or worse, depending on how successful they are in getting around, under, or over it. A safety note: Never travel in jammed boulder country alone.   LUIS ALBERTO URREA

box canyon

Box canyons are not, strictly speaking, canyons shaped like boxes; they are three-sided instead, an open box as it were, with steep, vertical walls of hard rock and lacking the floodplains of gentler and more traditional canyons. They can also be two-sided. As a 1900 brochure about Arizona's Grand Canyon describes, "You are hedged in by dark walls on the sides, with a reddish-yellow strip of river below and a corresponding blue strip of sky above. You are in a box—a box canyon." The walls of such canyons are unclimbable, and the lone exit route is often only the path of the river's downstream flow. Still, hikers and climbers often seek out such well-known examples as Idaho's Box Canyon State Park, the Box Canyon Park near Ouray, Colorado, and Box Canyon near Wickenburg, Arizona.   ANTONYA NELSON

braided stream

"You step in the same river only once/for an instant. Panhandle time with/the bruised fingers of what might have been." It always brings a fresh look, this tendency certain rivers and creeks have to branch and interlace. The Platte, for example, rebraids in its shallow meander channel after every flood. Technically speaking, sediment is brought downstream by stronger currents, and it falls when weaker currents present themselves; ephemeral subchannels open, sandbars emerge. The stream braids water back and forth, across accommodating land, until it reunites. One term for this phenomenon is intercommunicating. Intercommunicating is what moved Jim Harrison and Ted Kooser to write their small book of poems, *Braided Stream: A Conversation in Poetry*: it is the best map of a river's multiform channels forming a net across the land. "Only today / I heard / the river / within the river."   LUIS ALBERTO URREA

brake

A brake is a thicket, usually located in a low, flat, marshy region and composed of tall, hollow, canelike reeds *(Arundinaria gigantea)* that frequently grow to a height of thirty feet or more. Canebrake once typified true wilderness in the Mississippi River Valley: virtually impenetrable stands of woody, bamboolike grasses regarded by early pioneers as serious obstacles to progress and civilization. Davy Crockett in his 1834 autobiography describes crawling through a thicket "the best way I could; and if the reader don't know it was bad enough, I am sure I do. For the vines and briers had grown all through it, and so thick, that a good fat coon couldn't much more than get along." The term canebrake is used interchangeably with brake throughout the Mississippi River Valley to describe the same type of growth. In Louisiana, brake signifies a low, wet, sloughy area supporting dense strands of cypress and gum trees. And an Illinois pioneer once declared that he had seen canebrakes "in which buffalo, deer, horses, and other animals were completely housed and sheltered, and I may add, fed during the winter storms." Before the great middle section of the continent could be agriculturally developed on a large scale, the brakes had to be cleared—daunting work, requiring that the land be drained and the thickets destroyed by fire. The soil supporting a canebrake was rich in nutrients, it turned out, and eventually yielded generous amounts of cotton and corn.   CONGER BEASLEY, JR.

brazo

Literally, a *brazo* is a Mexican's arm. (An older Castilian form of the word includes "strength" in its meaning.) The celebrated Rio Grande is known in Mexico as El Río Bravo (sounds like "brave," is more like "fierce," "strong," "wild"), but some sources suggest an earlier name was Río Brazo, and a perusal of cowboy fiction and old cowboy movies will easily turn up misadventures on the Brazos River in Texas. Figuratively, then, a brazo is an arm of a river, and the Brazos could be translated as the river Arms. Flowing between Fort Worth and the Gulf of Mexico, the Brazos can be seen to bend slightly at its elbow, as does the Rio Grande. When that arm flexes and shows its strength, trouble follows. For example, when the Brazos flooded on June 29, 1899, its bed spread to twelve miles in width in some places and its rampaging caused $10 million (in 1899 dollars) in damages. A narrow ocean inlet is *un brazo del mar*. A *brazo muerto* (dead arm) is a section of river that has become isolated from its main stream except when floods come and periodically recharge it in a brief connection with the original flow. LUIS ALBERTO URREA

breaks

Breaks, in the western United States, are tracts of rough, broken land, similar to badlands, that are of little commercial or utilitarian value—stretches of terrain, cracked and fissured by arroyos and ravines, nearly impossible to negotiate for any distance on foot or by horse. A dramatic example is found in the Texas Panhandle, where the course of the Canadian River abruptly fractures the smooth face of the Llano Estacado into a virtual bedlam of steep hills and tight passages. The distinction between breaks and badlands is minimal. The primary erosional mechanism for both is the freeze/thaw cycle, which loosens surface particles and carries them off in running water. *Breaks* also describes a line of irregular cliffs at the edge of a mesa or plateau. Cedar Breaks National Monument near Cedar City, Utah, for example, is a huge natural amphitheater. Dotted with scrub cedars and eroded out of the western edge of the Markagunt Plateau, it measures three miles across and cuts 2,500 feet deep into the surrounding land. "Cedar" is a misnomer in this instance; the tree is actually a juniper, which because of its shape and shaggy bark was mistaken by early pioneers for the famous cedars of Lebanon in the Middle East. CONGER BEASLEY, JR.

breathing cave

Air movement in caves is a common occurrence. Cool air displaces warm air seasonally, for example, and barometric pressure shifts cause cave air to stir. A breathing cave features a particular kind of air movement, a resonance phenomenon most easily understood by blowing across the opening of a bottle. Inside the bottle, successive waves of high and low air pressure vibrate with such rapid frequency that they produce an audible sound wave. A breathing cave, with its analogous shape, exhibits the same phenomenon on a larger scale. Air moving across the cave opening triggers an undulating movement of air inside, but the cave's greater volume slows these undulations so dramatically that what is created is not a sound wave but a rhythmic periodic "breathing." Cavers can feel this breath on their hands and face or might watch it sway a candle flame. This is how Virginia's Breathing Cave got its name. CAROLYN SERVID

brecha

Brecha means "breach" in Spanish. In south Texas and throughout Mexico a brecha is a walking trail, or a path

through forest or brushlands made by deer and cattle.
Sometimes ranchers will call a rough road made by a
pickup truck a brecha.   ARTURO LONGORIA

briar patch

A briar patch is simply a piece of land overgrown with
a tangled mass of thorned plants. The term was once a
widely used figure of speech, a vivid way to suggest a
difficult place or problem, a prickly situation in life. Joel
Chandler Harris used both the literal and metaphoric
meanings in *Uncle Remus: His Songs and Sayings* (1881),
a collection of southern stories incorporating Native
American and African trickster tales. In "How Mr.
Rabbit Was Too Sharp for Mr. Fox," Rabbit tricks Fox
into flinging him into the briars. When Rabbit has safely
escaped to the far side of the patch, he sits "cross-legged
on a chinkapin log koamin' de pitch outen his har wid
a chip" and brags that he was "bred en bawn in a brier-
patch."   CHARLES FRAZIER

bridal veil fall

A steeply vertical waterfall of gently expanding or bil-
lowing length acquires the obvious metaphor of a bride's
veil. More specifically, a high cataract of low flow that
entirely mists out before striking the pool below gives
the impression of gauzy cloth. Such falls are favored in
fault zones, where blocks of earth slip past one another to
create cliffs; and where bedrock fractures and falls away
from a resistant lip, as in the Columbia River Gorge
basalts. Smaller streams of steep gradient with constrain-
ing, steep sides to the upstream flow are more likely to
make bridal veil falls than larger, shallow-gradient, less
constrained rivers, which tend toward broader waterfalls.
Where streamcutting frees loose boulders instead,
cascades form rather than high falls. Glacially stranded

hanging valleys may also terminate in bridal veil falls, as in Yosemite National Park. Post-glacial, flood-ripped coulees or canyons may do so as well. The Columbia Plateau and Gorge of Washington and Oregon are therefore rich in such falls, including the eponymous Bridal Veil and Horsetail Falls and the much larger, double-trained Multnomah Falls.   ROBERT MICHAEL PYLE

brink

A brink is a verge, a threshold, with an element of risk; the edge of a steep place; the end of land bordering a body of water, as a river, lake, or sea. If one walks out to the tip of the Hopi village Walpi on First Mesa, one stands at a brink: on a clear day, when the vast expanse stretches for miles, one can look south and glimpse the San Francisco Peaks in the far distance. The Brink on the Sevier Plateau in Utah provides another such threshold.   ARTHUR SZE

broken ground

Broken ground may mean uneven terrain, as when Edgar Rice Burroughs wrote in *The Lost Continent*, "There was nothing but rough, broken ground covered densely with weeds and brambles, and tall, rank grass." When used interchangeably with plowed ground, however, the term means tilled soil. Here, broken ground, like a broken horse, is tamed, reduced to human control. The violence implicit in the phrase can be heard in sod-busters, a contemptuous name first applied by ranchers and herders in the West to anyone who plowed the land. Because we break ground for new construction, we often speak of any pioneering endeavor as ground-breaking. By contrast, well-plowed ground is a piece of intellectual real estate so thoroughly worked over as to be exhausted.   SCOTT RUSSELL SANDERS

brown land

In an urban setting, abandoned parcels left to fall to ruin are referred to as brown land. This is land both abandoned and damaged through processes of neglect and industrial use. The phrase encompasses run-down and unoccupied buildings (including former single residential dwellings) and other structures in an advanced state of disrepair, such as buildings with unsound roofs or boarded-up properties, as well as vacant lots and other potentially habitable, fertile, or undeveloped ground, occasionally supporting or surrounded by "trash woods." The Environmental Protection Agency uses the official term brownfield to identify abandoned or underutilized properties subject to expansion or redevelopment.

The agency has established several cataloging programs, involving ten regional "brownfield coordinators" across the United States. One survey estimated that as many as 400,000 brownfields exist in the United States. Another found more than 21,000 brownfields in 232 major American cities. Long before this urban designation, T. S. Eliot evoked the sense of it in his celebrated 1922 poem "The Waste Land": "The river's tent is broken: the last fingers of leaf/Clutch and sink into the wet bank. The wind/Crosses the brown land, unheard. The nymphs are departed./Sweet Thames, run softly, till I end my song."   JEFFERY RENARD ALLEN

browse line

If you see a forest where the vegetation looks as if it has been neatly trimmed to a height of about five feet, this browse line is an almost certain sign that deer numbers have grown too high. With too few predators to control their numbers, and with favorable niches opened by agriculture and suburban development, deer numbers often explode, to the point that the animals first overgraze the herbaceous plants of the forest floor, and then stretch as high as they can reach for twigs and other woody browse. The realization expressed in "Thinking Like a Mountain," that a mountain therefore "lived in mortal fear of its deer," was part of what convinced Aldo Leopold to stop shooting wolves and help start the infant science of wildlife management.   BILL MCKIBBEN

brûlé

A term now mainly confined to Canada and Cajun Louisiana, brûlé—from the French *brûler*, to burn—means a burned-over area of forest or swamp. In the words of Canadian woodsman and mountaineer Curly Phillips, about a difficult moment in the mountains of British Columbia: "We lost the trail and had to cut through half a mile of brule." The term was carried to Louisiana in the eighteenth century by French Canadian exiles from Acadia (their name for Nova Scotia and adjacent areas). English-speaking pioneers of the Canadian West customized *bois brûlé*, burnt woods, into the more user-friendly "bob ruly." According to historian George R. Stewart, bois brûlé also meant the son of a French father and an Indian mother.   JOHN DANIEL

buckbrush coulee

Coulee, a word common to the West and the upper Plains, derives from French fur traders' incursions along the rivers of northern North America. Although *coulée* in French means flowing, like lava, to French Canadian trappers it meant a sluggish stream or a ravine that held occasional, seasonal water. West of the Missouri, however, a coulee is generally dry—except during pouring rain—a high-walled valley cut into a hill or escarpment, as along the Missouri Breaks. Its baleful cousin, the buckbrush coulee, is so dense at its base with the browse frequented by deer (the height of a buck, thus perhaps its name) that you might hear a rancher say to a newly hired hand on horseback, "Don't try to ride up that buckbrush coulee." LARRY WOIWODE

buffalo jump

The Plains peoples of North America hunted buffalo for thousands of years. One of their techniques was to find herds in a natural grazing area near a cliff or a steep bank over which the animals could be stampeded. The Cheyenne, the Kiowa, the Kiowa-Apache, the Lakota, and other Native peoples of the Great Plains constructed driving lines, sometimes with stone cairns, sometimes with logs, to funnel the herds to the cliffs. The sites had different names in different languages. To the Peigan-Blackfeet people of Alberta they are *pishkun*. In English they are buffalo jumps. The driving lanes, in the centuries before the horse reached North America, could be as much as ten or twelve miles long. The killing sites at the base of the cliffs are a compound of bones, stone rubble, and earth, sometimes to a depth of thirty feet with strata that go back 5,600 years. When Meriwether Lewis came upon a buffalo jump hunt in Missouri, he described the activities in great detail in a May 29, 1805, journal entry beginning with this: "Today we passed on the Stard. side the remains of a vast many mangled carcases of Buffalow which had been driven over a precipice of 120 feet by the Indians and perished; the water appeared to have washed away a part of this immence pile of slaughter and still their remained the fragments of at least a hundred carcases they created a most horrid stench." Well-known buffalo jumps among the remaining sites include the Vore Buffalo Jump in the Black Hills of northeastern Wyoming, Glenrock Buffalo Jump in central Wyoming, Madison Buffalo Jump State Park near Bozeman, Montana, and Head-Smashed-In Buffalo Jump near Fort McLeod, one of 150 jumps in Alberta. ROBERT HASS

bull pen

Bull pen here is not the board-wall or chain-link arena
where pitchers warm up, nor the stout enclosure near
outbuildings where bulls are contained until the season
to unleash them among heifers, but altitudinous meadows in the Rocky Mountains enclosed by the steep-
walled surrounds of a higher range. The designation
likely derives from the use to which they were originally
put. The unscalable (to cattle) walls of mountain rock,
with a single portal parted by nature or a watering
stream, could be walled shut with boulders or deadfall,
allowing bulls to be held in pasture until it came time
to release them to a herd. Calf Pen Canyon, near Pine
and Payson, Arizona, is named for just such a natural
use.   LARRY WOIWODE

buried soil

Soils comprise adjacent earthy layers of different texture,
structure, color, or composition, these layers called
horizons. Buried soil, or paleosol, is the horizon of
ancient land surface preserved beneath ash, sand, peat,
or other deposits, remaining remarkably stable over tens
of thousands of years. In many parts of North America,
buried soil marks the surface that existed before the
advent of agriculture as introduced by Europeans—it
was buried by a flood of sediment that eroded from those
early mismanaged fields. Buried soil is often analyzed for
information about human activity in a given period, or
the state of the environment at that time. For instance,
a recent excavation project in Richmond, Virginia,
called Cactus Hill uncovered evidence in buried soil
that suggested to some that Clovis people (thought to
have crossed the Bering Land Bridge 13,500 years ago)
were not the first to migrate to the Americas. Scientists
analyzed two sediments in this ancient sand dune. In the
paleosol they found chipping stone implements, burned

bone, and campfire remains—evidence, they believe, that confirms human occupation dating back nearly 18,000 years. Buried soil opens the door and offers tokens to explore former knowledge.   ELIZABETH COX

burn

A burn is a place where a wildland fire once was, such as the Tillamook Burn in Oregon's Coast Range, and more broadly a burn is a natural act, a human technique, and a regenerative ecological condition in a particular place. Native Americans throughout the continent set fires to drive deer, bison, alligators, and other animals for slaughter and, enhancing natural fire cycles, regularly burned to condition land to support game and wild or cultivated crops. Euro-Americans at first adopted these practices, but advancing settlement and Indian removal gradually brought the return of woods to landscapes that Native Americans had maintained as grassland or savannah. "The Great American Forest," writes Stephen J. Pyne in *Fire in America*, "may be more a product of settlement than a victim of it." Commercial forestry in the twentieth century vigorously suppressed wildfires and redefined the burn as an aesthetic and ecologic tragedy. As scientific understanding of fire ecology has deepened in recent decades, prescribed burning techniques have returned to land management practices. And, thanks largely to the writings of Stephen Pyne, the role of anthropogenic fire in the human ecological history of North America has been fully recognized.   JOHN DANIEL

burn pile

Burn piles are common sights in areas that are being harvested for timber or cleared for cultivation. Sometimes referred to as pum piles (*pum* is the Forest Service's acronym for "pile of unusable material"), they are more often called slash piles. Slash is the collective term for the limbs, tops, broken branches, stumps, root wads, and other "trash" left after a tract of land has been logged. This debris is piled or bulldozed into large heaps that are burned, generally in spring or fall, to get rid of dangerous fuels before the next fire season. To slash means to cut down trees in order to make a right-of-way or other clearing; more generally, it means "to cut or hack." Land that has been brutally cleared often looks ravaged. This is especially the case when slash and burn is employed, a method that involves cutting down an area of virgin or rejuvenated forest and piling the unsalvageable material, which is then allowed to dry before being incinerated. The phrase itself has become synonymous with any action or policy of malicious purgation.   KIM BARNES

burrow

A word whose obscure origins are at least as intriguing as its definition, burrow seems to be related to forms of the Old English *borough*, whose original meaning was a stronghold, and *bury* or *berry*, words whose roots belong to the notion of "shelter" or sometimes "a hillock," indicating protection. As a noun, burrow usually refers now to a hole or excavation made in the ground (often a hill or earthen mound) by rabbits and moles, foxes, and other animals and used as their dwelling places. But an early use of the word in English refers to the enclosures that the wintering Roman legions constructed for refuge, rather like modern foxholes, in flat and open fields that did not afford any protection from the elements or from advancing forces. The verb to burrow is often figurative, the imaged noun turned into an active verb suggesting the effort of finding shelter by digging or scratching a hidden space large enough to hold oneself, animal or human. To burrow can mean to seek safe haven from any encroaching danger or discomfort, as Willa Cather describes in her novel *My Ántonia*: "The burrow sloped into the ground at a gentle angle, so that we could see where the two corridors united, and the floor was dusty from use, like a little highway over which much travel went." PATRICIA HAMPL

butte

A butte is a mesa's orphan, the freestanding remnant of a larger landform. Protected from the erosional brunt of rain, frost, and wind by its overlay of hard caprock, the butte's mass stands flat-topped and steep-sided, always taller than it is wide. The parent escarpment may be but a gap of space away: imagine this gap filled with rock and you can picture the entire landform's sweeping, high-crowned continuity. Or the parent escarpment may be entirely eroded, leaving the outlier butte to evoke a terrestrial loneliness—a marker to help you find your way home in the desert, a gaunt cipher to align with summer stars. In *The Man Who Killed the Deer*, Frank Waters's classic novel, he writes: "The moon had risen high above the great, still trees. He could see between them, on one side, a jaundiced vista of the desert sloping up and away past a far, flat-topped butte to the long line of mountains lying like the upturned edge of the horizon." ELLEN MELOY

buttress

A buttress is a gargantuan prow of rock that sticks out from the side of a mountain, roughly analogous to the corner of a Manhattan office tower. Typically a buttress rises more steeply than a ridge, and is not as slender or as sharply chiseled as an arête. JON KRAKAUER

cairn

Human-created formations, cairns come in various shapes, styles, and categories. Rock piles and single stones used to mark the places of the dead are among the most widely known. These include the menhirs, dolmens, and barrows of Western Europe; the stupas of Buddhist Asia, along with the stelae and obelisks of other cultures; and myriad memorials and markers down to the humblest gravestone and the simplest pile of hand-placed stones at a burial site. In its usual, restricted sense, cairn refers only to the (most often) conical pile of stones used to mark boundaries; turning points along routes of travel; caches of food, water, and equipment; areas of danger; sacred sites; and places of private or personal importance. In a less restricted sense, cairn is applied in North America to the burial and effigy mounds, medicine wheels, herding chutes, stone figures (for example, *inuksuit)*, ground glyphs, and other stone structures created over many thousands of years by the Native peoples of the continent. Many of these sites are protected; others await the recognition that will afford them protection. Meanwhile, one stone atop another says a human being was here, feeling, thinking.   LINDA HOGAN

caldera

The Spanish word *caldera*, also spelled caldero, has varied meanings in the American Southwest and throughout Mexico. While the literal translation is "pot" or "kettle," in south and west Texas the term also means a cotton gin or steam engine. In ranch country, vaqueros call a bucket of feed a caldera. As a landscape term it is used to describe a volcanic phenomenon in which the violent propelling of magma creates a sudden void within the vent, thus allowing rock and molten debris encircling the vent to implode inward, forming a kettle-shaped orifice, as in the Valles Caldera National Preserve of New Mexico.   ARTURO LONGORIA

camelback

The rounded relief of a camelback suggests the arching back and hump of a dromedary. The name is given to several mountains but most notably to the iconic Camelback Mountain located in Phoenix, Arizona. Many lesser elevations also carry the camelback name, because they bear the characteristic profile of a sloping hummock. There are camelback features near Santa Barbara, California; Kiowa, Oklahoma; and Monroe, Pennsylvania. Camelbacks result from various geological processes, including erosion and glacial deposition. This sharing of a common name isn't because of the prevalence of camels in America; it could reflect the memory of a camel in a circus parade, a Bible illustration, or a picture in a spelling book: "C is for camel."   D. J. WALDIE

campo

In the Spanish language *el campo* is the countryside. Sometimes it refers more specifically to open country as opposed to forested or mountainous terrain. Used with a possessive rather than the definite article—*mi campo*—the term refers to land that has been tamed by human hands as an agricultural field.   BARBARA KINGSOLVER

cañada

Cañada means "dell," "ravine," or "cattle path" in the Spanish language. The word is also used to describe a wetland rich with river reeds (*caña* means "cane" or "reeds") as seen along arroyos and *resacas* (oxbow lakes). Cañadas choked with common reeds (*Phragmites* spp.) or cattails (*Typha* spp.) offer protective areas for waterfowl and aquatic mammals. Cañadas also harbor plants such as alders—Cañada del Aliso in Ventura, California—or grapes, as in Mary Austin's *The Land of Little Rain*: "Fifty-seven buzzards, one on each of the fifty-seven fence posts at the rancho El Tejon, on a mirage-breeding September morning, sat solemnly while the white tilted travelers' vans lumbered down the Cañada de los [*sic*] Uvas." Other cañadas include La Cañada Honda in New Mexico and La Cañada Simada in Fresno, California (in these contexts *honda* and *simada* both mean "deep"), as well as the Pima, Arizona, trail, Cañada del Oro. ARTURO LONGORIA

canal

A canal is a man-made watercourse constructed for navigation, drainage, or irrigation. Navigational canals either connect two similar bodies of water—the many canals of the Soo Locks connect Lakes Superior and Huron, for instance—or two very different waterways—the Erie Canal connects the Hudson River to the Great Lakes, employing, as most canals do, an ingenious system of locks to contend with differences in altitude. The rowdy life of nineteenth-century canalers who towed weighty barges with mule teams onshore was immortalized in the folk song "The Erie Canal," which boasts the line, "Oh the E-ri-e's a-rising and the whiskey's gettin' low." Canals also bridge unnavigable stretches of rivers such as the Mississippi and Ohio, and connect oceans with seaports that are not directly on the coast. Then there is the Panama Canal, which links the Atlantic and Pacific Oceans. DONNA SEAMAN

candle ice

"Ice," writes American writer Stephen J. Pyne in his book *The Ice: A Journey to Antarctica*, "connects land to land, land to sea, sea to air, air to land, ice to ice. . . . Out of simple ice crystals is constructed a vast hierarchy of ice masses, ice terraces, and ice structures." Like every other life form, ice, too, has a life cycle—it is created, it grows, begins to decay, then disintegrates, falling back into the water whence it was born. As ice ages, it is said to "rot." Candle ice, or candled ice, is a type of rotting sheet ice named so because in the process of decaying it forms in its interior clusters of vertical prisms resembling delicate, waxy tapers. Often forming directly beneath a seemingly solid layer of surface ice, this eight-to-ten-inch-thick substructure—sometimes called honeycomb ice for its resemblance to that kind of uniform lattice—presents a serious danger to ice travelers.   GRETEL EHRLICH

canyon

Canyon is a general term with a heady array of specifics. It may be as "simple" as a cleft between steep walls or as complex as the Grand Canyon or Mexico's Barrancas del Cobre—miles across, layered in their depths like ragged, inverted cordilleras. In the Southwest, canyons are assertive landscapes. Aridity sharpens their bones. Rivers may run through them—open arteries in a carapace of rock; others flow only with blow-sand and chokestones. Canyons come blind, box, side, slot, hidden. They stair down and pour off. They gooseneck. They hang. Muley Twist, Desolation, Snap, Lavender, Blue Canyon, Rain Canyon—canyons are where you want to live merely on behalf of their names. The Hopi word *pösövi* means "can-yon corners," as if one quirky, prismatic facet at a time were all you could manage in this seemingly irrational geography of space and rock.   ELLEN MELOY

cape

A cape is a point of land, a ridge, or rock, projecting into a sea or other body of water; related terms include promontory and headland. The word comes from the French *cap*, or head, referring to a projecting point or peninsula. Cape Horn, the most legendary of this type of landmass, is the southernmost point of South

America, first rounded by Europeans in 1616. The U.S. coastline features many capes, including The Cape in Cumberland, Maine; Cape Hatteras in North Carolina; Cape Meares in Oregon; Cape Island Point in South Carolina; and Cape Northumberland at Prince of Wales, Alaska. Cape Cod, perhaps the best-known and most distinctive cape in the United States, extends off the state of Massachusetts, and was described play-fully by Henry David Thoreau, in *Cape Cod*, as "the bared and bended arm of Massachusetts: the shoulder is at Buzzard's Bay; the elbow, or crazy-bone, at Cape Mallebarre; the wrist at Truro; and the sandy fist at Provincetown—behind which the State stands on her guard, with her back to the Green Mountains, and her feet planted on the floor of the ocean, like an athlete protecting her Bay,—boxing with northeast storms, and, ever and anon, heaving up her Atlantic adversary from the lap of earth,—ready to thrust forward her other fist, which keeps guard the while upon her breast at Cape Ann." LAN SAMANTHA CHANG

cap rock

Cap rock is the hard rock or stratum of rock that sits atop less hardy material, protecting that material from erosion. On a small scale, the effect is often a mushroom-like formation; on a large scale, you end up with the Cap Rock of the Texas Panhandle—the southern, rocky escarpment of the South Plains. It's a term common enough to locals that you often see it both in lowercase and as a single word, as in Walt McDonald's essay "Get-ting Started: Accepting the Regions You Own or That Own You": "My mother... said that when the wagon rat-tled up on top of the caprock onto the wide flat plains—nothing but sky and miles and miles of waving native grass—she said she sighed, took a deep breath, and felt at home." Somewhere between this small and large scale—

between individual formations and entire regions—are petroleum engineers, for whom cap rock indicates a stratum of impermeable rock sealing off a reservoir of oil or natural gas. So, effectively, an underground mushroom- or domelike formation miles wide, yet still functioning as a cap rock does aboveground: protecting what's beneath it from erosion. Only here, the erosion being protected against is of course the petroleum engineers' drilling efforts.   STEPHEN GRAHAM JONES

Carolina bay

Along the Atlantic shore, from the southern tip of New Jersey to northern Florida, the coastal plain is marked by marshy depressions known as Carolina bays. As the name suggests, these sinks—species of bay tree are the dominant vegetation—are most numerous in North and South Carolina. They all tend to be elliptical in shape, and, more curious, their long axes tend to parallel each other, suggesting they might have been created by a swarm of meteoroids plummeting to Earth on a slant, perhaps the fallout from an exploding comet. Carolina bays may be as short as fifty yards in length or as long as several miles. Swampy and crowded with shrubby evergreen vegetation, a Carolina bay is devilishly difficult to pass through and is a place where it is possible to wander in circles for hours. Over time these bays might slump even deeper, creating inland lakes. The cool, clear, and immensely popular White Lake and Lake Waccamaw, both in North Carolina, are flooded Carolina bays.   JAN DEBLIEU

cascade

Mountain streams like to descend in stair-stepped series of short falls and brief pools. In these cascades, water alternates between two energy states, much like air shifting between super- and subsonic flow. The white water of the falls is the fluvial equivalent of a sonic boom.

Cascade is used more broadly to mean a rocky stretch of whitewater less steep than a waterfall but steeper than a rapid. The Cascades of the Columbia River, formed several centuries ago when a massive slide filled the channel in the mid–Columbia Gorge, presented Lewis and Clark's Corps of Discovery with a three-mile stretch of chutes and falls, "boiling in a most horriable manner," according to William Clark's journal. Rafting or boating the gorge was the last leg of the Oregon Trail for many early immigrants. Some lost all they owned to the Cascades, and some lost their lives. Now drowned in slackwater behind Bonneville Dam, this reach of river gave the Cascade Range its name.   JOHN DANIEL

castle rock

A term inspired by castellated erosional forms in the western deserts, though the castle rocks of the upper Missouri River, commented on by Lewis and Clark and rendered in watercolor by Karl Bodmer in 1832, are among the most widely known examples of the form. Utah geologist Lee Stokes claims there are as many Castle Rocks in the American Southwest as there are Inspiration Points in the country's national parks. He goes on to say, in *Scenes of the Plateau Land and How They Came to Be*, that the related term monument is more properly "applied to those final remnants [of a previously massive rock structure] that are much higher than they are wide and which therefore bear some resemblance to living things or the works of man." Castle rock incorporates within its designation features typical of such formations: a broad palette of ocherous hues, vertical and horizontal banding, grooves and knobs, and turreted heights. According to some, a castle rock differs from a monument rock in that it stands more obviously within or upon the structure of its parent rock, not in isolation in an otherwise open landscape. Its towering shape can easily be imagined as having once been a section in a solid rock wall, which, eroded by water and wind, became a mesa, then a butte, and finally a spire. A well-known Castle Rock—also called locally Castleton Rock—stands as a sandstone beacon on the eastern boundary of the town of Castle Valley, Utah, an icon in the Colorado Plateau's Redrock Wilderness and a destination for rock climbers worldwide.   TERRY TEMPEST WILLIAMS

cataract

Early writers in English referred to the "cataracts of heaven" to describe the floodgates through which rain poured for forty days and forty nights to produce the flood of Genesis, which only Noah and the passengers of his ark survived. Such cataracts were great waterfalls, and so the term was classically applied. By the nineteenth century, however, cataract had come to describe not a single waterfall but a series of them. In this usage, a cataract differs from a run of rapids only in the scale of its magnitude. John Wesley Powell, in his exploration of the Colorado River, applied the term enduringly to a stretch of the river in southeastern Utah. On July 23, 1869, he wrote in his journal: "We come at once to difficult rapids and falls, that in many places are more abrupt than in any of the canyons through which we have passed, and we decide to name this Cataract Canyon." The following day he elaborated: "Large rocks have fallen from the walls—great, angular blocks, which have rolled down the talus and are strewn along the channel. . . . Among these rocks, in chutes, whirlpools, and great waves, with rushing breakers and foam, the water finds its way, still tumbling down."   WILLIAM DEBUYS

catena

A term that would seem to be a legacy of the early Spanish explorers, catena is actually from the Latin for chain, and is used everywhere from theological tracts (Aquinas's *Catena Aurea*) to planetary geology, where it describes a series of similarly sized impact craters. In the introductory soil science classroom, however, catenae really come into their own as a teaching tool, illustrating how a sequence of soils in a region can share the same parent material yet, due to the slightest variations in drainage and relief, differ radically in color, texture, smell, and pH—all the characteristics by which soil is measured. A catenary sequence drawn from the top of an incline or hill (with an auger) will usually bear little resemblance to a sequence drawn from the bottom of that same incline, forcing us to accept that topography isn't just contour, but an indication of what's going on beneath the surface as well. STEPHEN GRAHAM JONES

cat hole

Any Boy Scout, primitive camper, or soldier can tell you about having to dig a cat hole (a slit trench, a latrine hole). But the various areas in the eastern United States with the name Cathole appended (Cathole Mountain, Cathole Pass, Cathole Landing, Cathole Cave, and Cathole, South Carolina) are probably not celebrating the art of happy outdoor defecation. In southern Michigan, a cathole is a euphemism for a shallow bog less than an acre in size, usually left behind by a glacier. Geologist Rick Williams identifies cathole as a drilling term used among miners for a tight hole in which dynamite is to be placed. A tight hole is much closer to the root of cathole, since the word is, well, an anal allusion. It originated in coal mines in Lancashire, England. (Most Cathole townships are in mining country, and most cathole landscape features are either caves or tightly circumscribed *angosturas*, or narrows.) Harry Tootles, in his *Mining Dictionary*, offers this piquant definition: "Cat-arse or Cat-hole pit. Colloquial euphemism for a drift mine or an 'adit,' known in Lancashire as a 'sough.' Tantamount to peering into the upper rear orifice of a cat. 'It was dark, mucky, and it stinks.'" LUIS ALBERTO URREA

catoctin

When Henry David Thoreau stood atop the "hard matter" of Maine's Mount Katahdin and exalted in the glory of "the solid earth, the actual world," he was thinking in human, not geologic, time. In geologic time even the most solid forms erode, even mountains disappear—or, in some cases, rise up out of what once was flatter plain. The Catoctin Mountains in Maryland and Virginia, at the northeast tip of the Blue Ridge chain—where the presidential retreat Camp David is located—are examples of such forms. Most of the rock in the region was originally formed by lava flow, which cooled and was covered by seas and sediments. This lava, under pressure of heat and weight, changed, or metamorphosed, into Catoctin metabasalt and greenstone, a dark greenish-gray rock highly resistant to weathering. As the softer strata on top of and surrounding this rock wore away, the mountains emerged. Today Catoctin remains a proper name, rather than a geographic term more generally. The last part of the name Catoctin contains *tin*, a generic Algonquian indicator for "mountains"; the first part of the word is probably a form of Algonquian *ketagi*, which means "spottled or speckled," a name that comes in part from Potomac marble, a speckled marble that occurs in the region. This residual landform is also called an inselberg and, chiefly in New England, a monadnock. GRETCHEN LEGLER

catstep

A catstep is a narrow, back-tilted terrace or bench on a grassy slope, formed when a hillside slumps beneath its own weight. Several catsteps may form together, each only a few inches in height—a staircase fit for a feline; or an individual catstep may be as high as four feet. Some of the best examples are found in the deep, wind-formed loess deposits of western Iowa. These are particularly prone to small landslides. JAN DEBLIEU

cauldron

A particularly chaotic type of gaping river hole, a cauldron is characterized by "big, squirrelly, boily water," in the words of one river runner. River cauldrons form where rocks, which have accumulated on the riverbed at a spot where the river suddenly drops, scour out a bowl-shaped depression. The surface of the river churns and explodes here like soup boiling over in a pot. Sulphur Cauldron, on the upper Yellowstone River in northwestern Wyoming, is one of many famed river cauldrons. Cauldrons are also a seacoast feature. When ocean swells and breakers surge into constricted openings in the seaward face of the land, they sometimes produce ferocious hydraulics—violent whirlpools, geysers, and suddenly collapsing haystacks of white water. TERRY TEMPEST WILLIAMS

cave

A cave mouth is a door to mystery and beauty, the entryway to a mineral world of water and moving air that, over time, has become a sacred place. A womb of Earth. Many cave walls were once painted with animals and the history of different peoples. In far deeper caves, Earth has painted its own history. Some caves developed during the life-nourishing eruptions of the planet: lava tubes, where magma runs underground and leaves empty tunnels behind. Some are tectonic, created by quaking movements of the planet. And there are long-lived caves of ice. The caves most widely known in the United States, however, are those created by dissolution and erosion in karst landscapes. "The finest workers in stone are not copper and steel tools," wrote Henry David Thoreau, "but the gentle touches of air and water working at their leisure with a liberal allowance of time." Karst caves include passageways and rooms with mineral deposits in the form of stalactites and stalagmites, soda straws, and draperylike ribbons, all built up by trickles of calcite-bearing water. Patricia Hampl describes this water in *Romantic Education* as "running steadily, timelessly, making its slow, hypnotic mark on the stone, on the ear, on the brain." Caves have their own ecosystems and many animals and insects depend on them. Not just hibernating bears but resident blind crayfish and endangered cave fish. Many caves harbor bats and indigenous beetles and salamanders. Carlsbad Caverns in New Mexico shelters crystal formations in cathedral-like rooms. The stable temperature in caves near San Antonio preserves bat guano, once used to make gunpowder. Mammoth Cave in Kentucky is the world's longest cave system, with 350 miles of chambers and passages. LINDA HOGAN

cavern

A cavern is a large chamber within a cave, a subterranean hollow—some with astonishing dimensions. The word cavernous implies a place where body and psyche can be lost, a sanctuary where philosophical speculation, à la Plato, can blossom. The words cavern and chamber are sometimes used interchangeably with cave, but the cave is labyrinthine, a maze of subterranean chambers, galleries, and passageways, while the cavern is the biggest room of them all. Mark Twain described the discovery of such a space in *The Adventures of Tom Sawyer*: "Tom went first, cutting rude steps in the clay hill as he descended. Huck followed. Four avenues opened out of the cavern which the great rock stood in." Carlsbad Caverns National Park contains more than 100 limestone caves, outstanding in the profusion, diversity, and beauty of their formations. The details of caverns—drip-stone features such as stalactites and drapery—are fragile environments affected by human activities and natural processes both above and below ground.   GRETEL EHRLICH

ceja

In Mexico and the American Southwest, a line of trees at the edge of a meadow, or the thin strip of clouds above a chain of mountains, or a sliver of moon are called a ceja because each resembles an eyebrow—the meaning of *ceja* in Spanish. The term eyebrow scarp suggests the same connotation. In Cuba the word *ceja* means a "narrow path."   ARTURO LONGORIA

cenote

Rainwater drains rapidly into porous limestone rock; as the limestone dissolves, caverns and caves are created. In those places where the caverns collapse, deep, circular chasms are formed, creating natural freshwater wells called cenotes. Cenotes were the only source of water for the great cities of Mayan civilization. The artist Frederick Catherwood, in his travels through the Yucatán with John Lloyd Stevens in 1839, depicted Indians descending eighty-foot ladders to draw water from such wells. More ominous were the sacred cenotes, or sacrificial wells, first chronicled by the inquisitional Franciscan priest Diego de Landa in his sixteenth-century treatise on Mayan life. The Cenote Sagrado de los Sacrificios at Chichén Itzá is one of the best known and documented of these exclusively ceremonial wells. Believing that Chac, God of Rain, and other demanding if lesser deities resided in the depths, the Maya dispatched human victims to please them. Well into the sixteenth century, pilgrims from the valley of Mexico as well as Guatemala, Honduras, Costa Rica, Panama, and Colombia came to the sacred city and cast gold, silver, copper, and all manner of prized objects into the moody, murky waters. The largest single collection of artifacts ever obtained from a Mayan site was excavated from this cenote. As for human remains, the bones of fewer than fifty individuals have been found, most of them determined to be those of men and children.   JOY WILLIAMS

chaco

For Spanish-speaking people in the Southwest today, *chaco* refers both to tilled and irrigated land near a village and to an expanse of country cross-seamed by small watercourses that sustain swamps and lakes. A related Spanish word, *charco*, means puddle or pool; *charca*, the feminine form, commonly refers to a pond. Chaco Canyon, the site of an abandoned Anasazi pueblo in New Mexico's San Juan Basin, is a conspicuously dry desert valley with an apparently anomalous name. It's a shallow cañón to some, a broad wash to others, bounded by a set of low-lying, gapped mesas, the most southwesterly of which is called Charca Mesa. The area might have been named after the remnant evidence of a once vital agriculture, or for something else. El Gran Chaco, a vast swampland shared by Bolivia, Paraguay, and Argentina, is a landscape from which people are absent. One feels a similar absence at Chaco Canyon. The ghostly kivas, the five-story house walls, and the scattered potsherds, which still bear the fingerprints of their vanished makers, enhance a sensation of suspended time. It's a place where one inhales the pungent smell of plant resins, released by the first desert rains to follow on a dry spell, with an unusual degree of appreciation.   TERRY TEMPEST WILLIAMS

channel

A channel is a confined flow of water on the surface of the Earth defined by its banks. This insistent flow of water can be controlled and artificial (as in the related word canal), or a natural channel, the course of which is largely dependent on the resistance of the material the water makes its way through. Mark twain is an old Mississippi River term; it's the second mark on a line that measures depth to two fathoms, or twelve feet, a safe depth for a steamboat—helpful in finding the navigable channel hidden in the river. Although a channel through rock is fixed, in the soft sand and clay bed of the Mississippi the changing force of the water flow makes the channel dynamic: it shifts from day to day. Only by study can you learn the signs, the secrets, that will tell you where the channel lies. If you misread the river, the bottom may come off the boat, the cargo might sink, people could die. The river has a whole language, a vocabulary of signs. To read the river is to find the channel. Hence in *Life on the Mississippi* Mark Twain writes: "Piloting becomes another matter when you apply it to vast streams like the Mississippi and the Missouri, whose alluvial banks cave and change constantly, whose snags are always hunting up new quarters, whose sandbars are never at rest, whose channels are forever dodging and shirking, and whose obstructions must be confronted in all nights and all weathers without the aid of a single light-house or a single buoy." SUSAN BRIND MORROW

channel mouth bar

When a river enters an ocean or lake, losing velocity, its sediment load drops to the bottom and forms a bar. This underwater ridge may lie anywhere from the river mouth to twenty miles or more out to sea. If daily sea-level fluctuation is small, waves breaking along a stable line may reinforce the bar. Materials deposited at the outflow of an

estuarine stream disrupt currents and form a barrier to
navigation. The formidable bar of the Columbia River
discouraged explorers from entering the "Great River
of the West" for many years, until Captain Robert Gray
crossed it in the *Columbia Rediviva* on a mild May day in
1792. Since then, the Columbia River Bar has claimed
scores of ships and become known as "the graveyard
of the Pacific." Today skilled bar pilots, separate from the
regular river pilots, guide large vessels over the bar. Tennyson's famous elegy "Crossing the Bar" makes spiritual
metaphor from the mud that challenges every outbound
journey.   ROBERT MICHAEL PYLE

channeled land

Channeled lands are those gouged and trenched by the
urgent desire of glaciers to travel, to melt, and to flood.
The scablands of southeastern Washington are the only
extensive example in the United States of this type of
formation, in this case consisting of canyons, coulees, and
channels cut into the bare rock by catastrophic glacial
floods. It is land not only deeply but starkly scarred.
Channeled land, corrugated by the heavy push and scour
of glacial ice as it moves down a valley—bedrock left
furrowed by advancing ice in Washington's Okanogan
Valley is a good example—is what remained after
immense stretches of ice-age meltwater drained away.
Between fourteen and sixteen thousand years ago, in
what's now western Montana, an extensive and towering ice dam formed and collapsed repeatedly, creating
a series of Lake Missoulas, one after another. The high,
racing wall of floodwater, once loosed, overwhelmed
parts of Idaho, Oregon, and Washington. Each time it
roared unimpeded all the way to the Pacific, ripping
wider the Columbia River Gorge on its way. The water
crushed and scarified Earth, but also left in its wake a
diversity of ecosystems, from the vast, dry scablands of

Adams and Whitman Counties in eastern Washington, to small, rich pockets of life, such as the Turnbull Wetlands near Cheney, Washington.   LINDA HOGAN

C

chaparral

Chaparral refers to the low, scrub vegetation of the dry regions of California and the Southwest. *Chaparro* is the Spanish name for the tough, broad-leaved evergreen scrub oak that grows in thickets in a dry Mediterranean climate. The word may come from the Basque *txapar,* which means "thicket." It came into American English after the U.S. annexation of California and the inland West. Here is William Brewer, field leader of the first California geological survey, in a letter to his sister in early May 1861, describing the view of the Santa Lucia range from the Salinas Valley: "A very rugged landscape of mountains behind, steep, rocky, black with chaparral." In his 1938 story "Flight," John Steinbeck seems to be using the word a little more exactly: "As soon as the trail had parted from the stream, the trees were gone and only thick, brittle sage and manzanita and chaparral edged the trail." It can refer to different plant communities at different altitudes in different locations. The name has been attached to species as diverse as *Pickeringia montana,* the chaparral pea, which grows on dry hillsides in coast redwood regions, and *Yucca whipplei,* the chaparral yucca native to the San Bernardino Mountains. In casual use, it is a synonym for brush.   ROBERT HASS

charco

Throughout the American Southwest and into Mexico, the thunderstorms of the monsoon season sweep from above the sierras onto the deserts and brushlands, and within a few turbulent days the land receives much of its annual allotment of moisture. The pools and mud holes that form after these intense rains are called *charcos,*

91

which in Spanish means "puddles." The word is occasionally used when referring to the trenches dug under
fences by deer, javelina, or feral hogs as they cross from
one pasture to another, perhaps because the furrows fill
with water after a rain.   ARTURO LONGORIA

chattermark

In carpentry, chattermarks are the transverse gouging
of a plank, caused when a smoothing tool—a plane
or a sander, say—is not properly aligned, adjusted, or
employed. In glacial geology, chattermarks are small
curved scars in a brittle bedrock surface. They result
from the vibrational chipping action of rock fragments in
the base of a glacier. Each mark is roughly at right angles
to the direction in which the glacier was moving, rather
like rumble strips on a highway. The mark is usually
crescent-shaped. Chattermarks should be distinguished
from glacial striations, which are thin, sharply incised
furrows that run parallel to each other and to the
direction in which the glacier traveled; they result from
the scouring action of rocks embedded in the glacier's
base.   FRANKLIN BURROUGHS

chickenhead

Before it solidifies into stone, granite is a viscous pudding
of feldspar, quartz, and (usually) hornblende and/or mica.
These minerals vary in hardness, and their distribution within a given granite formation can be far from
homogeneous. The upshot is that a granite cliff, slab, or
boulder seldom erodes uniformly. More durable areas of
the rock surface will more stubbornly resist weathering,
sometimes creating fantastic, mushroomlike protuber-
ances—typically three to twelve inches across, and projecting a similar distance from the adjacent plane—as the
surrounding stone erodes away. These weird protrusions
are known as chickenheads or knobs. Snow Creek Wall

in the Wenatchee Mountains of Washington State and
several of the cliffs overlooking the western entrance to
Yosemite Valley are renowned for their abundance of
chickenheads.　JON KRAKAUER

chimney

As used to denote landforms, the term chimney most
commonly refers to slender rock towers that resemble
their man-made brick-and-mortar counterparts when
considered from afar. But the word is also applied to
aspects of the landscape that resemble masonry flues
when viewed from within—that is, parallel-sided slots
or grooves, approximately two to twenty feet across, that
cleave steep precipices. For instance, North Chimney,
Fields Chimney, and Alexanders Chimney, all of which
are located on the lower east face of Longs Peak in
Colorado. Historically, mountaineers have relied on
such chimneys to provide routes of ascent up otherwise
impassable rock faces. Sometimes a chimney will split
the underside of an overhang, in which case it is called a
bomb-bay chimney.　JON KRAKAUER

chine

A deep and narrow ravine cut in soft rock strata by a
stream descending steeply to the sea. (Ravine has a
similar, though not exact, definition: whereas chine
is most often associated with the coasts and cliffsides
of England, ravine connotes mountains and streams.)
England's Isle of Wight and the Hampshire coasts are
perhaps the best-known examples of this type of landscape, although such formations can also be observed
along the coast near Malibu, California, and Big Sur. In
a larger context, a chine is an open fissure in a surface;
a cleft, crack, crevice, or chasm; a ridge or crest of rocks.
The word itself is from Old French *eschine*, which in turn
blends the Germanic ancestor of English *shin* and the

Latin *spina*, which means "spine." Chine is also a joint of meat that includes part of the backbone, and the verb to chine means to cut meat along or across the backbone of a carcass—which may have given rise to the perception of water cutting down the spine of land.   KIM BARNES

chockstone

A chockstone is a boulder that's become lodged between the walls of a chimney, cave, or slot canyon, much like a cork jammed into the neck of a bottle. In 1931, the eminent mountaineers Robert Underhill and Fritiof Fryxell attempted the previously unclimbed north ridge of Wyoming's Grand Teton. While ascending a chimney on the vertical face of the ridge, they encountered a giant rock wedged across the slot's six-foot-wide throat, which halted their progress. The "chockstone [was] so big," Fryxell reported, "that it extended well out over our heads. I could touch the chockstone but nowhere find the slightest hold." With tremendous effort, the men managed to climb around the boulder and eventually reach the summit, completing what was then the hardest climb in the United States. The notorious passage that nearly thwarted their ascent was christened "Chockstone Chimney."   JON KRAKAUER

choke point

The choke point—the Achilles heel in a dynamic system where forces of flow and resistance bottleneck—has become a notion used in a variety of contexts. For land travelers, the choke point may be a narrow defile where a path crosses a ridge at a point hemmed tightly by flanking cliffs. For hydrologists, the choke point may be a constriction in a stream channel where sedimentation builds as flow is blocked. The restless drama of such a position in stream or path has caused this term to become a metaphor attractive to military strategists, economists, and computer consultants, whereby, for example, the clog of email may threaten worker efficiency, just as a wilderness hiker may need to exhale to slip through a tight spot. KIM STAFFORD

chop hills

Nebraskans use the term chop hills as an alternative to sandhills; both refer to a ridge of sand, or sand dune, in a region containing a series of hills either composed of or covered with sand. Nebraska's Sand Hills form a body of sandy landforms north and northwest of the confluence of the North and South Forks of the Platte River and include the marshes the hills nourish. The famed sandhill cranes, wading birds averaging four feet in height with gray plumage, a trumpeting call, and elaborately choreographed mating rituals, frequent the chop hills as a way station on their annual migrations. In "Wisconsin: Marshland Elegy," Aldo Leopold describes the magnificent sandhill cranes as "wildness incarnate," and writes: "When we hear his call we hear no mere bird. We hear the trumpet in the orchestra of evolution. He is the symbol of our untamable past, of that incredible sweep of millennia which underlies and conditions the daily affairs of birds and men." DONNA SEAMAN

chops

As a noun, chops once meant jaws. This sense of the word survives in locutions such as "to lick one's chops." Topographically, chops refers to a narrow passage or entryway, typically a forbidding one. This might be an alpine gap, but the term, like mouth, occurs most often in nautical contexts. Major Robert Rogers, leading a little armada of bateaux along the north shore of Lake Ontario in September 1760, describes entering "the chops of a river, called by the Indians the Grace of Man." James Sullivan, in his *History of the District of Maine*, mentions "the Chops of

Merrymeeting Bay—a strait where the ebbing and flowing tides are alike hazardous to navigation." This place is
now known to locals simply as the Chops. In Britain, the
southern end of the English Channel has long been called
"the Chops of the Channel." It, too, is famously hazardous
to navigation.   FRANKLIN BURROUGHS

chuck

Chuck is a Chinook Indian word, a vernacular term that
alludes to an intertidal inlet and water-filled tidal basin
at the terminus of a river where fresh and salt water mix
and are temporarily trapped. Thus sometimes salt chuck,
to distinguish saline coastal chucks from freshwater
chucks inland, where they're more commonly called
prairie potholes. Along the coast of southeastern Alaska,
as in the Petersburg Creek–Duncan Salt Chuck Wilderness, one can find sites called Chuck Creek and Chuck
Slough. These basins flood, then drain. A place called
Skookumchuck means "turbulent water," and refers to
the times that infusions of salt water roil with water that
is fresh. At Salt Chuck on Prince of Wales Island south of
Juneau, one local fisherman said the chuck was a unique
environment where he had caught "silvers, sockeyes, and
the occasional steelie." The word chuck also refers to
food, and so the kitchen—or chuckwagon—pulled across
the Great Plains and the western range, where meals
were cooked to feed cowboys.   GRETEL EHRLICH

chute

The term chute generally describes a swift fall of water,
caused either by a steep descent in a riverbed or a sudden
narrowing of a channel in a river or strait. Derived from
both the French *chute* and the British *shoot,* this word is
multifarious: it is also used to describe the trough of a
canal lock as well as any sloping channel or passage for
the conveyance of water or objects floating in water, such

as logs or rafts. Some U.S. game laws require the erection and maintenance of chutes for the passage of fish over dams. In a slightly different use of the term, whitewater river rafters and kayakers look for what is known as an island chute, the point at which the river's gradient steepens and the water is funneled around an island into a fast and very narrow channel. In *Life on the Mississippi*, Mark Twain explains how "once, in one of these lovely island chutes, we found our course completely bridged by a great fallen tree. This will serve to show how narrow some of the chutes were. The passengers had an hour's recreation in a virgin wilderness while the boat-hands chopped the bridge away; for there was no such thing as turning back, you comprehend." LAN SAMANTHA CHANG

ciénega

In Spanish, *ciénega* (also *ciénaga*) refers to a swamp or marsh. The term was generally applied to desert wetlands in the American Southwest. Lush meadow grasses and marshy plants dominated these surfaces until the mid- to late 1800s, when overgrazing, logging in the mountains, and other human effects carried their toll. Many ciénegas were drained out; those that remained formed valuable wildlife habitat. Fifteen miles southwest of Santa Fe, New Mexico, in La Ciénega, lies Rancho de las Golondrinas (Ranch of the Swallows), a living museum that bears testament to what life was like in a small farming community. In *All the Pretty Horses*, Cormac McCarthy writes: "They ate lunch under the trees at the edge of a small ciénega. The horses stood in the marshy grass and sucked quietly at the water." ARTHUR SZE

cinder cone

Cinder cones are small volcanoes born when lava, explosively ejected from a new vent, cools in air as glassy or gassy small particles, which rain down and form a hill

97

around the vent. Lava flows may appear around the base of the cone. Typically built in one eruptive period, cinder cones tend to occur in clusters, as in the region around Sunset Crater near Flagstaff, Arizona, or in the area of Newberry Crater in central Oregon. Most in the American West are of basalt or andesite, thus dark in color, and under a thousand feet in height. A large and famous cinder cone is Paricutín, born in 1943 in a cornfield southeast of Guadalajara, Mexico. The cone was observed to grow from a hissing six-foot mound to a 1,100-foot mountain in the course of a single year. A church tower is all that now shows of a buried village. JOHN DANIEL

cirque

A common feature of glaciated mountain ranges, a cirque is a semicircular rock basin or bowl, as the skiing term goes, framed by steep headwalls varying in height from a few hundred to several thousand feet. Glaciers are instrumental in hollowing out these rock amphitheaters. As they move, cirque glaciers tend to rotate on the bedrock, grinding out the cirque's floor and creating a characteristic rock threshold on the down-valley edge. The cirque's headwall is steepened by eroding freeze-and-thaw cycles both between the glacier and the rock and within the glacier's bergschrund. Some cirques contain active glaciers, while others are relics of past glaciation and may or may not be filled with ice and snow. Frequently they cradle small lakes called tarns. Back-to-back compound cirques can create knife-edge arêtes or sharp spire-shaped horns like the Matterhorn. Wyoming's Wind River Mountains feature a complex group of cirques and tarns carved by Pleistocene glaciers. CAROLYN SERVID

cistern

"Cistern. I say it aloud. Cistern. More magic" (William Kloefkorn, *This Death by Drowning*). Cisterns, whether man-made or nature-made, have seemed to be miraculous to most cultures. Kloefkorn speaks here of the cistern his grandfather dug, lined with rock and "connected somehow to a truckload of subterranean downspouts... thus when rain fell, it coursed and curved and sloshed its convoluted way down into the cistern." These dugouts were sources of drinking water and garden irrigation for farmers and ranchers through the millennia. The nature-dug cistern has many names. In Spanish, it is a *tinaja*. (You can find these in the Sonoran Desert of Arizona: Edward Abbey often drank at Tinajas Altas, a place where "illegal aliens" drink now if they're lucky enough to find it.) A bedrock cistern in the wild is an example either of chemical weathering or of rain excavating rock. The Navajo Sandstone Abbey encountered at Tinajas Altas weathers to form shallow pits that perform like cisterns. A steady drip or small cataract of rainwater grinds out and fills a bedrock basin. This bowl, or divot, deepens over the centuries, worked at, between rains, by wind and sand. A perpetual process of grinding. (Some cisterns grow from indigenous corn-grinding *metates*, as can be found in the Las Palmas Valley, south of Tecate, Baja California.) In *Walking Nowhere: Finding Home*, W. Andrew Beckham notes a series of cisterns so deep that they have been called "Giant Track." Truly, it was a giant who made a footprint so deep that wind cannot stir the surface of its water, and that giant is the rain cloud. Kloefkorn says, "If there is magic on this planet, it is contained in water." LUIS ALBERTO URREA

clearcut

A clearcut is where commercial forestry removes all or most of the standing timber on a tract of land. Companies justify clearcuts because Douglas fir, the most desirable replacement tree over much of the West, grows best in full sun, but the practice is driven chiefly by economies of scale and maximum short-term profit. Unless ecological costs are factored in, it is easier, cheaper, and more cost-effective to fall every stem on a given timber sale than to cut selectively. Square-edged clearcuts give a checkerboard or mangy appearance, most visibly from the air and in winter when snow accentuates the cut. Molding the cut-line to the contours of the land gives a softer visual aspect than rectilinear clearcuts, but it's more difficult to survey, cruise for stumpage, and carry out. While clearcuts promote forest fragmentation, they can develop into vigorous plant and animal communities when neither sprayed nor eroded. Related terms are logging side and logging show, and a current euphemism is "active stewardship." In "Elegy for a Forest Clear-cut by the Weyerhaeuser Company," poet David Wagoner describes "the slash and stumps" and "the cratered / Three square miles of your graveyard." ROBERT MICHAEL PYLE

clearing

A man-made clearing is a tract of land from which trees, roots, and stones have been removed, making it suitable for settlement and farming, while the surrounding forest is left intact. Such creation of open space has played a significant role in the environmental history of the North American continent. Early European colonists, encountering vast forests of hardwoods, firs, and white pines, began the backbreaking work of making the land suitable for plowing, as romanticized by James Fenimore Cooper in *The Last of the Mohicans*: "The trees of many acres had been felled, and the glow of a mild summer's evening had fallen on the clearing, in beautiful contrast to the gray light of the forest." White pines became ship masts, and stones were piled into boundary walls. In a few hundred years, as the country's agricultural center moved west, these clearings extended hundreds of miles to Illinois

and eastern Missouri. The farmlands of Iowa, once protected by a mosaic of gallery forests, prairie vegetation,
and wetlands, are now subject to erosion. But the northeastern forests are recovering. Today, a hiker in the New
England woods will find mossy remnants of stone walls
surrounded by birch trees and other hardwoods, signs of
the old forest's return.   LAN SAMANTHA CHANG

cleaver

A cleaver is a mountain ridge that has been sculpted by
glacial ice into uncommonly sharp proportions. The
usage is largely limited to Washington's Mount Rainier,
which boasts seven named cleavers. The majority of the
twelve thousand–plus climbers who attempt to ascend
Rainier each year do so via Disappointment Cleaver, a
dark blade of eroded lava that demarcates the Ingraham
and Emmons Glaciers on the dormant volcano's southeast flank.   JON KRAKAUER

cleft

A cleft is a sizable crack, fissure, crevice, or rift in a rock
surface. It is smaller than a cave or cavern, and, unlike
those landforms, it gives the appearance of having been
created by an abrupt fracturing or splitting action rather
than by a gradual process of erosion or subsidence.
Probably through a confusion with cliff, it is sometimes
spelled clift. The writer James Kilgo, in *An Inheritance
of Horses,* describes meeting a man named Roy in the
mountains of north Georgia. Roy tells a story of a hound
that fell into a rock clift. Kilgo asks him exactly what a
rock clift is.

"Why it's kindly like a hole."

"A hole in the ground?"

"No. It's where you have a clift in the rock." He
paused, then continued, "Hell, it's just a rock clift, is
what it is."   FRANKLIN BURROUGHS

cliff

Inland or on coastlines, a cliff rises as a nearly perpendicular rock face. Eight to ten miles of cliffs layer-cake
back from the Grand Canyon. Faults and joints crack
cliffs. Erosion carves and paints them. Hapless victims of
foul play are thrown off them. Prehistoric farmer-hunters
in the Southwest—cliff dwellers—tucked their masonry
pueblos into the natural alcoves of sandstone cliffs and
lived in vertical tan or rose-colored space. From a cliff
in New Mexico Mark Helprin, in *Refiner's Fire*, looks
into a world where golden eagles "returned to cliffside
aeries in graceful lines of flight, the sun diminished in a
perfect sphere beyond the curve of the horizon, the stars
appeared at first mildly then blindingly bright, and violet
bands stretched from heaven to the face of a darkened
peaceful earth—a planet of cool high desert and ruffling
insistent winds." ELLEN MELOY

closed basin

Areas where topography prevents the outflow of water
are called closed basins. With no outlet, all drainage is
internal. These rivers do not reach the ocean, and water
escapes only by evaporation or percolation. Closed basins
may be extensive: the Great Basin—which is actually a
collection of smaller closed basins—for example, covers
an area of nearly two hundred thousand square miles,
covering most of Nevada and large parts of Utah and
Oregon. Or they may be quite small: prairie potholes of
the northern plains cover just a couple of acres or less.
CHARLES FRAZIER

coal dig

Coal digs are commonly found in the western Dakotas
where lignite, a soft coal, resides near the surface, from
three to thirty feet underground. Trappers and home-

steaders began the digs, using shovels and bare hands, in regions where chunks of lignite erupted through the ground itself. Areas of coal digs regularly visited for fuel are still visible, their squared-off sides slowly sodding over in the manner of peat digs in the Western Hebrides. The digs range from the size of a pickup to an acre or more, and are often located along wandering creeks. Lignite usually arrived wet from such digs and had to be dried on racks before it could be burned. Lignite digs are also visible at river edges and in cutbanks, in hillsides fronting rivers, and in the mounded formations of the Theodore Roosevelt National Park badlands, where lignite lies in black slices across the colorful formations. A gasification plant near Beulah, North Dakota, where lignite is transformed into propane, uses a crane so huge to mine lignite that automobiles can be parked inside its bucket—a far cry from human hands. LARRY WOIWODE

coastal plain

Coastal plain is used especially in the Carolinas and eastern United States to refer to the land between the Piedmont and the ocean, from New Jersey all the way around to Texas's Balcones Escarpment. The term is understood to mean the belt of flat or almost flat land made of sand- and sea-deposited minerals reaching from the shore to the fall line. The coastal plain is characterized by pine forests, shallow lakes, white sandy soil. Cities such as Richmond, Virginia; Fayetteville, North Carolina; and Columbia, South Carolina, are set at the edge of the coastal plain where navigation was halted by rapids on the rivers and where the hill country begins. "At intervals, the Atlantic has advanced and retreated across the Coastal Plain," writes Michael A. Godfrey in *Field Guide to the Piedmont*. ROBERT MORGAN

cockpit

The cockpit country of Kentucky is the best North American example of a type of terrain in which limestone-based karst landscape is filled with depressions. The pits form when the underlying limestone dissolves and the surface of the ground subsides or collapses into subterranean channels or caves. The resulting small, enclosed basins vary in dimension, but are often of just the right size to contain a clandestine cockfight, a sport reputed to survive in parts of Kentucky.   BARBARA KINGSOLVER

cofferdam

Imagine a decorative wishing well, then imagine that well writ large. Next, understand that the well is not meant to contain water but to exclude it, so you must now envision a body of water surrounding your big, dry well. These are the kinds of structures erected by engineers in the middle of a river then pumped dry; the watertight wall enclosing the dry area is known as a cofferdam. In his book *Boulder Dam,* Zane Grey describes one such structure this way: "The truck road ended on the cofferdam, which was still forty feet above the river—a solid obstacle of lumber and sandbags." Built as temporary structures to facilitate the construction (or destruction) of aquatic edifices such as bridges or dams, cofferdams have been employed since the early days of modern dam building. In the early 1900s, large cofferdams were put in the great Mississippi River to hold back its water, allowing the construction of what was then the largest hydroelectric plant in the world—Keokuk Dam in Keokuk, Iowa.   ANTONYA NELSON

cold deck

In logging lingo, a cold deck is a pile, or deck, of logs that have been stacked up away from the immediate logging operation, usually outside of densely forested areas because of fire danger. Most people are familiar with cold decks as those towering stacks of logs seen in the yards of lumber mills—enough to keep a big mill going all winter and spring. During the era of log drives, landings along the river were lined with cold-decked logs awaiting spring breakup, when the logs would be pushed into the river for their journey to the mill. The opposite of cold decking is, of course, hot decking, part of a fluid logging operation in which the trees are felled, skidded, trimmed, and loaded with little delay. It is interesting to note that, in gambling, a cold deck is a stacked deck of cards held in the dealer's hand; therefore, cold deck has evolved into a general term meaning "to take unfair advantage of." Although it is difficult to say how these two definitions might inform one another, it is fair to speculate that early generations of bunkhoused lumberjacks were as familiar with one application as they were with the other.   KIM BARNES

colina

A colina is a hill. However, a hill is one thing to a mountaineer and another to a plainsman. A colina is less than the imposing elevation of a *montaña* (mountain) but grander than an *altozano* (a rise). *Cerro* and colina are nearly synonymous, though colina's topographic neutrality suggests an elevation that is neither particularly steep nor thickly forested. Unlike an *otero*, a colina does not lord over a lowland in solitude; it's a neighborly, everyday hill.   D. J. WALDIE

collapse sink

A collapse sink occurs when an underground cavern becomes so enlarged by solution and/or erosion that its upper surface collapses, or slumps, creating a shallow basin or funnel-shaped depression in the landscape. Size and shape vary; a collapse sink may create a shallow depression of many acres. Like other categories of sinkholes, collapse sinks have numerous synonyms, including collapse doline, shakehole, and swallowhole in the United Kingdom; the more musical *polje* and *ponor* of Serbo-Croatian; and cenote, very common in Florida and in Mexico's Yucatán.   KIM BARNES

comb ridge

A comb ridge is a sharp mountain crest eroded by glaciers or water to look jagged, saw-toothed. Because of the pinnacles and notches along its crest, a comb ridge—the expression is often used interchangeably with arête—resembles a rooster's comb. It is the acute and rugged divide between two aggressive glacial arenas. In the dryland west, a comb ridge is a single fold of upturned rock that has sharp teeth cut by water erosion. An example is Comb Ridge, near Bluff, Utah. Other comb ridges can be seen in Grand Staircase–Escalante National Monument, Utah.   ROBERT MORGAN

commons

A common, or commons, is land that belongs to an entire community. More specifically, it is open land held in common by the people of a town for shared pasturage or the gathering of firewood. As noted in *A Gazetteer of Illinois* in 1834 by J. M. Peck, "A common is a tract of land . . . in which each owner of a village lot has a common but not an individual right. In some cases this tract embraces several thousand acres—the common attached to Cahokia extends up the prairie opposite St. Louis." In her book *Red: Passion and Patience in the Desert*, Terry Tempest Williams notes that "most lands in the American West are public lands, a commons if you will, held inside a national trust: national forests, Bureau of Land Management lands, national parks, monuments, and refuges." These are the commons of a global village, preserved with common sense and commitment to the common good.   DONNA SEAMAN

The place where streams converge and unite is their confluence. North America's two great rivers, the Missouri and the Mississippi, meet on the northern edge of St. Louis. The confluence of the Allegheny and Monongahela Rivers in Pittsburgh forms the Ohio River. Similarly, the Kansas River, formed by the confluence of the Republican and Smoky Hill Rivers, flows about 169 miles eastward to its confluence with the Missouri River at Kansas City. And a place called The Confluence, in Canyonlands National Park and named by John Wesley Powell, is where the Green and Colorado Rivers meet. Many of the early thriving communities in the American colonies began at a confluence, since rivers were necessary for trade and the transportation of goods. Such trade often required the construction of forts to protect traders from the real or perceived threats of local Native Americans or competing settlers and traders. Hence, Washington Irving notes in his book *Astoria; or, Anecdotes of an Enterprise beyond the Rocky Mountains* (a glorified history of John Jacob Astor's fur trade empire): "At length it was found necessary to establish fortified posts at the confluence of the rivers and the lakes for the protection of the trade, and the restraint of these profligates of the wilderness." Writing about confluence sites in the Great Plains, Ian Frazier notes: "The reason no city grew at the confluence of the Missouri and the Yellowstone is that in 1866 the Army built a post called Fort Buford a few miles east of Fort Union, and in 1868 created a thirty-mile-square military reservation with the post at the center. Since the reservation was closed to all settlement, the city which people eventually built was farther down the Missouri, at the junction of the Little Muddy River. Today this city is called Williston, North Dakota, and it gets much of its income from oil, and its long commercial highway strips wax and wane." JEFFERY RENARD ALLEN

Continental divides are clearly definable lines, usually
running along the ridgetops of mountain chains, that
separate one drainage basin from another. In a journal
entry dated August 12, 1805, Meriwether Lewis writes:
"After refreshing ourselves we proceeded on to the top
of the dividing ridge from which I discovered immence
ranges of high mountains still to the West of us with their
tops partially covered with snow. I now decended the
mountain about ¾ of a mile which I found much steeper
than on the opposite side, to a handsome bold running
Creek of cold Clear water. here I tasted the water of the
great Columbia river." He and the other members of the
Corps of Discovery had just crossed the east-west continental divide at Lemhi Pass on today's border between
Montana and Idaho. Shortly before crossing, Lewis had
straddled a rivulet trickling from a spring on the east side
of the line that slipped downhill to join other streams
heading east and south for the Missouri River and the
Gulf of Mexico. Two additional divides frame the vast
interior basin of the Missouri-Mississippi river system.
The first lies to the north at Browns Valley, a town on
the Minnesota–South Dakota line, where water from the
Red River, which rises in Minnesota, turns north toward
Canada. The second lies to the east, along the north-
south crest of the Appalachian Mountains, between the
Atlantic coast and the rivers of the interior. The Pacific,
Gulf of Mexico, and Hudson Bay watersheds meet at the
summit of Triple Divide Peak in Glacier National Park.
To the west the peak drains into the Flathead River,
thence to the Pacific via the Columbia River. To the
northeast it flows into the Saskatchewan River and on to
Hudson Bay. On the southeast its waters enter the Marias
River and flow on to the Gulf via the Missouri and
Mississippi. In "Once by the Pacific," Robert Frost writes:
"You could not tell, and yet it looked as if / The shore was

lucky in being backed by cliff / The cliff in being backed by continent." CONGER BEASLEY, JR.

copse

A copse is a wood filled with small growth, a thicket of brushwood. While copse is sometimes used interchangeably with coppice, there is a difference. Although having the same etymological root, coppice means a small wood subject to periodic cutting, or "coppicing." (*Webster's Collegiate Dictionary,* Tenth Edition, defines the term as "to cut back so as to regrow in the form of a coppice; to sprout freely from the base.") Copse, meanwhile, conjures the image of a limited area of trees, as in a stand or a grove. Both words enjoy more currency in the language of Ireland and Great Britain. This might reflect the degree to which their original forests have been reduced and domesticated, compared to the larger woodlands still found in North America. CONGER BEASLEY, JR.

coral reef

Whereas a reef is merely a line of rocks in the tidal zone of a coast, and an artificial reef is just junk—from old railroad cars to scuttled destroyers—dumped for the benefit of divers and sports fishermen, a coral reef is a living underwater Xanadu constructed from the slowly, slowly growing exoskeletons of individual marine polyps. There are over two thousand species of soft and stony corals, and coral reefs—the most diverse ecosystems on Earth—harbor twenty-five thousand species of fish and other invertebrates. These extraordinary sea gardens survive within an exceedingly narrow range of water temperature, clarity, and purity. Warming ocean temperatures have caused deadly bleaching of corals; air, water, and land pollution—sewage runoff and the phosphorus-laden, nutrient-rich wastewater produced by agriculture—endangers their survival further. A living reef erratically runs the length of the Florida Keys on the Atlantic side—the Keys themselves are ancient dead coral islands—and is increasingly being eaten away by a variety of diseases, its colorful complex world reduced to pallid rubble. *Aspergillus* is one of the most recent culprits in this decline; a fungus found in soil, it shreds coral as moths shred lace.   JOY WILLIAMS

cordillera

A cordillera is a series of more or less parallel mountain ranges, including their ridges, basins, and tablelands. To this definition, one geographic reference adds the quali-fication, "belonging to a single orogenic belt." Orogeny is the process of mountain building, especially the processes of faulting and folding that raised the great mountain ranges of the Earth. The term cordillera came into English from the Spanish, from the word *cordilla*, which means "string" or "rope." It was first applied to Las Cordilleras de los Andes, and came to be used to describe North Ameri-can ranges, especially the Sierra Nevada and the Rockies. The *Oxford English Dictionary* cites a description of the Andes from 1833 that uses the term to mean lesser divisions of a mountain chain: "At the northern limit of the group of Loxa . . . the main range divides into two subordinate chains, or cordilleras." Finally, the term has been used to mean the crest ridges of a mountain range. That seems to be Jim Harrison's sense of it in *Legends of the Fall*: "By noon they crossed a divide, a cordillera, and turned to take a last view of the ranch."   ROBERT HASS

cornice

As windborne snow crystals accrete and bond atop a storm-swept ridge, they are apt to solidify into a cornice. Sometimes cantilevered spectacularly over the leeward side of the ridge crest on which it forms, a cornice resembles nothing so much as breaking surf frozen in mid-curl. When large cornices collapse—from rising spring temperatures, under the weight of careless skiers and mountaineers, or when they simply become too heavy to support their own unstable bulk—they can trigger cataclysmic avalanches.   JON KRAKAUER

corridor

Corridor was once used primarily to describe an architectural feature, a passageway connecting two separate buildings, but recently it has taken on a broader, conceptual meaning as an area that distinguishes itself from its surroundings by either the access or passage it provides. We now speak of air, recreational, transportation, environmental, high-tech, economic, migratory, retail, stream, and heritage corridors. Greenway corridors made up of streams, floodplains, open space, and woods in cities and suburbs are essential for the survival of native animal and plant species, the maintenance of ecosystems, and the preservation of geological formations. Organizations such as the Lackawanna River Corridor Association in northeast Pennsylvania and the Mississippi Corridor Neighborhood Coalition in Minneapolis have formed to protect and advocate for degraded and endangered rivers that pass through their communities. The Springwater Corridor in Portland, Oregon, is a rail-to-trails project that has created 170 miles of recreational pathway for hikers, joggers, and bicyclists.   MICHAEL COLLIER

coteau

Coteau (as a large-scale landscape feature) is chiefly an American usage of a French word for a hillside or the terraced slope of a vineyard. Americans use the word, borrowed from French Canadian frontiersmen, to name the steep ridge above and between lower elevations to either side or to describe hilly ground overlooking a plain. The name also is given in Louisiana to a substantial mound of

solid ground in a swamp or marsh. The Missouri Coteau/
Coteau du Missouri is a narrow plateau beginning in the
northwest corner of North Dakota. Its western escarpment forms the bluffs of the Missouri River. The Prairie
Coteau/*Coteau des Prairies* is an extensive plateau in South
Dakota and Minnesota that was processed into its current form at the end of the last North American glaciation. The Prairie Coteau is a hilly, hummocky complex
of moraines, basins, and pothole wetlands. Many of these
features were formed by dead ice.   D. J. WALDIE

coulee

A coulee is a deep gulch or ravine carved out by water
erosion, or a dry canyon forged by the Pleistocene floods
that cut formations into lava beds of the Columbia
Plateau thousands of years ago. That is, glaciers in that
area retreated, leaving tremendous amounts of meltwater
to flood the landscape and carve many landforms, including coulees. These broad, shallow depressions, which
often have an underfit stream (a stream that seems too
small for its valley) flowing through them like a ribbon,
are a familiar part of the western landscape. The Grand
Coulee, located in central Washington State, was an
ancient dry riverbed six hundred feet above the Columbia River. Now it is the site of the massive Grand Coulee
Dam—the largest concrete structure in the country—
built under President Franklin D. Roosevelt to irrigate
the arid areas of the Pacific Northwest. In 1941, when the
dam was completed, the plan for irrigation was forgotten
in lieu of the greater demands of war. Electricity from
the Grand Coulee Dam was used to power aluminum
mills and support production of uranium for the Manhattan Project; after the war, irrigation resumed. In the
book *Northwest Passage: The Great Columbia River*, William
Dietrich describes how "one can see the geographic logic
of an idea that utterly changed the Pacific Northwest.

The mesa is a kind of attention-getting monolith that almost demands to be climbed to its hurricane deck, but instead of a boat stair there is a steep, crumbling trail up a draw in the volcanic cliffs to the 800-foot-high plateau on top. . . . Paths wind away through bunch grass to its abrupt cliff, giving grand views of the Coulee, the reservoir, the blue bluffs of the distant Okanogan Highlands, and in spring a pencil line of green wheat along the Coulee's rim." ELIZABETH COX

couloir

Couloir comes to us from France, where the word's primary meaning is "corridor." Since the eighteenth century, however, the term has also been applied to vertiginous mountain gullies. In October 1872, upon cresting a divide in the Sierra Nevada, John Muir observed (in *The Mountains of California*): "There, immediately in front, loomed the majestic mass of Mount Ritter, with a glacier swooping down its face nearly to my feet. . . . The entire front above the glacier appeared as one giant precipice. . . . The head of the glacier sends up a few finger-like branches through narrow couloirs; but these seemed too steep and short to be available, especially as I had no axe with which to cut steps. I could not distinctly hope to reach the summit from this side, yet I moved on across the glacier as if driven by fate." A few hours later, after nearly falling to his death ("I became nerve-shaken for the first time since setting foot on the mountains, and my mind seemed to fill with a stifling smoke"), Muir emerged from the top of one of these sheer couloirs to make the first ascent of 13,157-foot Mount Ritter. JON KRAKAUER

country rock

Among geologists, mountain climbers, and other aficionados of the continental crust, granite and its closest igneous cousins tend to be held in higher esteem than most other varieties of rock. This bias is evident in the term country rock, which is used to describe the motley body of nonigneous rock that surrounds an igneous intrusion. Simply put, country rock is everything in the Earth's geological mix that isn't granite. In the Brooks Range of Arctic Alaska, for example, there are a few isolated batholiths that culminate in arresting clusters of granitic summits (most notably the jagged spires of Mount Igikpak and the Arrigetch Peaks), surrounded by lovely but considerably less dramatic scarps of limestone, shale, and conglomerate, which march toward the horizon in a seemingly endless procession. This latter vastness of highly complex, nonigneous geology is summarily dismissed as country rock.   JON KRAKAUER

cove

Whether found deep in a range of mountains or hidden along a stormy shore, a sheltered basin is known as a cove. The word is most commonly applied to a water-filled niche along a coast encircled on three sides by land, as if by protecting arms. These watery coves are found inside bays and are often homes to settlements and fleets of fishing vessels. Inland, a plain or valley that extends into mountains is often called a cove. In the southern Appalachians, coves are gently sloping valleys surrounded on all sides by peaks. Even in this use they have a connection to water: the shape of the land tends to funnel moisture into such valleys, creating damp enclaves with tremendous plant diversity. Perhaps the most famous is Cades Cove in the heart of Great Smoky Mountains National Park. In addition, the term is sometimes used to describe a small, cirque-like nook in a cliff worn into the land by weathering or erosion.   JAN DEBLIEU

cove forest

In the mountains of the South, cove refers to a remote valley hidden away between high mountains, or in the natural amphitheater of a mountainside. As opposed to a mere hollow or valley, a cove is most often found on the north slope, so sunlight only reaches the floor in the middle of the day. Because the soil and leaves and other detritus drift down the sides of the cove over the centuries, and because water flows down those sloped sides, the topsoil on the floor is especially deep and rich. As a result, trees in a cove forest grow bigger, taller, older. Giant tulip poplars, white oaks, yellow buckeye thrive in the deep humus. The Joyce Kilmer Memorial Forest in western North Carolina's Nantahala National Forest contains outstanding examples of virgin cove forests. Cove forests in the Great Smokies are known to have some of the greatest botanical variety of any places in North America. Because of the valleys' isolation after the last ice age, many ancient species are trapped and protected in the coves: mosses, ferns, flowers such as the Oconee bell. The forests preserved in the coves shelter rare lichens, liverworts, fungi, and include basswood, sugar maple, sweet buckeye, yellow birch, beech, bitternut hickory, white ash, cucumber trees. Because of the constant shade, understories are haunted by flies, spiders, and mosquitoes in the summer.   ROBERT MORGAN

cowbelly

It is along the banks of slow-moving creeks, where the current slackens completely, that the very finest particles of sediment settle out of the water. A barefoot wader, stepping tentatively into the shallows from the bank here, feels no suggestion of the creek's flow, only a change of temperature. At the boundary where water becomes silt, the bottom is so plush the sinking foot barely registers the new medium, only a second change of temperature. Silt soft as a Holstein's belly.   CONGER BEASLEY, JR.

coyote well

As a mythological figure, Coyote is alternately heroic and foolish, lewd and gullible, benevolent and greedy. He does some good things, but basically he's a trickster, a despoiler. In the Tohono O'odham Indian country of southwestern Arizona and Sonora, Mexico, there are coyote melons, coyote tepary beans, coyote cotton, even coyote devil's claw, foul-tasting or useless plants that mimic helpful ones. One could so surmise that a coyote well is desert water that Coyote has despoiled in some way, or that it is a hole holding something that only seems like water. Still, real coyotes are known for their ability to find water when other animals cannot. In *The Land of Little Rain*, Mary Austin writes: "The coyote is your true water-witch, one who snuffs and paws, snuffs and paws again at the smallest spot of moisture-scented earth until he has freed the blind water from the soil. Many water-holes are no more than this, detected by the lean lobo of the hills."   JOY WILLIAMS

crack

Great rock monoliths such as Half Dome and El Capitan in Yosemite, or Stone Mountain in Georgia, are not in fact monolithic—they are riddled with fractures, which are known as cracks or joints in the parlance of climbers and geologists. Mountaineers categorize cracks according to the size of the body part that can be effectively wedged into a given crevice to enable ascent—that is, a finger crack has the dimensions of a finger; a hand crack is the width of a jammed hand; and a fist crack conforms to the span of a human fist. When a crack is broader than fist size but narrower than a chimney, it is known as an off-width, and can be very difficult to climb. In certain types of rock (most notably Wingate Sandstone and some varieties of granite) cracks may be astonishingly uniform and run for hundreds of feet without interruption; such perfect fissures are termed splitters.   JON KRAKAUER

cranny

A cranny is a narrow hole or opening. Synonyms include notch, cleft, crack, jag, niche, chink, crevice, and fissure. The origin of the word is disputed. It may come from Old French, *cren* or *cran*, where it meant "notch" and was used as a technical term in reference to fortification—from which we also get the word crenellated. The earliest use of the expression "nook and cranny" cited by the *Oxford English Dictionary* comes from 1836. Poets have used the word as a verb—in Arthur Golding's sixteenth-century translation of Ovid's *Metamorphoses*, "The ground did cranie everywhere, and light did pierce to hell"—and also as an adjective. Byron in *Childe Harold*: "All tenantless, save to the crannying wind." Tennyson: "Flower of the crannied wall, I pluck you out of the crannies." The word came into North America bearing this genealogy. There is a Cranny Spring in Cassia County, Idaho, a Cranny Crow Overlook in Lost River State Park in West Virginia, and among northern California skiers the adventurous are always on the lookout for the challenge of "nook-and-cranny mountains," such as Alpine Meadows near Lake Tahoe in the Sierra Nevada. American poets have also had their way with the word. Here is Edna St. Vincent Millay: "Holds Heaven not some cranny, Lord, / For a flower so tall and blue?"
ROBERT HASS

crater

Craters are the footprints of a dramatic geologic event involving eruption, impact, or collapse. Broadly speaking, a crater is a depression in the Earth, but the word most readily evokes the interior of the steep-sided bowl produced in explosive volcanic eruptions. This classic shape (Mount Fuji is the prototype) can be seen today atop several active Alaskan volcanoes, including Shishaldin on the Aleutian island of Unimak. Shield volcanoes (such as Kīlauea Volcano in Hawai'i), which eject a more fluid basalt than composite volcanoes, form craters after erupted magma drains away and, over time, through the breakdown of shield walls. Shield volcanoes may also develop pit craters, if magma intrudes just below the surface and then withdraws, leaving an unsupported terrain prone to collapse. Until late in the nineteenth century it was believed that the moon's craters were caused by volcanic activity. A later analysis of lunar craters, spurred by accumulating scientific evidence, suggested, for example, that a mysterious mile-wide depression near Flagstaff, Arizona, now called Barringer Meteorite Crater, was formed by the impact of a meteoroid. Over 150 large impact craters have now been identified on Earth, the largest being the Sudbury Crater in Ontario, Canada, around 140 miles in diameter.   PAMELA FRIERSON

crater lake

When rainwater or groundwater accumulates in the crater (or caldera) of a dormant or extinct volcano, it is called a crater lake or caldera lake. Perhaps the best-known example is in Crater Lake National Park in Oregon, formed partly by explosive eruptions and mainly by subsidence of the magma at the top of a composite volcano. Crater Lake's Wizard Island is a small volcanic cone with a crater at its summit.   KIM BARNES

creek

Creek is a word that has been transformed by the North American continent. The British usage of the term was its first meaning here, and this definition still applies

along the Atlantic coast from North Carolina to Maine:
a saltwater inlet narrower than a cove; the estuary of
a stream. But as settlement probed inland beyond the
coastal plain, following watercourses upstream well past
the influence of salt and tides, the word creek held on
for any flow smaller than a river, even when the water in
question eventually became a clear, leaping Appalachian
stream narrow enough to step across. In a few places,
though, a distinction was retained. M. Schele DeVere,
in his 1872 *Americanisms: The English of the New World*, put
it succinctly: "The kill of New York is a brook in New
England, a run in Virginia, and alas! a crick or creek,
almost everywhere else." CHARLES FRAZIER

crevasse

Informally, crevasse refers to any deep crack or fissure
in the earth. A breach in a riverbank or levee is called a
crevasse, as is a rift in the Earth's surface caused by an
earthquake. Crevasse most commonly refers to a fracture
in glacier ice, however, created by the glacier's flow over
uneven terrain or down a steep slope. Crevasses, some
of which are too deep to measure accurately, can form
both across a glacier's flow and parallel to it. These
longitudinal crevasses splay apart where the ice spreads
in a fanlike formation. Chevron crevasses, pointing up-
valley, form along a glacier's edge where ice movement
is restricted by valley walls. Multiple crevasses in one
section of a glacier constitute a crevasse field. In his
narrative of the 1899 Harriman Alaska Expedition, John
Burroughs describes a view at Glacier Bay of "a perfect
wilderness of crevasses, the ice ridged and contorted like
an angry sea." CAROLYN SERVID

cripple

Cripple is an anglicized version of the Colonial Dutch
kreupelbosch, which means "thicket" or "underbrush."

From its earliest use in America, however, cripple has been associated not only with thickety areas but also with wetlands. Describing the vernacular speech of the residents of the New Jersey Pine Barrens, John McPhee writes in *The Pine Barrens* that "a low, wet area where Atlantic white cedars grow is called a cripple. If no cedars grow there, the wet area is called a spong, which is pronounced to rhyme with 'sung.' Some people define spongs and cripples a little differently, saying that water always flows in a cripple but there is water in a spong only after a rain. Others say that any lowland area where highbush blueberries grow is a spong." (Note that the American use of spong may trace to the nineteenth-century East Anglian dialect, in which a spong was a long, narrow strip of land.) Many eastern place-names derive from cripple, including Big Cripple Swamp, in Delaware; Cripple Brush Creek, in Vermont; and Kripplebush, New York. There are also dozens of Cripple Creeks found across the country—from Tuscaloosa, Alabama, to Denali, Alaska. A few of these creek names arise from the English sense of cripple; for example, a surveyor once cut his foot with an axe at an Oregon stream, which has since been called Cripple Creek. But the majority of Cripple Creeks are entirely free of links to either accidents or thickets. Folklorists speculate that as the original Dutch meaning faded, people continued using cripple as a name for creeks because of the pleasingly alliterative and faintly poignant sound the two words create together.   EMILY HIESTAND

cuesta

Lay a writing tablet on a flat surface, then place a ruler on edge under one length of it, and you have a miniature of a cuesta—a clifflike face, with a long gentle backslope. Hogbacks, massive tilted rocks formed as a result of dramatic uplift, are a related landform, though cuestas are far less steep. Cuestas tend to appear along the tributaries of rivers that "open wide valleys in weak rock," writes O.D. von Engeln in *The Finger Lakes Region: Its Origin and Nature.* The faces of these beds of rock are the cliffs; the beds of strata inclined on a gentle slope are their backsides. Cuestas are distinguished from escarpments by their range; escarpments may extend into several states, while cuestas are local and sometimes viewed, as in the Finger Lakes Region, as "parallel rows of hills each with one steep slope and one gentle slope. These hills are designated by a Spanish term, cuesta, which signifies a hill of such profile," according to von Engeln.   LARRY WOIWODE

cul-de-sac

Cul-de-sacs (French, literally the bottom of the bag) feature prominently in housing developments, where they establish the quiet loop of a dead-end street. A city's blind alleys are also cul-de-sacs. Similarly, a cul-de-sac may be a blind lead in a cave, a passage that has but one entrance and exit. The term also refers to a swallowhole down which a stream once disappeared, but which is now abandoned and partially filled in. A cul-de-sac is both a turn-around and a turn-away. A tranquil if limited space. The pause before the return.   DONNA SEAMAN

cutbank

The outside bank in the bend of a stream that experiences erosion, a cutbank is normally high and steep, and is formed as part of the process of a stream meandering across its floodplain. Often, a cutbank is the only vertical relief in an otherwise flat landscape. A stream is deeper and flows faster on its cutbank side. Opposite the cutbank, on the inside of the bend, lies the point bar, an area of shallow water, a crescent-shaped accumulation of sand and gravel. Someone might, for instance, spread a blanket for a picnic or sunbathing on the bank of a point bar and wade in the shallow water there, while someone else might look for fossils uncovered by erosion on the cutbank or fish in the deep water of the stream on the cutbank side. "Cutbanks can offer you a great shot at a trophy fish," writes Dave Hurteau in "Big Trout Hideouts." PATTIANN ROGERS

cut-off

When a flooding river is powerful enough, it may force its way across the neck of a meander and erode a more direct channel, which is called a cut-off. The gradient of a cut-off is necessarily steeper than that of the meander it replaces, which results in an increase in the river's energy. The river may in turn dissipate this energy by forming a new meander, which ultimately it will bypass with a new cut-off, as the self-reinforcing cycle continues. Not all cut-offs form naturally. According to Mark Twain in *Life on the Mississippi*, little excavation was required to make a cut-off on the Lower Mississippi. "When the river is rising fast, some scoundrel whose plantation is back in the country and therefore of inferior value, has only to watch his chance, cut a little gutter across the narrow neck of land some dark night, and turn the water into it, and in a wonderfully short time a miracle has happened: to wit, the whole Mississippi has taken possession of that little ditch, and placed the countryman's plantation at its bank." Twain also reported that many cut-offs were made for the sake of shortening the distance riverboats and other craft had to travel, so much so that between 1706 and 1882 the length of the Mississippi from Cairo, Illinois, to New Orleans, Louisiana, shortened from 1,215 to 973 miles. Never one to shy from the absurd, Twain extrapolated that rate of change into the distant future, concluding that "seven hundred and forty-two years from now, the Lower Mississippi will be only a mile and three-quarters long, and Cairo and New Orleans will have joined their streets together, and be plodding comfortably along under a single mayor and a mutual board of aldermen." WILLIAM DEBUYS

C

dale

A dale is a broad, open river valley primarily associated with the north of England, where the inhabitants were called once dalesmen. The mountains and hills forming such valleys are called fells. Dale and fell are native English words that, after the Norman Conquest, were supplanted by the French-derived words valley and mountain. Etymologically, dale is similar to dell, the roots of both words meaning "deep or low place." Dale appears frequently in Romantic and Victorian-era verse, and phrases such as "over hill and dale" or "up hill and down dale" are conventional phrases used by many writers, including W. E. B. Du Bois, Charles Darwin, and Theodore Roosevelt, to describe the repetitious ascent and descent when traveling across a terrain marked by hills and valleys. Dale is not used much in the United States except to fabricate meaningless place-names such as Scottsdale or Glendale, two suburbs of Phoenix, Arizona, where the Sonoran Desert dominates and the uplands of Great Britain could be nothing but wistful chimeras.   MICHAEL COLLIER

dalles

The word dalles is generally thought to derive from the French plural of *dalle*, meaning "gutter" or, possibly, "tube" or "conduit." Dalle is also French for flagstone, a natural material historically used to line gutters. Local history suggests that The Dalles, Oregon, a place where the Columbia River once moved swiftly between steep canyon walls, was named by French Canadian trappers: the steplike rapids created by the flow of water over columnar basalt might well resemble water moving through an enormous gutter lined with flagstone. The Grand Dalles refers to the great rapids east of the present town, which were inundated by the backwaters of the newly built Dalles Dam in 1957, described by Robert

Michael Pyle in *Chasing Monarchs: Migrating with the Butterflies of Passage*, this way: "It is now a prefab village above the reservoir beside the freeway, the home of those who remained after The Dalles Dam did its dirty work of drowning the falls, wrecking the fishery, and killing what was left of the river culture in 1956." Indeed, Celilo Falls, also erased by the resulting slackwater, was one of the most important and sacred Indian fisheries in North America. In some regions, dalles may also be synonymous with dells. In Wisconsin, the geologic feature called the Dells is a channel system cut into Cambrian sandstone, through which the Wisconsin River flows. In fact, the ravine complex was originally called the Dalles.

KIM BARNES

deadening

From the verb "to deaden," the term deadening refers to an area where timber has been decimated by fire, flooding, insects, or disease, or to a clearing in which trees have been systematically killed by girdling, that is, having rings cut about their trunks.   KIM BARNES

dead ice

The advance of even a continent-sized ice sheet eventually grinds to a stop. This stalled, slowly melting ice (think of a landlocked iceberg) is said to be dead. Dead ice has a potent afterlife, however, despite its name. Large tracts of remnant blocks of ice created the wet, jumbled, pothole-and-hummock landscape of the coteau uplands of North and South Dakota. Debris in the ice and soil deposited on its surface was shed from the melting ice as a semifrozen gumbo of gravel and earth to form dead-ice moraines. Where the surface of the dead ice was insulated by a thicker crust of sediment, variations in the melt of the underlying ice allowed the soil to collapse into landscape features as round as a doughnut (a ring of glacial debris) and boggy as a kettle (a sink formed when a core of dead ice surrounded by earth eventually melts). These features collect rain and snowmelt and are favored by migrating waterfowl.   D. J. WALDIE

debacle

In the spring, when warming temperatures bring snow-melt and rainfall to the watersheds of frozen northern rivers, the flow of rising waters breaks up the winter cover of river ice and floats it downstream. Where these floes jam and raft up—often where the channel narrows—ice jams, or dams, may impede the flow of water until the river's forcing pressure fractures and destroys the dam. The headwall of floodwater that bursts through and scours the banks for some distance downstream is called a debacle, a word often used in other circumstances to describe a similarly stunning mess.

ELLEN MELOY

debris cone

A debris cone is commonly made when rock from a high-up narrow slit or gorge falls into a flat-floored valley. Here the soil and loose materials are deposited, leaving a mound of conical shape. While an alluvial fan is formed when flowing water rushes rock and soil down a slope, debris cones come from a dry process known as "mass wasting"—that is, gravity pulling loose materials downslope. Such mounds can reach sizes large enough to obstruct river channels. Similar deposits can also be found lying on boulders moved by a landslide, or on a glacier, where a cone-shaped mound of ice or snow may be covered with a veneer of debris thick enough to prevent the underlying ice from melting. A debris cone is also called a dirt cone or cone of detritus.   LAN SAMANTHA CHANG

deer yard

Once winter snows reach a foot or so, deer have a hard time digging down for moss, ferns, lichen, and other food. Not only that, but snow travel is difficult on slender deer legs. So the animals head for deer yards, often conifer stands that offer some protection from wind and snowfall. Once they've "yarded up"—in spots that may have been used for generations—the animals beat out a series of trails as they forage for twigs and leaves. Depending on snow depth, these trails can turn into corridors as tall as the deer themselves, and competition for accessible food can be fierce; as soon as the snow depth starts to drop with the spring thaw, therefore, the yarded-up herds melt back into the forest.   BILL MCKIBBEN

defile

In military terms, a defile is a path so narrow that only a single file of men can move along it. (In England, the French word was often pronounced with an -*ee* at the end, but being generally written -*e* without accent, it has come to be treated as *e* mute.) In a larger context, defile means a long, narrow, steep-sided pass through hills or mountains, often forming the approach to a larger pass. In *The Man Who Killed the Deer,* Frank Waters writes: "There where the pines at last stood back to let him pass, he saw rising before him the two rocky points of a parted cliff, between them a steep, narrow defile. Carefully he felt his way up the old, almost obliterated trail rising crookedly beside a small stream."   KIM BARNES

deflation hollow

Water may be the main sculptor of rock and the surface of the planet, but wind is also a carver and shaper. On a beach, wind can scoop out a hollow in hours, pushing and tossing away one grain of sand at a time until a bank or ridge or dune appears hollowed out, deflated. Inland, wind also carves a slope to its fancy, as sure as it can carve a drift of snow. Wind abrades and blasts one particle of the slope at a time, over centuries, over millennia, until the soil or rock is hollowed out by the prevailing draft of air armed with abrasive grit, tiny wind-carried teeth. On the high mountain peaks of the southern Appalachians prevailing winds not only bend and stunt the growth of trees, but also hollow out bins and wallows, sometimes called tumbles by the local people, on the balds and high unprotected ground. The largest deflation hollow in the contiguous United States is Big Hollow in Albany County, Wyoming. It's forty square miles and a perfectly suitable sight in a state known for wind.   ROBERT MORGAN

dell

While chiefly a literary word, dell was once used to describe a small, secluded hollow densely overgrown with trees, vines, and shrubs. As a prop in pastoral verse, poets have idealized it exhaustively, so that there are flowery, sunny, shady, dewy, woody, pleasant, shadowed, placid, and tangled dells. Nevertheless, its root comes from Middle English *delle*, a deep hole or pit, and Old High German *telle*, a ravine. Spenser in *The Shepherd's Calendar* has an ewe "fall headlong into a dell." In Ainsworth's 1783 *Latin Dictionary*, dell is translated as *fossa*, which brings to mind Dante's *fossi*, the pits and holes (the *malebolge*) that contain the sinners of his Inferno. If this darker meaning of dell was ever applied, it no longer does. Instead the most familiar context for the word is found in the nursery rhyme "The Farmer in the Dell."
MICHAEL COLLIER

delta

A flat, low-lying area located at the mouth of a river and created over many years by sediments and nutrients deposited when the regular flow of river water mixes with the relatively still water of a lake, gulf, bay, or ocean, the term delta was first used by Herodotus in the fifth century B.C. to describe the mouth of the Nile River, whose shape resembled the triangular Greek letter of the same name, with the apex pointing upriver. Herman Melville in *Moby-Dick* makes literary use of this compelling geographical image: "The old man's purpose intensified itself. His firm lips met like the lips of a vice; the Delta of his forehead's veins swelled like overladen brooks." America's most famous delta is the bird-foot or lobate delta at the mouth of the Mississippi, on the Louisiana coast. To citizens of the state of Mississippi, however, "Mississippi Delta" means something different. It's the fertile alluvial land running tabletop flat "from the lobby of the Peabody Hotel [in Memphis, Tennessee] to Delta Hill in Yazoo City [Mississippi]," land bounded to the east and west by, respectively, the Yazoo and Mississippi Rivers. This "inland delta," isolated and farmed for cotton by generations of black slaves, has been a cultural treasure trove, giving fertile rise to grand southern literature and the plaintive originality of black gospel, blues, and rock music. As an adjective, delta is used to describe a wide range of related geographical features. There are delta terraces and bars, delta plains and shorelines, and delta lakes. The latter are formed along coastal areas when sediment bars build up across an embayment or when part of the sea is entirely captured by the growth of deltaic deposits. Small deltas the size of a dinner plate may form where a creek enters a lake (technically, a lacustrine delta). A cuspate delta, the opposite of the fan-shaped or arcuate delta, forms where ocean waves reduce the width of the delta to a point as it enters the larger body of water. The bird- or bird's foot delta takes its name from the narrow lobes

of land that carry trunks of the same river separately to
the sea.   MIKE TIDWELL

den

In North American usage, a den is typically the habitation of a large wild animal. A burrow is a hole in the
ground that is the habitation of a small wild animal.
Bears, wolves, mountain lions, and bobcats use dens;
badgers, rabbits, gophers, mice, and some birds live in
burrows. When Barry Lopez writes about polar bears in
Arctic Dreams, he uses the word den as verb, noun, and
adjective: "Before she dens, usually in late October or
early November, a female bear must put on a heavy layer
of fat." Also: "The variety of structures denning females
build is great." And Wallace Stegner, writing about the
plains of Saskatchewan in his childhood in *Marking the
Sparrow's Fall,* recalls a picket-pin gopher's response to a
coming storm: "The gopher disappeared as if some friend
below had reached up and yanked him into his burrow."
As for birds, there is *Athene cunicularia,* the burrowing owl,
and the dream-bird in Terry Tempest Williams's *Refuge*:
"The purple bird turned gold, dropped its tail, and began
digging a burrow in the white sand." It's interesting to
note that the 1828 *Webster's Dictionary* defines the word
lair as "the bed or couch of a boar or wild beast." In
his essay "The Conduct of Life in 1860," Ralph Waldo
Emerson can use the word this way: "Every creature—
wren or dragon—shall make its own lair." In modern
North American usage, lair tends to be associated with
large cats. In William Davis and David Schmidly's *The
Mammals of Texas,* a mountain lion is described as being
"accidentally flushed from its daytime lair in a thicket."
Perhaps because of this association of lairs with stealth,
the term was regularly transferred by popular western
novelists to the hideouts of robbers. Their lairs occur

in the stories of Zane Grey, Max Brand, and Louis
L'Amour.   ROBERT HASS

dendritic drainage

From a bird's-eye view, it is easy to see why dendritic
pattern drainage was named after the Greek word for
tree, *dendron*. Branching irregularly and at variable
angles, the streams and rills in dendritic drainage
systems closely resemble the limbs and twigs of a bare
deciduous tree. This most common of drainage patterns
occurs in terrain where the underlying rock is uniform
in composition and has only very minor jointing and
faulting. Lacking features that would direct the course of
streams, such a terrain yields the somewhat random patterns of dendritic drainage. By contrast, a trellis drainage
pattern occurs over terrain where several structural features of the landscape combine to strongly influence and
direct the course of streams. For example, in a landscape
where narrow valleys are separated by parallel ridges,
tributaries flow down the steep ridge scarps and join the
mainstream in the valley at a nearly perpendicular angle.
The resulting rectilinear configuration, remindful of a
horticultural trellis, is sometimes also called grapevine
drainage pattern.   EMILY HIESTAND

derelict land

Land that has been used, ruined, and consequently abandoned by humans is peculiarly described as derelict—
as if the land itself had become careless of its duties.
BARBARA KINGSOLVER

derramadero

The spillway or overflow of a dam, a flooded river, a dry
streambed that carries water during intense rainfall, or
even an overfilled dump is described by this term, der-
ramadero, which derives from the Spanish verb *derramar*,

meaning "to spill, pour, scatter," or most picturesquely when used with *sangre*, "to shed blood," as in *derramar su sangre por la nación*. BARBARA KINGSOLVER

desert

The word desert has no fully agreed upon meaning among geographers. Many prefer, in fact, the terms dry lands or arid lands. Part of the problem in arriving at a definition that will satisfy everyone is that many popular images of North American deserts—bleak expanses of sand, lizards seeking shaded cover from a broiling sun, saguaro cactus—don't begin to fit all of North America's deserts. Saguaros grow only in the lower Sonoran Desert; no lizards inhabit the polar deserts of Alaska; and much of the Great Basin Desert is covered with brush and grasses, even open stands of piñón pine and juniper. To biologists, deserts are dry habitats that accommodate many fewer species than other habitats such as forest land or tall grass prairies. Desert habitat is further characterized by plants and animals with unique strategies for finding and conserving water. And they are set apart from other lands by low humidity and scant rainfall, and by sometimes striking fluctuations in daily and seasonal temperatures. For nonbiologists, what makes deserts distinctive is not ecosystems but landforms—stony plains of desert pavement, arroyos cut by flash floods, dune fields. Excluding the polar deserts of Alaska and the arid, volcanic landscapes of Hawai'i, there are four deserts in the United States. The "warm" Chihuahuan and lower Sonoran Deserts of California, Arizona, New Mexico, and Texas; and the "cold" deserts—the upper Sonoran of Arizona, New Mexico, and Utah; the Mojave of California and Nevada; and the Great Basin Desert, stretching all the way to Canada and taking in parts of California, Nevada, Utah, Colorado, Idaho, Oregon, and Washington. The most arid of them all is the Mojave.

In the "high desert" of eastern Oregon and Washington, desertification caused by overgrazing has converted large stretches of dry grassland into landscapes dominated by sage and scrub vegetation and by such exotic plants as Russian thistle (tumbleweed) and cheat grass. Scientists are still discovering new forms of life in the desert, contradicting the persistent notion that deserts are barren, lifeless, worthless.   BARRY LOPEZ

desert pavement

In extremely arid places (usually with less than seven inches of annual rainfall) a combination of extreme environmental forces may combine to form desert pavements: broad, barren areas of closely packed stony material, winnowed by the wind and abraded by sand. Cima Dome in the Mojave Desert is one example, a place where lava flows of recent age, geologically speaking, partially covered by younger soil layers, developed the stony carapace of a desert pavement. In a region with more precipitation, such mosaics might be broken up regularly—or prevented from forming—by the persistent force of plant growth. In hyper-arid areas, no seeds germinate on pavements. The more they are hardened by environmental forces, the more unlikely their breakup becomes; in the rare event of rain, all water flows quickly into runnels between the pavements. Viewed from the air, these pavements shine like nude, muscular interfluves veined with narrow bands of vegetation.   BARBARA KINGSOLVER

desert varnish

Desert varnish, also called rock varnish, is a small miracle of resistant rocks. It occurs widely but is most conspicuous in arid environments. It is a brown to black patina, only nanometers thick, composed largely of clays combined with manganese and iron oxides, and it gives exposed rock faces, be they scattered cobbles on the desert floor or entire mountain or canyon sides, a distinctive, wind-burnished coloring. Where a high proportion of iron is present, the patina tends toward red; the more manganese dominates, the blacker the "varnish" becomes. The most remarkable characteristic of desert varnish is that it is alive. Until relatively recently, geologists thought that desert varnish was an artifact of weathering—a result of slow oxidation—but anomalies discredited that explanation: rocks that contained little manganese were found to bear desert varnish with high levels of manganese oxide. In time, researchers learned that certain bacteria with powerful abilities to capture, metabolize, and concentrate trace amounts of manganese from windblown dust colonize the often superheated and usually moistureless faces of varnished rocks. These microorganisms appear to be the principal agents in the slow and steady accretion of oxides. Moreover, the varnish forms at such an even rate that it can be used to determine the date of rockslides and other events that initiate the exposure of rocks to the elements. Sometimes that exposure is human-caused: for several thousand years, natives of the North American Southwest have hammered at rock surfaces to remove the desert varnish and reveal the lighter-colored rock beneath it. In this way they have etched images—petroglyphs—of infinite import and variety into the landscapes of the region. While the "meaning" of much "rock art" remains a mystery, the date of many glyphs' creation can now be determined by radiometric techniques that measure tiny bits of carbon in the varnish and, hence, the length of time the varnish has been forming.   WILLIAM DEBUYS

desire path

A close look at any city park or green will typically reveal footpaths that break away from paved walks, trails that countless pedestrians have worn into the grass. Such a trail is a desire path: the route people have chosen to take across an open place, marking a human pattern upon a landscape. "A 'desire path' is what hikers or walkers have worn thin through finding a better way, or a shortcut, to a desired place," writes Mary Morris in *Acts of God*. Today, many planning agencies make use of such patterns when designing a public space. They first clear the land and then, after a few weeks or months, examine the ground for evidence of a human trail before choosing where to lay the path.   LAN SAMANTHA CHANG

despoblado

The Spanish term *despoblado* suggests an area that is not just empty but has been depopulated, abandoned, or sacked. The Big Bend region of Texas, along the Rio Grande, is often referred to as *el despoblado,* or the "Texas Despoblado." Put analogically, despoblado is to place as feral is to pet.   ANTONYA NELSON

detroit riprap

Car bodies embedded in the cutbanks of streams and rivers to stem erosion are called detroit riprap. The adjective detroit refers, of course, to the American home of car production, Motor City, though the practice of lining up autos nose down and door-to-door in water-ways is not limited to the Midwest. Indeed, it was once a popular way, countrywide, to put old cars to use. While car bodies might be cheaper than manufactured materi-als used in the construction of riprap, abandoned cars, with their residues of grease, paint, oil, and rust, placed in waterways are neither environmentally safe nor sound. The practice is now rare.   JEFFERY RENARD ALLEN

diggings

A diggings is not a dig, that archeological haunt, but a place of excavation by a prairie dog, fox, coyote, badger, or other digging species, including a human being, especially one at the controls of a human-built machine. Diggings is also a designation for the visible leavings outside an excavation. Human diggings may be for a precious stone or ore of importance, including gold, as at a placer mine; for the construction of a building; for a souvenir, such as petrified wood or mica; for a burial; or for imagined or actual buried treasure, a Mason jar of coins or white lightning whose exact location has evaded memory—as everywhere across the continent we encounter unexpected, mysterious diggings.   LARRY WOIWODE

dike

In popular usage, a dike is a wall or embankment constructed to control the threatening surge, tide, rise, or flow of a sea or river. In geology, a dike is a mass of molten rock that has penetrated vertically through layers of older rock and solidified, forming an intrusion often harder than the surrounding rocks. (A similar horizontal intrusion forms a sill.) Dikes form either when volcanic magma rises through an existing fracture in the country rock, or when it generates a new crack by exploiting a weakness in existing rock. Dikes often appear as dark-colored vertical bands set in rock of a lighter color. Hundreds of dikes might intrude in the cone and inner core of a volcano, forming a dike swarm. The Independence Dike Swarm is one of the largest and most visually striking dike formations in North America, extending all the way from the White Mountains of the southern Sierra Nevada to the southern Mojave Desert in eastern California, offering some of the most beautiful vistas in the American landscape.   JEFFERY RENARD ALLEN

dip

A dip is a gentle depression in an otherwise flat landscape in which rain or snowmelt gathers seasonally.

Neither a pond nor a marsh, which are longer lived, a dip is still sufficiently different from the surrounding terrain to create its own small-scale ecology born of subtle changes in moisture, nutrients, and sedimentation. Dip, dip slope, and angle of dip all refer to the degree to which a surface, as in a layer of rock embedded in a geologic formation, deviates from the horizontal. Dip has another sense as well: A compass needle aligns with the lines of the Earth's magnetic field. When the compass is brought close to where these force lines converge, at the north and south magnetic poles, the pivoting needle is also pulled down from the horizontal. This magnetic dip further complicates directional navigation in the far north and south.   D. J. WALDIE

discordant landscape

To be discordant is to be at variance, quarrelsome, in conflict, dissenting. For a landscape to achieve this contentious state, it must display topographical uncon-formity and eschew parallelism in its rivers, hills, and mountains. A discordant landscape features cross-cutting and intersecting relationships between its layers of rock rather than neat layering. In a discordant landscape—be it coastal or inland, a drainage basin or a mountain hollow—one element boldly goes against the grain, as do such unconventional individuals as artists, environmen-talists, and other visionaries.   DONNA SEAMAN

ditch

Ditch suggests a waterway dug out by human labor to serve a specific purpose. A ravine or gully seems natural in origin, whereas a ditch or trench is artificial. *Webster's Dictionary* of 1828 defines ditch as "a trench for draining wet land, or for making a fence to guard inclosures, or for preventing an enemy from approaching a town or fortress." A ditch is a utilitarian device, then, that alters a landscape. We dig ditches in cities for laying pipes and cables. Irrigation ditches serve farmers' needs for water. We excavate ditches to drain off swampy land, to make it productive for agriculture. Conversely, after draining off much of the water, say along the bottomlands of the Missouri and Mississippi Rivers, we might then dig ditches to carry water from wells and lagoons to flood these fields in the fall, to attract wild fowl for hunters. In the agricultural Midwest, drainage ditches are often lined with perforated tile after they're dug, then buried and smoothed over. Ditches flow both ways; they can denature a habitat or restore it to its near-original condition. CONGER BEASLEY, JR.

dog-hair pine

In South Dakota, rising up the flanks of the Black Hills, dog-hair stands of ponderosa pine as dense as 20,000 to 40,000 stems per acre seem to provide a green wall of serenity during the day; at night, they deepen the experience of full darkness. The heavy growth results from a lack of harvesting, or an unnaturally reduced incidence of fire. Such isolated forests, also known as dog-hair thickets, occur in northern Arizona and the southeastern states, as well as anywhere pine trees grow. The term is used around Yellowstone National Park to describe thick "toothpick" stands of lodgepole pine. Competition for water in these overgrown areas stunts many trees, and the woods are said to stagnate; foresters argue that if some trees are removed, the remaining trees will likely return to health. Even though growth is typically slow, the strength and persistence of many pine species are evidenced in the taproots of the young seedlings. These roots might extend five feet into the ground, while only a small shoot of growth appears above ground. Deep roots give pines the ability to survive drought, to thrive even when oppressed by surrounding trees. ELIZABETH COX

dome

In almost every granitic mountain range (but especially in the Sierra Nevada of California) enormous,
astounding hemispheres of naked stone—called domes,
appropriately—stand above the surrounding terrain to
catch the eye and fuel the imagination. In 1870, during a
field trip to Yosemite, the renowned geologist Joseph Le
Conte described the domes of the Sierra as "concentric
structure[s], on an almost inconceivably grand scale."
Among the features that most impressed him was "the
grand mass of Half Dome," which is probably the world's
most famous granite dome.   JON KRAKAUER

domer

To envision a domer, begin with a slick of river riding
over and partly submerging a boulder. From upstream,
the domer resembles a wet tortoise. On the downstream
side, a pourover drops abruptly into a squall of turbulence. It takes a quieter flow to produce a pillow, the
cushion of water on the upstream side of a protruding
rock, or where the river current hits a wall at an abrupt
angle. On his 1869 Colorado River journey, Major John
Wesley Powell took a pillow ride: "The river turns
sharply to the right and the water rolls up against a rock
which from above seems to stand directly athwart its
course. As we approach it we pull with all our power . . .
but it seems impossible to avoid being carried headlong
against the cliff; we are carried up high on the waves—
but not against the rock, for the rebounding water strikes
us and we are beaten back and pass on with safety, except
that we get a good drenching."   ELLEN MELOY

downwind

Downwind indicates a direction in which the wind
blows: toward or on the lee side. The term also holds a
political meaning both in North America and abroad.

Residents who live downwind from a factory or oil refinery often complain about the bad smells resulting from emissions and often assert that such emissions cause them to suffer from a variety of health problems, ranging from allergies and breathing difficulties to cancer and lung-related ailments and diseases. Factory emissions are not the only danger. A study conducted by an oncologist at the University of Bristol in Great Britain found that people living downwind of overhead power cables are more likely to develop lung cancer, accounting for perhaps three thousand premature deaths in Britain each year, more than from road accidents. Many people who feel they've become sick or poisoned because of their location, including those in northern Arizona and particularly southwestern Utah who lived near fallout from the nuclear testing in the southern Nevada desert, call themselves Downwinders. "The more I learn about what it means to be a 'downwinder,' the more questions I drown in," writes Terry Tempest Williams in *Refuge*.

JEFFERY RENARD ALLEN

draft

In two distinct regions of the country, a gully, gorge, or steep ravine that contains a creek or small river is known as a draft. Ramseys Draft, in Virginia's George Washington National Forest, is a cool slit of rock and soil lined with a roaring creek. The term is applied commonly in the mountains of north-central Pennsylvania and the deeply folded Appalachian peaks near the Virginia–West Virginia border, and almost nowhere else. JAN DEBLIEU

drain

Depending on the region of the country, a drain may be variously a ditch dug for draining off water; a tributary more diminutive than a creek; a little spring in a small hollow; a gully or ravine; an ebb tide; or a channel in a saltwater marsh. In many places, including South Carolina and Maine, the word is pronounced, and often spelled, dreen. During the Prohibition era in America, Appalachian moonshiners liked to situate their whisky stills on what they called dreens—springs located very far up on particularly steep slopes, thus obscured from all but the most ardent revenuer. Even today, in Maine, lobstermen and clam diggers may refer to especially low tides as dreen tides, and a Maine tide may be said to "dreen out." In *Beautiful Swimmers*, author William Warner indicates how drain is used in the vernacular of the Chesapeake Bay watermen: "Down every tidal gut and through every big 'thoroughfare' and little 'swash' or 'drain,' as the breaks in the marsh are called, there comes an enormous and nourishing flow of silage."   EMILY HIESTAND

drainage pattern

Natural drainage patterns are created where stream courses follow the lead of a landscape's geological history and features. Characteristics of the underlying rock, steepness of slope, faults and joints in the Earth's surface, the specific shape of particular geological formations, and the soil's susceptibility to erosion are among the factors that affect the pattern established for the flow of water in a particular place. Drainage patterns, generally rectangular to circular, might be elongated like a feather, braided at certain points like a net, or broken up by natural impoundments like lakes. They might, like the spokes of a wagon wheel, radiate from a center such as a peak, or converge toward a point, as in a closed basin. The pattern might fan out over a delta or collect myriad, many-pronged branches into a central stem. Because the shape of the pattern is determined by the land itself, it's a useful image in analyzing and understanding the rocks and geologic structures of a particular drainage.
CAROLYN SERVID

drapery

When a drop of water runs sinuously down the slanted ceiling of a cave, it leaves behind a minute record of its passing in the form of a microscopic trail of calcite or aragonite. When other drops follow this original trail and deposit their own particles, over vast periods of time they form a delicate folded curtain of minerals that may descend as much as twenty-five feet and can be thin to the point of translucence. This speleothem, or cave feature, is called drapery. As the water enters the cave and its atmosphere, calcium compounds evaporate out, adding to the drapery feature. When such formations include distinct bands of color, usually a reddish cast from iron, they are referred to as bacon rind. Spectacular examples of this formation may be seen in the Drapery Room of Mammoth Cave, Kentucky.   CHARLES FRAZIER

draw

A draw is a small natural watercourse or gully, shallower and more open than a ravine or gorge; also known in some areas as a blind creek if water routinely flows beneath its dry surface. A draw is typically dry and subject to flooding in heavy rains. A woody draw is a troughlike depression, choked with shrubs, thickets, and small trees, that usually leads to a valley from a gap between hills. Woody draws regulate the runoff from rainstorms and help filter pollutants. They also provide havens for wildlife. On the Great Plains, woody draws offer a shady respite from the searing summer light, and a place to ride out the worst of a winter storm. A draw's ability to conceal, suddenly and surprisingly, is conveyed in Cormac McCarthy's *All the Pretty Horses*: "The riders were fanned over the open country a mile below him and he counted not four but six of them before they dropped from sight into a draw." Gulch, a similar term, was used in the Pennsylvania Appalachians before making its way west to become a common mining term. To be "dry gulched" was to be ambushed in a secluded draw. CONGER BEASLEY, JR.

drawdown

Drawdown is a measure of a lowering of the water level in a reservoir, well, or other body of water as the result of direct pumping or the general lowering of a water table, most often when more water is pumped from an aquifer than enters it through recharge, such as rainfall. Power demand, flood control measures, and irrigation all cause temporary, long-term, or sometimes effectively permanent drawdowns. Sometimes drawdowns are a remedy for specific environmental problems. For example, lowering the water level of a lake or reservoir can reduce or eliminate exotic plant populations and reduce aquatic weed cover, leading to the recovery of native plant and fish populations. Regular drawdowns, however, can deprive waterfowl of habitat and can make it difficult for native aquatic vegetation—the superior food for native fish and wildlife—to establish itself, thus putting all these forms of flora and fauna at risk. The expanse of muddy terrain exposed by draining a reservoir is sometimes referred to as "the drawdown." JEFFERY RENARD ALLEN

drift

In his *Dakotah Sioux Indian Dictionary*, Paul War Cloud translates drift as oh-KAH-poh-dah, suggesting a Native need to define the phenomenon. A drift may be of sand, clay, or topsoil, as along a fence line over a season of drought, or a buildup of wind- or water-borne materials—though in the northern Plains drift commonly defines the depth of snow in its windswept accumulation: a three-foot drift. Snowdrifts depict scaled-down versions of landscape and the effects on it of erosion—cliff faces (some with pocked holes as if dwellers are present), cutbanks, buttes, and the mounded hills shaped by glaciation. Drift is also "the general term for any glacial deposit," according to Edward J. Tarbuck and Frederick K. Lutgens in *Earth Science*; the name for material driven or carried by water, thus sandbars and their muddy cousins; the measure of velocity of flow in rivers and sea currents; and the wrack washed up by waves. A word as multiform as the miniature landscapes visible in snowdrifts.   LARRY WOIWODE

D

drift fence

A barbwire fence across open pasture, strung in a curve to keep cattle from drifting or from bunching up, as cattle do when fences meet at ninety-degree angles, is called a drift fence. The term refers also to a broad fenced lane used to drift cattle to rail junctions. A more common drift fence is the northern snow fence of sienna-colored laths, slats of the sort once used under horsehair-enriched plaster in the walls of a house. The slats are bound together, equally spaced (air flow is essential, or winds and blizzards take the fences down), by strands of twisted wire. Living snow fences, carefully spaced rows of evergreen trees, are used in several areas of the West to keep sections of road prone to drifting from being buried. In plains areas of the worst winds, constructions of spaced two-by-sixes, angled into the wind and anchored to platforms, are employed. All such drift fences are set back from roads and yards to snare drifts. At Denver International Airport, lining the entrance road, a snow fence of bright-orange plastic pierced with baseball-sized holes has lately been used (perhaps temporarily) to replace the originals of wood slats, its color so stunning against fresh snow it can induce a cross-eyed headache.   LARRY WOIWODE

drowned valley

When the level of a lake or sea rises dramatically, its waters may spill into river valleys and the crevices between hills, creating drowned valleys. Drowned valleys are not as steeply sided or deeply cut as fjords; indeed, they include the gently sloped basins of coastal estuaries such as the upper Chesapeake Bay. The term ria, now considered synonymous with drowned valley, originally referred to inlets where landforms rise from the water at precise right angles. Drowned valleys are common along the North American East Coast, where water covers shorelines exposed ten thousand years ago during the last major ice age. Many of the coves and inlets now plied by oyster boats and recreational boaters were once feeding grounds for the land animals of the Pleistocene. In coming centuries, as sea level rises and pushes inland, drowned valleys will likely become more numerous around the world.   JAN DEBLIEU

drumlin

Drum is a Scottish term meaning a "narrow hill" or "long ridge." A drumlin, derived from the Irish Gaelic *druim*, is a low, elongate oval hill of glacial drift, composed mainly of boulder clay or glacial sands and gravels. Drumlins are sometimes described as having the shape of inverted spoons, and though their genesis is debated, they are believed to have been formed when glacial ice, moving over the land, compressed the earth into specific patterns. The long axis of a drumlin is parallel to the direction of former ice movement, while the steep end faces the direction from which the glacier advanced. Drumlins often appear in groups called fields, pods, or swarms; three thousand drumlins lie in southern New Hampshire and eastern Massachusetts, and close to eleven thousand drumlins lie in New York between Rochester and Syracuse, north of the Finger Lakes.

Some of the drumlins in this area rise to sharp, sloping ridges and are called razorbacks, as they look like razorback hogs sleeping on the open land. "Watching the shifting light above the drumlins . . . I felt a darkening within myself," writes Ben Howard in his poem "Midcentury." PATTIANN ROGERS

dry-bottom swamp

Dry-bottom swamp and hard-bottom swamp are terms from the Pine Barrens of New Jersey, foxhunting country. The different kinds of swamp alternate in a patchwork in most sections of the region. A dry-bottom swamp has less standing water throughout the year, and Atlantic white cedars grow right out of its gravelly soil and peat moss. In places where water tends to stand on sphagnum moss, the cedars grow out of hassocks, which are clusters or "knees" of roots and soil bound in cushions about a foot in diameter. The densely woven hassocks are very tough and hard to walk through. These swamps with hassocks are called hard-bottom swamps. Dry-bottom swamp is seasonal, while hard-bottom swamp is constantly flooded. The terms are used by local foxhunters, and are recorded in *One Space, Many Places: Folklife and Land Use in New Jersey's Pinelands National Reserve* by Mary Hufford. The swamps are described as "acoustically magnificent" for carrying the voices of the foxhounds. ROBERT MORGAN

dry fall

A waterfall lacking the important attribute of water is called a dry fall. Georgia O'Keeffe responded to one with the painting *Cliffs Beyond Abiquia, Dry Waterfall*, and a dry fall in Grand Canyon's Obi Canyon is often cited as a prime example. The most dramatic dry fall in the world, three and a half miles wide with a drop of over four hundred feet, is in Sun Lakes State Park, Washington. The skeleton of the greatest waterfall known to have existed on Earth, it is a feature of Grand Coulee Canyon, part of the Channeled Scablands that cover nearly half of eastern Washington. Though unenthusiastically described by some viewers as a wide, bare canyon-walled hole, Dry Falls has an impressive geological pedigree. Fourteen to sixteen thousand years ago, when vast lakes in present-day Montana repeatedly broke through glacial dams, the Missoula Floods raced across the Northwest. Tremendous waters pushed along the ancient course of the Columbia River, gouging rock and sculpting precipices. This ancient giant cataract was so powerful it couldn't sustain itself. Retreating, it vanished.   JOY WILLIAMS

dryki

Dryki refers to an area where trees have been killed by flooding, usually as a result of a river or stream being impounded behind a dam and spilling out beyond the natural banks. A more general usage suggests a slew of dead branches and underbrush, unfit for lumber but suitable for firewood—for instance, driftwood stranded on a sand or gravel bar. Another example would be the ring of trees around Cook Inlet near Anchorage, Alaska, that died in the aftermath of the 1964 earthquake. The faulting that accompanied the quake permanently shifted the local sea level, inundating the trees adjacent to the shoreline. Choked by salt water, the trees eventually died. A ring of woody skeletons marks the landscape decades later.   CONGER BEASLEY, JR.

dry pond

A depression in the ground, after a good rain, will appear to be a shallow yet stable pond. Come back a few dry days later, however, and the pond will be even more shallow, or empty, as its sandy bottom can't hold water. Though naturally occurring—this is how rainwater

becomes groundwater—dry ponds are also man-made to
deal with stormwater runoff in urban areas. While dry
ponds are short-lived in dry climates, in the Southeast
they can hold their water for a whole season or longer,
drawing insects, frogs, alligators, and, because children
come to watch the alligators chase the frogs, fences.
What separates a dry pond from a wet pond is the type
of soil: dry ponds are sandy and porous, while wet ponds
have clay bottoms. STEPHEN GRAHAM JONES

dry valley

A dry valley is a valley once created by a flowing stream
that now has little or no running water. Some dry valleys
are relatively minor indentations, others much deeper
chasms. Possible reasons for the disappearance of the
initial stream include lack of rainfall and a consequent
lowered water table. Or the stream may have been
beheaded—diverted at its source, perhaps by another
stream. Another possibility is that a significant climatic
shift dried up the flow of water over time. A dry valley in
limestone karst could have lost its stream down a joint in
the rock or to a collapsed underground cavern. The name
Dry Valley has been given to valleys across the United
States, from California to Tennessee, Idaho to Georgia,
Alabama to Arizona. CAROLYN SERVID

duff

In eastern deciduous woods, the forest floor usually
contains five to ten years' worth of leaves and twigs
not entirely decomposed, but the same surface layer in
western coniferous forests, where summer drought slows
decay, may hold the accumulated needle-, cone-, and
twig-fall of fifty years. The upper horizon of a coniferous forest floor is properly called litter, and the lower,
partly decomposed layer, duff, but duff is also used more
broadly to mean all debris in a coniferous forest above

the humus and mineral soil. Fires can smolder in duff, erupting days or weeks after surface flames have been snuffed. A Scots term for boiled flour pudding, duff may have been transferred to the stuff of forest floors because of its mixed composition and its soft and yielding quality. Forest duff may or may not be etymologically related to the informal term for the portion of the human anatomy that resting hikers apply to it.   JOHN DANIEL

dugout

The term dugout is mostly used in Canada and by people on the prairies in the United States. Equivalent to the farm pond or a rancher's tank, a dugout is a small, on-farm reservoir dug into the ground and located in a particular watershed area. Prairie farmers look for land with sufficient drainage area that slopes toward a central point in a field: this is a perfect place to build a dugout. The water held there is for farm maintenance—livestock or crop—and is usually sufficient (an average size is two hundred by seventy feet on the surface, with a twelve- to sixteen-foot depth) to withstand drought conditions. In parts of the West and Southwest, dugout refers to a half-house, half-basement residence; Dugout Ranch, open to tourists in south-central Utah, features an example.

ANTONYA NELSON

dugway

A striking example of a dugway exists on the south end of Cedar Mesa in southern Utah: Moki Dugway—a dirt road that drops over two thousand feet in two miles without a switchback, looking something like a furrow slanting down the sidewall of an open pit mine. A dugway can be a road cut across the slope of a hill (if it's bulldozed it's often called a cat road, for Caterpillar tractor) or one excavated to run below the surface of the land. It can also refer to a place on the steep bank of a stream graded down by human means to let cattle and other traffic enter or leave the water. Wallace Stegner describes such a place in *Marking the Sparrow's Fall*, when one character "peered and squinted for the sight of the dugway that would lead them out of the channel and up the cutbank and across a little flat to the final security, so close now and so much more desperately hard to reach with every step." The Dugway Range in Utah is known for its beautiful geodes. More infamous is the Dugway Proving Ground, located in the desert of western Utah—a controversial U.S. Army site because of its tests of chemical and biological warfare agents. KIM BARNES

dune

Wind and a generous supply of granular material are needed to make a dune, which can arise in arid places or along the shore of a lake or ocean, or even along the banks of a river such as the Arkansas River in western Kansas. Dunes are classified by their shape, which is a function of sand and topography interacting with the wind. Sand particles begin to move when wind velocity reaches about eleven miles per hour. The particles move by skipping over the ground, a motion called saltation. The grains are kicked briefly into the air and then fall with a forward glide, hitting other grains on the ground and putting them into motion as well. Relatively fine sand collects this way to produce dunes with a clearly marked crest that drops off to a steep slip face on the sheltered, leeward side. Coarse sand produces rounded dunes without these features. One of the largest dune fields in the United States is the Algodones Dunes, extending southeasterly more than forty miles from Glamis in Imperial County, California, to the southwestern corner of Arizona and into Mexico. The highest dune on America's East Coast is the 140-foot high Jockeys Ridge on the Outer Banks of North Carolina; it's an example of a coastal dune. Sometimes, continuing wind causes dunes to move—as at White Sands, New Mexico, where the dunes of loose gypsum sand move twenty-four feet a year. If the winds and sand supply diminish, an advancing or migrating dune might acquire a covering of vegetation and settle down as a fixed or stabilized dune. The dune environment often has unfamiliar acoustic properties and dune-created wind patterns that sculpt the features of the dune field. Wanderers among dunes may feel a thrill in their alien presence, be enchanted, or, like early saints, see visions in mirages and hear voices in the falling sand.   D. J. WALDIE

dust bowl

A semiarid tract of land from which wind has blown the surface soil exposed by frequent plowing or overgrazing is known as a dust bowl. During periods of drought, these lands, rendered infertile, give rise to dust storms. The term came into popular usage in the 1930s, after parts of the southern Plains were stricken with severe drought, specifically during three very dry years, the worst of it coming in 1934 and 1935. Fields were abandoned and strong winds raised huge clouds of sterile dust, which then settled into drifts. The resultant Dust Bowl became a primary symbol of the Great Depression. This area—the panhandles of Oklahoma and Texas, eastern Colorado, western Kansas, southwestern Nebraska, and the corner of northeastern New Mexico—emerged as the very figure of a desolate rural landscape marked by human isolation and poverty. The marginalization included even the small bands of criminals that preyed on banks in the area during this time. Led by the likes of John Dillinger and Pretty Boy Floyd, these gangsters were called "dustbowl desperados," in contrast to the more organized and urbanized gangs, headed by men like Al Capone in Chicago. More than any other writer, John Steinbeck deserves credit for the nearly mythic stature the Dust Bowl took on in the American imagination. In *The Grapes of Wrath*, his celebrated 1939 novel about Oklahoma farmers driven off their land by soil erosion, Steinbeck gives us many memorable descriptions of the afflicted landscape, as in this passage from the book's opening pages: "Little by little the sky was darkened by the mixing dust, and the wind fell over the earth, loosened the dust, and carried it away. The wind grew stronger. The rain crust broke and the dust lifted up out of the fields and drove gray plumes into the air like sluggish smoke." JEFFERY RENARD ALLEN

D

dust dome

The dome-shaped formation of stagnant and polluted air above a city is known as a dust dome. As any summer city-dweller eager to get to the country for a cool weekend knows, the air in an urban environment is often significantly warmer than air in the surrounding rural area, creating a phenomenon called the urban heat island. Industrial machinery and furnaces, manufacturing complexes, cars, and even air conditioners heat up the city's air; building materials such as concrete, asphalt, and brick retain and radiate that heat well into the night. The large number of windows and other reflective surfaces serve to trap heat, and the lack of areas of open water sustains it. Soon the city is cooking; an inversion layer forms, which, because it's capped at a relatively low level in the atmosphere, causes a dome of air pollutants to form over the city. If there is no wind, the dust dome remains intact, its pollutants sometimes growing a thousand times more concentrated over the urban area than in a nearby rural area. If the winds begin to blow strongly enough, however, the dust dome will elongate downwind, forming a dust plume. The city's pollutants are then spread to its neighbors in the country. JEFFERY RENARD ALLEN

dustwell

A dustwell is a glacial feature caused by patches of dust, dirt, and small stones deposited on the surface of the ice. Because these darker materials have a lower albedo, or reflectivity, than the surrounding ice and snow, they absorb more solar radiation and create small pockets of increased temperature. The ice around these pockets melts more rapidly than the surrounding area, and this differential melting results in holes, bowls, and pits in the glacier's surface. CHARLES FRAZIER

earth pillar

As rainfall gullies a glacial moraine, columns of loose till may be left standing, each with a boulder hat that protects it from erosion. These earth pillars, among the most transient of landforms, typically taper outward toward the bottom. In the French Alps they are called *demoiselles*, perhaps for their delicacy or the winsomeness of their headwear in the eyes of mountaineers long afoot. When the capstone falls, the column quickly follows. Earth pillars also form in badlands, where sandstone slabs of various sizes cap columns of unconsolidated sand. It is possible to watch generations of miniature pillars form and die within the course of a single rainstorm.

JOHN DANIEL

eater

An eater, or swallowhole, is a reach of stream or a tidal area given to violent currents and waves that often upset and/or suck under boats and kayaks and the like as they are attempting passage. When tremendous volumes of water flow over a ledge or plunge over the downstream edge of a boulder in the bed of a channel, eaters can drive boats down to the streambed before spitting them out again, farther downstream. Large rapids in the Grand Canyon, especially during high water, are for good reason known as eaters because of the frequency with which boats disappear into them. The term swallowhole also refers to the place where streams disappear into rock faults, lava breaks, and tubes. Lost rivers are well known in active volcanic regions such as the Craters of the Moon National Monument in Idaho. The Williamson River in Oregon, below ancient Mount Mazama, which exploded to form Crater Lake, vanishes into a rocky ridge only to resurface again as a full-blown river a mile or so below. Such lost waters have been used as a literary metaphor for disappearing values. WILLIAM KITTREDGE

echo hall

An underground chamber large enough to create echoes. Tennessee's Camps Gulf Cave, a five-mile system, for example, contains what may well be the largest underground chambers in the Southeast, including its third room, known as Echo Hall. An echo hall can also be an acoustically resonant grotto, natural amphitheater, or side canyon. Saxophonist and composer Paul Winter explored the Grand Canyon in search of a "great acoustic place" that would capture the majesty of the canyon. After several quests, he found his dream "sound-space," a sanctuary enfolded by an eight-hundred-foot wall of Navajo Sandstone. Winter named this place Bach's Canyon, and he writes that within it "the sound was sublime, with the same seven-second reverberation time as in the Cathedral of Saint John the Divine in New York." Bach's Canyon is the setting for two of Winter's recordings, *Canyon* and *Canyon's Lullaby*. DONNA SEAMAN

ecotone

The area where two or more distinct habitats adjoin is called an ecotone. Because it is a border zone where multiple sets of resources and opportunities become available, an ecotone tends to support greater biological diversity than either of the systems it mediates between. Delineating an ecotone, however, can be problematic. Like habitats and ecosystems, ecotones are not self-defining, as, for example, individual species are. They are human constructs, which derive their shape and character from the qualities their observers find most salient. Much depends on scale. The zone of contact where the prairies of the Great Plains meet the first foothill trees of the Rockies is an ecotone. At such a broad, regional scale, a woodland savanna might be described as ecotonal between the dense forests of the mountains and the grasslands of the plains. Closer up, however, the savanna's edge, where trees and grassland meet, constitutes another ecotone. Other transition zones emerge as one reduces the scale further: at the scale of a beetle, the border between the edge of a clump of bunchgrass and the moat of soil and other plants around it is also an ecotone. In scientific terms one might say that the world is composed of gradients with relative discontinuities. Put simply: things change nearly everywhere, and so nearly every place is the edge of something and shares the qualities of an ecotone.   WILLIAM DEBUYS

eddy

An eddy is a swirling of water or air in a direction contrary to that of the main flow within a larger system. Eddies refer to the swirling currents within high- or low-pressure zones in the atmosphere as well as to river features that develop where the current encounters an obstruction and turns back on itself upstream of the main current. Those that form a completely circular system are called back eddies, and in the right conditions can form whirlpools. Ann Zwinger, in *Downriver*, describes an eddy in the Grand Canyon this way: "The bore of fast water from the rapid emerges and encounters the slower water along the edge of the river, a shear line forms that sets the slower water spinning the opposite direction; the eddy flow is firmly upstream." Water in eddies flows more slowly than the main stream, averaging a foot per second, and in smaller streams the silt and sand thus transported settle into spits and bars, which in turn evolve into spawning beds for trout and salmon. Eddies are also significant resting places for waterfowl. As a result, techniques for rebuilding streambeds to encourage the formation of eddies are important to artisans restoring wildlife habitat.   WILLIAM KITTREDGE

eddy line

An eddy line is the seam between a river's faster, main jet of current and the slower current of an eddy. Crossing a placid eddy line gives pause on quiet waters—time, perhaps, to leave the mainstream and admire a pale ellipse of sand draped along the bank. In formidable white water such as the Colorado River through the Grand Canyon, the shear zone between a screaming downstream current and the upstream spin of an eddy may turn the eddy line into an eddy fence. The two countercurrents rip along each other, separated by a purgatory fault that can surge several feet high. A boat on the eddy side of the fence may be looking "uphill" into the main flow, perhaps in the precarious state of either being eddied out or made an eddy prisoner. Eddy hydraulics are tactile reminders that flowing water has shape and form, that river topography is terrain in motion.   ELLEN MELOY

embouchure

Derived from the French verb meaning "to put in or to the mouth," embouchure refers to the mouth of a river, to the opening out of a valley into a plain, as well as to the shape of lips and mouth in blowing on a musical instrument. In observing landscape, we sometimes overlay our language onto the land, transmute sight into musical sound. In a specific conflation of landscape and musicality, Walt Whitman employs embouchure and its antonym, débouchure. In *Song of Myself,* Whitman writes: "I blow through my embouchures my loudest and gayest" for the dead, and later, close to the end, "I perceive that the ghastly glimmer is noonday sunbeams reflected,/and debouch to the steady and central from the offspring great or small."   ARTHUR SZE

embudo

The Spanish word *embudo* means "funnel." As a landscape term it refers to any place where something is confined or restricted, and thus funneled. For example, the word is commonly used within the ranch country of Mexico and south Texas to describe cramped cuts in the brush where cattle are routed toward corrals. Embudo can also mean a place where a dry canyon narrows or—as the Rio Grande does in Embudo, New Mexico—a river's flow becomes constricted.　ARTURO LONGORIA

encinal

In the savanna regions of the Texas Rio Grande plains and coastal prairies, thousands of oak thickets stand amid weed-covered eolian sands, as if they were castles encircled by desert moats. Each thicket is called an enci-nal, from the Spanish word for a type of oak, *encino*. Primarily composed of post oak, *Quercus stellata*, and live oak, *Q. virginiana*, the encinals serve as nesting habitat for Rio Grande turkey and provide an abundant source of protein for white-tailed deer and javelina. The term is also used to describe oak-dominated ecological commu-nities in Arizona mixed with juniper and piñón pine.
ARTURO LONGORIA

ensenada

An ensenada is a cove or inlet suitable for harborage (one form of the word in Spanish suggests a corral or stock pen). The city of Ensenada, Mexico, is best known as a tourist destination on the Pacific coast of Baja Cali-fornia, but it is also one of Mexico's largest seaports. Explorer Sebastián Vizcaíno named its crescent-shaped bay Ensenada de Todos los Santos (All Saints Cove) a few days after the Feast of All Saints in 1602. The town was established in 1887, when its founders, Californian financiers together with their Mexican partners, acquired eighteen million acres of desolate rangeland and laid out the port to exploit both the climate and land—making this the kind of hybrid place that defines the frontier between Mexico and the Southwest.   D. J. WALDIE

entrenched stream

An entrenched stream or river is one on a flat plain that has cut a trench deep enough to contain its flow, even in flood conditions. A stream becomes entrenched when some change takes it out of equilibrium—a change in climate or land use, for example, or the uplift of land over which the river flows. Depending on the gradient of the stream and the make-up of the terrain it cuts through, the stream will be classified as heavily, moderately, or slightly entrenched. The sinuous meanders and terraced banks of the Colorado and Little Colorado Rivers in Arizona are the dramatic results of entrenchment, as is the expressive gooseneck formation of the San Juan River in Utah.   MICHAEL COLLIER

ephemeral stream

A stream or reach of a stream that flows only during and for short periods following precipitation is known as an ephemeral stream. Also called a stormwater channel, it receives no extensive long-term water supply from melting snow or other sources, and its channel is, at all times, above the water table. Such streams are common throughout the United States, even in the humid East, where it is small, finger-width streams—rills or rivulets—that are ephemeral. Although stream types are commonly divided according to their behavior over time—ephemeral and perennial—a stream may also be classified as exotic where it flows with a volume of water all out of proportion to the land through which it passes, such as the lower Colorado, incongruous in the eastern Mojave Desert.   JEFFERY RENARD ALLEN

erg

What some call sand seas are also known as ergs, from an Arabic word for any vast area covered by sand. The only active erg in North America is the Gran Desierto of northern Sonora, which extends into southwestern Arizona and southeastern California and includes the Imperial Sand Dunes northwest of Yuma, Arizona, the "Saharan" landscape of many Hollywood movies. The floor of an erg usually lies below a floodplain and downwind of dry riverbeds, a source of sand. Ergs become established in dry, wind-eroded regions where transported sand builds up, grain by grain, in distinctive forms. Sand moves like a fluid before the wind, creating rippled surfaces and rising into wave forms that, depending on the wind, may come to dominate one area of an erg—pyramids and crescents and, sometimes, where crosswinds blow, star-shaped dunes. Grain by grain. The power of the small. It was an ancient erg that eventually became what today is known as the Navajo Sandstone layer of the Colorado Plateau.

LINDA HOGAN

erratic

As glaciers melt and retreat, they leave behind rocks and boulders, some of which have been carried great distances. These erratics, aliens in their new geologic communities, stumped scientists until the mid–nineteenth century, when Louis Agassiz realized they provided strong evidence for his new theory of glaciation: they were blazes marking the former trail of the ice. Those boulders most easily linked to the geology of some more distant region are called "indicator blocks," and have been found 750 miles or more from their source. According to one history of New England, patches of great erratic boulders are called bear dens. Erratics often give further testimony to their past in the crisscrossing striations that mark their surface, a result of their tumbling, churning tenure in the ice.   BILL MCKIBBEN

escarpment

Escarpment is related to escarp, an old military fortification term for a slope or banked wall that lies at the foot of a rampart. In the nineteenth century, naturalists began using escarpment to mean a long line of cliffs, a continuous ridge, or a series of hills that because of faulting or erosion rises abruptly from a level or gently sloping plain or plateau. The dramatic and impregnable features of a cliff escarpment are on display in the three-hundred-mile-long, two-thousand-foot-high, yellow-to-gold-to-white limestone of the Mogollon Rim that forms the southern edge of the Colorado Plateau in Arizona. Less spectacular but perhaps more important is the Balcones Escarpment that cuts across central Texas, manifesting itself as a line of low hills. It divides Texas's coastal plain from its western hill country and marks the boundary between the cattle-ranch culture of the American West and the traditional agrarian and farming culture of the American South and East.   MICHAEL COLLIER

esker

Esker derives from the Irish Gaelic word *eiscir,* meaning "ridge of gravel." Also called serpent kames, eskers are long, narrow, usually twisting ridges, formed by meltwater streams that ran beneath the ice of a retreating glacier. They remain today across the Earth. Excellent examples of serpentine eskers are found in Manitoba, Canada. Since prehistoric times, eskers with their winding hills of gravel, sand, and water-smoothed rocks have been used by humans and migrating animals as roadways above the sunken marshy bogs surrounding them. One might imagine the seemingly endless, icy plain of an ancient glacier shining like fire in the sun, creating riverbeds as its huge mass melts and the rocks and gravels it carries are dropped into the rushing waters. Swollen, soggy lands were everywhere then. One might imagine the tracks of horses and oxen coming later, the rattling of carts and wagons, the sounds of humans with all of their retinue following back and forth along the paths of those old riverbeds. Where were they going? For what?

PATTIANN ROGERS

esplanade

From the French meaning "promenade," an esplanade was originally the unsettled area between a citadel and the closest houses of town; now it's a level stretch of open grassy ground, often with a view, as over a meadow, lake, or river. The term is applied to any flat and open area that serves as walkway and overlook—and so Esplanade is a prevalent park name in California, with that state's singular outlook on the Pacific.   LARRY WOIWODE

estero

Estero is Spanish for inlet or estuary—as in the Estero Bay areas of Lee County, Florida, and San Luis Obispo County, California. In south Texas and parts of Mexico the word is used to describe bottomland or those segments of an arroyo that remain filled with water after the rainy season. These esteros hold water for only a short time after a heavy rainfall. In Taos County, New Mexico, the term is applied to a swampy area called Los Esteros.

ARTURO LONGORIA

estuary

That part of the mouth of a river where the river's current meets the sea's tide, and where salt and fresh waters mix, is the estuary. A pleasing word, lovelier than the brackish conditions it implies, for an estuary is defined by prosaic and precise measures of salinity. The

true estuarine nature is divine: estuaries are nurseries
where nascent marine life is nurtured and protected.
Florida Bay, lying between the tip of peninsular Florida
and the Upper Keys, is a large and important estuary
whose health depends on fresh, clean water from the
Everglades. Pollution and decades of flood control are
turning this once crystalline and productive environment into a hypersaline, muddy, superheated lagoon.

JOY WILLIAMS

everglade

An everglade might be defined most easily as a swampy
tract covered with tall grass and dotted with occasional
trees. In practice, however, the word almost always
refers to the grand marsh of southern Florida, which is
so flat that a broad sheet of water flows slowly across it
on the way to the sea—a river with a valley so shallow it
is measured in inches. The system is so finely balanced
that minute variations in elevation can lead to dramatic
changes in flora and fauna. The etymology of everglade
is obscure, but "ever" may have been used to mean
"interminable." If so, it was a misnomer, for changes in
land use and irrigation north of the Everglades have
altered the flow of water and driven the area's unique
plants, animals, and processes to the point of extinction.
As the twenty-first century begins, it is the site of the
largest attempt at ecosystem restoration any place on the
face of the globe, an expensive and desperate attempt to
keep the concept of everglade alive.   BILL MCKIBBEN

exfoliation

Devotees of cosmetics, who may cherish their exfoliation scrubs designed to peel away a thin layer of skin,
will understand intuitively what the word means to a
geologist: the weathering of granite rocks in great sheets,
instead of through grain-by-grain erosion. Stone Moun-

tain in Georgia and Independence Rock in Wyoming are fine examples of exfoliation; the classic case may be Yosemite's Half Dome.   BILL MCKIBBEN

exotic stream

A stream found in an area too arid to have spawned such a flow is called exotic, the stream's headwaters being in some far moister region. Permanent desert lakes, such as Pyramid Lake northeast of Reno, Nevada, are formed either from permanent springs or from the flow of an exotic stream whose source is in a nearby mountain range. Pyramid Lake is fed by waters from the Truckee River, flowing down from the Sierra Nevada. Some of the world's great rivers are exotic streams. The Nile is perhaps the most famous of these, while the Rio Grande is the grand exotic stream of the American arid zone, with a length of 1,885 miles, making it the twenty-fourth largest river in the world. Receiving its water from the melting snows of the Rocky Mountains in Colorado and New Mexico, it flows through desert for much of its length, taking contributions from a few major tributaries, the Conchos, Pecos, and Chama Rivers, and rising with the runoff from summer thunder-showers. The upper Rio Grande essentially terminates at El Paso, Texas, where it is entirely diverted from its channel for human use. It does not resume significant flow until its confluence with the Rio Conchos 250 miles downstream.   JEFFERY RENARD ALLEN

eye

The point where an underground spring suddenly bursts to the surface is known as an eye. It is a place of mystery, where dry ground becomes soaked with life-giving water, and nature gives us a glimpse of all that happens out of the realm of human vision.   JAN DEBLIEU

face

The sides of mountains, cliffs, and other scarps are referred to as faces or, less commonly, walls—for example, the east face of Mount Whitney and the west face of Lembert Dome in the Sierra Nevada of California; the Emperor Face of Mount Robson in the Canadian Rockies; and the Painted Wall in Colorado's Black Canyon of the Gunnison.   JON KRAKAUER

fall line

Fall line is a phrase both metaphoric and literal. In broader terms, it means the zone where the Piedmont foothills level out into the coastal plain, where sandy soil derived from marine deposits replaces rocky rolling land. On some southeastern rivers, such as in the Carolinas and Virginia, the Fall Line is a specific place where shoals and rapids once stopped navigation from the coast because ships couldn't pass through. Cities such as Richmond, Fayetteville, and Columbia sprang up at the head of navigation, and mills and factories were built to take advantage of the water power at the falls and rapids. The abrupt change of elevation caused industry and commerce, courts and seats of government, to take root in those areas.   ROBERT MORGAN

fallow land

Cropland, when it is allowed to lie idle in either a tilled or untilled condition for a year or more, is called fallow. The soil is allowed to rest in order to encourage an abundance of the microscopic organisms necessary to fertility, and to build up nutrients and moisture. Where such methods as brush fallowing, green fallow, or false bedding are practiced, the land is left untilled for as long as a decade, and grasses, weeds, and shrubs are left uncontrolled until plowed under as a way of restoring vitality to the soil. In low-rainfall areas, like the short-grass plains of western North America, acreages of croplands are seeded every other year. During fallow years they're tilled to form a sealing dustcoat on the surface. The tilling also keeps the land bare of weeds that absorb moisture. Leaving the land fallow encourages blowing soil in drought years, notorious examples being the Dust Bowl of western Kansas during the 1930s and, recently, agricultural areas of northern China. It also contributes to desertification. Yet the practice is still extensive, as can be seen in photos taken over the Golden Triangle northeast of Great Falls, Montana, where alternating strips of wheat and bare ground reach to the horizon.   WILLIAM KITTREDGE

false pass

A false pass is a hoped-for passage that, once found, leads nowhere. A dead end. At sea, it's a natural passage incompletely transecting a barrier reef or perimeter reef, usually less than thirty feet deep and blocked by reef growth or sediment deposition. One place in the United States named for the feature is False Pass, Alaska, a tiny village located on a strait on the eastern shore of Unimak Island, the first of the two hundred islands of the Aleutian chain that stretches toward the Kamchatka Peninsula of Russia. This "false pass" did indeed represent a hoped-for passage between the Pacific Gulf of Alaska and the Bering Sea, but proved too shallow for large vessels. The area was originally settled by a homesteader in the early 1900s, and grew with the establishment of a salmon cannery in 1917.   GRETCHEN LEGLER

fan terrace

A fan terrace is a fan-shaped or conical alluvial deposit formed by a stream or a river at the edge of a plain where it becomes less steep. The natural sequence of land formation in a river valley is fan, terrace, floodplain. Terraces

may be alluvial, or they may be strath terraces consisting of a flattish bedrock surface created through lateral
erosion by a river, with a thin layer of alluvium on top.
If a floodplain is isolated from the active channel—for
example, if the channel is deeply cut—then the floodplain
becomes a terrace. So—from a geographer or geologist's
point of view—the distinction consists in whether the
land adjacent to a river is susceptible to flooding. If it is,
it's floodplain. If it isn't, it's terrace.   ROBERT HASS

fast ice

Alaskan painter Toni Onley once described an Arctic
shoreline as "great blocks of ice thrown up in confusion—like a Cubist's dream." Similarly, standing on the
Beaufort Sea's shore, writer Annie Dillard (in *Teaching
a Stone to Talk*) contemplated a "mess of ice . . . standing floes, ice sheets upright, tilted, frozen together and
jammed—which extended out to the horizon." This chaos
occurs at the floe or flaw edge where pack ice, driven by
wind and current, rips and shreds the seaward edge of an
otherwise stable, flat, often gently nubbled, sometimes
vast sheet of sea ice anchored to the land. In *Shadow of the
Hunter,* Richard Nelson writes: "Finally the pack pressed
in against the fast ice, and huge ridges began grinding
together. The sight was awesome, even for men who had
seen it many times before. Colossal boulders of ice turned
and fell, sending shivers through the floes. Low rumblings
gave voice to the incredible power before them, as the
faces of ice mountains met in slow, pulverizing collisions."
Fast ice forms anew each year, with wind and ocean
depth playing the most important roles in determining its
extent. Iñupiaq people call this motionless expanse *tuwak.*
Fast ice may or may not be separated from pack ice (the
perpetually moving floes of annual and multi-year polar
ice) by stretches of open water, called flaw leads. Eskimo
hunters regularly traverse fast ice to hunt at the flaw lead,

where sea mammals associated with pack ice—seals, bowhead whales, belugas, and narwhals—congregate to breathe. Here, too, is where polar bears, drawn to the floe edge by the concentration of prey, often come ashore across the reach of fast ice. From miles away hunters on *tuwak* may spy steam rising from a flaw lead or see a patch of dark cloud, both revealing open water. Other names: landfast floe, *tuaq* (Yup'ik), flaw ice. Global warming, by delaying the seasonal formation of fast ice, is threatening the ice-dependent universe of polar bear, bowhead whale, Eskimo. EVA SAULITIS

fault

When rock strata in the Earth's brittle crustal layers fracture under stress, the blocks slip past each other to a point of equilibrium along a fault line that may be inches or hundreds of miles in length. These sudden breaks trigger earthquakes, and faults of three different sorts are the result. When the crust is pulled apart, a normal or tension fault occurs, with one side of the fractured strata dropping vertically, sometimes leaving the other block exposed as a prominent cliff, or fault scarp. When the Earth's crust is compressed, one side of the fracture rises abruptly above the other—a reverse fault. (A thrust fault, when one side overrides the other at a low angle, is a type of reverse fault. When two fault blocks rotate past each other by pivoting at the same point, the result is a scissor fault.) When movement along a fault line is horizontal rather than vertical, the break is called a strike-slip or transcurrent fault. California's six-hundred-mile-long San Andreas fault system is perhaps the best-known North American strike-slip fault. Lateral shearing, in contrast to the cliffs that vertical shearing produces, creates rift valleys and offsets, sometimes spectacular ones. In *Assembling California,* John McPhee compares the dissimilarity of the two sides of Tomales

Bay, a flooded San Andrean rift valley thirty miles north of San Francisco, writing: "A tan cotton sock on one foot and a green wool sock on the other could not represent a greater mismatch.... The granite on the west side of the Tomales broke away from the southern Sierra Nevada and has traveled north along the fault at least three hundred miles, an earthquake at a time." A river may be offset by strike-slip faulting where it's forced to follow the fault line, sometimes for miles, in an abrupt dogleg until it reconnects with its displaced channel. In some places—California, the Rocky Mountains, Alaska's Prince William Sound—the history of thousands of slip-faults is starkly visible. Many such breaks were violent responses to stress, but McPhee writes that blocks along some faults "assume an almost steady creep," leaving behind a seismic record of barely detectable tremors. Faulting leaves its signature in many features—scarps, offset rivers, sag ponds, desert oases, and the smooth friction polish on a rock surface known as slickenside.   EVA SAULITIS

fault spring

When an aquifer encounters a vertical fracture in the Earth's crust, it sometimes emerges from the fault as a surface spring. Halted by an impermeable rock wall, the water is forced up along the fault to a place where it bubbles out onto the landscape as a fault spring. If the aquifer's subterranean path takes it near hot, young rock, it emerges as a hot spring—Pilgrim Hot Springs on Alaska's Seward Peninsula is a good example. Fan-palm oases in the Mojave and other deserts are typically associated with cool-water fault springs.   EVA SAULITIS

fell field

Fell is a very old English word for hill or mountain. It also meant a wild, high mountain slope or stretch of pasture, fell-pasture probably having been shortened to fell. In current usage, a fell field refers to a particular alpine habitat, a flat rocky area above tree line with low-growing vegetation that is often related to desert species. As Mary Austin observes in *The Land of Little Rain,* "Extreme aridity and extreme altitude have the same dwarfing effect, so that we find in the high Sierra and in Death Valley related species in miniature that reach to a comely growth in mean temperatures." Fell fields occur as low as 9,500 feet in the Sierra Nevada and as high as mountain summits. A recent publication has described the fell fields of the Sierra as nature's own Zen rock gardens and mentions Donner Pass, Devils Postpile, and Sonora Pass as places where they can be visited. The related term felsenmeer comes from German and means a "rock-sea." It refers to any large field of angular boulders, of the kind formed by frost or the action of glaciers.   ROBERT HASS

fen

A series of mucky lowlands, the fen, or water-meadow, is home to water-loving plants that decay to form peat. Unlike a bog, which has acid soils, the fen is alkaline or neutral, and often occurs above a limestone bed. The name comes from the fenlands of eastern England, now mostly drained for agriculture. America's most famous fen is—or was—in Boston. Frederick Law Olmsted converted this "noxious tidal swamp" into part of his Emerald Necklace of parks, but the name remains attached, among other things, to the Hub's beloved ballyard, Fenway Park.   BILL MCKIBBEN

field

A field of cleared or open ground is presumed to have some purpose: a cornfield, a pasture field, a minefield, and a fallow field all have their special jobs to do. Even a field of wildflowers is so described because of its value as a spectacle; otherwise it would just be a meadow. And so it is that field has crept increasingly into our language as a means of describing a specific area of cultivation, albeit of culture or the mind: the field of anthropology and a baseball field share in common the task of drawing each one's adherents into a dedication to its unified purpose.   BARBARA KINGSOLVER

F

field pattern

Geographers use field pattern to describe how the countryside is divided up into allotments for cultivation or grazing, reflecting the history of ownership and administration. The term may also refer to the way in which individual fields are plowed. The typical field pattern in New England is a crazy quilt of small, irregular parcels, their boundaries influenced by the contours of the land. Along rivers in Louisiana and the Southwest, fields are often laid out according to the old French and Spanish system of narrow long lots running at right angles to the watercourse. Meanwhile, in the Midwest the dominant pattern, dictated by the Land Ordinance of 1785, is a checkerboard of mile-square sections, their sides running due north-south or east-west, without regard to hills, streams, or other natural features. A corrugated field is one in which neighboring strips are plowed in opposite directions, thus creating distinct ridges and troughs, to reduce erosion or guide irrigation water. An envelope field, which suggests the merging of the triangle folds on the reverse of an envelope, is a type of corrugated field.   SCOTT RUSSELL SANDERS

fil du courant

A Cajun French term meaning "thread of the current," fil du courant is used to describe the optimal navigation course within a bayou or river. The fil is often visible as a glassy-smooth pathway through the otherwise ripping water. Louisiana shrimpers follow the fil du courant to avoid underwater obstructions and to secure sufficient depth for skim nets that extend winglike from either side of the vessel.   MIKE TIDWELL

fin

Fin is a general term for a thin ridgeline of rock resulting from fracturing and the effects of erosion, as with some sandstone formations such as The Organ and others, generally, in Fin Canyon in Arches National Park, Utah. Arches are formed when moisture seeps into fractures of fins, then freezes and expands to break off fragments and sheets of rock (spalling). Clearly likened to the fins of fish and sea mammals, the term was transferred to the projection on the share or coulter of a plough, and to standing ridges on a usually hot object, such as a radiator or cylinder head of an engine. In volcanic activity, as with Mount St. Helens in Washington State, a fin is a standing and often rising ridge of extruded rock within the caldera, radiating heat at very high temperatures.   JOHN KEEBLE

finger drift

Narrow, elongated drifts of dry snow, or drifts of sand in dryland areas, that are blown across open, firm-surfaced areas, such as a highway.   WILLIAM KITTREDGE

finger lake

On a map, the long, narrow, and roughly parallel troughs of the lakes of western New York look as though they might have been gouged by giant hands reaching south from Lake Ontario. These are the imaginatively named Finger Lakes, of which Seneca and Cayuga are the largest. The gouging agent, however, was not a pair of hands but a series of massive glaciers that dug U-shaped valleys in the underlying bedrock. Today finger lake is applied to any body of water occupying a similarly shaped valley.   WILLIAM DEBUYS

finger-rafted ice

A floating piece of ice that meets and overrides another creates rafted ice—because one piece uses the other as a raft. When two pieces of rafting ice interlock with one another in narrow, alternating strips, like the fingers of folded hands, the ice is said to be finger-rafted. Rafting is the usual way fractured young or new ice, such as nilas, joins together to develop floes of larger size and greater thickness. As floes grow larger, instead of rafting when they collide, they fracture and buckle. The debris from these dramatic impacts creates the hummocks and pressure ridges that commonly distinguish the surface of pack ice.   GRETCHEN LEGLER

fire line

A fire line is a break in fuel continuity. It can be a natural barrier, such as a river or cliff, but in wildfire containment, fire lines are more commonly human constructions. A rule of thumb holds that the width of a fire line on reasonably level ground should be one and a half times the height of the flames to be contained, and considerably wider on steep slopes. Fire lines dug down to mineral soil before an oncoming fire are known as hot lines. Burned-out areas are known as cold trails. Lines put down by human labor are hand lines, and preliminary lines are scratch lines. Fire lines constructed by use of equipment such as bulldozers are known as cat lines, tractor lines, or plow lines. Lines involving chemicals, foam, or water are called wet lines or retardant lines. Those put down to contain backfiring, the burning of fuels ahead of the main fire in hope of replacing an uncontrollable fire with one that's more likely to be controlled, are known as back lines.   WILLIAM KITTREDGE

fishhook dune

A dune made up of a long, slightly S-shaped ridge
(the shaft) ending in a crescent (the hook) is a fishhook
dune. Examples can be found in central California's
Guadalupe-Nipomo Dune Complex.   D. J. WALDIE

fissure

A fissure is an extended surface crack or fracture that
creates a distinct separation in rock. These rifts in the
earth are often associated with areas of volcanic and seismic activity, and are being studied in such places as the
Inyo Crater area in Long Valley, California. Fissures can
form in the sides of lava domes and serve as outlets for
volcanic gasses or openings through which lava flows in
fissure eruptions. Such eruptions, through fissures rather
than through a central vent, have occurred repeatedly
on the flanks of the Hawaiian volcanoes Mauna Loa and
Kīlauea. Up to seventeen million years ago, extensive
basalt flows from innumerable fissure eruptions built up
the Columbia Plateau, an area of over 200,000 square
miles in Washington, Oregon, and Idaho. Fissures have
recently opened within the city of Phoenix, Arizona,
apparently caused by a severe drawdown of the local
water table.   CAROLYN SERVID

fjord

Fjords are created when a rising sea floods a glaciated
coastal valley. A fjord (sometimes spelled fiord and also
known as a sea loch) begins as a U-shaped trough up to
a hundred miles or more in length, gouged out by an
advancing glacier plowing debris ahead of it. At its fur-
thest reach, the glacier's snout floats on a frozen or open
sea. When the glacier retreats, it leaves behind a line of
glacial debris—a terminal moraine, which later becomes
an underwater sill near the fjord's entrance. Multiple sills
mark the temporary stopping points of some glaciers.

When a rising sea enters these gouged troughs, it eventually forms long, finger-shaped, steep-sided inlets, commonly over a thousand feet deep. In many fjords, niche or cirque glaciers still hang from the mountain-sides, ghosts of the fjord's Pleistocene past. In summer, multiple waterfalls may spill down a fjord's sides from these glaciers, the thin streams spiraling away in mist. In certain fjords, the parent glacier might survive still, as a tidewater glacier at the head of the inlet, where it now calves centuries-old ice that is still advancing seaward from the land's interior. College Fiord and Chatham Strait in Alaska are among North America's many fjords. In *The Blue Bear,* Lynn Schooler writes that the Hoonah Tlingit, who call Glacier Bay, Alaska, their traditional home, say "a foolish woman insulted the glacier and caused it to rampage down from the mountains. . . . Since then, the ice has been placated and withdrawn, grumbling and complaining, more than sixty-five miles back into the mountains," creating in its wake the fjords of Glacier Bay National Park. The Norwegian word *fjord* came into English usage in 1674 when the Norse volume *Scheffere's Lapland* was translated.   EVA SAULITIS

flake

Over the ages, powerful forces such as frost wedging and exfoliation will cause scales or sheets of rock to split away from the face of a cliff. Eventually these rock scales may become completely detached and fall to the ground, but before that happens they can remain partially affixed to even a very steep precipice for millennia. While still in situ they are known to climbers and geologists as flakes. Flakes can be as small as a dinner plate, or they can measure thirty feet thick and encompass as much vertical terrain as a basketball court. Sometimes particularly large or distinctive flakes are given names that gain wide usage; Boot Flake, for example, which is shaped like

a huge gumboot, towers fifty feet from heel to cuff, and
tenuously adorns the upper southeast face of Yosemite's
El Capitan. JON KRAKAUER

flash flood

Slow-moving thunderstorms, or a series of storms, that
move across the same area again and again are frequently
the cause of the phenomenon known as flash flooding, and the number of deaths from flash flooding has
exceeded deaths from tornados since 1985. Craig Childs,
in *Soul of Nowhere,* evokes the seriousness this way: "The
sound becomes familiar. Next I smell it, and that too is
familiar. It is the musty scent of death, the unmistak-
able smell of a flash flood." What happens during a flash
flood is that too much water falls in too short a time for
the terrain to absorb or safely channel it. Whether the
water falls on the rocky slopes of a Colorado canyon or
onto the flat desert in Arizona, or whether what's trying
to hold the water back is a dam, levee, or ice jam, the
abrupt and excessive combination becomes deadly. York,
the only African American member of the Lewis and
Clark expedition of 1804–1805, and a slave since birth,
is remembered for having saved William Clark's life
when he plucked him from a flash flood on the Missouri
River near Great Falls in present-day Montana.
ANTONYA NELSON

flat

The transformation of North America from wilderness to
marketable real estate needed flat land to farm and build
towns on, and to make crossing the continent possible.
One way to advertise land that could become farmland,
a town site, or a roadbed was to name it Flat or Flats.
Some flats point out the local vegetation: Cedar Flat,
Oregon; Hickory Flat, Missouri; Yucca Flats, the Nevada
nuclear test site; and Piney Flats, Tennessee. Some flats

just locate the site: Yukon Flat in Alaska, Rail Road Flat in California, and Flatgap in Kentucky. Other flats are a problem: there are more than fifteen potentially unpleasant locations in the West named Alkali Flat or Flats. Then there's a Dead Ox Flat in the aptly named Malheur County, Oregon. The term is evocative, however it's used. Flat is one of the words with which writers quickly sketch the West, as in this scene from Zane Grey's novel *The Light of Western Stars*: "Far below lay the cedar flat and the foothills. Far to the west the sky was still clear, with shafts of sunlight shooting down from behind the encroaching clouds."   D. J. WALDIE

F

flatiron

A flatiron is a tilted, triangular rock outcropping, usually on the flank of a mountain, a type of hogback ridge composed of coarse sandstone and conglomerate. Flat-lying sedimentary rock is pushed upward by geological uplift, creating a core area edged with steeply uplifted sedimentary rocks. Water erosion cuts through the uptilted edge, forming a series of V-shaped valleys with triangular rock masses in between, resembling a smooth row of sharklike teeth. The name comes from the fact that the triangular slabs resemble the irons used to press clothes. Some of the best-known flatirons are found near Boulder, Colorado, where they tower above the town on the east-facing flank of the Front Range. Others are found in the Garden of the Gods in Colorado Springs, Colorado. Flatiron has an architectural application, as well, as in the Flatiron Building in New York.   CONGER BEASLEY, JR.

flatwater

Flatwater is the section of a river flowing smoothly downhill over the bed of its own creation, broken by obstacle or turbulence. Though the term is also used to describe water in lakes and reservoirs, flatwater to a boater is the river cruising. Steep-gradient rivers can lose elevation by a repeated physics of pools and drops. Flat-water is often described as any "pool" between the drops, or rapids. Nevertheless, much goes on along flatwater's laminar flow. The river's velocity is checked, its flow a "garment of motion," in James Dickey's poem "Inside the River." The surface may seem glassy and sluggish, the current not discernible, but it is there in the deepest channel, gentle and resolute.   ELLEN MELOY

---

flatwoods

Dominated by longleaf pines, slash pines, pond pines, and low-growing saw palmettos, the trees in flatwoods are a major part of the terrestrial ecosystem in Florida, cover-ing nearly fifty percent of the state's land area. People who made their homes in the backwoods of the Florida flatwoods, once known as "Crackers," are described by Lois Lenski in her children's story *Strawberry Girl*: "They came to the flatwoods at last, where their feet made a soft patter on the pine-needled path. Innumerable tall straight trunks of giant pines rose up on all sides to join their tops in a green roof overhead." Flatwoods trees grow on level ground created by sea level changes during the glacial period. Increases in sea level caused floods on the flatlands, which were covered with thick layers of sand. Pine trees eventually established themselves in that sandy soil. Settlers who came upon these lands found that pine flats had such open underbrush that a man could easily drive a wagon through them. In areas such as Illinois, flatwoods grow on clay hardpan—a layer of firm, finely textured clay particles. Hardpan forms a barrier to rooting, so the majority of these trees have shallow roots. White-tailed deer, black bear, fox, squirrel, and the rare red-cockaded woodpecker are among the many animals that depend on a flatwoods environment. These habitats are also important breeding areas for amphibians; in the northern flatwoods, the blue-spotted salamander is common, while the southern flatwoods are the habitat of the northern crawfish frog. Tales of strange, alien flatwood creatures have also loomed large—a story told long ago in the town of Flatwoods, West Virginia, described the sighting of one slimy giant in the hills of Braxton County. The rumor has been retold and passed down through generations—the area is known to this day as the "Home of the Green Monster." ELIZABETH COX

F

flaw lead

A flaw lead is a navigable passage between floating pack and landfast ice. One side of the lead, the pack, is in more or less constant motion. The other side is motionless, a sheet of fast ice firmly attached to the shore or to an ice front, the seaward edge of an ice shelf. Fast ice may extend anywhere from a few feet to nearly two hundred miles from shore, and flaw leads are often temporary, their creation always subject to shifts in the direction of the wind. (Grounded or floating icebergs sometimes develop aprons of "fast ice," but open water at the edge of such ice constitutes one of the floating pack's many transitory "open leads.") When a sheet of landfast ice rises more than six and a half feet above water, it can be reclassified as an ice shelf and it creates a special type of flaw lead. British explorer Robert Falcon Scott, sailing in the flaw lead of Antarctica's Ross Ice Shelf, a mass of ice the size of France, described its ice front as "a relentless coast of high ice cliffs," much of it more than one hundred feet high (and descending, he was unaware, hundreds of feet below his ship). In the Arctic, this type of flaw lead is rare. Far more common is the dynamic system of opening and closing flaw leads maintained by alternating on- and offshore winds, an unpredictable situation that makes navigating in the flaw leads dangerous—and frustrating. GRETCHEN LEGLER

floating island

A floating island in a marsh or swamp is formed by a mass of decayed vegetation held together by interlacing roots. Created from plant litter, the mat adds to itself year by year, as its vegetation thrives on rich decay, building a raft or platform, stitching moss and humus together until it grows thick and heavy. It may eventually come to rest on the pond floor. Floating islands in the lakes of Wisconsin are described by May Watts in *Reading the Landscape of America* as drifting tamarack logs on which moss and seedlings take root, and mats of entangled vegetation, bulrushes, sphagnum moss, leatherleaf, and sundew. "An island came bobbing alongside our rowboat. It consisted of a floating log, with a minute tamarack seedling riding it, in a crack beside a knob of moss."

ROBERT MORGAN

floe

An area or expanse of floating ice that is not fast—not anchored to the shore or to any grounded iceberg, glacier face, or ice wall—is called a floe. "Once embedded within the pack, a floe enjoys a collective identity," writes Stephen J. Pyne in his book *The Ice*, but until then, floes are solitary creatures. Floes gathered together in unconsolidated pack ice create fantastic patterns of many-sided, blue-tinged shapes floating in dark water. From above they seem like icy puzzle pieces on a liquid table. Floes are classified according to an international system of reference: giant (over 10 km), vast (2 to 10 km), big (500 m to 2 km), medium (100 to 500 m), and small (20 to 100 m). Even smaller than "small" are ice cakes. The largest of these floes, then, can be fifty miles or much more across, while the smallest are no more than six feet wide. After that, such small floes are generally called brash ice.

GRETCHEN LEGLER

floodplain

The area of a flat valley floor that a river, swollen by spring melt and spring rains in some parts of the country, and by hurricanes and tropical storms in others, will cover when it overflows its usual course or banks is its floodplain. It is an area in which you will probably not be able to buy flood insurance from a private company. Floodplain incursions are measured according to a river's history—a variety of frequencies depending on the region's hydrology and the upstream control by dams. The hundred-year floodplain is inundated once a century; the one-year floodplain, annually. The means of managing floodplain regions includes dikes, floodways, and zoning and building codes—these regulated by community or state law, unless they do not meet federal government, especially Federal Emergency Management Agency (FEMA), minimum standards; then federal law applies. LARRY WOIWODE

floodway

A floodway is a man-made channel built as a branch or a neighboring bed to a river that tends to flood. It provides a secondary course for the river's swelling waters during high-water stages. (The U.S. Army Corps of Engineers also uses the term to refer to that part of a floodplain with rapid downstream flow.) Floodways are more common to Canada than the United States, and one striking example (as viewed in vertiginous aerial photos) is a bypass of the Red River around Winnipeg. The narrow Red, which defines North Dakota's eastern border on its route to Hudson Bay, is so tempestuous it can flood to a width of sixty miles, as it did in 1997. Floodways have also been constructed on the Colorado, below Davis Dam; on the Missouri, their mechanics here located within a series of Army Corps of Engineers dams; and on other

rivers whose regular flooding has caused devastation
to property.   LARRY WOIWODE

flume

If you are in the White Mountains of Arizona and ask
for the nearest flume, you will be shown a water pipe
or trough. In New Hampshire's White Mountains
with the same request, helpful locals will take you to a
ravine. Thus, flume seekers should know which White
Mountains they're in. Flume refers to both artificial and
natural water channels. A westerner's flume is usually the
engineered one, an inclined chute or pipe built to carry
water for irrigation, mining, and other uses. Easterners
refer to the geomorphic flume, a steep-sided ravine with a
stream that descends in a series of cascades. New Hampshire's famous flumes, which formed when water eroded
a dike of basalt or soft rock, unplugging fissures in harder
rock, include Crawford Notch, Sabbaday Falls, and The
Flume at Franconia. Flowing mountain water stair-steps
down these chasms, smoothing granite streambeds and
plunging into spring-clear pools.   ELLEN MELOY

fluting

Another geologic term with architectural origins, fluting is
applied to formations that have the appearance of orna-
mentation, corrugation, gutterlike channels, or elongated,
streamlined depressions, suggesting the shapes of flutes
(the musical instrument) laid more or less parallel to each
other. The word has numerous applications, often describing the effect of weathering and erosion on coarse and
exposed, unstratified rock, such as granite, particularly
in arid and mountainous regions. This may be the result
of water erosion, or of glacial effects, and with the latter
a part of a continuum including drumlins, rogen (parallel ridges of glacial drift), and hummocky terrain. In the
upper Midwest, fluting refers to the small-scale gouges

created by glaciers dragging an ice-embedded boulder across a rock surface, of which the most famous are on Kelly's Island on the southern edge of Lake Erie. Yet seemingly, fluting can occur on any scale, as suggested by the geologist and climber Clarence King in his *Mountaineering in the Sierra Nevada* (1872): "Every fluting of the great valley was in itself a considerable cañon." JOHN KEEBLE

fold mountain

A fold mountain is one created by the bending of strata, a tectonic process. When continental plates collide with one another or with oceanic plates, their margins exert immense compressive forces that buckle the Earth's crust and crumple sedimentary layers. This slow deformation results in a corrugated series of folds called synclines (concave) and anticlines (convex). Differential erosion of these rock structures can make fold mountains out of anticlines, and low points in the local relief from synclines, but can also produce anticlinal valleys and synclinal ridges. When erosion sheers off the humps of the folds, it may leave sharp-edged scarps that resemble fault-block mountains. Actual faulting takes place under extreme pressure, as does metamorphosis, turning shale into slate, sandstone into quartzite, and limestone into marble. The Appalachians are old fold mountains created by the collision of two continental plates, then exposed by the erosion of thousands of feet of strata laid down above. One sees the north-south trend of these ancient folds when traversing the ridge-and-valley region of Pennsylvania. The Rockies and Andes arose from complex interactions between oceanic and continental plates.
ROBERT MICHAEL PYLE

foothill

The base of a mountain or a mountain range is usually ringed or lined by a series of low rises. These are called foothills. The western slope of California's Sierra Nevada offers a spectacular example of a complex and manifold system of foothills. Starting east of Sacramento it begins as soft, elevated undulations that develop into rounded but steeper and eventually sharper hills, morphing into one of the most sublime North American mountain ranges. A more gentle and extended range of foothills is the Piedmont area of the Middle Atlantic States, stretching from Maryland through the Carolinas. Compared with the ascendant and aristocratic peaks and ridges presiding above them, foothills are like steady commoners who occupy a middle ground between flatland and mountains. One feels at home in this proletarian landscape, consoled and reassured by its human scale.   MICHAEL COLLIER

footwall

The lower-lying side of a reverse (compression) fault is called a footwall. The rock mass that towers above the footwall is called a hanging wall. These terms were first used by English miners working such faults: they stood on the footwall and hung their lamps from the overarching hanging wall. With a normal (tension) fault, though, it's the higher side of the inclined fracture that's called, somewhat incongruously, the footwall and the lower side that's called the hanging wall.   DONNA SEAMAN

ford

A ford is a shallow place in a river where a man or an animal can cross by wading. The title of Mary Austin's 1917 novel of the Owens Valley, *The Ford,* uses the word in both its literal and metaphorical senses. For a sort of gorgeous stippling with the word, here is Cormac McCarthy in *Cities of the Plain:* "He looked at the horses across the creek where they stood footed to their darkening shapes in the ford with their heads raised looking toward the house and the cottonwoods and the mountains and the

red sweep of the evening sky beyond." The Spanish is
vado, and is preserved in the name El Vado Reservoir
on the Rio Chama in northern New Mexico.

ROBERT HASS

foredune

Wherever the sea meets the beach, grains of sand are
blown landward by ocean breezes. A few yards from the
tide's edge, the sand gathers itself in a lone wrinkle that
runs the length of the shore, parallel to the surf. This
first pinch of land is the foredune, formed where bits of
shell or debris cause the flow of wind to slow and drop
grains of sand in a long pile. It usually stands several
yards landward of the beach face (the zone where waves
wash across the sand) and the berm (where the land rises
gradually and sunbathers love to recline). The foredune
may vary in height from a barely discernible ridge to one
that is thirty or forty feet. It is generally covered with
vegetation, which traps grains of sand and holds the dune
in place. If plants covering a portion of this coastal ridge
are destroyed by traffic or erosion, sand will again fly free
and the foredune will breach. The broken link within
the dune line will begin to migrate, blown inland by the
force of the maritime wind.   JAN DEBLIEU

foreshore

The foreshore is that zone of a beach or seashore that
lies between the average low-tide mark and the average
high-tide mark. It is fully exposed at low tide, hence its
synonym, beach face. While in the United States the
foreshore is regarded as public space, in Britain this
part of any beach is owned by the Crown or its grantee.
Because of its association with tide markings, foreshore is
not typically used to refer to freshwater lakes but rather
to any large body of water—usually the sea—affected by
the tide.   PATRICIA HAMPL

forest

Of four basic life communities—forest, grassland, scrub (including desert), and savanna—the forest requires the most water to develop peak biotic density. In forests, trees provide a closed canopy that fosters a complex, self-sustaining realm. Forests create their own humid and thermal environments, and provide tempering effects on water and weather systems beyond their boundaries. The root of forest, the Latin *foris*, signifies a woodland outside the common bounds of property, though this meaning regarding ownership has become largely lost, as it is now common in America to refer to commercial forests and to managed forests, within common bounds of property. Still, a dichotomy has existed for all of human history between woodland owned for timber production or cleared for agricultural application and forests reserved for an escape from human law and commerce. In North America, forest systems include the taiga or boreal forest (a nearly continuous belt of conifers across North America and Eurasia overlying once-glaciated lands); deciduous forest systems farther south; the rainforests of the Pacific coast and the tropics; and local forest systems of redwood, pine, or other species.   KIM STAFFORD

fork

A fork is a stream that drains into a larger stream. Easterners are likely to call these watercourses branches, tributary is also appropriate, and those in west Texas would call smaller forks prongs. They are most often named by their geography—that is, the west branch of the Sacandaga, the North Fork of the Flathead. And then there's the North Prong of the Little Red River Fork of the Prairie Dog Town Fork of the Red River, in Briscoe County, Texas. Playfair's Law holds, among other things, that tributary forks almost always join the main river at its level instead of with a sudden drop.   BILL MCKIBBEN

fosse

A fosse is a long narrow depression that lies between the front of a moraine and its outwash plain. Nantucket, an island of singular beauty off the coast of Massachusetts, is the easternmost point reached by the great glacial land transformers of millennia past, and strikingly exhibits the varied work of the ice sheet. All the topographical phenomena that result from the morainal margin are clearly present—kame hills, fosse, contact slope, and an apron plain. Widening and shrinking, rising and sinking, at times to near sea level, this particular fosse winds though almost the entire length of the twelve-mile island. Nantucket Town lies in the fosse.   JOY WILLIAMS

fossil bed

A layer of identifiable fossiliferous material preserved in sedimentary rocks, fossil bed is also a common term for a fossil landscape buried by deposits and revealed only when denuded by wind, rain, or excavation. (The alternative term, exhumed landscape, is perhaps preferable.) The National Park System is rife with fossil bed sites: the John Day Fossil Beds in the John Day River basin of Oregon, noted for the discovery there of the small three-toed horse named Miohippus; the Agate Fossil Beds along the banks of the Niobrara River in Nebraska, an important source for 19.2-million-year-old mammal fossils; and the Florissant Fossil Beds just west of Pikes Peak in Colorado, where, 35 million years ago, an enormous volcanic eruption buried the valley and petrified huge redwood trees. The Ashfall Fossil Beds in northeastern Nebraska hold not just remnants but articulated remains with bones still joined together in their proper order—a product of the animals having been quickly buried in volcanic ash.   KIM BARNES

fourteener

A mountain peak whose summit exceeds 14,000 feet above sea level. The name has been used for many years in Colorado, a state with fifty-four or so fourteeners—more than any other. Climbers and hikers speak of "bagging fourteeners" and collect them like destination badges tacked to an alpenstock. Individual fourteeners have their particular lore, such as when a climbing party from New Haven built a cairn atop Mount Yale (14,196 feet) in Colorado's Collegiate Range so that it overtopped nearby Mount Princeton (14,197 feet). Pikes Peak (14,110 feet), easily the most famous fourteener, and Mount Evans west of Denver (14,264 feet) have automobile roads to their summits. In the Pikes Peak summit house, flatlanders find souvenirs, postcards, coffee and donuts, and oxygen masks.   ROBERT MICHAEL PYLE

freshet

A freshet is a species of flood—a relatively sudden surge, brought on by heavy rainfall, rapid snowmelt, or the two together, that sends streams and small rivers over their banks. Spate and flush suggest the same phenomenon. Around the term's usage area—chiefly the mountainous Atlantic states and the northern tier of the United States—the definition of freshet varies locally. In the maritime Northwest, it is as Robert Michael Pyle writes in *Wintergreen*: "Big, long rains on a warm west wind that really raise the rivers and bring superhigh tides, the two together deeply flooding everything in reach for a few days." Henry Thoreau, in *Walden*, speaks of freshets as signs of the inexhaustible vigor of Nature. The word may still be uttered here and there in an older sense, to mean a stream of fresh water, and a related meaning was probably important to nervous European explorers poking at the margins of North America—a region of fresh water beyond the mouth of a seagoing stream.   JOHN DANIEL

freshwater lens

The aquifer beneath south Florida is called the Biscayne Aquifer and is one of the most permeable in the world. Rainwater entering it is rapidly discharged into surrounding coastal waters. The Florida Keys consist, for the most part, of porous limestone, remnants of an ancient coral reef. However, on the large islands of the Lower Keys—Key West, Sugarloaf, Cudjoe, and Big Pine—a thick caprock of fine-grained calcium carbonate retains water in thin lenses that actually float on top of the heavier underlying saltwater. The size and extent of the lenses vary depending on the elevation of the key beyond the reach of tides, the season, and, of course, the amount of rainfall. Lenses are of maximum size and freshness during the late-summer wet season and are closer, at that time, to the surface. A freshwater lens— varieties of which occur in many coastal areas of the world—is highly beneficial for wildlife, but any large-scale pumping for human use can quickly exhaust it, and saline water could be rapidly drawn into the aquifer. The Keys rely on water piped from wellfields in Florida City, 130 miles from Key West. The original pipeline was built by the U.S. Navy in 1940.   JOY WILLIAMS

frost hollow

Topographic depressions susceptible to frequent, even unseasonable, frosts while the temperature of surrounding hillslopes remains above freezing are called frost hollows. Air, as it loses heat by terrestrial radiation at night, becomes more dense. Draining downhill by the force of gravity in a katabatic flow, this cold dense air can accumulate in frost or pocket hollows. In Nathaniel

Hawthorne's fanciful sketch "A Visit to the Clerk of Weather" (uncollected by the author in his lifetime for good reason), a Mr. John Frost is described by the fetching maiden Spring as "that misshapen wretch . . . that soulless withering demon" forever intent on delaying her arrival. She promises, however, to appear early in the coming year, for "Mr. Frost is obliging to take a journey to the North to find a polar bear for his wife, who has lingered amongst you with her husband so long that she affects some of your customs, and must have a substitute for a lap-dog." JOY WILLIAMS

frost line

In arctic and subarctic landscapes, the frost line is the lower limit of permanently frozen ground (permafrost). In places such as Barrow, an Iñupiaq Eskimo village on Alaska's Arctic coast, the frost line is more than a thousand feet deep. On a fool's errand in 1881, Lt. Henry Ray, the leader of the first Arctic science station in Barrow, supervised the digging of a pit to measure temperatures of frozen ground. Of this experiment, Charles Wohlforth writes: "According to local legend, he wanted to find the bottom of the permafrost." Weeks of digging produced a pit over thirty-seven feet deep. "We have no record of what the Natives thought of this activity," Wohlforth writes, "but practically enough, an Iñupiaq family appropriated the hole as a prodigious ice cellar." It was used to preserve whale meat for over one hundred years. In temperate climates, frost line has a different meaning, and is as important to farmers as tides are to mariners, as it indicates the maximum depth that ground freezes in winter. Those who have crops at stake speak of the frost line of a particular winter, of a series of winters, of the most extreme depth ever recorded. Even warm, mountainous places such as the Hawaiian Islands

have their frost lines: altitudes below which freezing
doesn't occur.   EVA SAULITIS

fumarole

Fumarole, sometimes spelled fumerole, is an Italian
word for a hole or vent in the Earth's surface from which
fumes, smoke, or vapors issue. Fumaroles are found at the
surface of lava flows, in the calderas and craters of active
volcanoes, and in areas where hot, intrusive, igneous rock
bodies occur. They emit powerful jets of volatile con-
stituents—steam, hydrochloric acid, sulfur dioxide, and
ammonium chloride—at high temperatures, sometimes
reaching one thousand degrees Celsius. Although usually
associated with volcanic landscapes that are dormant or
declining, the fumarolic stage may actually precede volcanic eruptions, as was the case with Mount St. Helens
in Washington State in 1980. Other areas of fumarolic
activity include the Valley of Ten Thousand Smokes
near Katmai Crater in Alaska; Yellowstone National
Park; and Bumpass Hell on the flanks of Mount Lassen
in northeastern California. Fumaroles may stay active for
decades or even centuries if they are above a persistent
heat source, or they may disappear within weeks to
months if they occur atop a fresh volcanic deposit that
quickly cools.   KIM BARNES

gallery

A gallery, an enlarged passageway within a cave system, links one cavern or chamber with another. Its ceiling is high enough and its floor broad enough to make it seem more accommodating than other parts of the cave. It is a place where one can actually view one's surroundings.   GRETEL EHRLICH

gallery forest

A gallery forest grows along the banks of a river in open savanna and prairie country. Sometimes, but not always, the trees on either side intertwine their canopies, forming a tunnel-like corridor over the water. (The term is adapted from the Spanish word *galería,* meaning an overhanging balcony.) Historically, gallery forests provided shade, fuel, refuge, and a source of food and water for people crossing huge, daunting spaces. They also served (and still do) as conduits by which wildlife migrate back and forth between wetter climates east of the hundredth meridian and drier locales on the High Plains.   CONGER BEASLEY, JR.

ganderbrush

In the dense backwoods of the New Jersey Pine Barrens, swampy sinks are commonly filled with a shrubby plant called leatherleaf. These plant communities, known as ganderbrush, grow over deep peat soils. Ganderbrush is notoriously thick. Fox hunters describe it as pushcover, because dogs in chase can only push slowly through it, while the fox slips away by following a deer path. "Ganderbrush ponds, we call 'em. . . . You sink right down in that to your hips," reports Jack Davis, a fox hunter from Brown Mills, in Mary Hufford's book *Chaseworld: Foxhunting and Storytelling in New Jersey's Pine Barrens.* Ganderbrush grows alongside ponds and in the riverside and pitch-pine savannas of the Pine Barrens. In the 1870s these places were highly sought after by farmers seeking to establish cranberry bogs. If an area could support leatherleaf, growing conditions were perfect for cranberries as well. Although thousands of acres of ganderbrush were destroyed by cultivation during the late nineteenth and early twentieth centuries, many cranberry farms have since been abandoned or placed in conservation, and the native vegetation is creeping back in.   JAN DEBLIEU

gap

Traveling minister James Smith's journal, 1792: "We started just as the sun began to gild the tops of the high mountains. We ascended Cumberland Mountain, from the top of which the bright luminary of day appeared to our view in all his rising glory; the mists dispersed and the floating clouds hasted away at his appearing. This is the famous Cumberland Gap." Gap appears in the literature as a synonym for pass, and it is often used interchangeably with gorge. In Pennsylvania, a gap is a "deep sharp notch" in a mountain ridge. Water gaps are gaps near a mountain's base through which water passes. And here we get close to what a gap actually is: the course of a stream, one that cut down into the land as the land rose or one that's still a waterway, still cutting down through an older land feature. The Cumberland Gap is an old streambed, "discovered" by Dr. Thomas Walker in 1750. It can be assumed that deer, bears, lions, and coyotes discovered it long before Dr. Walker, and the Cherokee used it for centuries before Daniel Boone promoted it as a pathway through the Appalachians, into Kentucky. Boones Trace, as it was originally known, was widened to allow Conestoga wagons to navigate it. Today, if you drive U.S. Highway 25E through the gap, you drive among a parade of ghosts. It may seem reasonable to assert that gap is, then, a regional colloquialism for pass; however, a gap is clearly narrower than most passes and related to water—

closer in nature to (but not as daunting as) a gorge. Note: if a watercourse does not complete its cut, or the land rises and the water diverts, the subsequent opening in the hills is known as a wind gap.   LUIS ALBERTO URREA

gate

The term gate, from the Anglo-Saxon *geat,* or opening, can refer to a valley through a low range of hills, a broad opening between hilly areas, a defined section of a river, hence Hellgate Canyon on the Rogue River near Medford, Oregon, or an opening to a bay or harbor between promontories, hence the Golden Gate in San Francisco Bay. A gate is grander in scale than a gap. Golden Gate is more than a mile wide between the Marin headlands and Fort Funston, and the two portals for which Gates of the Arctic National Park is named, Boreal Mountain and Frigid Crags, frame an opening five miles wide across the Koyukuk River in Alaska's Brooks Range.

ROBERT HASS

gendarme

In the mid–eighteenth century, inspired by sojourns through the Alps, aesthetes and Romantics embraced the notion of the Sublime, thereby popularizing a radically new way of regarding wilderness. High, imposing mountains still inspired fear and disquietude, as they always had, but the fear was now permeated with transcendent awe. Suddenly, the great peaks and glaciers of France and Switzerland were thought to be beautiful. Their breathtaking features were climbed, rendered on canvas, and named. Which explains why a great many geomorphologic terms in wide use today are of European origin—*gendarme,* for instance, which is the French word for policeman, and is used to describe lofty rock towers that stand like huge petrified sentries (for example, Cerberus Gendarme, a prominent sandstone spire that famously watches over a

horseshoe bend of Zion Canyon in southwestern Utah).
Such towers may also be labeled pulpits, pinnacles, spires,
minarets, needles, and aiguilles—the latter being the
French term for needles. JON KRAKAUER

geode

Spherical stone nodules of plain exteriors with wondrous
hollows of crystal within, geodes typically range from
walnut size to the dimensions of a small melon (though
one was reported at several hundred pounds and four
feet in diameter), and in some locations have weathered
from their native beds of limestone or shale to be found
as discrete objects of the rockhound's quest. Because
of its hand-friendly size and shape, the geode serves
as popular entry point for geological commerce—the
roadside stand; the diamond saw and polish of the hob-
byist. Thunder egg is the colloquial name, coming from
Oregon native folklore in which angry spirits of Mount
Hood and Mount Jefferson hurled at each other rocky
eggs stolen from the mythical thunderbird. Cut open, a
thunder egg holds a crystal cavern held in the hand like
a cup of miracle tea. Thus the geode serves children as
an example of one of the most important experiences
in nature: plain surfaces can hide delicious revelations.
Rich collecting sites include locations in Iowa, Utah,
Nevada, Oregon, Arizona, and the Hauser Geode Beds
in California's Imperial Valley. KIM STAFFORD

geothermal field

These "reservoirs" of the Earth's heat—geothermal
fields—lie several miles below the surface in areas of
geologically recent volcanic activity. The heat is generated by the decay of radioactive substances in rocks lying
even farther below in the Earth's crust, and from compression as the rock becomes deeply buried by geological
processes. The land in and around Yellowstone contains

such large fields, as evidenced by the numerous "surface thermal displays" of hot springs and geysers, spectacular but merely visible signs of the much deeper, bigger, and more complex ecosystem below. Yellowstone's geothermal wonders were the original justification for the park's creation in 1872, and the area is now legally defined as a geothermal resource. Of the major geyser areas of the world, only two—Yellowstone and the Kamchatka Peninsula of extreme eastern Russia—have not been massively disrupted by energy development. Many in the mining industry contend that the exploitation of geothermal fields would provide clean energy, but fail to fully address the many ecological problems—not the least being the radioactive contamination of rivers and streams—that would result. JOY WILLIAMS

G

geyser

When superheated water, rising under pressure from areas of molten rock beneath the ground, bursts through cracks and crevices in Earth, sending water and steam skyward, the eruption is called a geyser. When water from Earth's great depths, heated above its boiling point but under too much pressure to turn to steam, encounters cooler surface water, the eruption is sometimes a violent gush. These conditions—intense heat generated underground from volcanic activity, water under pressure, and surface springs—must all be present to sustain Earth's thousand or so geysers. A geyser might be considered the half-sister of an artesian well; the tight necks of its containment keep the water from rising easily and provide limited avenues of escape. When a geyser shoots skyward, it is usually at regular intervals. Geysers are as restless and changing as other parts of Earth. Occasionally new ones erupt, sometimes in quiet forests, killing trees. More than half of Earth's geysers are found in Yellowstone Park. LINDA HOGAN

geyser pool

Unlike hot springs, the small bodies of very hot water known as geyser pools are part of a geyser system. They develop on the surface at places where Earth's underground volcanic pressures have diminished so much that pooling has replaced eruption. Most geyser pools are deep, and beneath some, magically, are flooded caves. Because they're part of a geyser system, the water level in geyser pools often drops just before an eruption. Many geyser pools support life. Those lower in temperature are sometimes brown with microorganisms. Others support larger life forms, including insects. Many Yellowstone pools contain the bones of buffalo and elk that have stumbled into them. One preserves, in its clear water, the complete skeleton of a coyote.   LINDA HOGAN

glacial drift

The random spoils of a glacial incursion over land, whereby detritus is picked up in one place and set down in another, is called glacial drift. Occupying the time stratum between the drifting of snow and the drifting of continents, glacial drift represents the products of abrasion between resident earth and moving glacier. A drift map thus shows the deposition pattern of superficial material, which is left by glacial movement to overlie the bedrock features of a geologic formation. Drift materials may consist of erratic stones, landforms such as massed terminal and lateral moraines, drumlins dozed up by moving ice, or broad sheet deposits such as till or outwash, which are shaped by ice and left when glaciers retreat.   KIM STAFFORD

glacial polish

A vagabond sits on an outcrop in open country and suddenly knows the story: the sheen on exposed bedrock, or the tactile silk feel of polished stone, reports glacial passage. The marks in bedrock left by glaciers, called glacial striations, are clues to the glacier's direction of movement. The land here was skinned and the surface of bedstone made smooth by the abrasive action of moving glacial ice, or by rocks, grit, or glacial rouge embedded in the ventral skin of the glacier as it passed. A graceful remnant sign of massive movement.   KIM STAFFORD

glacial valley

A glacial valley is distinguished by its distinctive U-shape: a broad flat floor flanked by high walls of rock. Such a valley has been bulldozed wide by a glacier scraping its way down an existing V-shaped valley, created by a preglacial river. Glacial valleys are common in the mountains of the American West and Alaska. In Prince William Sound and southeast Alaska, some of these classic-shaped valleys start deep in coastal mountain ranges and run into the sea later to become water-filled fjords. California's Yosemite Valley is one of the United States' most celebrated glacial valleys, and John Muir was the first to explain its icy origins. In his 1912 book *The Yosemite,* he writes: "These bald, westward-leaning rocks, with their rounded backs and shoulders [facing] the glacier fountains of the summit-mountains, and their split, angular fronts looking in the opposite direction, explain the tremendous grinding force with which the ice-flood passed over them."   CAROLYN SERVID

glacier

A tremendous accumulation of snow, compacted by weight and turned to ice, often carrying rock and sediment debris with sometimes a meltwater river below, a glacier moves with gravity due to its own mass. Glaciers may flow—and always in a distinct direction—from a few feet to several miles per year. A glacial system can be as large as a continent, or it can fill a small valley between mountains—an alpine or valley glacier. From the high cirque where snow recrystallizes into firn, then ice, and begins to move, down valleys that shape and are shaped by the moving mass of ice, to the terminal snout where low-altitude temperature ends the ice journey, the alpine glacier reveals geologic processes accessible to perception in human time. Glaciers, past and present, cause massive changes in our landscape; more change would be wrought if, for example, the Greenland glaciers were to melt and flood the world's seacoasts. Glacial ice cores are texts for ancient pollen and atmospheric conditions. The weight of the great continental glaciers not only shaped in passage but also physically depressed whole landscapes so severely that the land continues to rise ("isostatic rebound") thousands of years after the melting of the glacial ice. In motion, glaciers shape and polish bedrock features, convey and deposit erratic rocks and massive moraines, grind rock flour that turns meltwater streams milky, and in their accumulation and ablation exhibit evidence of climatic change.   KIM STAFFORD

glade

A glade is a small, open, light-filled space, usually in a forest or woods, cleared either by man or resulting from natural conditions. When Willa Cather described an "open glade like an amphitheatre," she was responding to the feeling of release that Anglo settlers experienced in their early encounters with the American plains. But glade can also describe a feeling of enclosure and safety, respite from a forest's dark impenetrability. In New England a glade can be a patch of open water on a frozen lake or river. In sunlight this kind of water-glade will ripple with a chiaroscuro as busy as any leaf-dappled glade.

Now glades are inextricably linked with the Everglades of Florida, and as such this speaks to the quality of endlessness that abides in light and open space. Finally, by the time of the Romantic and Victorian poets glade had become a literary device that evoked an ideal place, a "bower" as Wordsworth wrote, or was often employed as a noun for such adjectives as silent, rocky, forest, swampy, and bee-loud.   MICHAEL COLLIER

glory hole   G

The term glory hole can refer to a cylindrical feature in a reservoir, built right in front of the dam, designed to keep the dam from being overtopped—that is, if the water gets too high, it flows into the glory hole and is transported under the dam and downstream. However, glory hole is most often used as a mining term. Originally conjured during the gold rush to describe the process employed by those miners who could not afford conventional and more sophisticated extraction methods, the glory hole was the single shaft dug straight down in hopes of hap-pening upon a gold seam. The Glory Hole near Central City, Colorado, for instance, was once part of the most productive gold mining area in the world. In modern mining, the term has come to signify the belowground cavern—whether natural or man-made—from which material is mined. This contemporary sense, ironically, harks back to another colloquial use of the term to mean any small room or cupboard, or, in the instance of Jack London's novel *Michael, Brother of Jerry*, the hidden locker at the stern of a ship. Connotatively, the expression indicates both the means to, and the chamber of, secret and sequestered booty.   ANTONYA NELSON

goat prairie

Goat prairie was perhaps originally an ironic term for steep, rough terrain, often including a hilltop that presumably only an animal as nimble as a goat could hope to reach for grazing. This rocky, dry area, a result of glacial drift in the Midwest, often abounds in wildflowers and prairie grasses. The nine-acre Kaufmann Prairie in Iowa, with rugged, rocky ridgetops and steep inclines, is a typical goat prairie. In recent years such areas, once considered valueless, have become the focus of passionate reclamation and restoration efforts in Minnesota, Wisconsin, Iowa, and Illinois, where the term seems most used.   PATRICIA HAMPL

gooseneck

That rivers and streams seldom flow (naturally) in straight lines is a gift of beauty. Otherwise we would not have canyons that bear the shape of moving water. The river's meandering pattern forms sinuous, sweeping bends. Goosenecks are meanders so tight in succession that their bows nearly meet one another. The Goosenecks of the San Juan River in southern Utah are a classic canyon complex of deeply entrenched meanders. Here the river coils like a sidewinder through russet, terraced walls a thousand feet high. From one tight, looping bend to the next, the canyon layers up squarely on itself, an even set of folds. The saddle of the high cliff on your left is the saddle of the next cliff on your right, just around the bend.   ELLEN MELOY

gore

A small, triangular piece of land—the result most often of a surveyor's error or a mistake in a deed description—is called a gore. Highway engineers apply the term to those useless sharp juts left on a mountain slope after the construction of a series of hairpin curves. Both departments of transportation and law enforcement agencies refer to the triangular area between an entrance or exit ramp and a freeway as a gore. Some states, including

Arizona, have drawn up particular laws regarding the gore: for instance, a traveler is often not permitted to stop in one. The term is most commonly used to designate a small triangular parcel on flatter ground in New England—called by some a hiatus—either unpopulated or of undetermined ownership. One gore—Hibberts, Maine—has a population of one. Another, Averys Gore in Essex County, Vermont, has a population of zero. Gores may become homesites, be turned into river parks, or be ignored by tax authorities. They are often fought over—in some cases, legislation is required to finally decide ownership. Some gores simply provide breathing space to stand and observe the world. The Gore Range in Colorado, one of the most rugged parts of the southern Rockies, was supposedly named for an English sportsman, Sir Saint George Gore, but the serrated range is punctuated by many sharp peaks that thrust their triangular points into the sky.   ELIZABETH COX

gorge

Gorge (French for throat) most often refers to a deep, steep-sided, rocky river valley, such as the Columbia Gorge of the Columbia River that forms the border between Washington and Oregon, or the Royal Gorge of the Arkansas River in Colorado. Gorges are considered to be smaller than canyons, with walls more vertical than those of ravines, and are sometimes the result of cave collapse or of the downcutting power of the river being greater than the processes of valley-wall erosion. Wallace Stegner, describing his exploration of Glen Canyon and the Colorado River in *The Sound of Mountain Water,* notes that "the most innocent opening, apparently a mere keyhole of an alcove, may be the door to a gorge a quarter of a mile deep and heaven knows how long, sometimes rods wide, sometimes less than a yard. Often the water has cut down irregularly, so that the walls waver and overhang and cut off the sky." Gorge may also refer to a narrow defile or passage between hills or mountains, or, infrequently, a mass of something obstructing a passage, especially a mass of ice blocking a river.   KIM BARNES

graben

Where fault lines in the Earth's crust run parallel, the land between them may subside into a long trough or rift valley called a graben (the German word for ditch) as the adjacent blocks, lying on the opposite sides of each fault, are thrust upward into horsts. For instance, the San Luis Valley is part of the Rio Grande Rift system, extending from central Colorado southward through New Mexico and west Texas into northern Mexico. This valley, which has been called the highest, largest mountain desert in North America, formed long ago when a large graben sank along deep bounding faults.   BARBARA KINGSOLVER

grade

A tilt in the landscape is called a grade. We know grade viscerally in steep country, and in more subtle ways where the tilt is slight. Water's "line of desire" is directly down, but the nuances of grade translate this simple urge to myriad expressions of declination and flow in streams, from falls to rapids, to fast water and long reach, to pool and slack. One may "climb the grade," or "go over the grade" at a low point of the ridgeline. Generally, the term refers to gradient: the climb up, and the going down. The Lewiston Grade in Idaho, bane of truck drivers until furnished with escape ramps, is one spectacular example. In scientific writing, grade is a term of some complexity, referring to the equilibrium between erosion and deposition in streams—ideas developed in the West.   KIM STAFFORD

graded shoreline

A graded shoreline is typically a steep line graded to a gentler slope by heavy equipment and frequently involving the placement of hard structures, such as riprap. Designed to protect against erosion from waves or ice, or simply to enhance aesthetics and public access, graded shorelines are common along lakes, ponds, and rivers in urban parks from New York's Central Park to Seattle's Washington Park Arboretum.   MIKE TIDWELL

G

graded stream

A river or stream seeks comfort over its own bed. It scours its channel, wears down obstacles, carries sand grains and boulders drawn from its outback, runs its course with the sheer weight of its will. By erosion and deposition a river modifies the slope of its bed until its rate of flow can transport its load efficiently. A river or stream that reaches such equilibrium is called a graded stream. A graded stream is a somewhat theoretical stream—explained by fluid mechanics, felt as mystery. Flow is never perfectly even; interruptions and changes abound. Some stretches of the same stream may flow at grade, while others do not. Flood, drought, rock that resists, sandbars that succumb—flowing water constantly responds to variables. Thus, equilibrium is a dynamic rather than steady balance of energy and resistance—gravity as a fluid medium, reading the land it traverses.   ELLEN MELOY

grand bois

Among Cajun Americans *le bois* can mean any forested area, while *le grand bois* denotes a wooded area of exceptional size and isolation, a region often regarded as both sublime and tinged with danger. "La Valse de Grand Bois" (Waltz of the Big Woods) is a classic Cajun song about a spurned lover, heartbroken, lonely, and surrounded by a forest that provides little comfort: "The animals will eat me out there in *le grand bois.*" In Lafourche Parish, Louisiana, deep in the bayou country, there is a village called Grand Bois made up of about two hundred mostly Houma Indians living amid dark stands of live oaks draped with Spanish moss. Several U.S. towns and cities incorporate the word bois in their names, most notably Boise, Idaho. Purportedly, French trappers, coming on the site early in the nineteenth century after hard travels through the area's bare foot-hills and bleak high desert, yelled "Les bois! Les bois!" Idaho's capital, which grew up on the setting, has ever since been known as "The City of Trees" for its riverside stands of cottonwood, willow, and aspen, which grow in abundance there.   MIKE TIDWELL

grassed waterway

Runoff following rainstorms and spring snowmelt can create small rills in bare, unprotected farmland. Left untended, these rills can quickly deepen into gullies, carrying away tons of valuable topsoil. Conservation-minded farmers often grade these unnatural waterways into broad, shallow channels, then seed them with deep-rooting grasses. The resulting grassed waterways slow the flow of water and direct it to a suitable outlet. The grass cover not only helps protect the drainageway from gully erosion, but it may also filter out harmful farm chemicals like pesticides and herbicides carried by the runoff water. Small animals and birds may also find food and shelter in the grasses.   MARY SWANDER

grassland

Grassland is one of the four major vegetation types (or biomes) of the Earth, along with forest, savanna, and shrubland (which includes desert). Grasslands, which thrive in arid to subhumid conditions where ten to thirty inches of rain fall annually, easily contend with drought and fire because their root systems are extensive and hardy. Grassland of one kind or another once covered about forty percent of the United States. The largest area is found in the American Great Plains, stretching from the tallgrass prairies of the Midwest to the mixed-grass and shortgrass prairies that run to the foothills of the Rocky Mountains. West and south of the Rockies sparser grassland proliferates in the Sonoran and Chihuahuan Deserts and the Great Basin of Nevada and Utah. It was not long ago that bluestem and Indian grass rippled horse high from horizon to horizon in many of these areas, frightening and astonishing early settlers with its ocean-like vastness. Richard Manning in his book *Grassland* suggests that the Rocky Mountains are islands in a sea of grass, an archipelago rather than a boundary or divid-ing line. This apt metaphor speaks to the surrounding endlessness of grasslands, whether they are the Russian steppes, African veldt, Argentine pampas, or English downs. The tallgrass prairie of the Sheyenne National Grassland is part of the nearly 1.3-million-acre system of the Dakota Prairie Grasslands that straddles North and South Dakota and also includes the Little Missouri, Cedar River, and Grand River National Grasslands.

MICHAEL COLLIER

greenbelt

An officially designated area of open countryside encircling a town or city in which development is severely restricted is called a greenbelt. Greenbelts have four important functions: to prevent the unrestricted sprawl of large built-up areas; to provide areas of unspoiled countryside where people can find recreation and enjoyment; to provide habitat for some plant and animal species; and to provide for the continued use of

farmland, woodland, or common land. In Boise, Idaho, the Boise River Greenbelt illustrates how transformative greenbelts can be. Up until the 1960s the river area was dumping ground for trash, industrial waste, and raw sewage; today twenty-two miles of greenbelt through the city provide towering trees and abundant wildlife.
ARTHUR SZE

groin

The term groin, sometimes spelled groyne—possibly from the Old French *groyn*, for the snout of a pig—is a construction either of wood or stone, or sometimes concrete, that extends out into the sea for the purpose of preventing the erosion of beaches, stopping the closing of channels from sedimentation, or to defend a pier or harbor from the action of the waves. Groins that project out into currents that run parallel to the shore work by disrupting the flow of the current and triggering the deposition of sand or other sediments. The word isn't included in the 1828 *Webster's Dictionary*, but it appears in a 1923 article by Philip P. Farley in the *Municipal Engineers Journal*: "Groynes of all types and sizes and more than thirty in number had been in existence along the Coney Island shore for many years." It is in current use mostly on the Atlantic coast, where beach preservation has been an engineering issue. Cornelia Dean, in *Against the Tide: The Battle for America's Beaches*, writes, "Groins, often incorrectly referred to as jetties, are short rock ribs that begin on the sand under the beach and run into the sea, sticking out like fingers into the surf to trap sand." A group of groins is a groin field.   ROBERT HASS

grotto

A small cavern scooped in a cave wall, usually by erosion, is called a grotto. The term vaguely suggests protection,

shelter, or sustenance. As a river term, grotto usually
refers to a small, shaded hollow at the foot of a cliff that,
most often, leads back to a hidden spring or rivulet.
Harriette Arnow, in *Seedtime on the Cumberland*, describes
a type of grotto worn into the base of a limestone cliff
by a river of stream, an undercut feature known in that
country as a rockhouse.   ARTHUR SZE

ground

In discussions about land, ground means soil or, more
generally, the surface of the Earth. The solid surface,
to be more precise: a ship runs aground when it meets a
reef, a shoal, or the stubborn shore. Just how solid Earth's
skin might become was suggested by Willa Cather in
O Pioneers! when she described the winter landscape of
Nebraska: "The ground is frozen so hard that it bruises
the foot to walk in the roads or in the ploughed fields. It
is like an iron country, and the spirit is oppressed by its
rigor and melancholy." The word may also mean a space
designated for a certain purpose, as in tent ground or circus ground. For nineteenth-century Americans, a revival
ground and campground were often the same thing: a
place for holding religious revivals. That's the sense of
the term in the Civil War song "We're Tenting Tonight
on the Old Campground."   SCOTT RUSSELL SANDERS

ground ice

Ground ice is a collective term used to refer to all types
of ice found in permafrost, the layer of ground—often
hundreds of feet thick—where temperatures usually
remain below zero degrees Celsius. When moisture
mixed with soil in this ground freezes, ice patterns
known as polygons may appear on the surface, a jigsaw
puzzle of stone-rimmed figures extending across a plain.
Called fairy rings in Ireland and patterned ground in

parts of the United States, these polygons are generated by expansion—when ice forms, it takes up a volume about eleven percent greater than the volume of water used to create it. Larger solid particles are moved to the outside edge of "bubbles" formed by the freezing process, and stones collect at the junction, forming the fairy rings. Pore ice, which fills each opening of any available porous material, is one of five types of ground ice. The others are segregated ice, pingo ice, ice wedges, and ice lenses. The latter is a horizontal accumulation of ground ice in a small area, while segregated ice describes a more extensive area of pure ice that grows because of active migration of water from some nearby source. Ice wedge refers to a vertically oriented wedge-shaped piece of ground ice that forms in the "active" (that is, not permanently frozen) layer of permafrost. And then there's pingo ice, created by the freeze-thaw cycle in the active permafrost layer. The active layer begins to freeze in winter, first at the surface and then at an increasing depth below the surface. At some point this advancing "freeze front" approaches the permanently frozen layer, compressing the remaining free water. Forced upward through narrow openings to the surface, this water raises the upper soil layer in a mound, often with an opening in the middle where any remaining free water comes out (and freezes, of course). These mounds, called pingos, can be found throughout the Mackenzie Delta of northern Canada, though they occur in Alaska, too. The phenomenon is most commonly seen on deltas and other layers of lake sediments in permafrost regions. Scientists searching for proof of past climate change often search for fossil ice wedges—not ice, but a cast in the ground where ice once occurred—and have found them in places such as Pennsylvania, an area of permafrost during the late Pleistocene.   GRETEL EHRLICH

groundwater

Water lying under the surface of the ground and contained within the space between rocks is known as groundwater. It may be either original water introduced by magmatic processes (water that has never been in the atmosphere, some of which is thousands of years old), or meteoric water collected via the percolation downward of rainwater, snowmelt, or seepage from surface bodies (and which can also be thousands of years old). Groundwater's erosive action on permeable rocks results in the formation of underground streams, rivers, and caves. Far more freshwater is found beneath the Earth's surface (ninety-five percent or more of the planet's usable freshwater) than in its rivers, lakes, and wetlands, and it is therefore a crucial resource, and an endangered one given groundwater's vulnerability to pollution and humankind's ever-increasing demand for fresh water.   DONNA SEAMAN

G

grove

A small wood free of underbrush, a grove is often the last remaining patch of a once immense forest. A grove is also a planted stand of nut or fruit trees. Ancient groves were often considered sacred. The Babylonian *Epic of Gilgamesh* features a sacred cedar grove, and sacred groves figure prominently in the myths of ancient Europe, Greece, and Rome. In North America, many Native American peoples believe that trees have souls, and the Ojibwe, for instance, rarely cut down living trees. As Ralph Waldo Emerson writes in a poem titled "Good-Bye," a grove is "a spot that is sacred to thought and God." In our day, grove is often used in place-names, whether a community still possesses one or not. Chicago is ringed by Buffalo Grove, Downers Grove, Elk Grove, Fox River Grove, Long Grove, Morton Grove, River Grove, and Sugar Grove.   DONNA SEAMAN

gulch

In the western United States, gulch is a word for a small ravine. Deeper than a gully, generally narrow and steep sided, shallower than a canyon. Miners often found gold or other minerals concentrated in a gulch's swash channel. The Blue Cloud Gulch and the Old Dominion Gulch in Montana each yielded gold, silver, and copper for many years. Dublin Gulch in the Yukon attracted a steady stream of miners during that gold rush. Artifacts of ancient civilizations are also sometimes exposed in a gulch. In Grand Gulch, Utah, for instance, the Anasazi left their mark in red sandstone. Dwelling places, pottery, and tools were eventually uncovered by centuries of moving water in that area. In the profusion of gifts offered by gulches, none was more spectacular than the one discovered by a miner in New Mexico in 1987. He saw the tip of tusk in a gulch; the remains were later identified as those of a Columbian mammoth. Public and scientific interest brought about a full excavation of this site, now known as the Dry Gulch Mammoth Site, exposing a grail of bones. ELIZABETH COX

gulf

Principally applied to the largest of several forms of inlets of the sea—larger than bays, much larger than coves—gulfs are partially enclosed by usually extensive sweeps of land, as with the Gulf of Mexico and Gulf of Alaska, which produce an intricate interaction of eddies and back-currents. The term may also refer to a large, landlocked portion of sea with an opening through a strait or inlet, such as the Gulf of Boothia in Canada's Northwest Territories. Gulf has several other, looser, and sometimes quasi-figurative applications, perhaps invited by its onomatopoetic quality—for instance, its use as a synonym for whirlpool, sinkhole, fiery volcanic opening, gorge, chasm, or abyss, as H.W. Longfellow suggests in

Tales of a Wayside Inn: "The headlong plunge through eddying gulfs of air." JOHN KEEBLE

gully

A channel worn in the earth by a torrent of water carving out a deep ditch is called a gully. Gully erosion happens after a rill, a high-velocity rush of water, has removed large amounts of soil along a depression or drainage line. As water wears away the land, the rill—the geomorphic feature—becomes a gully; cutting farther down, the headlong water makes a gulch, until the cellar doors open into a canyon. On its smaller scale, gully erosion, or gullying, is the bane of farmers. It disrupts field operations, creates access problems for trucks and stocks, and uproots crops. Farmers learn to look for rabbit burrows, old root holes, cow or horse tracks on slopes, and lines of drainage, so they can stop gully erosion before it starts. But not everyone thinks of a gully as evidence of a necessarily destructive force. Sometimes the term is used to describe a placid waterway, as in this passage from *Betty Zane*, by Zane Grey: "Two hours of still-hunting found him on the bank of a shallow gully through which a brook went rippling and babbling over the mossy green stones." Geographers distinguish between gullies, washes, and arroyos on the one hand, and cañadas on the other, according to the materials involved. Cañadas—like cañoncitos—slice through bedrock. Arroyos and washes cut through flat layers of valley deposits; and gullies and gulches erode hill-slope materials. ELIZABETH COX

gumbo

Gumbo is clayey soil that is extremely waxy and sticky when wet, as during times of thaw or during or after a rainstorm. Gumbo terrain is referred to as "ape-shit flats" by cowboys on ranches in north-central Wyoming, who are well acquainted with the gooey substance. Early Midwest settlers also struggled with the difficult soil, as indicated by Emmanuel and Marcet Julius Haldeman in their 1921 bestselling book *Dust*, about farm life in Kansas: "It had rained earlier in the week and Martin was obliged to be careful of the chuck-holes in the sticky, heavy gumbo soon to be the bane of pioneers." Gumbo is found throughout the south-central United States, where a number of shallow seas once covered wide areas of marine shales and mudstones. Gumbo does have its good uses: the soil makes excellent adobe mud for structures, and bentonite, a type of gumbo created from volcanic ash, is used for well casing and to line duck ponds. A synonym for gumbo is burnout soil.   GRETEL EHRLICH

gunk hole

In coastal New England, a gunk hole is a small, out-of-the-way harbor or a nearly unnavigable shallow cove or channel. Dictionaries insist that gunk enters the language as the trade name of a "self-emulsifying colloidal detergent solvent" patented by the A.F. Curran Company of Malden, Massachusetts, in 1932. But citations of gunk hole go back to at least 1908. Either way, the word connotes greasy, gooey, yucky, mucky stuff, whether found in a tidal marsh or in the sump of an engine. Gunk hole seems uncomplimentary, as though implying the deepwater sailor's disdain for the shallows. But in fact the term is generally used affectionately, and gunk holers constitute a secret fraternity of navigators who happily abjure marinas, mooring fees, and the beaten track.

FRANKLIN BURROUGHS

gut

The term gut is a reduction of gutter, and along the East Coast it applies to a number of water features with gutterlike characteristics of drainage, outflow, narrow passage. In tidal areas a gut is a small channel through a marsh. Farther inland it may be the outlet stream draining a lake or swamp. Alternatively, it may be a narrow passway through a swamp, or simply a narrow section of a creek or river. In the South it is sometimes used to designate a cut-off—or nearly cut-off—meander of a river. It appears frequently as a place-name: Devils Gut along the Roanoke River in North Carolina, Horsepen Gut in the Congaree National Park of South Carolina. John Bartram, an eighteenth-century American naturalist, used the word this way in his Florida journals: "Near the store was a deep gut with a middling stream of water, which headed about a quarter of a mile up in the pine-lands." CHARLES FRAZIER

guzzle

In coastal New England and the Canadian Maritimes, a guzzle is (1) a natural spillway across a beach, affording a temporary connection between the sea and the marshes behind the beach, according to John Stilgoe's *Shallow Water Dictionary*; (2) a small harbor, barely bigger than a gunk hole, according to John Gould's *Maine Lingo*; (3) any small creek draining a tidal marsh or a wetland adjacent to it. Hunters and fishermen commonly use the word in this last sense. The author of *The Partridge Creek Chronicles* finds snipe in "the guzzle that empties the meadow" in coastal New Brunswick. A Massachusetts fishing guide mentions "dozens of bass parading down a guzzle" near Barnstable Harbor. Anatomically, guzzle as a noun once referred to the throat. This explains its connection to the verb "to guzzle"—to imbibe immoderately, like some undergraduates and all SUVs. FRANKLIN BURROUGHS

habra

The Spanish phrase *una habra* means "an opening." It is commonly used in mountainous Mexico to describe a pass or cut between two mountains. In the brushlands of south Texas and northeastern Mexico the phrase refers to a meadow within the *monte*.   ARTURO LONGORIA

hammock

The great naturalist William Bartram recorded the word hammock in his journal in 1765. In Florida it refers to a low hillock or knoll rising above level ground. Sometimes the word is used interchangeably with hummock, which means elevated ground in a swamp—clumps of trees on soil surrounded by water. But hammock refers more particularly to a boss of soil or rock that rises on level dry ground. Hammocks are often knolls of hardwoods standing above the level plain of a sawgrass prairie or in a pine forest (called flatwoods) in the southeastern United States, and especially in the St. Johns River area of northern Florida.

ROBERT MORGAN

hanging glacier

Hanging glaciers are isolated masses of glacial ice flowing in high, detached valleys and protruding over the cliff edge that defines such a valley's lower limit. They're termed hanging because they never reach the valley below intact. They bend under the force of gravity to hang suspended above the lower landscape. From time to time, the vertical section of the glacier fractures and falls because of the tremendous unsupported weight. It's this plummeting ice (not to be confused with an icefall) along with avalanches, and not continuously flowing ice, that finally brings the hanging glacier's store of moisture to the land below.   WILLIAM KITTREDGE

hanging valley

A high valley that converges with, and breaks off abruptly into, a deeper valley, often over a cliff, is known as a hanging valley. Hanging valleys occur when glaciations or water flow erode the main valley to a depth well below that of its tributary valleys. A hanging valley might include a hanging glacier, or end in a waterfall such as Bridal Veil Falls in Yosemite or Bird Woman Falls seen from the Going-to-the-Sun Highway over Logan Pass in Glacier National Park. Seacoast streams that fall over sea cliffs, which result from erosions caused by wave action and tectonic uplift, emerge from hanging valleys. Washes in the American Southwest often form hanging valleys, such as the seventy-five-foot cliff where Johns Canyon ends above the gorge of the San Juan River in the Grand Gulch country of southern Utah.   WILLIAM KITTREDGE

hardpan

Hardpan is a pale, unyielding substratum of soil that is much denser than the horizons above and below. It forms over thousands of years as materials from the upper soil layers dissolve and percolate downward. When the water evaporates within the lower soil layers, these dissolved materials, such as silica, aluminum, iron, and calcium, precipitate onto the surrounding soil particles. The result is a compacted, cemented layer that interferes with the movement of moisture, hinders the growth of plant roots, and is difficult to cultivate. In some regions, this layer is called claypan, and in the desert Southwest, where it occurs at the surface and not just at depth, it's known as caliche. A hardpan layer can be from a few inches to several feet thick. The shallow soil above the pan dries out quickly but becomes easily saturated, since rainwater cannot drain. Writing about the 1930s Dust Bowl conditions of the Great Plains, poet Archibald MacLeish described "dead quarter sections with the hardpan clean as weathered lime and the four-room flimsy ranch houses two feet deep in sand." CHARLES FRAZIER

hassock

Hassock is a very old word indeed, recorded in English at least as early as the tenth century. Derived from the Welsh, hassock refers to a clump of sedges or a tuft of grass in boggy ground. Sometimes the word is also used for a clump of trees in sedge or wetland brush. In the New Jersey Pine Barrens, hassock refers specifically to cushions of roots interlaced with soil out of which cedars grow in the areas called hard-bottom swamps. Tussock, which is probably derived from the word tusk, refers only to clumps or tufts of grass, sedge, or sprouts; however, the two words are often used interchangeably. ROBERT MORGAN

haystack

Haystacks occur in karst terrain, generally in tropical regions with high humidity. Remnants of ridges or plateaus, they represent one form of tower karst. Haystacks are in effect vestiges of an earlier, more elevated topography; they simply have not subsided as far or as fast as the surrounding landscape. Their characteristically weathered and slump-shouldered forms may resemble slightly lopsided haystacks, loaves of bread, or traffic cones, and they tend to be covered by shrubs, vines, and small trees. Haystacks are common in Cuba, where they are generally called *mogotes*, and in northern Puerto Rico, where they are called *pepino* hills, and range in height from a few feet to a maximum of about 150 feet. They give a landscape an odd, arbitrary, and discontinuous look, and invite mythological speculation. FRANKLIN BURROUGHS

headland

Anatomically, the head is the most prominent feature of the human body—and a headland, in geographic terms, is an equally bold promontory jutting far out from a coast. Virgil, in *The Aeneid*, emphasizes the loftiness of the feature in describing "the towering bluffs of Pachynum's headland brow." Headlands, with their accompanying bays or fjords, signal a coastline that has not yet succumbed entirely to the erosive energy of waves, which tend to concentrate on the most prominent coastal features. Headlands are found along rocky, geologically youthful coastlines: the edges of the Pacific Northwest provide a good example. Along this actively eroding coast, rivers and glaciers have carved rugged hills and valleys. With rising sea levels after the Ice Age, water encroached upon the land, filling valleys and creating bays and headlands. On volcanic islands, however, headlands may signal ancient erosion: On Kaua'i, the oldest major island in the Hawaiian chain, streams have carved deep valleys in their run to the sea, producing dramatic headlands along the Nāpali Coast. In the nature of wave action against coasts, however, the rough shall be made smooth, and the Nāpali headlands will eventually give way to a coastline of straight cliffs.   PAMELA FRIERSON

headwall

When a landslide gives way, it leaves a steep vertical face, or headwall, at the top of its scar. (The toe slope is the face of the rubble field at the bottom of the slide where the failed material settles.) Headwall also applies to the wall at the back of a glacial cirque. Mountain climbers often seek out headwalls because of the challenge of their steepness. The Coleman Headwall, above the Coleman Glacier on Mount Baker, Washington, is such a place.
WILLIAM DEBUYS

headwaters

Most people visualize a headwater as a powerful gush of water over a falls or a single bubbling brook high in the mountains at the source of a stream. But in fact, rivers have no single source. A network of springs, creeks, streams, and tributaries drain into the upper portion of a river's system to form its headwaters. These network waterways are often found in the mountains but may also include desert springs and seeps, wet meadows, or even bayou-like channels. The headwaters of a reservoir are the waters at the far upstream end, where the river empties into the lake. Headwater streams are critically important to the whole river system, providing habitat to the flora and fauna of their own ecosystems and delivering nutrients and organic material to downstream regions. Headwaters can also carry pollution and damage downstream. For example, the Mississippi River begins in Minnesota, carrying agricultural runoff pesticides and farm chemicals all the way to its mouth in New Orleans. The chemicals flush into the Gulf of Mexico, where they create a lifeless region of oxygen-depleted (hypoxic) water called the Dead Zone. In *Moby-Dick*, Herman Melville wrote metaphorically of headwaters: "Our grand master is still to be named; for like royal kings of old times, we find the headwaters of our fraternity in nothing short of the great gods themselves." MARY SWANDER

hedgerow

Distinguished from a windbreak by the lower height of its plants, a hedgerow is quite simply a line of bushes and trees with accompanying undergrowth. Common to the British Isles and now under protection by custom and law in England, hedgerows provide a semipermeable fence around pastures and fields, and a partial restoration of habitat, especially for birds, otherwise compromised by tillage. Hedgerows are an agricultural concept brought to the United States by the earliest British settlers in the Northeast, though predated by indigenous agricultural cultures throughout the Americas. On large and corporate farms, naturally arising hedgerows along fence lines—pejoratively called dirty fences—are eliminated by mowing and herbicides, while advocates of sustainable agriculture argue in favor of such hedgerows for their beneficent effects on habitat, water conservation, erosion control, and insect control by resident birds. Hedgerows—"dirty" and otherwise—remain common in agricultural regions, particularly where farming is intensive, as it is in parts of New England, the South, and California. In his poem "The Clerk's Tale," Spencer Reese writes: "We dart amongst the aisles tall as hedgerows." And in *The Gift of Good Land*, Wendell Berry quotes the anthropologist Stephen Brush on the agricultural practices of the Andean peasants of Peru: "They protect their land against erosion by . . . the use of hedgerows and horizontal plowing, and by field rotation."

JOHN KEEBLE

heights

Heights is a general term for an elevated landform that provides a vantage point from which to view surrounding countryside. Hills, cliffs, mesas, plateaus, palisades, and bluffs can be thought of as heights. Brooklyn, Morningside, Harlem, and Washington Heights in New York City were named for the promontories they occupy. Across the United States there are dozens of well-known suburbs, such as Shaker, Hacienda, Dearborn, and Arlington Heights, that employ the name. In a suburban context, heights carry a kind of middle-class pretension or snobbery, as if higher ground, real or nominal, makes a better neighborhood. This is why Sinclair Lewis set much of the action of his scathing satire of the American middle class, *Babbitt*, in the Floral Heights section of the mythical town of Zenith.   MICHAEL COLLIER

hell

In nineteenth-century America, hell was a generic term for a rough or difficult stretch of country, such as the wildly eroded Hell's Half-Acre in Wyoming. Similarly, the thermal features of Yellowstone Park were originally called Coulters Hell, after the explorer and mountain man John Coulter. The word was also used to designate the most lawless sections of frontier towns like Fort Worth and San Antonio, as well as particularly dangerous and rough parts of the urban landscape, such as Hell's Kitchen in New York City. In the southern Appalachians, a hell is a dense, extensive growth of laurel or rhododendron. Horace Kephart, in *Our Southern Highlanders,* defined the term this way: "A 'hell' or 'slick' or 'wooly-head' or 'yaller patch' is a thicket of laurel or rhododendron impassable save where the bears have bored out trails." CHARLES FRAZIER

high bank

Rivers may cut deeply and sharply into the earth, they may slowly make modest impressions in the ground, or, like some Great Plains rivers, they may flow only a couple of feet below the surface of the surrounding land in a shallow channel. Further, a single river may have a wide variety of gradients. Whatever the depth of the channel or the slope of the bed, most rivers are framed by banks that separate the flow of their water from the surrounding floodplain. High bank is a relative term used to distinguish a river's farther banks—which sometimes mark the boundary of the river's floodplain—from a parallel set of low banks closer to the river. Riverbanks may be more—or less—apparent, depending on the degree of downcutting and the frequency and pattern of flooding. A river in flood may spread past its low banks to create minor flooding, or breach its high banks in a major flood. MARY SWANDER

high desert

A high desert is arid country at high elevation or latitude, also known as cold desert. The High Desert Museum near Bend, Oregon, celebrates and interprets the inland Pacific Northwest and the organisms elegantly adapted to it such as coyotes and big basin sage. Much of the Great Basin, with valleys averaging 3,000 to 6,000 feet above sea level, qualifies as high desert. Playas such as the Alvord Desert in southeastern Oregon and the Black Rock Desert in northwestern Nevada are deserts within the high desert. This landscape often goes unappreciated. As Barry Lopez wrote in *Desert Notes*: "He would drive out then into the great basin over arroyos and across sage flats dotted with juniper and rabbit brush . . . where the government was trying to grow crested wheat grass, trying to turn the high desert into grassy fields for bony Herefords with vacant eyes. . . . He would see, on a long stretch of road, a golden eagle sitting on a fence post." ROBERT MICHAEL PYLE

high plains

Incorrectly referred to, often by residents themselves, as prairie (prairie refers to the vegetation, plains to the landform), the high plains extend southward from near the South Dakota boundary with western Nebraska, encompassing portions of Wyoming, Kansas, Oklahoma, Texas, and Colorado, as if in preface to the altitudinous reach of the Rockies and western ranges. The high plains are distinguished by low hills and buttes overlaid with remnants of shortgrass prairie and an average annual precipitation, including snow, of ten to twelve inches. So they are semiarid, with temperatures ranging from 110 degrees in the summer to 40 in the winter, the precipitation often arriving in cataclysmic thunderstorms and blizzards. Home of bison, deer, and antelope, all still present in diminished herds over its swooping landscape; viewed by earlier eyes as "stretching away and away, beyond the range of vision, over hill, valley, and plain, the skyline unbroken by trees, except a fringe along the course of a stream" (Melvin R. Gilmore, *Prairie Smoke*).   LARRY WOIWODE

hill

The main problem in defining hill involves knowing where it ends and mountain begins. Both are natural elevations of the Earth's surface. Sometimes an upper bound for a hill is set at a thousand feet, but you can take a "hill trek" in the Himalayas at fifteen times that height. If there are no craggy peaks in the area, then hills are the rounded prominences that form the skyline; if there are mountains, then hills, however high, are what stand in front of them. For some, the hill has a softer edge. In *Ceremony*, Leslie Marmon Silko writes: "Years of rain and wind had weathered away the adobe plaster, exposing the symmetry of the brown adobes which were beginning to lose their square shape, taking on the softer contours of the mesas and hills." In eastern Washington's Palouse country, hills too steep to plow and that stand like forested islands in a sea of wheat are called eyebrow hills.   BILL MCKIBBEN

hill country

Hill country is a term that has been associated with poverty, the reason being intrinsic to the nature of hills—erosion on sloped land: soil vulnerable to being washed away is poor. Another aspect of the nature of hills is relative inaccessibility. "The hills" are a place of isolation, meaning rural character. Think Appalachia: hillbillies come from the hills. Rural character traditionally suggests not only a coarse ruggedness but also toughness and independence. When richness of soil no longer matters, the hill country (like the Texas hill country outside of Austin) is ultimately sought as a place of authenticity, regionalism as a kind of aesthetic. Another feature of hills is that one can easily hide in them—as the Scottish highlanders, outlaws of the American West, and the mujahideen of Afghanistan have demonstrated; the hill country traditionally serves as a fortress also for fierce guerrilla fighters who descend from them to sack the cities in the rich flatland below. The hills as manageable mountains accord refuge—hence the Old Testament verse, "I lift mine eyes to the hills"—and were the refuge of anchorites who went to find religious retreat outside a nearby community. The shapes of hills form a knowable landscape. They connote permanence, something to go toward and back to, as Arlo Guthrie sings in an old folk song: "Way down yonder in the Indian nation riding my pony on the reservation in the Oklahoma hills where I was born." Something familiar, remembered, home.   SUSAN BRIND MORROW

hogback

A hogback is so called because of its resemblance to the dorsal ridge of stiff hair on a wild hog's back. A long, narrow-crested ridge of exposed rock, geologically it is stratum that has been tilted until the originally horizontal beds are nearly vertical. (The beds must be tilted at least thirty-five degrees above the horizontal to be called hogbacks; otherwise they're cuestas.) Hogbacks are common in the Black Hills of South Dakota, where sedimentary rock was uplifted by the intrusion of Black Hills Granite. Some of the most striking hogbacks occur in Colorado, in such places as Garden of the Gods and near the city of Boulder, whose storied geological backdrop, the Flatirons, is a type of hogback. The Navajo term for a hogback a few miles northeast of Mexican Hat, Utah, is *Dził Na'neest'eeʻi*, "Mountain That Is Twisted." Hogbacks are sometimes called razorbacks.   BARBARA KINGSOLVER

hole

Hole is a term with at least two meanings. To a river runner, it designates a dynamic feature in flowing water, suggesting a potential for trouble and the need for deft maneuvers to avoid catastrophe. When the term refers to a feature of the land, it has the opposite meaning—it promises refuge, a safe harbor. A mountain hole is a sizable valley, often rich with wildlife, which offers good grazing and protection from the harshest kind of winter weather. A river hole identifies a spot in the (usually) swift and voluminous flow of water where the current spirals down so strongly it can trap a boat or a person, offering no timely escape to either. Holes appear and disappear in a river according to the volume of water moving through, though some holes are more or less permanent features. In Westwater Canyon on the upper Colorado River, near the Colorado-Utah border, water forced under at Skull Rapids surfaces violently in a whirlpool of a hole called the Room of Doom. Many people have lost their lives here, unable to fight free of the current. Jackson Hole, Wyoming, protected against heavy weather coming in from the west by the Teton Mountains and composing a winter range for thousands of wapiti on the National Elk Refuge, is the archetypal sheltered mountain valley, first designated a "hole" by trans-Mississippi fur trappers. Hole can also be used to mean an isolated corner in unfrequented country, a lair where someone might reasonably expect to see few other humans. Edward Abbey evoked such a sense of self-protecting isolation when he suggested in *Abbey's Road* that it was "best [for him] to stay in Wolf Hole, behind the Virgin Mountains, near Dutchman Draw and Pakoon Springs, the kind of place where an anarchist belongs." TERRY TEMPEST WILLIAMS

hollow

Throughout most of the North American continent, a hollow is a scooped-out place in the land. The term is used to describe many features: a small, sheltered valley,

as in Washington Irving's *Legend of Sleepy Hollow*, or, in the
Catskill Mountains of New York State, a notch or pass in
mountains. In *A Lady's Life in the Rocky Mountains*, Isabella
Bird writes of "the blue hollow at the foot of Longs Peak
. . . where the hoar frost crisps the grass every night of
the year." Deep within the Appalachian Mountains,
however, the word is pronounced "holler" and is used to
describe the seam where two mountains join. In a holler,
land rises on three sides, up the crease (along which a
stream usually flows) and so up the flank of each mountain. The sun shines into a holler only a few hours a day,
and the woods within are dark and dense. "Most hollers
don't have no view," observes Granny Younger in Lee
Smith's novel *Oral History*. Small hollows are sometimes
called cloves, likening them to the space in a goat's
splayed hoof.   JAN DEBLIEU

homestead

In colonial America, a homestead was understood to
be a plot of land adequate to support a family. The
Homestead Act of 1862 granted a quarter-section (160
acres) of U.S. public land to any head of family, on the
condition that the settler live on the parcel for five
years and "improve" it, typically by clearing fields for
cultivation and by erecting buildings. In *Wolf Willow*,
Wallace Stegner, recalling his boyhood on the Canadian
border, writes: "The homestead, though it was a stead
of sorts, was never a home. There was only a handful of
real homes on either side of the Line. Most houses were
like ours, shacks made to be camped in during the crop
season; and some were like Pete and Emil's, never meant
to be lived in at all, but only to satisfy the law's require-
ment." The act eventually carved out hundreds of thousands of farms in the West, many of them far too small,
in such dry country, to maintain a family. Although
agrarian in origin, homestead has come to be defined in

the laws of many states as a person's principal residence, whether urban or rural. So defined, a homestead may be exempt from certain taxes and protected from seizure by creditors.   SCOTT RUSSELL SANDERS

hondo

Hondo means "deep." (Although it looks like Honda, the *h* is silent.) Hondos are low spots in arroyos; they can also turn up in quebradas and canyons. It is a term heard often in the Southwest. Mary Austin, in *Land of Journeys' Ending*, features a New Mexican hondo: "After it issues from the Culebra into the valley of Taos, there is no sound but of the river's own making in the Arroyo Hondo, where it runs, or perhaps as it passes Valdez and the village of Hondo." If a book, like Austin's, is profound, it is *muy hondo*. Where land is lower than its surroundings, as in a hollow, vale, or depression, the area often gets called a hondo, though the proper word would be *hondonada*. Various lakes and features like meander scars bear the name Hondo, as do creeks and towns in the American Southwest. One can readily see, though, that these features are usually in, or near, a lowland feature.

LUIS ALBERTO URREA

hoodoo

Hoodoos are fantastically shaped stone pillars in deserts and badlands of the North American West. Classic hoodoo groupings, such as those in Bryce Canyon National Park and Goblin Valley State Park in southern Utah, form by sporadic, intensive rainfall erosion of steeply sloped but horizontally layered sedimentary rock, leaving freestanding pinnacles, each with an overhanging cap of resistant stone. They abound on the Colorado Plateau, where smaller specimens are sometimes called goblins, but occur also north through the Rockies and have been reported on Baffin Island in the Arctic. The term dates back at least to the mid–nineteenth century. Walt Whitman, in *Specimen Days*, regrets that he never saw "the 'hoodoo' or goblin land" of the Yellowstone country. That these arresting features should have been tagged with a variant of voodoo seems almost inevitable. Their suggestively spirited forms, whether taken as malign, whimsical, or transcendently elusive, exert spells to which many humans are susceptible.   JOHN DANIEL

hook

Features named Hook are found on both land and water. On water, hook is the term for an acute, hooklike bend in a river or stream; the Hallowell Hook in the Kennebec River of Maine is an example. As a landform, hook is another name for a recurved spit—the low, tonguelike shoal of land that extends from shore into a body of water that then curves back landward. The hooked shape of a recurved spit is sculpted by a complex interplay of natural forces, including winds, wave refraction, and opposing ocean currents. The dynamic nature of a recurved spit can be seen at Sandy Hook, a compound recurved spit that extends into the major channel leading into New York Harbor: due to the ongoing northward expansion of the shoal, the lighthouse built on Sandy Hook in 1764, which originally stood five hundred feet from the tip of the hook, now stands one and one half miles inland. As a word for a landform, hook seems related to the Dutch *hoek*, which means "corner" or "nook"; in nineteenth-century usage, a cornerlike scrap of land was sometimes called a hook.   EMILY HIESTAND

horizon

The horizon or sensible horizon is, first of all, the visible place where earth, or sea, and sky appear to meet. At a hundred feet above sea level, the horizon is approximately fourteen miles away. The word has other technical meanings. A true, astronomical, or celestial horizon in astronomy is the circle on the celestial sphere whose plane is at right angles to the visible horizon. In geology, the horizon is the plane of a stratified surface containing a particular series of fossils. In soil science, it is a layer of soil in a cross section of land. In literature it is, of course, often a symbol for opportunity, especially if it is out of reach. Here is Zora Neale Hurston in *Their Eyes Were Watching God*: "Ships at a distance have every man's wish on board. For some they come in with the tide. For others they sail forever on the horizon, never out of sight, never landing until the Watcher turns his eyes away in resignation." In the plural horizons can be sequences of days, as in this seascape from Wallace Stevens's "The Idea of Order at Key West": "Theatrical distances, bronze shadows heaped/On high horizons, mountainous atmospheres/Of sea and sky." ROBERT HASS

horn

A horn is the pyramidal peak of a mountain, created by several glaciers carving away at different sides of the same mountain; that is, cirques on all sides are eroding backward into the mountain mass. It's no accident that the best horns occur on mountains that are being rapidly uplifted, where gradients are steep and erosion is fast. The Matterhorn in the Alps is the classic example, but Bloody Mountain in California and Forbidden Peak and Mount Shuksan in the Washington Cascades are also fine examples. ROBERT HASS

horseback

A New England term for esker, or a long narrow ridge of remnant glacial debris, is horseback. As in whaleback or hogback—common names for ridges in the Northeast— and, in Kansas, swayback, the word contains the obvious visual: a horse's back is not straight but has a declivity, a sway, between shoulder and haunch, as an esker so strikingly does from end to end.   SUSAN BRIND MORROW

hot spring

A hot spring is a concentrated discharge of groundwater to the surface. Unlike springs in general, the emergence of hot springs, also known as thermal springs, is enhanced by the pressure created from the heat of warm rocks within the Earth. Thus, such springs are most common in tectonically active regions. The temperature at which a spring becomes "hot" is an anthropomorphic ninety-eight degrees Fahrenheit. Hot springs are relatively common in the Americas. They may contain mineral properties thought to be beneficial to health, and in some locations their waters are contained and deployed as spas. In 1804, President Jefferson sent William Dunbar and George Hunter to explore what would become the Hot Springs Reservation in Arkansas (the oldest area in the National Park system). Dunbar reported that "the temperature of their waters is from 130 to 150° of Farheneits' [*sic*] thermometer. . . . I found by the aid of an excellent microscope, both Vegetable and animal life, the first a species of moss, the latter a testaceous bivalve of the size of the minutest grain of Sand." Of his mid-nineteenth-century sojourn in the region of the Yellowstone River, Osborne Russell, in *Journal of a Trapper,* observes: "Near where we encamped were several hot springs which boil perpetually."   JOHN KEEBLE

hourglass valley

The adjective in the term hourglass valley draws on the outline of this ancient timepiece to suggest a geographic shape, as seen from above. The upstream part of such a valley narrows to the width of its watercourse before entering a pinched canyon, usually quite short. Where the watercourse emerges, the valley broadens again to form its lower reach. Mosaic Canyon in California's Death Valley, with a floor composed of tessera-like,

water-polished rocks of black, gray, and white, is one
such valley. During a thunderstorm, water piling up
at the head of the narrow canyon flushes through this
midsection with a noticeable increase in velocity, then
runs out freely over stones where the valley broadens
out again. In a wineglass valley, an alluvial fan at the
mouth of a steep, narrow canyon is seen to form the
base or foot of the glass, the adjacent lower part of
the canyon its stem, and where the canyon widens,
higher up, one gets the impression of a final piece, the
cup. Probably the full range of wineglass shapes, from
champagne flute to red-wine goblet, is to be found in the
western canyons. The Black Mountains on the east side
of Death Valley, California, include a number of such
valleys, among them Gower Gulch, Tank Canyon, and
the canyons between Badwater and Mormon Point.

TERRY TEMPEST WILLIAMS

hueco

A hueco is a depression eroded into a rock that will often
stand water long after everything else has gone dry. It's
a naturally occurring stone tank, essentially, usually
elevated simply because that's where the exposed stone
is. In the Old West of westerns, huecos saved countless
parched cowboys and allowed whole bands of Indians
to keep to trails that, due to an apparent lack of water,
seemed otherwise impossible. Temporary (reliant on
rain) and often purposely poisoned with a dead animal,
however, huecos marked the end for perhaps just as many.
The term itself translates from the Spanish to "hollow"
or "cavity," and seems to carry with it the idea that a
hueco is recessed, hidden, nearly inaccessible—behind
something else. Which, for it to stand water for any
length of time, is necessary: with no shade, the water
would quickly evaporate. Another spelling of hueco is
waco, as in the Waco (Wichita) Indians of the Brazos

and Guadalupe Rivers of Texas, rivers that, in many places, have wide stone beds pocked with little hollow bowls, seemingly made to hold handfuls of water. Waco, Texas, is of course named after these Waco Indians; Hueco Springs, Texas, and Hueco Tanks State Historic Site, also in Texas, come by their names more directly.   STEPHEN GRAHAM JONES

huérfano

Huérfano is Spanish for orphan. In this case a perfect description of the landform—a solitary spire or hill left standing by erosion apart from kindred landscape features. Also called a "circumscribed eminence," a lost mountain, or an island hill, it is a kind of existentialist monument, an island in the sky: no man is an island, but a huérfano is. You could make the argument that Devils Tower in Wyoming is the mother of all huérfanos. Alternately, a huérfano can be a hill or mountain of old rock completely surrounded, but not covered, by younger rock. A disk-shaped huérfano is known as a tejón. A huérfano is also known as a lost mountain and an island hill. In 1842, John C. Frémont, a second lieutenant of the newly formed Army Corps of Topographical Engineers, was greatly enthusiastic about Huérfano Butte in southern Colorado. Once considered a geological mystery, its origins were the subject of some debate: was it a volcanic plug or something else? Evidence suggests that this solitary cone, sitting adjacent to I-25, is the remnant core of an igneous intrusion—a volcano that never erupted; when the surrounding layers of rock subsequently eroded away, they left what writer and photographer Curtis Von Fange calls "an orphan in stone." These orphans will always serve as cinematic and literary short-cuts to a western mythos. In *Sinister Pig,* Tony Hillerman writes: "It was a pleasant location with a fine view . . . of traffic speeding along New Mexico Highway

44, of Chaco Mesa far to the west. . . . Visible through the side window were the towering walls of Huérfano Mesa." A section of the Sangre de Cristo Mountains of Colorado and New Mexico has the local label The Huérfano.   LUIS ALBERTO URREA

huerta

There are two main words that mean "vegetable garden" in Spanish and they are *huerta* and *huerto*. Technically they should be different in meaning, but they are often used without consideration to differences. Huerta should refer to a larger vegetable garden, while a huerto should be smaller. In some areas a distinction is made about the purpose of their respective products. The vegetables and fruits of a huerta are usually cultivated for sale, while the huerto is generally intended for family use. Also, strictly speaking, the huerta should have more vegetables than fruits. Both words can also mean "fruit tree orchard," although some people say that huerta should be completely reserved for vegetables and huerto for fruit trees. Huerta can also mean simply "irrigated and cultivated land."   LUIS VERANO

hummock

Hummock, also spelled hommock, was originally hammock, a nautical term feasibly drawn from the image of hammocks folded and stowed in a net suspended above the deck. The diminutive ending, as with hillock, is an indicator of size, and the word may have conflated with Low German *hümpel* (or its variants), which means a small height or eminence. In geography, the term can refer to a mound of broken sea ice forced upward by pressure, as within a floe, or to a small knob of damp earth in subpolar and alpine regions, but more commonly it is applied to a mound or cone-shaped piece of ground elevated above a swampland, especially in the southern

United States, and most especially in Florida, where it is sometimes confused with hammock, a dryland feature. Hummocks often have trees and other dense growth on them. Also, in the southwestern part of the Florida Everglades, and elsewhere in the South, the mounds built up of shell fragments or other detritus by pre-Columbian inhabitants may be called hummocks. In *Wolfert's Roost*, Washington Irving observes: "When Florida was ceded by the Spaniards . . . the Indians . . . retired . . . [into the] intricate swamps and hommocks and vast savannahs of the interior." JOHN KEEBLE

hundredth meridian

Of all the mapmakers' imaginary lines inscribed on North America, the most famous is the one curling north and south to the poles, one hundred degrees west of Greenwich, England. In the United States, the hundredth meridian runs from the Dakotas through Nebraska, Kansas, the panhandle of Oklahoma, and the heart of Texas. It became famous after John Wesley Powell, explorer of the Grand Canyon, observed that this meridian roughly coincides with the twenty-inch annual rainfall line: land to the east receives more than twenty inches of rain per year, enough to grow crops without irrigation, while nearly all land to the west receives less, and thus requires irrigation. We should therefore be cautious, Powell argued, in how we settle the arid region beyond the hundredth meridian. Because this caution has been flagrantly ignored, western aquifers, such as the Ogallala, are being rapidly depleted, and rivers such as the Colorado are being drained. SCOTT RUSSELL SANDERS

ice dam

Ice dam is sometimes used as a synonym for ice jam, a clog of fractured river ice at spring breakup. A different sort of ice dam can develop out of sight beneath a glacier, where it may back up a large lake and release it suddenly in a glacial outburst. A third and larger variety produced epic floods in the Pacific Northwest only 14,000 to 16,000 years ago. A lobe of the Cordilleran ice sheet periodically plugged the canyon of the Clark Fork River in northern Idaho, giving rise to ancient Lake Missoula, which covered three thousand square miles of western Montana to a depth of nineteen hundred feet. When the ice plug melted and broke down—or popped up like a cork—surging waters scoured out the channeled scablands of eastern Washington, swelled the Columbia River a thousand feet deep at Wallula Gap, overtopped Crown Point in the Columbia Gorge, and repeatedly made a deep mud puddle out of Oregon's Willamette Valley, bequeathing three hundred feet of rich, exotic silts that Oregon Trail pioneers would declare the firmament of a New Eden.   JOHN DANIEL

icefall

Where a river encounters a steep cliff, it descends as a waterfall. Likewise, where a glacier encounters a steep cliff, it descends as an icefall. To an observer, the icefall appears as immobile as a sculpture; however, compared to the glacier's normal velocity, the ice actually "pours" down the cliff at speeds of hundreds of yards per year. Ice on the underside of the curving glacier moves over a shorter distance than ice at the top, causing the surface to fracture into a fantastical ice scape of crevasses, seracs, ogives, septa, and pinnacles. John Muir and his dog Stickeen, on a hike across a glacier in Alaska's Glacier Bay in 1880, came upon an icefall that "in the form of a magnificent ice-cascade two miles wide, was pouring

239

over the rim of the main basin . . . its surface broken into wave-shaped blades and shattered blocks, suggesting the wildest updashing, heaving, plunging motion of a great river cataract." At an icefall's base, glacial movement is arrested. The ice thickens, compressed now, restoring a smoother surface to the glacier's flow. With valley glaciers, an icefall often separates a glacial plateau from a glacial basin. The chaotic, collapsing walls of icefalls intimidate even great mountaineers, as suggested by the name of one on Alaska's Mendenhall Glacier: the Suicide Icefall. EVA SAULITIS

ice stream

In *Innocents Abroad*, Mark Twain described how he once camped on a glacier, hoping it would transport him miles while he slept. He wanted to hitch a ride on an ice stream, a term that refers to the movement of a whole glacier down a valley. Twain was disappointed; the imperceptible creep of such a glacier might be better compared to the slow, plastic flow of warm putty than to the swift flow of water. If it adheres to the bed and walls of a valley, an ice stream moves by slow deformation. Other ice streams slide forward on sheets of meltwater. When glaciers from side valleys push into a valley glacier, the result is a compound glacier, made of two or more ice streams "flowing" side by side. These parallel streams are visibly delineated, separated by long, sinuous black stripes called medial moraines, as the encroaching glaciers deposit trails of rock debris scraped from the valley walls onto the trunk glacier's surface. Ice stream also refers to another phenomenon. Within ice sheets and ice caps, ice streams—narrow zones of faster-moving ice—are bounded by broader regions of slower-moving ice. The border between fast and slow ice is marked by spectacular crevasses. A bird's-eye view reveals ice streams as bands within the ice that "overflow" the ice margin. The forces that cause ice streams are not fully understood, though landscape features under the ice sheet may be factors. For instance, ice flowing over buried valleys increases in velocity in the same way that a flooding river flows faster in its deep channel than it does over its floodplain.   EVA SAULITIS

ice wall

At its seaward edge, the face of a glacier, ice shelf, or ice sheet normally drops steeply to the water. When this mass of ice doesn't float but actually sits on the bottom, its ice front is called an ice wall. The rock floor beneath an ice wall can be at or below sea level. In 1854, polar explorer Dr. Elisha Kent Kane described the front of an Arctic ice sheet as "a glassy wall three hundred feet above the water, with an unknown, unfathomable depth below it—a long, ever-shining line." In a loose sense, anywhere ice exists in nature one might come up against an ice wall: at a frozen waterfall, on a mountainside ice cliff, or at a glacial icefall. Depending on one's perspective, such features may be impasses, scenic wonders, or substrates for ascension with crampons, pitons, ice screws, ice axes. In 1879, John Muir clambered up an ice wall—the face of a glacier—in southeastern Alaska, its surface "gashed and sculptured into a maze of shallow caves and crevasses—clusters of glittering lance-tipped spires, gables, and obelisks, bold outstanding bastions and plain mural cliffs—every gorge and crevasse, groove and hollow, was filled with light, shimmering and throbbing in pale-blue tones of ineffable tenderness and beauty." EVA SAULITIS

ice volcano

When waves that would otherwise break on an open shore are instead forced underneath an apron of shore-fast ice, the surge may spout violently through small

holes in that ice. If it's cold enough, the water, falling
back, will splatter and freeze around the opening. If the
air is calm and the spout is strong and sufficiently high,
the freezing water will build up around the spout hole
in the shape of a cone, sometimes to the height of five
feet or more. The process compares with the way spatter
cones are created around fumaroles, the vents on active
volcanoes. Ice volcanoes continue to grow until the surge
subsides or the vent freezes shut. They sometimes occur
in clusters, as is commonly the case along the winter
shores of Lake Superior.   BARRY LOPEZ

imbricated rock

Rocks are imbricated when their edges overlap, like roof
shingles or the scales on a Douglas fir cone. (The Latin
root is *imbrex*, a curved tile.) For a geologic sense of the
range of the term, imagine very big imbrication (overriding land masses piling up like slumped stacks of giant
pancakes); odd, scary imbrication (boulders layered on
a coast, likely dominoed there by the wave action of a
tsunami); and streambed imbrication (cobbles overlapping and angled by moving water). Imbricated rock
lets you hold solid and see fluid. In a stratum of fluvial
sandstone, water-worn cobbles pile edge over edge in a
shingle pattern, their long axis aligned with the current.
Such dipped and titled cobbles imply paleo-currents, the
direction of flood and deposition in a river that flowed
millions of years ago.   ELLEN MELOY

impact crater

Just look at the moon. The term is terse and exact: an
impact crater is the footprint of an impact by an unspeci-
fied foreign object, often causing a major landscape
feature to develop. These tend to be round and symmetrical holes, sometimes mistaken for calderas or volcanic
lakes. The science fiction film *Starman* made good use of

America's premiere impact crater—Meteor Crater, east
of the Grand Canyon in northern Arizona. (It forms part
of the geological trifecta of that section of I-40: Grand
Canyon, Petrified Forest/Painted Desert, and Meteor
Crater.) LUIS ALBERTO URREA

incón

This obscure word, incón, also written as encón, is a
colloquial New Mexican term for a bay or a cove. It can
also be a beach, as in a riverbank. Or it can be a bend in
a river, where a pool has formed; also a sandbar rising in
the middle of a river or stream. It is a remnant of antique
Spanish. Gaspar Castaño de Sosa, in his *Memorias de
descubrimiento* (*Memoirs of Discovery*) of 1590–91, writes:
"On the thirteenth of said month, we left our *paraje*
[camp] and we went to sleep three leagues from there;
in an encón was the village we had departed from, a
league away from us." LUIS ALBERTO URREA

infant stream

An infant stream is a small, gathering watercourse at
the very upper reaches of a watershed. Such a stream
has only begun its erosive mission of redistributing the
materials of the land downhill. Infant streams are not
generally protected by buffers or setbacks from logging
activity, as higher-order streams downstream may be.
In heavy rains, the flow in embryonic rivulets grows
from a trickle to a wash. When the slopes that give rise
to infant streams are denuded by clear-cutting, steep
soils become saturated. Without well-established roots
to hold them, entire sheets of sediments surrounding the
network of infant streams may slide over the underlying
bedrock, taking with them whole headwalls of the upper
watershed. Such headwall failures contribute greatly to
the siltation of salmon spawning grounds downstream.
For this reason, and as cradles of the watersheds, infant

streams deserve the same protection given mature
watercourses in the lowlands.   ROBERT MICHAEL PYLE

inlet

An inlet is an arm stretching inland off a larger body
of water. Lakes and large rivers have inlets, but the
mightiest, of course, are found along ocean coasts. In
the Pacific, Cook Inlet stretches 150 miles to Anchorage,
while the largest inlet on the East Coast is Chesapeake
Bay.   BILL MCKIBBEN

intermittent stream

A stream that flows seasonally when the water table
is high, such as during and after periods of heavy or
steady rain, is called intermittent. Such streams may
be connected with natural reservoirs in hills or mountains. When the reservoir exceeds maximum holding
capacity, water spills over the rim and siphons down
toward lower ground. This flow ceases when water
levels fall below the reservoir rim. During the dry
summer months, intermittent streams may cease to flow,
causing the channels to appear dry, although in fact
water continues to travel through the stream bottom or
underground. At the height of flow, intermittent streams
may temporarily fill dry lakebeds in desert regions to
form bodies of water called playa lakes. Sometimes
intermittent stream is used as a synonym for ephemeral
stream.   JEFFERY RENARD ALLEN

iron range

When European explorers first ventured into the upper
reaches of the American Midwest, they dismissed the
area as a barren, worthless wilderness. Then in 1844,
William Austin Burt, a land surveyor, noticed a strange
movement of the needle of his compass near what is now

Negaunee, Michigan. A Native American led Burt to the site of a large deposit of iron ore, and so the mineral was "discovered." For centuries, Natives had been using the iron ore for pigment and hammering it into beads, buttons, and chisels. In 1849, the first blast furnace was put into operation, and large-scale mining began in the region. It continues to this day, even though the reserves of high-grade hematite iron are now exhausted and, instead, lower-grade taconite deposits are being worked. Iron ore was found in large deposits throughout the Lake Superior area—not only in the Upper Peninsula of Michigan but also northern Minnesota and northern Wisconsin. The region came to be known as the Iron Range, and over the past 150 years it has produced more than one billion tons of iron ore. The iron deposits were laid down in the Precambrian era, when the entire region was covered by a shallow sea and great masses of iron in the water accumulated over troughs filled with sediments of sand. When the waters eventually receded, vast thicknesses of iron and sand deposits were left in the ground.

MARY SWANDER

irrigation circle

A series of irrigation circles viewed out a jetliner window might convert the uninitiated to a belief in crop signs. An irrigation circle is, actually, a burgeoning crop of alfalfa or corn or wheat or soybeans, its shape dictated by a huge irrigation system that rotates in a circle from the pivot point of a central tower. The driving mechanism resides in the axles of twin rubber-tired wheels on struts that support the irrigation booms, which are fitted at intervals with waterers similar to those used on lawns, some of the twirlybird type, though much larger. The benefit of circle irrigation is that no ditches need to be dug and no ground pipes laid or moved once the system is in place; besides, little crop is damaged or local habitat disrupted, the only marks on the land being the trails where the paired tires trace their unending circles.   LARRY WOIWODE

island arc

An island arc is a curved linear chain of volcanic islands produced by the midocean collision of two crustal plates. One plate is gradually subducted, or pushed under, by the other, chiseling a deep trench as it plunges down. Friction and the heat of the Earth's underlying mantle melt the leading edge of the subducted plate, and where molten rock rises to the surface it forms a line of volcanoes along the edge of the overriding, or obducted, plate. The Aleutian Islands, extending 1,200 miles southwest from the Alaska Peninsula, make up a classic island arc, bordered by the deep (over 24,000 feet at some points) Aleutian Trench. In *Basin and Range,* John McPhee explains why the volcanic islands emerge in an arc by comparing an oceanic plate pushing under a continental plate to a knife slicing at a forty-five degree angle into an orange: "The incision becomes an arc on the surface of the orange. If the knife blade melts inside, little volcanoes will come up through the pores of the skin, and together they will form arcs, island arcs."   PAMELA FRIERSON

islet

An islet is most simply a little island, anything markedly differing in character from that by which it is surrounded. Archly poetic and connoting the diminutive, even the fanciful, islet is not a terribly serious term, though it has been used by no less an eminence than the naturalist Archie Carr. Though general usage has not adopted Carr's approach, he uses the term in place of hammock or tree island, providing an opportunity for digression here on the subject of Florida tree snails, genus *Liguus.* Specific in color and design to individual isolated hard-

wood hammocks of the Everglades—their sole habitat—
the exquisitely patterned lovely "ligs" are considered a
microzoogeographic classic.   JOY WILLIAMS

isthmus

Bordered on two sides by water, an isthmus is a relatively
narrow strip of land that links larger land masses, such
as two islands, a mainland coast with an offshore island,
or even two continents. An example of the last is the
Isthmus of Panama, which extends from the southern
border of Costa Rica to Colombia—linking the North
and South American continents. An isthmus that acts
as a corridor along which animals and plants migrate
from one continent to another is sometimes called a land
bridge. In *From the Earth to the Moon*, Jules Verne observes
that an isthmus can also transport a mountain range: "On
the west," Verne writes, "arise the Rocky Mountains,
that immense range which, commencing at the Straits of
Magellan, follows the western coast of Southern America
under the name of the Andes or the Cordilleras, until it
crosses the Isthmus of Panama, and runs up the whole
of North America to the very borders of the Polar Sea."
The term appears in various coastal place-names, including Isthmus Bay in Alaska; Isthmus Brook in Penobscot,
Maine; and Isthmus Slough in Coos Bay, Oregon. While
many landscape terms derive from analogy to our own
anatomy—neck, mouth, finger, etc.—isthmus seems to be
the rarer case in which a geographic term is applied to an
analogous feature of the body: anatomically, an isthmus
is a narrow band of tissue connecting two larger parts of
some corporeal structure.   EMILY HIESTAND

jackstraw timber

Visually, jackstraw (or jackstrawed) timber resembles the
child's game of pick-up sticks, writ large: a pile of fallen
trees, most often conifer. Jackstraw timber provides
both protection for new growth (inhibiting browsing
of vulnerable aspen sprouts) and fodder for forest fire.
Jackstrawed timber occurs naturally—the result of
mortality, of blowdown, of fire aftermath—and is also
orchestrated by humans to discourage browsing by
animals. With poetic license, various writers have used
jackstraw to describe both the chaotic arrangement of
all manner of objects, man-made or natural, literal or
figurative, and the delicacy one must employ in moving
one piece without disturbing the rest. As Charles Simic
writes in his poem "Jackstraws," "My shadow and your
shadow on the wall / Caught with arms raised / In display
of exaggerated alarm, / Now that even a whisper, even a
breath / Will upset the remaining straws / Still standing
on the table."   ANTONYA NELSON

jaral

You have seen the jaral in a score of spaghetti westerns.
These Italian genre movies made great use of the vast
desertlike vistas found in the western Mediterranean
landscapes of Spain. As is often the case in the American
Southwest, place-names trace the progress of conquest:
the jaral became the Texan–New Mexican land where
sandy soil supported low, sparse shrubs of the same
type found in Spain. Jaral encompasses the famous *llanos*
(scrub plains) that so fascinate Misters McCarthy and
McMurtry in their novels. The Chihuahuan Desert
is prime jaral territory. In microcosm, a jaral can be a
willow thicket on a sand bank. For many, it's synonymous with chaparral. The root of the word is the jara,
a rockrose that grows in tangles; indeed, jaral can also
be used as slang for a tangled, confused situation. It is a

landscape, like a cactus field, where the vegetation makes progress difficult: it's hell on horses. Also known as a chamizal: literally, the place where *chamizos*—tradition- ally thatch-roofed huts, often with adobe walls—are found. When we see Clint Eastwood riding out of the jaral, he squints at the *peones* as they hurry into the safety of their chamizos in the great, dangerous, eternally hot chamizal.   LUIS ALBERTO URREA

jetty

A jetty is a structure, usually of wood or stone, built out onto water. The term can refer to a built structure at the entrance to a harbor, or running out into the sea or into a lake, to defend the shore from the action of the waves; a structure built into a river to divert the current in order to prevent erosion or to shape a channel by control- ling the deposit of sediment; an outwork of piles or timbers protecting a pier; or the lightly constructed and projecting portion of a more heavily constructed wharf or landing pier. Thus a maritime jetty usually func- tions as a breakwater, and freshwater jetties are usually structures built parallel to the bank at or near the mouth of a river to control the shape of the channel. The most famous example of this latter use is the series of jetties constructed by James Buchanan Eads in 1879 to create a dependably navigable channel from New Orleans to the Gulf of Mexico. Jetties that serve as breakwaters are usually built in a straight line and more or less perpendicular to the shore. Hence, the name of Robert Smithson's earthwork *Spiral Jetty* on the Great Salt Lake must be intended to be paradoxical. However, the matter is really not this simple. Jetty comes from the Old French *jetée*, which describes the action of throwing something outward. There are a lot of names for structures built out over water. And they are so often used interchangeably; it is a question whether jetty, groyne or groin, mole, wharf, quay, pier, breakwater, and seawall are synonyms, words for distinct structures, or for similar structures with different uses, or whether they have simply meant different things in different times and places. Here's a Cape Cod jetty from Conrad Aiken's poem "Letter to Li Po": "The tide/scales with moon-silver, floods the marsh, fulfils/Payne Creek and Quivett Creek, rises to lift/the fishing boats against a jetty wall." And here is a North Carolina jetty from Bland Simpson's *Into the Sound Country* that is almost a still-life: "Not far from Little River jetty stood a curved-top, rural mailbox on a post in the dunes, a sandy park bench nearby, aimed out to sea." North Carolina also produced the 1950s and 60s band Homer Briarhopper and the Jetty-jumpers. ROBERT HASS

J

jolla

The word jolla, as in La Jolla, California, is widely translated in that area as "jewel," but this is in fact a figurative meaning of the term and represents a common confusion with *joya*, the Spanish word for jewel. Jolla means hollow, which is, apparently, what the settlers of La Jolla originally had in mind. Elsewhere in the Southwest, jolla always means a low, flat place adjacent to water and noticeably richer in vegetation than the area surrounding it. The popular stopping spot on the Colorado River in Grand Canyon called Elves Chasm is a jolla—and for many in that parched landscape a joya. LUIS VERANO

kame

Kame is a Scottish name for a steep-sided ridge, a hummocky deposit at the front of an ice sheet. A kame terrace is typically formed between the lower edge of a glacier and the valley below, where trapped meltwater coming from under the ice carries sediment and then deposits it. Once the glacier melts, that deposit constitutes a ridge on the slope, usually composed of sand and gravel.

WILLIAM KITTREDGE

karst

A German word derived from Kras, the Serbo-Croat name for a region of rugged limestone plateaus in the Dinaric Alps near the Adriatic coast of Croatia, karst refers to limestone areas riddled with extensive subterranean streams and caves, and an aboveground terrain that collapses into these underground channels, leaving distinctive hollows, pits, and sinkholes. This kind of landscape typically develops in humid uplands (such as southern Indiana, Florida, and Kentucky) where thick, strongly jointed limestone underlies the soil and abundant rainfall provides water to drive the carbonate-solution process that generates caves.   BARBARA KINGSOLVER

kettle

Taking its figurative cue from the domestic vessel for boiling water, similar to a pot or cauldron, the geological kettle refers to a hollow scoured in a rocky riverbed or under a glacier. Kettles are often found embedded in moraines. They are formed by depressions left by the melting of an ice block lodged in a deposit of till or drift. Sometimes known as potholes or sinks, these cavities can be of irregular size and depth and are often numerous in glacial regions. Kettle hole is a synonym. Kettle Hole Woods State Natural Area in Wisconsin is a good example of this topography, as is the Kettle Hole Trail in Long Island,

New York. Thoreau's Walden Pond is another example. Places where especially large kettle holes are filled with water are called kettle lakes.   PATRICIA HAMPL

key

Key derives from the Spanish word *cayo*, or little island. Keys are composed of sand and coral fragments built up just above sea level on a reef flat. The Florida Keys curve southwest from Biscayne Bay to the Dry Tortugas, a distance of some 180 miles. The distance accessible by car is 106 miles from Key Largo to Key West, with the many genuine *cayos*, as well as a few fill islands, linked by forty-two bridges. Numerous other keys in the chain, uninhabited and accessible only by boat, are protected by linked wildlife refuges and marine sanctuaries. The Keys rest on an ancient fossilized reef, but the upper keys are composed of porous limestone, while the lower keys have a layer of caprock, up to thirty feet deep, of finely grained calcium carbonate called Miami oolite. Rainfall drains quickly through the limestone but is retained in the compact, dense oolite, resulting in considerable differences in the natural environment. The bay—or Gulf—side of the Keys is called the backcountry. The Atlantic side is actually the Straits of Florida, where Hawk Channel runs out from the shore to the living reef. Beyond the reef is the Gulf Stream—"outfront"—and beyond that, the ocean. When Ponce de León sighted the Keys in 1513, he dubbed them Los Martires—the Martyrs—and sailed on.   JOY WILLIAMS

kill

In the Dutch language, *kill* is used to describe streams and river channels, and is literally translated into English as brook. So it is not surprising to find the term commonly applied to the parts of the American East originally settled by the Dutch. On maps of the upper Hudson

Valley and the Delaware Valley one can find landforms, rivers, and towns containing the word—the Catskill (Cats Creek) Mountains of southeast New York State, and the mighty Schuylkill River (or "Hidden Channel River") that flows through Philadelphia. Although the Dutch also settled the lower Hudson Valley, kill is not widely used there, perhaps because the Dutch culture was subsumed after 1664 when the English captured the colony of New Netherland and renamed it New York. Elsewhere on the continent, landforms and communities are named for the act that involves the taking of life. A mountain in North Dakota, once known by a Sioux phrase, *Tah-kah-p-kuty*, "the place where they kill the deer," is now simply Killdeer Mountain. JAN DEBLIEU

K

kīpuka

A kīpuka is a raised island of native forest and plants situated in the middle of a recent lava flow. Because of its elevation, a kīpuka is spared burial and incineration. Hawaiians say a kīpuka is an oasis saved from Pele's embrace. The word is a variation of the Hawaiian word *puka*, which means "hole." It can refer to an opening of blue sky among high clouds, or a calm in the middle of rough seas, or a safe time and space where one perceives things clearly. Kīpukas also exist in New Mexico, in the El Malpais National Monument, and in the lava flows in Oregon's Cascade Mountains, but it is generally thought of as a Hawaiian term. The Kīpuka Puaulu provides excellent habitat for the two species of butterflies native to Hawai'i, the Kamehameha Lady and the Hawaiian Blue, or Blackburn's Bluet. PATTIANN ROGERS

kiss tank

Walking across the hot, dry lands, through saltbush and snakeweed and desert sage, the tired travelers longed for the sight of a kiss tank, a pool of water left from the last rain and its runoff in a naturally formed rock basin. Ranchers call these pools of water kiss tanks because, when such a pool is found, all creatures of the desert, as well as cattle and horses and humans, put their dry lips and thirsty mouths to its water eagerly, with a kind of passion. And they rise refreshed. Such basins filled with the water from snowmelt can also be found in mountainous regions. A basin on top of the Maiden, a sandstone spire near Boulder, Colorado, for instance, contains freshwater shrimp that have evolved to survive the dry seasons. A kiss tank is also called a tinaja, which is Spanish for a big, earthen jar. PATTIANN ROGERS

knob

A knob is a rounded hill, a prominent, isolated, rounded mound or knoll. Knobs are a familiar landform to people in the South and Midwest. They are usually smaller than neighboring mountains, less angular than buttes, and more symmetrical than hills. George R. Stewart, in his book *Names on the Land*, says early English settlers had no word "for a mountain standing up sharply by itself," so they used the word knob (from Middle Low German *knubbe*, meaning "knot" or "bud"). Knobs are formed by the weathering of sandstone or granite, both of which tend to erode into rounded forms. The soil between knobs is usually quite fertile. In the Ozarks, a knob crested with open, grassy glades is known as a bald knob. Bald knobs are also found in the Appalachians, which persist as grassy meadows in otherwise forested terrain. Cherokee Indians used such high, open locations as lookout posts to guard against raids by rival tribes. CONGER BEASLEY, JR.

knoll

A small, low hill distinctive for its round shape is a knoll. *Knollen* and *Knolle* in German, and *knolle* in Dutch, mean, variously, "clod," "ball," "turnip," "lump," and "knot." A knoll is usually something that can be walked around, like a hillock or mound, and is self-contained and singular, rising out of a flat landscape such as a plain or situated on a plateau or mesa. Along with glen, dale, dell, and ridge, to name a few, it has suffered debasement at the hands of developers who christen their communities with names such as Wood Knolls, Lake Knolls, or, more pretentiously, The Knolls. Similarly, a knoll is a poeticized hill, as in Wordsworth's "rocky knoll," although Robert Frost gets it right in "The Cow in Apple Time" when he writes, "She bellows on a knoll against the sky." The most famous knoll in America is the "grassy knoll" of Dealey Plaza in Dallas, Texas, from which it was initially thought the shots were fired that killed President John F. Kennedy.   MICHAEL COLLIER

K

krummholz

Krummholz is a German word meaning "crooked wood." It is used to designate the dwarfed and deformed coniferous vegetation of the transition zone between subalpine forest and the treeless alpine tundra. Because of a mixing of species from each region, the krummholz, an ecotone, has a richer flora than either alone. Wind speeds may exceed one hundred miles per hour in krummholz, snow can accumulate to depths of twelve feet, and the growing season is often less than two months. The crowns of trees here often become one-sided as their windward branches fail to develop. The result is a low deformed wood of asymmetrical "flag trees" and low-branching, interwoven mats of foliage. Krummholz systems in the southern Rocky Mountains run in a band between 11,000 and 12,000 feet of elevation. These trees are surviving at their environmental limit, so growth is slow and irregular. Trees several hundred years old may have a trunk diameter of four inches, and may be only a few feet tall.   WILLIAM KITTREDGE

kudzu

In large portions of the southeastern United States the kudzu vine, rapacious and fast growing, has overtaken the countryside, "covering Dixie like the dew." Growing sixty feet or more in a season, this woody, hairy vine, originally a native of Japan and China, can completely engulf large trees, telephone poles, abandoned cars, small sheds, little-used country roads. Kudzu is believed to cover more than seven million acres of rural areas in the South, and has been found as far north as New York, as far west as Texas, and commonly in the Midwest, including Ohio, Indiana, Illinois, Missouri, and Kansas. Luckily, winter frost kills the vine, although its roots survive. People residing in kudzu country have adopted the vine good-naturedly as an emblem of their homeplace and enjoy telling tall tales about it. For example, there's the one about an escaped prisoner who fled into a kudzu patch and is still unaccounted for. The Kudzu Kings, a musical outfit, advertise themselves as the "purveyors of Southern roots rock drunken country jungle boogie Americana from Oxford, Mississippi." PATTIANN ROGERS

labyrinth

As applied to natural geographical features, labyrinth
adopts the intricate structure of the man-made maze to
describe phenomena of cave and canyon, land and sea.
In both instances, the structure is built of interconnect-
ing passages through which it is difficult to find one's
way. The point in constructing a labyrinth is to lose
or confuse; the result in encountering one is often the
same. In Greek mythology, the Minotaur was punished
by confinement in a labyrinth designed by Daedalus.
Naturally occurring labyrinths—such as the one in
Mammoth Cave in Kentucky, one in the Canadian
Arctic Archipelago, and Utah's Labyrinth Canyon,
on the Green River just upstream from its confluence
with the Colorado River in Canyonlands National
Park—were formed, and continue to be altered by, time
and water rather than man or god. "In these years we are
witnessing the gigantic spectacle of innumerable human
lives wandering lost in their own labyrinths," wrote
Spanish essayist José Ortega y Gasset in *The Revolt of the
Masses.* ANTONYA NELSON

lacustrine deposit

Pertaining to, produced by, or inhabiting a lake, the
adjective lacustrine designates a lake-specific rather
than marine quality or aspect. There is, for instance, a
lacustrine age, a prehistoric period when lakeside dwellings were common. Lacustrine often refers to animals
and plants inhabiting lakes, and also to the ecology
of a lake area. Thus, lacustrine deposits are stratified
geologic materials of the lake bottom. Sometimes the
term indicates that these deposits have been exposed
and made visible by the lowering of the water level or
by the elevation of the land. Because, in contrast to seas
and oceans, lakes are smaller, nearly closed systems with
finer-grained sediment (silt and clay)—and are often

rich in organic shales, which, in turn, are important
rock sources of petroleum—this distinction is not only
geographically significant (indicating a lake rather than a
sea) but also geologically important (referring to certain
deposits peculiar to lakes). Lacustrine deposits are
found even in the Sahara, where the Cenozoic era left a
sand sea of wide, shallow basins filled with alluvial and
lacustrine drift.   PATRICIA HAMPL

lagoon

A shallow body of water located adjacent to a larger body
such as a river, lake, or ocean, yet partly separated from
it by a thin strip of land, is known as a lagoon. The separating barrier may be a sand bank, reef, barrier island, or
spit. Lagoons related to coral reefs occur in two forms:
one is situated between a barrier reef and the coast and
can be of almost any shape; the other is found within an
atoll, a circular reef with the lagoon at its center. Tourism
brochures have strongly linked the term to faraway tropical places, like Coconut Lagoon in Kerala, India, or any
of the classic half-moon reef lagoons of the Pacific atolls.
This may owe to the fact that "marooned" and lagoon
rhyme so nicely in the poetry of getaway fantasies.
Notable American lagoons include the shallow inden-
tions along the south shore of New York's Long Island,
flanked by dunes, and the coastal lagoons around Sitka,
Alaska, prized by sea kayakers for watching gray whales.
River lagoons in the American heartland commonly
shelter natural wonders, as described by Willa Cather in
O Pioneers!: "The Bergson wagon . . . skirted the margin
of wide lagoons, where the golden coreopsis grew up out
of the clear water and the wild ducks rose with a whirr of
wings." And lagoons have long offered coveted shelter for
human settlements. Lagos, the Nigerian capital, derives
its name from the Portuguese word for lagoon.
MIKE TIDWELL

laguna

The Spanish equivalent of lagoon, that is, an enclosed bay, inlet, or other narrow or shallow body of water, the word *laguna* commonly appears as a part of place-names in the Spanish-speaking Americas. For example, Laguna Mar Chiquita and Laguna de Términos in Mexico. Not restricted to marine environments, in Spanish the term also refers to a large diffusion of stagnant water, or to country in which marshy ground and wetlands abound, such as La Laguna Flamingos system in the Mexican state of Tamaulipas. A laguna may also be a shallow pond or small lake in a bolson where waters ephemerally gather in basins. One of the best-known occurrences of the term is Laguna Pueblo, located in west-central New Mexico near the paths of the Santa Fe Railroad and Interstate 40, and so named for a former small lake along the Rio San Jose, which, by way of the Rio Puerco, is a tributary of the Rio Grande. In *Wah-to-yah and the Taos Trail*, Lewis H. Garrard writes of a discovery in the Rio Rayado vicinity of northeastern New Mexico: "On the summit, a level bare spot and a brackish body of water— El [*sic*] Laguna—presented itself—its margin grown with slime-covered sedge." JOHN KEEBLE

lahar

Javanese for rapid mudflow associated with volcanic activity, a lahar is created when volcanic ash is converted into a mobile paste by water from torrential rain, snowmelt, or breaching of the walls of a crater lake. This fluid landslide may spread many miles from the source volcano when confined along preexisting valleys: the five-thousand-year-old Osceola Lahar of Puget Sound in Washington is up to five hundred feet thick and extends over two hundred square miles. When the Electron Lahar that swept from Mount Rainier about five hundred years ago was excavated in 1993, remnants of an old-growth forest were exposed. Associated with lahars are *nuées ardentes*, French for glowing clouds—highly mobile, turbulent, and sometimes incandescent clouds erupted from a volcano and containing large amounts of ash and other pyroclastics. Such a mixture, once it settles, is quite fluid, and it can move rapidly down even a gentle slope. When the mixture comes to rest, the hot glass fragments meld together, forming a welded tuff. It was an eruption of this kind from Mount Vesuvius that buried the city of Pompeii in A.D. 79. In 1985, more than twenty-three thousand people were killed by a lahar that swept through Armero, Colombia. Lahars are, in fact, often catastrophic and the cause of most volcanic fatalities, which is why the United States Geological Survey recently instituted a pilot project in Washington called the Mount Rainier Volcano Lahar Warning System.   KIM BARNES

lake

A lake is a considerable body of water surrounded by land; or, sometimes, an expanded part of a river (as Lake Pepin, the massive widening of the upper Mississippi River between Red Wing and Wabasha, Minnesota). Lake has traditionally denoted a body of water large enough to present itself as a geographic feature, perhaps opening to rivulets and streams, thus potentially part of a larger, interrelated water system. But lake has proved to be a wonderfully, or perhaps perversely, flexible term and is applied to freshwater forms as diverse as the Great Lakes, which constitute vast inland seas, and small constructed ornamental lakes in parks or even private properties. Lake is also a red pigment composed of a coloring agent combined, usually by precipitation, with metallic oxide or earth to create striking hues such as madder lake (a fierce yellow). The etymology of lake has been traced to early forms meaning play, fun, sport, glee, games, and tricks, and sometimes "to fight" and occasionally "to please." In early

Middle English, "to lake" indicated an offering, a sacrifice, finally a gift. These verb forms are very old, almost forgotten except in lexicons, but they provide testimony that argues persuasively that lake's etymology is best found in the earliest traces of English out of its Teutonic roots, not, as might logically be assumed, from the Latin *lacus*. Lake is unobtrusively onomatopoetic, the *l* and *a* together forming a plangent, serene sound, combined with the kick of the *k*, like the soft lapping of a wave. Lake often serves as a descriptive or evocative adjective, as in lake poets, lake country. Two particularly voracious fish, the bow-fin and the burbot, are sometimes called, in jest, lake lawyers. In Minnesota, a regional usage—"We're going up to the lake this weekend"—often confuses visitors who assume there is a single lake to which the speaker is referring, when in fact "the lake" pertains to any lake in the state but also, in the spirit of affectionate possessiveness, to a specific lake that is the speaker's destination. Used in this way, lake is both a place and a condition, rather in the spirit of its earliest root in play and fun.   PATRICIA HAMPL

L

laminar flow

Laminar is a term used by hydrologists, river scientists, rafters, and other experienced river watchers to describe the smooth and even flow of a river unimpeded by rocks, trees, or other obstructions. This condition is as close as a river can come to the laminar flow used by physicists in their description of all fluids: a state in which all particles move in the same direction, perfectly in parallel. Some textbooks liken the flow to layers of playing cards sliding over each other. In a river, a rock, hole, or sudden narrowing of channel width can cause more complicated flow structures, such as vortices and eddies, to form. Particles begin to move in different directions. When this occurs, laminar flow is no longer present, and the flow begins to be described as turbulent.   LAN SAMANTHA CHANG

land bridge

A land bridge forms a link between two continents across which plants and animals may move to colonize a new habitat. This bridge may stand in the present—such as the Isthmus of Panama—or it may have existed in the past before it was lost to continental drift or a change in sea level. Anthropologists and biologists who study modern distributions of flora and fauna take special note of these places that have served as migratory routes for the dispersal of terrestrial, landlocked animals, recognizing, for instance, the possibility that humans discovered America many centuries ahead of Columbus by walking across land that now lies beneath the Bering Strait.

BARBARA KINGSOLVER

landing

At its most rudimentary, a landing is simply any convenient, safe place to come ashore on a river, lake, or ocean. As such useful places were developed, the word also came to incorporate the proximate docking and staging areas for cargo or passengers. From the town of Landing, New Jersey, near the southern end of Lake Hopatcong, to Jim Cullum's Landing, a jazz club on the San Antonio River, landings are associated with good facilities and transfer areas on bodies of water. Because they were naturally strategic sites, landings established for commercial water traffic sometimes grew into full-fledged communities. An example is Moss Landing in California, a town that once flourished as a whaling station and survives as a small fishing community on Monterey Bay. Today, new landings are being proposed for sites along the Allegheny, Monongahela, and Ohio Rivers as one tool to help reclaim the rivers and the riverfronts of the old steel communities of southwestern Pennsylvania. In the lexicon of marine fisheries, landing is the word for catches of fish brought ashore, in aggregate. Finally, landing is also a logging term, referring to the flattened-out place on a mountain where loggers pile recently cut trees until they are ready for transport to a sawmill.   EMILY HIESTAND

landslide

A landslide is distinguished from mudslides, avalanches, and other forms of mass wasting by the relative dryness of the soil or rock in it. Earthquake, freeze-thaw weathering, and the domino effect of falling debris are among the perturbations that can trigger the spontaneous downward movement of a landslide.   WILLIAM DEBUYS

lava blister

Like a glassblower who blows air into molten glass to create a goblet or vase, gas released from lava may force the thin, glassy crust of a lava flow to form a large circular bubble or blister. Blisters may also form through hydrostatic or artesian forces in the lava. They are usually one hundred to five hundred feet in diameter, with a maximum height of one hundred feet, and are hollow. The largest may form blister caves, although the geologic situations where this happens are rare, the most common being a calm volcanic eruption. Generally, blisters are too small to enter, but the more tenacious the lava is, the bigger the bubbles can become. The largest blister caves are found at Mount Fantale, Ethiopia. The basaltic lava flows of the Kīlauea Volcano in Hawai'i have created smaller but no less defined lava blisters.   KIM BARNES

lava cave

Water is the creative force behind most caves. Lava caves, however, are usually formed during the transformation of fluid basalt into solid rock (the exceptions being the small caves created during the uplifting or buckling of congealing lava crust). Lava flowing downhill tends to develop a central channel of faster-moving magma. This molten

river forms its own levees, and cooling and congealing lava, rafting the surface, catches on the sides like a
snagged log, narrowing the channel edges until they crust
over in a roof. The molten river below, eroding its way
deeper and deeper, is now encased in a tunnel or lava tube
of its own making; where well insulated, it can continue
to flow for miles. If a change or an end to the eruption
reduces or stops the flow of lava, the fiery river will drain
out of its tube, often leaving a series of horizontal ridges
like stone bathtub rings on the walls as the fluid level
drops. The world's longest lava tube cave, the Kazumura
Cave on the east slope of Kīlauea Volcano, Hawai'i Island,
is over thirty miles long.   PAMELA FRIERSON

lava field

As lava issuing from a vent or fissure cools, it forms a
surface crust, which often is broken by continued movement underneath into a rubble of sharp-edged hunks,
until eventually the entire flow cools to a halt. Thinner
lavas flow faster, with less surface breakage, sometimes
hardening with ripple marks intact. A lava field is an
area of acres or a few square miles covered by such flows,
relatively unweathered. A lava plain is a larger land
area, usually several hundred square miles, underlain by
lava flows—the Snake River Plain is an example. A lava
plateau is a yet broader, regionally defining feature. The
Columbia Plateau of Oregon, Washington, and western
Idaho was built by a series of voluminous basalt lava
flows that inundated sixty-two thousand square miles
to a maximum depth of nearly three miles. The engine
driving these extraordinary outpourings was the magma
plume that enlivens Yellowstone today. The plume has
held its place in the planet's mantle as the continental
tectonic plate has shifted overtop of it to the west for the
last sixteen million years, at the rate of one or two inches
a year.   JOHN DANIEL

lava fountain

When very fluid lava erupts through the constricted
opening of a narrow volcanic vent, expanding gas bubbles
may cause it to jet, like water from a hose, in a fountain
of glowing, molten rock. The earliest visible event in
the eruption of a shield volcano may be a series of such
fountains, called a "curtain of fire," spewing from a
fissure at the top of the volcano or along a rift zone. On
Hawai'i Island in 1959, lava fountained for several weeks
from a pipelike vent in Kīlauea Iki Crater, adjacent to
the main caldera of Kīlauea Volcano. The vent acted
like a high-pressure nozzle, spraying lava as high as 1,900
feet and spewing cinder downwind for several miles.
That height record was broken by a lava fountain on
Izu-Oshima Volcano in Japan in 1986 that reached over
5,000 feet. The Galileo spacecraft has photographed lava
fountains with an estimated height of one mile on Io, one
of Jupiter's moons. PAMELA FRIERSON

lava tongue

Oceanic basalt volcanoes (such as the Hawaiian volcanoes) produce fluid lava that may advance over these
shield-shaped mountains' gentle slopes in tonguelike
flows. According to volcanologist Robert Decker, such
tongues are typically a few dozen feet wide and a yard
deep, flowing at speeds of from three to thirty miles per
hour. Smaller flows are often called fingers. At the front
of a slow-moving pāhoehoe flow, molten rock pooling
behind the cooling surface of the advancing lava wall
constantly splits open the hardening crust, to emerge in
glowing red bulbous toes. Humans have long referred to
their own anatomy when describing landscape features,
but the uncanny "aliveness" of a fiery, creeping lava flow
perfectly embodies attributes of the Hawaiian volcano
goddess, Pele. In Hawaiian tradition, all aspects of
volcanic creation and destruction, from flows that alter

the landscape to the red ʻōhelo berry bushes that colonize recent lava flows, are considered *kinolau* (literally, "body forms") of the volcano deity. PAMELA FRIERSON

lawn

The older meaning of lawn involved a lot less work, for it derived from the same root as land, referring to a moor, heath, or glade, where nature did the trimming. In eighteenth-century England, the grassy glades designed by Capability Brown and others as parks surrounding stately homes were kept trimmed by sheep, on occasion, and more often by groundskeepers swinging scythes. The invention of the lawn mower in the mid–nineteenth century enabled people of modest means to imitate the romantic parks by sowing their yards to grass. With help from the U.S. Golf Association and the manufacturers of herbicides, fertilizers, sprinkler systems, and gas-powered gear, the vision of a neatly clipped, uniform carpet of green, unblemished by dandelions or other "weeds," has spread across the United States, from wet Boston, where it is merely costly in pollution and dollars and time, to parched Los Angeles, where it is utterly crazy. SCOTT RUSSELL SANDERS

lead

"It doesn't make any sense to try to conquer ice," Peter Høeg has a character say in his novel *Smilla's Sense of Snow*. "I can feel how the sea wants to close us in, how it's merely because of a coincidental, passing constellation of water, wind, and current that we're allowed to continue." Such is the mercurial nature of leads—openings in the ice through which boats and larger vessels can navigate. There is irony in the word, for it suggests a direction one might follow; but leads, short or long, jagged or straight, narrow or wide, often close abruptly, as abruptly as they open—and even if they remain open, they might soon freeze over. Dynamic systems of leads connected to areas of nearshore open water called polynyas permit more light to enter the water, thus stimulating photosynthesis. Like leads, some polynyas may be temporary. (Submariners use the term skylight for polynyas that have recently frozen over, and call an ice canopy full of such polynyas "friendly ice." "Hostile ice" is thick, tight, unrelieved.) Leads provide not only channels for vessels but also breathing space and migratory routes for whales and seals, hunting grounds for polar bears, feeding grounds for sea ducks and alcids, and, occasionally, access for all to open water at the floe edge. Large leads provide dramatic passage for large ships; it is the small leads, however, kayak-size and smaller, that are so vital to wildlife and indigenous culture. Leads also permit the ocean itself to "breathe." This transpiration of heat between the ocean and the atmosphere sometimes creates sea smoke or rising water vapor, or, one might say, the ocean's breath.   GRETCHEN LEGLER

L

ledge

Ledge has applications in mining, architecture, shipbuilding, carpentry, printing, and geology, and is used to describe the outside boundary or overhanging edge of a surface. Ledges can be jagged outward projections, or they can run in long narrow shelves from mountains, cliffs, or buildings. Standing on a ledge, one feels both the precariousness of being suspended above and over a space and the thrill of looking out and being drawn to the beauty and mystery of an expanse. Certainly this is what one experiences when standing on the brittle and crumbling sandstone ledges along the top of Canyon de Chelly in Arizona. And when William Meredith writes, in "The Wreck of the Thresher," "I stand on a ledge where rock runs into the river/As night turns brackish with morning, and mourn the drowned," one fathoms not only the depth of the sea that waits beyond the ledge but the depth of grief that leads the poet to elegize the lost submariners. MICHAEL COLLIER

lek

Lek is a word of Scandinavian origin identifying a particular, traditional area of land or water to which various species congregate, year after year, to enact mating rituals. Among the creatures that mate at leks are pipefish and marine iguanas, and, above all, certain species of birds—notably prairie grouse, sage grouse, and woodcocks. At the avian leks, male birds display in an array of ingenious ways, variously leaping, jousting, strutting, drumming, spiraling into the air, then plummeting to earth in zigzags—all behaviors evolved to attract females of the species. After observing the displays, female birds choose mates based on signs of prowess, including, in some species, the male's ability to maintain a position in the center of the lekking ground. The spectacular events at the leks on the American prairies also impressed the Sioux, Cheyenne, and Shoshone peoples, who incorporated stylized elements of lek displays into some of their dances. Today, many traditional lek grounds have been fragmented or erased altogether by such activities as grazing and agriculture, mining, subdivision and highway construction, and chemical treatments. As suitable lek territories have diminished, the populations of American lekking birds have also declined steeply. Happily, in some areas, including the eastern Texas Panhandle, sustainable ranching techniques are restoring both native grasses and good lek territories. EMILY HIESTAND

levee

A levee is an embankment along a river that resists the overflow of the stream. Derived in the eighteenth century from the French levée, meaning "act of raising," the word refers in modern times especially to the elevated ground along the Mississippi and its tributaries. Natural levees are built up year after year by the deposit of sandy soil on the banks of the flooding river. As the floodwaters rise over the banks, no longer held by the channel, the velocity of the current drops, along with the water's ability to hold sediment. Coarser materials fall out first, and finer silt and clay are carried into the back swamp areas of the floodplain, where they drop out of suspension as the water slows even more. The levees themselves are made of sand and coarser sediments. Man-made levees are constructed to control flooding and protect populated areas along the river. Extensive levees have been built along the Mississippi system. The most famous use of the word is perhaps in the Don McLean song celebrating rock and roll and lamenting the death of Buddy Holly: "Drove my Chevy to the levee/but the levee was dry."   ROBERT MORGAN

L

lick

Salt licks are places, often along rivers and streams, where naturally occurring salt deposits attract animals that come to lick the earth for its mineral gifts. These areas tend to be rich in both biotic and human history. A good example is the Licking River, earlier known as Great Salt Lick Creek, a 320-mile-long river arising in eastern Kentucky and flowing north into the Ohio. The salt licks along its banks drew down mastodons and other great mammals of the Pleistocene whose skeletons are today embedded in the substrate; they so greatly influenced the migratory routes of eastern bison that early European explorers counted more than one thousand at a time at the licks, and Daniel Boone told of seeing buffalo "more frequent than I have ever seen cattle in the settlements." Later, these same springs along the Licking became centers for the human industry of salt-making, strategically important Civil War sites, and, during the nineteenth century, home to bottling plants and grand hotels touting the health benefits of the waters from their springs. The craving of mammalian species for mineral salts is strong and timeless. BARBARA KINGSOLVER

littoral cone

When lava flows into the sea, explosions occur. Fragments, blocks, bits, chunks, and spatters of molten rock are hurled into the air, and some land back on the shore. These pieces of volcanic debris, called according to their forms Pele's tears, Pele's hair, and *limu o Pele* (seaweed of Pele)—all honoring the power and force of the Hawaiian goddess of fire—sometimes accumulate in cone-shaped mounds or hills up to two hundred feet high and four hundred feet across. Called littoral because they're created along the shoreline, in the littoral zone, the cones can be soft and rubbly or solid and craggy, with shells of hardened lava. They may become permanent features of the shoreline or be washed away by waves and storms. There seems no more elemental process of creation than that of the volcano spewing forth hot rock from the center of the Earth, giving newly born land up to the forces of wind, water, and time. Hawaiian myths and chants celebrate the powerful creative and destructive force of Pele and her sister, Hi'iaka. American author Pamela Frierson, in her book *The Burning Island*, quotes one such chant sung by a mythic chief in honor of Pele: "For whom do I make this offering of song?/... For Pele, and for Hi'iaka the land—/This solid ground that swings and floats/Beneath the o'erhanging arch of heaven." GRETCHEN LEGLER

littoral drift

Littoral means of or pertaining to the shore, and littoral drift is material moved along a beach by a littoral current, a current carried by waves breaking at an angle to the shoreline and moving parallel to and adjacent to the shoreline within the surf zone. Littoral drift is, then, the material waves and wind work to shape coastlines, depositing and rearranging the sand, rock, gravel, bits of shell, and other debris to form shoals, spits, bars, and beaches. One example of a high-littoral-drift zone is California's Santa Cruz Harbor, where up to 327,000 cubic yards of drift is deposited each year, enough to cover a football field to a depth of 184 feet.

GRETCHEN LEGLER

lobe

Fluid earth and glacial forms—clay slides, lava flows, sheets and caps of ice, glacial drift—extend themselves from time to time in rounded, tonguelike projections called lobes, sometimes vast in scale. Lobes of the great Pleistocene ice sheet, such as the Des Moines Lobe and the Green Bay Lobe, extended for hundreds of miles, leaving lobate moraines—curvilinear hills that snake across the landscape, marking the terminus of the ice and pauses in its position as the glaciers melted back thousands of years ago. Henry Thoreau, in *Walden,* riffs grandly on much smaller examples. Observing the forms assumed by thawing sand and clay in a raw railroad cut, he finds "moist, thick lobes" suggestive of internal organs verging into leaves, feathers, and wings of "the airy and fluttering butterfly." "The very globe continually transcends and translates itself, and becomes winged in its orbit," he exults, and concludes: "There is nothing inorganic." JOHN DANIEL

loblolly

Loblolly pine, *Pinus taeda,* occurs widely throughout the southeastern United States. Aurally, the luscious assonance and mellifluous liquidity of its given name are sufficient to evoke some moonlit, blossom-saturated southern dreamscape all on their own. Loblolly is in fact a rather unpoetically onomatopoetic word—one meant to suggest the bubbling and plopping of a pot of thick glop simmering on a stove. In British nautical usage, it referred primarily to any gruel or porridgelike entree not greatly relished; secondarily, it referred to any unappetizing medicine of similar consistency, for which reason the ship's surgeon's assistant was called a loblolly boy. In America, a loblolly was a mudhole—a gooey, gelatinous mess suggestive of naval cuisine. Loblolly pine could tolerate low bottomlands, where loblollies were the bane of loggers trying to extract them from the swamps. As a noun, loblolly is now obsolescent, if not obsolete. The tree preserves it. FRANKLIN BURROUGHS

loess

Loess is windborne dust found in vast deposits in North America, north-central Europe, and Asia. Blown from glacial outwash plains at the edge of Pleistocene ice sheets, from deserts, and from river floodplains, it has accumulated in vast deposits. Thirty percent of the United States is blanketed in this ice-age eolian silt, which, along with other elements, has developed into the fertile agricultural soils of the Mississippi Valley, parts of the Great Plains, and the Palouse Hills of the Columbia River basin. Iowa's Loess Hills feature an extraordinarily deep deposit, two hundred feet thick in places. Loess is generally yellowish brown. Its silty particles make it porous, crumbly, and prone to erosion. Still, loess can stand in vertical, albeit vulnerable, cliffs. Scientists believe this is because loess is well sorted, allowing particles of similar size and geometries to pack together. CAROLYN SERVID

long-lot field

Before the township-and-range survey grid was imposed on most of the western two-thirds of the United States,

land along rivers was often divided into narrow strips
running at right angles to the stream, like ribs stretching away from a spine. Such long-lot fields gave the
maximum number of settlers access to the river for
transportation and, in dry regions, for irrigation. Crops
needing the most water could be planted near the stream,
while crops needing less could be planted farther back. In
Spanish America, the width of these lots was measured
in lengths called *varas* (eventually defined by the Texas
legislature as thirty-three inches), and thus early deeds
for allotments on the Rio Grande and other southwestern
rivers refer to such fields as vara strips. In Quebec, along
the St. Lawrence and its tributaries, the ratio of length
to width of these long-lot fields ranged from 10-to-1 to
100-to-1.   SCOTT RUSSELL SANDERS

longshore bar

Visible at low tide as a sand bar, or a ridge of beach sediment sharing the general contour of the shoreline itself,
a longshore bar is actually a feature sculpted by the push
and pull of years of waves. It only seems to share the
general contour of the shoreline because the break point
of the waves (a point determined by depth) tends to be
equidistant from shore—which itself has of course been
rounded off or leveled by waves—lending any bar that
shares its contour a generally level, or straight, appearance. However, this is just a function of the break point:
the bottom current necessary to feed the shoreward
current of a wave pulls silt in with it, then, the moment
the wave breaks, deposits it, in the same place, time after
time. That deposit—that steady accretion of silt—is the
longshore bar. Due to the redistribution of silt, there
will often be a trough between the longshore bar and
the beach itself. Seaward of the longshore bar are other
longshore bars at the break point of larger waves. A distinct but related action is longshore drift, which results

when the waves strike the beach at an angle instead of straight on. Instead of forming a stable longshore bar, beach sediment is pulled deeper and deeper into the breaker zone—"passed back," effectively. If groins (small jetties extending from shore) aren't erected to trap this sediment and redistribute the effects of longshore drift downcurrent, the erosion can radically resculpt the shoreline. STEPHEN GRAHAM JONES

looking-glass prairie

Nineteenth-century settlers were astounded by the grandeur of prairies on the western plains, particularly those christened looking-glass prairies for their elegant curving shapes and their surprising reflectivity. These gleaming prairie wetlands (circumnavigated by prairie schooners)—great shallow basins of sedges, reflecting sky and landscape and nurturing fish, waterfowl, and other animals—were initiated by glaciers retreating from the Central Lowlands, which stretch west from the Mississippi River across the Great Plains. The term is generic, although it can be specific, as in the 1829 third volume of *Travels in North America*, where B. Hall writes of one prairie that was "particularly beautiful of its kind, and named Looking Glass Prairie." Such prairies engender optical illusions and mystical revelations, and it's worth noting that L. Frank Baum set his Oz books in the magical prairies of Kansas. But alas, most settlers considered looking-glass prairies useless impediments, and busily drained and plowed them. DONNA SEAMAN

lookout

From Cape Lookout on the Core Banks of North Carolina to Tecate Peak lookout on the California-Mexico border, a lookout is an eminence or prominence from which a useful view is possible. (Overlook carries the same meaning in some parts of the country.) There are scores of Lookout Mountains across the continent, each, no doubt, with a story of its naming. The founders of a settlement near Tennessee's Lookout Mountain picked for the town's name the Creek Indian word for "rock rising to a point," spelling it Chattanooga. From the beginnings of North American history, Indians, explorers, settlers, cattlemen, soldiers, and outlaws in need of an improved outlook have made use of countless natural lookouts. Put a tower on a peak and a fire guard in the tower, and lookout means the peak, the tower, or the person, all in two quick syllables.   JOHN DANIEL

louderback

Named after the geologist G.D. Louderback, who first described the phenomenon, the term louderback refers to a tilted ridge or slope that's been capped by a lava flow. In the Basin and Range province, where louderbacks are common, it's easy to see how the lava flowed onto the surfaces before they were tilted. If it can be established that the lava flow is of late geologic age, there is justification for assuming that associated scarps were produced by faulting.   ANTONYA NELSON

lover's leap

It is not known whether each of the sites listed under this name by the United States Geological Survey commemorates a tragic jump by one or more doomed lovers. But these fifty-two places hold enough topographical features in common to warrant a definition. Lover's leap is a colloquial term describing a landmark, typically a cliff or bluff, varying in height from fifty to two hundred feet, but usually possessing the following: a promontory where a troubled lover, or lovers, might contemplate a final act; a beautiful, often exceptional view; and a quota of free fall with necessary dramatic effect, often including a swirling lake or river below. There are eight lover's leaps in Missouri and four in Texas. Mark Twain once wrote that there were at least fifty such high bluffs up and down the Mississippi River alone.   LAN SAMANTHA CHANG

lowland

The central interior of the United States, a region bordered by the Rocky Mountains on the west and the Appalachians on the east, is a vast example of a lowland, or a low-lying, level expanse of countryside. During the Pleistocene ice age, huge glaciers moved into the region from Canada, covering most of the great wedge of land between the Missouri and Ohio Rivers, smoothing and flattening its contours. This glacially modified region is today called the Central Lowlands.   MARY SWANDER

mainland

The term mainland suggests some immense solidity, as opposed to the fragmentation of land into islands. An island is limited and has a periphery, but the mainland is thought of as an indefinite mass, which goes on to the horizon. Mainland is always a relative term. The American continent was perceived by the first European explorers as an island in the way of China, and they pushed inland to get to the end of it. The state of Maine takes its name from "the main," the mainland as opposed to the many islands the explorers found off the coast. One geographical dictionary gives this example of the use of the term: "Two islands, north of Newfoundland, were given over to the fiends from whom they derived their name, the Isles of Demons. The passing voyager heard the din of their infernal orgies . . . 'and all who dwelt there have fled for refuge to the main.'" Mainland is used by residents of Hawai'i for the continental United States, and used frequently in the summer colonies on Nantucket, Martha's Vineyard, and Fishers Island in the common phrase "I'm going over to the mainland to buy . . ." As Elizabeth Bishop once wrote about her New Haven, Maine, home, "The cows come here and get island sick & have to be taken for a trip to the mainland." There is some question as to whether the word comes from the Greek *monos* (single) or *megas* (big). Donne's "no man is an island, alone unto himself, but every man is a part of the main" presents the paradox of the human condition, the mystery of whether, or how, in the mass of humanity, there can be such a thing as an individual.   SUSAN BRIND MORROW

malpais

Often the test of endurance in western adventure novels, the malpais of the Southwest are regions of basaltic lava and mesas very difficult to cross, especially on foot or horseback, as more than suggested in Cormac McCarthy's

Blood Meridian: "On the day following they crossed the malpais afoot, leading the horses upon a lakebed of lava all cracked and reddish black like a pan of dried blood, threading those badlands of dark amber glass like the remnants of some dim legion scrabbling up out of a land accursed... a cinderland of caked slurry and volcanic ash as imponderable as the burned-out floor of hell." As McCarthy establishes, malpais translates into English simply as "badlands." As his "pan of dried blood" suggests, to both the Pueblo and Navajo peoples of the region the malpais is the blood of a great monster slain by hero twins. Either way, the message is clear: the malpais is hostile, unforgiving. While in general usage badland can refer to any area of loose soil or rock radically eroded by rain and runoff, malpais tends to be reserved for that area of northwestern New Mexico that features a combination of lava and sandstone formations—flows, cinder cones, tubes, bridges, pressure ridges, bluffs—and, of course, all the animals who call the malpais home, and who don't think it's that bad a place.   STEPHEN GRAHAM JONES

manche

French for the sleeve, *la manche* is used as a proper noun in France to describe that body of water known to the British—more possessively—as the English Channel. Similar long and narrow waterways carry the name in French-influenced parts of North America. For instance, Newfoundland's La Manche Provincial Park is named for the sleevelike harbor near St. John's, a thin watery strip with high, steep sides.   MIKE TIDWELL

mangrove swamp

To poet Elizabeth Bishop, mangroves made up the "celestial landscape" of Florida, with herons in "tiers and tiers of immaculate reflection" shining whitely among the leaves. She compared the roots of one mangrove, a red mangrove, *Rhizophora mangle*, to Gothic arches because of its distinctive bower of aerial roots and numerous finger-like breather roots—pneumatophores—rising from the mud. Though mangroves flourish worldwide in tropical and subtropical areas, this particular one, the red, can be found only in Florida, while the white and black are found in Florida and elsewhere. Possessing all three of these salt-loving, tropical-zone trees, Florida has luxuriant mangrove "forests." The red is the great colonizer, its foot-long seedlings dropping and rooting in the protective tangle of detritus below, or drifting off in storm-season tides to implant themselves elsewhere. Mangroves are essential to many water birds for rookeries and rest—the brown pelican nests almost exclusively on mangrove islands—and the watery, airy mazes the trees provide are favored by lobster, tarpon, and manatee alike. A peculiar environment, the mangrove swamp: displeasing to man in its tangled impenetrability, but celestial to a great and lovely multitude that is not man. JOY WILLIAMS

M

marais

Marais is French for marsh or swamp, but in Louisiana French it means pool, slough, or even bayou. American place-names that incorporate the term range from Marais Saline Lake in Arkansas to Marais des Cygnes, a noted waterfowl area in Kansas. MIKE TIDWELL

marine terrace

A marine terrace is a coastal landform, usually a broad, horizontal platform made up of sediments and broken, water-ground and water-polished material cut from sea-cliff faces by breaking waves. South of Monterey, California, the terrace and wave-carved cliffs of the Carmelo formation show the history of life at the edge of Earth, relics of sea creatures embedded in sandstone, fossilized worm burrows, and the preserved remnants of collapsed canyon walls and ancient underwater landslides. These cliff faces reveal where lava once flowed, which is even now being broken and rounded into the sheets of dark pebbles and cobbles that mark parts of the terrace. At the edge of the Pacific plate farther south, at Torrey Pines State Beach, the forces of water carved a lagoon, which filled with mud when the sea rose. Terrace features of the Delmar formation there include flat expanses of exposed rock and, underneath the layers of mudstone and sandstone, a bed of fossilized oyster shells. Middens left by earlier people sometimes turn up in the cliffs, layers of ancient trees come to light. The ocean's force breaks all of it down and works it, wave after wave, into the terrace slope. A drop in sea level or continental uplift can leave marine terraces isolated as marine benches. In areas such as Big Sur and Bodega Bay, California, a series of old marine terraces with steep front slopes and gently inclined tops descends to the sea.   LINDA HOGAN

marsh

A wetland tyro may find himself wondering whether he is standing in a marsh or a swamp. Looking down will not solve the problem—his feet will be wet in either case. But if he surveys the area and finds it composed primarily of grasses, rushes, reeds, and cattails, he can be confident it is a marsh he inhabits—swamps are dominated by trees. If he dips a finger in the water and raises it to his lips, he will know if he is in a coastal salt marsh, whose hay is much prized by gardeners for mulch. In general terms, marshes are likely to be found in the North and called swamps in the South, with ciénega the preferred term for marsh throughout parts of the West. Fresh or saline, tropical or temperate, marshes are crucial and fecund habitat, having lent their name to species as diverse as the marsh hawk and marsh marigold. As the author Bern Keating writes, "Poets who know no better rhapsodize about the peace of nature, but a well-populated marsh is a cacophony." BILL MCKIBBEN

massif

The word massif is French, meaning literally "massive." It refers to a compact and more or less independent mountain mass, either protruded through the Earth's crust or depressed as a unit and often bounded by faults. Not to be confused with the summit alone, massif refers to the entire configuration. A massif is composed of rocks more rigid than those of its surroundings, and from a different, often more ancient time. Examples are the Chain Lakes massif in the northern Appalachians and the Yukon Territory's Mount Logan, the second highest mountain in North America. JOHN KEEBLE

meadow

M

Land covered with grasses, or a grassy field, or other discernable area of grassland either mown for hay or used as pasture is known as a meadow. Also, though rarely, the hay that is mown from this area. The term is used either to denote a "natural" (uncultivated) meadow or one planted to enhance the presence of particular flowers or to discourage the invasion of others. This distinction between an uncultivated and cultivated meadow usually depends on the context in which the word is used. Thus, a meadow can be wild or landscaped, but in general a healthy meadow has fifty percent of its surface in some form of grass. (Subalpine meadows, however, are dominated by herbaceous plants.) In North American usage, meadow refers most often, though not exclusively, to a tract of uncultivated grassland, often along a river or in a marshy region, as described by James Galvin in *The Meadow*: "There is an island on the island which is a meadow, offered up among the ridges, wearing a necklace of waterways, concentrically nested inside the darker

green of pines, and then the gray-green of sage and the
yellow-green of prairie grass." Though rare, meadow
can mean—chiefly in Newfoundland—an area of sea
ice where seals come out of the water in large numbers,
thus also seal meadow. Meadow is often a modifier
or part of a compound noun, as in meadow flower,
meadowlark, meadow mouse. This modifying habit
is especially notable in the names of plants, denoting
species that thrive in meadows, such as meadow barley,
meadow buttercup, meadow campion, meadow clover,
and meadow crocus. Sometimes the linkage creates an
entirely new and figurative meaning, as in meadow silver,
an obsolete term for a cash payment made in lieu of the
feudal service of mowing. Meadow thatch is another such
term, meaning the coarse grass or rush used for roofing a
cottage. There is as well the term salt meadow, which is a
grassy area subject to flooding or overflow by salt water.
The etymology of meadow is directly related to mead,
the alcoholic beverage made by fermenting honey and
water. And mead, in turn, may have been a noun-form
of the adjective meaning "sweet" in many old forms of
languages as diverse as Frisian, Dutch, Icelandic, Swedish, Gothic, Sanskrit, Irish, Breton, and Church Slavonic.

PATRICIA HAMPL

meander

Although humans more often name the land in terms of
themselves (finger lake, headwall, a neck of land, etc.),
sometimes the reverse takes place and a human behavior
takes its name from a feature of the Earth. The river
Menderes, which rises in what is today western Turkey
and was known among the ancient Greeks as the Maian-
dros of Phrygia, flows to the Aegean with such seeming
reluctance that it continually doubles back on itself,
wreathing its floodplain in loop after serpentine loop of
wandering channel. The name of the river, descended to

modern English from Greek, gives us meander, which is
our best verb for expressing randomness in thought and
movement. The coinage is not without its irony, however, for the meandering of a river is only superficially
random. If one thinks of a river or stream as energy
moving through terrain, one can begin to see the ordered
sinuosity of a meandering channel as the expression of
how that energy is spent by the river and absorbed by
the land. A river does two kinds of work: it transports its
volume of water downhill, and it also transports some
amount of earthen freight consisting of silt suspended in
water (suspended load) and rocks and gravel tumbling
and skipping along the riverbed (bed load). If by virtue of
velocity or volume a river has more energy than it needs
to accomplish its work, it will spend that extra energy
to reshape its course. Sometimes a river will incise its
channel, ultimately lowering its bed, which is a way of
diminishing the gradient at which it moves downhill; this
in turn diminishes its velocity and the energy it has to
spend. In other instances a river will extend its channel
laterally by carving a series of curves or meanders. Here
the river diminishes its gradient by lengthening the
distance over which it descends a given amount of elevation. Meander formation is especially characteristic of
rivers that flow through soft material and lack the erosive
tools (i.e., bed load) to incise their channels. The Mississippi, twining from Cairo, Illinois, to New Orleans, is a
classic meanderer, while the canyon-carving Colorado
River is the Mississippi's incisive opposite. (The famous
goosenecks of the San Juan River in southeastern Utah
are an anomalous hybrid of both processes. They consist
of meanders incised into canyons hundreds of feet deep,
the formation of which no one fully understands.) The
physics of meandering are consistent across all scales of
flowing water, from great streams like the Mississippi to
rivulets of meltwater on the surface of a glacier. Notably,

M

the distance from the apex of one meander to the next, known as the wavelength of the meander, tends to be seven to fifteen times the width of the channel. Also noteworthy is the fact that meandering is not restricted to terrestrial waters and distractible humans. Ocean currents like the Gulf Stream meander, as do the jet stream and other currents of air.   WILLIAM DEBUYS

meander scar

When a flooding river straightens its channel by eroding a cut-off across the neck of a meander, it leaves behind an abandoned loop of former channel, a meander scar. If groundwater seepage or overflow from the river fills the scar with water, it becomes an oxbow lake. Eventually, however, sediment and vegetation accumulate in an oxbow to such an extent that only the depressed scar of the former channel remains. Meander scars develop at multiple scales, from small creeks to great rivers. They are typically wetter and biologically richer than surrounding lands, and seen from above, their crescent shapes impart a dimpled beauty to the land.
WILLIAM DEBUYS

meander valley

A meander valley winds sinuously through the landscape in deep, large, sweeping curves that repeat themselves in shape and size. The valley's slopes are steep on the outside bends of the meander, more gentle on the inside. Many such valleys once contained large rivers, but now are home to smaller streams that carve their own scaled-down meanders through abundant alluvium deposits on the valley floor.   CAROLYN SERVID

medano

Medano is a Spanish word meaning "a sand dune that exists along a seashore." To American geologists, however, this term has come to signify a bare dune of immense proportions that migrates in the wind, consuming everything in its path. Just downwind (east-northeast) from Great Sand Dunes National Park in Colorado's Sangre de Cristo Range is Medano Pass. Medanos ranging in height from twenty-five to one hundred feet once dotted the mid-Atlantic coast south of the Chesapeake Bay, but since the early twentieth century they have tended to flatten out, a trend hastened by coastal development. Once common, fields of open sand have been replaced by houses with grassy yards, leaving scant loose sediment to nourish the great dunes. In the 1970s Jockeys Ridge, a well-known medano on the North Carolina Outer Banks, stood at 110 feet, the highest dune on the East Coast. It now measures less than eighty feet. Nonetheless, the dune has shown itself to be indomitable. Blown by the wind, it is migrating quickly southwest, covering houses and roadways as it moves.   JAN DEBLIEU

M

meltpond

Meltponds form on polar sea ice when temperatures rise during summer months. They are more common in the Arctic, where they often originate at the site of seal-breathing holes, than in the Antarctic. Some (bottomless) ponds appear almost black; others take on a striking turquoise hue from the sea ice beneath them. Because meltponds are darker than the surrounding ice, they absorb rather than reflect the twenty-four-hour Arctic summer light and warmth. The balance between this absorption and reflection of the sun's energy is a significant climate factor in the Arctic. Scientists know that the Arctic sea-ice cover has decreased significantly in the last thirty years, and are monitoring the ratio of meltponds to ice during summer months to determine the extent to which the ponds accelerate sea-ice melting.

CAROLYN SERVID

mere

Now chiefly regional or poetic, mere is a lake or a pond, or sometimes the sea or an inlet of the sea, even a marsh or fen. In rare, obsolete usage, mere means a siren or mermaid, and sometimes simply mother (from Old French). A mere also indicates a boundary and is often commemorated by a place-name, such as Lake Windermere. The boundary between two fields might be marked by merestones or a mere path. In English mining terminology, mere is a linear measurement along a vein of ore, or a division of a vein of ore allocated to a miner. The etymology of mere can be traced back through a dense network of early European languages that denote, in various forms, the sea.   PATRICIA HAMPL

mesa

In the North American landscape a mesa, which in Spain is merely a dinner table, occupies a grander scale: a flat-topped mountain or rock mass, usually capped with a weather-resistant rock stratum, it stands above an arid plain as a remnant of eons of erosion. Mesas and their smaller relatives, buttes—a butte is taller than it is wide, a mesa wider than it is tall—figure in place-names through-out the semiarid lands of Utah, New Mexico, Arizona, and Colorado. The world's most famous mesa-and-butte landscape, in the Navajo Nation Monument Valley Tribal Park of northeastern Arizona and southeastern Utah, has so regularly served as the backdrop of cowboy movies and other manufactured visions of the American West that these unusual landforms are mistakenly assumed, throughout the world, to be the dominant feature of the western landscape. Mesas, in art, also commonly co-occur with another cliché of the Southwest, the saguaro cactus with its pair of raised arms, even though that plant has a limited range and does not grow within two hundred miles of Monument Valley.   BARBARA KINGSOLVER

mezquital

The mezquital is an ecoregion in southwestern Texas through which the Lower Rio Grande flows. While it contains coastal tidal flats and brush-covered dunes, the mezquital is characteristically a savannalike grassland broken by open woods of mesquite trees with an understory of lesser shrubs. Mezquital also describes the scrub vegetation that reclaims rangeland, often with relatively uniform stands of the mesquite trees that outperform other early colonizers of abandoned land in southwestern Texas. A mezquital is an unruly and haphazard zone, as remembered by one Laredo resident to his local newspaper: "If we got some beer, we would cruise the streets being ever wary of the police.... Our favorite drinking spot was the lush mezquital where Nixon High School now stands." D. J. WALDIE

midden

M

A midden is a mound, of varying size and composition, created by animals or human beings. The middens of desert wood rats (*Neotoma lepida*), also called pack rats, are often constructed around the base of prickly pear and cholla cactus, where they form virtually impregnable fortresses against predators. In addition to bones, fur, teeth, and other collected animal remains, their midden nests include twigs and hardy plant material, as well as found objects, from walnut shells to belt buckles. Some preserved pack-rat middens are large enough and old enough to contain many thousands of years of evolutionary history for a single species—a meadow vole, say—offering scientists an unprecedented record of how a species has changed and evolved, and how its evolution has been affected by climate change. Middens created by human beings comprise all the leftovers from village life—worn out clothing, broken pots and tools, unrepairable toys. In *Wind in the Rock*, Ann Zwinger writes of an

Anasazi midden at the base of Junction Ruin in Grand Gulch, Utah, that produced "pieces of corn cob, soft cotton string, shreds of bark (used for bedding and diapers), turkey feathers" used in making blankets and capes, and yucca fibers, for which the Anasazi had many uses. In her memoir *Already Home*, Barbara Gates painstakingly describes one of the more than 425 shell mounds found around the rim of San Francisco Bay, writing that these middens were composed mainly of charcoal, ash, and shells—kitchen life.   TERRY TEMPEST WILLIAMS

middle ground

Ground need not imply dry land. Its original meaning was closer to "bottom." Thus ground fish, like cod or haddock, are species that feed on the seafloor. The grounds of coffee are the dregs, the sediment that settles from the brew. Middle grounds are sandbars or mudflats found in the middle of a tidal channel; water flows on either side of them. They characteristically occur near the entrance or exit of a constricted passage. They are sedimentary deposits, like coffee grounds, and are precipitated by eddies and counter-currents. They may or may not be visible at low tide, but, at some stage of the tide, they are near enough to the surface for vessels to run aground on. The politician infallibly steers for the metaphoric middle ground, the shifting shallows created by current events. Not so the honest sailor.   FRANKLIN BURROUGHS

milk gap

A term once common in Tennessee, the Carolinas, Kentucky, and Arkansas, a milk gap is, variously, any outdoor place where cows are milked; the structure that encloses such a place; or, in mountainous areas, an actual gap or notch in the hills through which farmers bring their cows for milking. In keeping with the variations in meaning, milk gaps can be located at some distance from the main farmhouse (in *Smoky Mountain Mysteries*, Juanitta Baldwin writes: "Lucius and Almarine lit lanterns, picked up zinc buckets, and set off over a path up the hill to the milk gap") or fairly close by (in an oral story collected by Silas Turnbo, a resident of Wileys Cove, Arkansas, reported that "near 10 o'clock in the night while the calves were at the milk gap I heard a great racket out there—I knew a savage beast had attacked the calf but having no dog and as the night was very dark I was afraid to run out to the milk gap to try to scare the beast away"). The sense of a milk gap as a physical structure is given in Robert Morgan's *Brave Enemies*, a novel set in the eighteenth-century Carolinas: "'We must all do our share to help your darling mother,' Mr. Griffin said. He said it while he leaned on the milk gap and I carried leaves to spread in the cow stall." EMILY HIESTAND

M

mima mound

Mima mounds are sometimes called pimple mounds and vice versa, but the two formations are geographically and geologically distinct. Mima mounds derive their name from the Mima Prairie, near Olympia, Washington, where they abound. They occur in dry, grassy upland areas of the West. They are up to six feet high and up to 30 feet across. They are often attributed to the subterranean exertions of pocket gophers, over many generations. Writing from southern California, Alfred Wallace advises filling a shallow pan with eggs, lying on their sides and with their axes unaligned, then pouring fine sand into the pan until the eggs are half buried. This, he says, "gives a fair representation" of a mima plain. Such plains are colloquially called hog wallows. One presumes some poetic soul saw the low mounds and thought of recumbent swine. FRANKLIN BURROUGHS

mineral spring

Mineral springs contain a high proportion of mineral salts in solution, including calcium carbonate, magnesium sulfate, potassium, and sodium sulfate. Formed through natural geological processes and through the decomposition and fossilization of animals, the mineral matter gives water a definite taste, distinct from ordinary drinking water. A mineral spring is often described in terms of its principal characteristic constituent—for example, salt spring or sulfur spring. Given their therapeutic value for the treatment of rheumatism, arthritis, skin diseases, and various other ailments, sulfur springs have become popular sites for spas and resorts worldwide, such as those at Saratoga Springs in upstate New York. The United States and Canada have over two hundred commercial hot springs and mineral springs, along with thousands of smaller noncommercial springs.

JEFFERY RENARD ALLEN

misfit stream

A misfit stream is one that is out of proportion to its valley. The reference is usually to a stream significantly smaller than the valley might accommodate. One place that exemplifies this term better than any other is Paradox Valley, near the settlement of Bedrock in southwestern Colorado, where the Dolores River flows across rather than along the valley. This is David Lavender's impression of this stretch of the Dolores, in *One Man's West*: "It pierces the bastion wall in a titanic, crimson-cliffed canyon of singular beauty, spills sluggishly over the table-flat valley floor in a series of horseshoe coils, gathers itself, and plunges out the northern side in another echoing gorge." A less dramatic misfit stream is found in nearby Unaweep Canyon. Misfit streams may have lost water to climatic changes, to the capture of their water source by another stream, or to the seepage of water down into the floodplain. They are sometimes found in larger meandering valleys, where they carve new smaller meanders into the alluvium deposits on the valley floor. And occasionally misfit streams come about because the valley itself was enlarged during glaciation, though the right term here is usually underfit stream. Valleys cut by glacial meltwaters but whose stream channels today gather only the runoff from rainfall are common in the middle United States, but these disproportionate watercourses are also properly underfit streams.   CAROLYN SERVID

mofette

French for noxious gas and similar to the Italian word *mofeta*, meaning "noxious exhalation," a mofette is a type of fumarole (a vent in the Earth's surface from which gases erupt) characterized by its high carbon dioxide emissions at temperatures much below the boiling point. Mofette refers both to the opening itself and to the gas emitted, which, along with carbon dioxide, can contain oxygen, nitrogen, and water vapors. Mofettes indicate a late stage in minor volcanic activity, such as in the Phlegraean Fields near Naples; at Auvergne in central France; in Java; and at Yellowstone National Park.
KIM BARNES

mogote

While the Spanish word *mogote* can mean "knoll" or "hummock," in south Texas it refers specifically to patches of impenetrable thorny brush growing in clay-loam soils mainly along the coastal prairies, and especially in Cameron and Willacy Counties. (The Spanish use of *mogote* for knoll is found on the American landscape at the western edge of the San Luis Valley in Colorado—Los Mogotes.) Mogotes serve as ideal bird-nesting areas and are the primary habitat for endangered ocelots and jaguarundi. A small patch of this ultrathick brush is called a mogotito. Occasionally, the word is used to describe a stack of corn. In *A Vaquero of the Brush Country*, John D. Young and J. Frank Dobie write: "Here are mogotes (thick patches) of the evergreen, stubborn, beautiful *coma* with dirk-like thorns, and, in season, with blue berries which the Mexican dove likes so much that it constantly coos—if we are to believe the Mexican folk—*comer comas, comer comas*, saying that it wants to eat coma berries." ARTURO LONGORIA

mogul

When skiers turn their way down a slope, the ruts they cut outline bumps called moguls. Once the mogul has begun to raise its head, subsequent skiers tend to follow similar paths around it, deepening the grooves and hence raising the bump. Ski resort operators take two opposing tacks with these human-caused landforms. On some slopes they groom them flat each night to make the skiing easier; on others they allow them to grow, in hopes of attracting the most intrepid downhillers. BILL MCKIBBEN

monadnock

Though all land erodes, that erosion is never perfect; where harder rocks resist, an isolated mountain or hill called a monadnock can rise above the reduced plain, an unassimilated remnant of the loftier previous geology. The word comes from the Abenaki Indians, with one possible meaning of "mountain that stands alone." They used it to name the classic example of the formation, a 3,165-foot peak that rises from the flatter lands of south-west New Hampshire. Divorced from any range, it offers spectacular views in all directions; because of that (and its convenience to Boston), Mount Monadnock lures more hikers than any peak on Earth save Mount Fuji. In the climactic chapter of *Moby-Dick*, Melville describes Ahab as "fairly within the smoky mountain mist, which, thrown off from the whale's spout, curled round his great, Monadnock hump." BILL MCKIBBEN

monte

The Spanish word *monte* can mean "mountain," "woodland" or "forest." But for Mexico's indigenous people, and for *la mestizaje*—those of mixed European and Indian blood—the word carries an intrinsic spiritual significance, for the monte is not simply a place of corporeal sustenance but also a site of metaphysical renewal. Historically, the people found edible plants and animals as well as medicinal and curative herbs, or *yerbas,* within *el monte.* Whether atop a mountain or beneath the sheltering shades of myriad trees, the *monte* also possessed religious and ethereal symbols and signs—a power, it seemed, creating a sanctuary that aided in directing one's life. In recent times, monte has been used to refer to any place "out of town," from which one infers a locale removed from the stresses of city life, an area of tranquillity and quiet. ARTURO LONGORIA

moraine

One could do worse than simply to quote Joseph Le Conte, from *A Journal of Ramblings through the High Sierra of California,* published in 1875. Le Conte, the first professor of geology at the University of California, was on a hiking and exploring trip in Yosemite with John Muir when he made the following notes: "On the surface, and about the foot of glaciers, are always found immense piles of heterogeneous debris consisting of rock fragments of all sizes, mixed with earth. These are called moraines. On the surface, the most usual form and place is a long heap, often twenty to fifty feet high, along each side, next to the bounding cliffs. These are called lateral moraines.

They are ruins of the crumbling cliffs on each side, drawn out into a continuous line by the motion of the glacier. If glaciers are without tributaries, these lateral moraines are all the debris on their surface; but if glaciers have tributaries, then the two interior lateral moraines of the tributaries are carried down the middle of the glacier, as a medial moraine. There is a medial moraine for every tributary. In complicated glaciers, therefore, the whole surface may be nearly covered with debris. All these materials, whether lateral or medial, are borne slowly onward by the motion of the glacier, and finally deposited at its foot, in the form of a huge, irregularly crescentic pile of debris known as the terminal moraine." We might add to this the term ground moraine, which refers to a thinner veneer of glacial till laid down over a broad area. Spectacular nested lateral and end moraines extend out from the eastern front of the Sierra Nevada at Lee Vining Canyon. Lakes are found occupying the valleys behind many of these landforms. Kettle Moraine State Forest, northwest of Milwaukee, Wisconsin, is also the site of numerous moraines. On the other side of the country, Cape Cod owes its shape to the terminal moraine there, though some of the cape's outlines have been modified by waves.   ROBERT HASS

morro

A morro is a promontory overlooking a harbor or a hill with good prospects for armed vigilance. Fortified heights in the Spanish Americas often contain *morro* in their name. Morro is sometimes confused with moro. A morro is a sentry hill, while moro is both the name of the North African Islamic culture driven from Spain by 1492 and a color that ranges from dark brown to near black. Still, a morro may be a hill as round as a turban and dark as Othello. El Morro, on the trail to the Zuni Pueblo, is the towering "Inscription Rock" on which the

Spanish reconquest of New Mexico in 1692 was recorded, along with a thousand other travelers' graffiti before and since. Morro Rock in Morro Bay in central California is one of a line of exposed volcanic plugs called the Nine Morros, named in 1542 by the explorer Juan Rodríguez Cabrillo.   D. J. WALDIE

moulin

A moulin is a sinkhole forming a vertical shaft in the surface of a glacier. It is worn into the ice and sometimes into the rock beneath, by the circular movement of meltwater, swirling down it. The name, from the French word for mill, as in Moulin Rouge, comes from the motion of the water. The following observation by an experienced mountaineer may help one keep in mind the distinction between a crevice and a moulin: "Falls into crevices are often not serious, or at least are survivable (even unroped if you are lucky), but a fall into a moulin is instant death."   ROBERT HASS

M

mound

To baseball fans, a mound is where the pitcher stands to throw the ball; to geographers and archeologists, respectively, it's a rounded elevation or small hill, or an artificial mount or rounded earthwork made of piled stones or soil. Artificial mounds may be angular or rounded at their base, raised in the shape of a cone or a pyramid, but with a flat top, or built up in the shape of an animal, a so-called totemic mound. Archeologists have studied a wide variety of mostly burial mounds erected by a succession of Native American cultures, beginning with Adena societies about four thousand years ago in the upper Ohio River valley. Adena structures were followed by a more diverse array of earthen mounds constructed on a much grander scale by societies of the Hopewell culture, who carried this architecture farther down the Ohio, to its confluence with the Mississippi. With the decline of the Hopewell culture around A.D. 500, societies of the Mississippian culture further diversified mound building, and these massive and extensive forms—one Hopewell earthwork enclosed an area of four square miles—spread from the upper Mississippi River valley into the American South, as far east as New York State, and out into the Great Plains. Susan Brind Morrow describes such a site in upstate New York in her book *Wolves and Honey:* "The first settlers to farm the land around Kanadesaga agreed not to disturb the burial mound of raw earth, five feet high and forty feet around, that stood in an open field where a Mrs. Campbell, a captive from the massacre at Cherry Valley who was still alive among them, had witnessed one of the last of the Seneca tribal rituals: the sacrifice of a white dog at the end of winter." Today, the range of artificial mounds, from simple structures that might have been built by just a few people in a day or two to structures that must have required the labor of thousands of people over a period of years, are preserved at such places as Mound City Group National Monument, Ohio; Effigy Mounds National Monument, Iowa; and Ocmulgee National Monument, Georgia. The word is also widely used to refer to piles of soil created at tunnel entrances by burrowing animals such as gophers, badgers, prairie dogs, and coyotes.   ELIZABETH COX

mountain

A mountain is land that rises above the surrounding plain. But it is not simply higher than a hill; the very word mountain also implies a brand of majesty. On a mountain, normal processes are magnified—their steep slopes, for instance, mean streams flow faster and carry more rock of larger size, accelerating erosion. Mountains can create their own weather, as clouds dump their cargo on the windward side. And they carry their own heightened psychological charge as well: Thoreau, in a spiritual fright as he bushwhacked up Maine's Katahdin, imagined that "some part of the beholder, even some vital part, seems to escape through the loose grating of his ribs as he ascends." Though by conventional measurement the planet's tallest mountains are all in Asia, Hawai'i can claim its most massive: by the reckoning of one geologist, measuring from the seafloor, the Mauna Loa volcano is the "largest projected landmass between Mars and the Sun." BILL MCKIBBEN

mouth

Applied to land features, mouth is a term for all manner of surface openings, including the crater of a volcano as well as the entrances and exits to canyons, valleys, and caves. A mouth is also the place where one waterway empties into a larger body of water, for example where a river flows into the sea. (The mouth is considered the last identifiable portion of the smaller tributary before it merges with the larger entity.) Place-names derived from mouth include the Mouth of River Styx Landing, in Mississippi County, Arkansas; and Mouth of the Maravillas, at Bourland Canyon, Texas. Other American place-names arise from two Algonquian words for mouth: *sawacotuck*, which means "mouth of the tidal stream," is the basis for the name of Saugatuck, Michigan, a town located at the mouth of Kalamazoo River. *Saco*, the Algonquian word for "flowing out" or "river-mouth," is the source for several town names, including Saco, Missouri; Sac City, Iowa; and Saco, Maine. Still other kindred American place-names arise from *boca*, the Spanish word for mouth, including the historic town of Boca, California, located at the mouth of the Little Truckee River. Based on these typical examples, it would seem likely that Boca Raton, Florida, would also be located near the mouth of a river. Yet the

M

history of that city's name illustrates instead the mutability of landscape language. Boca Raton and nearby Lake Boca Raton take their name from Boca Ratones, which is shown on an eighteenth-century Spanish map. This Boca Ratones, as it turns out, was merely a bay inlet, and not a mouth. Moreover, its location was nowhere near the present-day city of Boca Raton, but far to the south in Biscayne Bay near Miami. For reasons now unknown, the name migrated north up the Florida coast and was applied first to the lake (although the lake did not then have a connection to the sea) and some years later to the emerging coastal settlement of Boca Raton. During this process, citizens of the new Florida city shortened the original adjective *ratones*—colloquially, "thieves"—to the apparently more suitable *ratón*, Spanish for rat.

EMILY HIESTAND

mudflat

A mudflat along a coastline is a level area of fine silt continually exposed by low tide, never quite drying out before high tide returns; it's usually associated with or sheltered by coastal estuaries, sand spits, shingle bars, barrier islands, or cheniers. In a lake, river, or wetland, however, a mudflat, while also associated with such sheltering formations as islands or wide, lazy bends in a river, gets its water not so much from tides but from extremely gradual contours of the land. Such contours allow the lake or river to periodically wash up and cover the mudflat in shallow water, which drains slowly, both downslope to the river or lake and straight down to a shallow water table. In either case—fluvial or marine—a mudflat is characterized simply by a big, flat, often bad-smelling expanse of mud, one that, because it strands insects and small animals, tends to draw birds (though in the case of Olympia, Washington, the local mudflat draws Evergreen College's graduating seniors for a nude race). The main difference in fluvial and marine mudflats, aside from sources of water, is that while a fluvial mudflat has dry periods, in which the mud on the surface acquires a salty crust and cracks, a marine mudflat stays wet year-round, sometimes even—as happens in Alaska—trapping the occasional person in a suction grip while water steadily rises. The trick in that circumstance is to run a stick or handle down your leg and move it sharply to the side, allowing enough air in to break the suction. And then take your stick with you, for the next step. STEPHEN GRAHAM JONES

mudflow

A mudflow is a moving mass of earth made motile—fluid—by rain or melting snow. These are the rain-driven landslides of mud that often take out houses and roads in California and Oregon. Not so much a formation as an event, mudflows, though temporary—fast-moving, even—are often given names, such as the Kautz Creek Mudflow or the Osceola Mudflow. One type of mudflow is a lahar: pyroclastic material or water-saturated volcanic debris sliding down the flank of a volcano. Midway between a mudflow and a lahar is what happened on Mount Shasta's Konwakiton Glacier in 1924: meltwater built up until the land in front of it gave way, releasing all the water at once and triggering a sudden, dangerous laharlike mudflow. A distinct though related type of flow is a debris flow, a mass of earth moving downslope. Only here, the debris and the slope are both significantly drier. STEPHEN GRAHAM JONES

M

mud pot

Located in the geothermal areas of Yellowstone National Park, only three miles above the Earth's molten rock, are gurgling, sulfurous pools of viscous boiling mud. These mud pots are a type of hot spring formed when water is in short supply. What seems to happen is that the smelly hydrogen sulfide present in hot springs creates sulfuric acid, which eats away at the surrounding rock and turns it to clay. When the clay gets thick enough, the water source gets clogged and, eventually, the spring becomes a mud pot. These curious pools contain clay, volcanic ash, and other mineral matter that can give them unusual colors; one very well known group of mud pots in Yellowstone, arranged along the Artist Paint Pot Trail, includes reddish, yellow, blue, and green pools. Often the boiling mud squirts over the edge of the pool, resulting in a mud volcano, which can rise to a height of three to five feet. LAN SAMANTHA CHANG

mudslide

If the sudden, vertical slip of a mass of soil from a hillside consists of dry material, both the event itself and the aftermath, or remnant, of the event are called landslides. If the material that slumps or shears away is saturated with water, it's a mudslide. Like landslides, mudslides can be small- or large-scale events, though typically mud-slides occur over a smaller area than landslides. (It was a landslide that created Earthquake Lake, Montana, on the Madison River.) Mudslides most often happen when vegetation that served to hold soils in place is removed, exposing the ground to sudden saturation and slippage. Ordinary earth tremblors might then trigger a full-scale slide—on the banks of a road cut, on overgrazed slopes, or on forest clearcuts. Mudslides occur naturally wherever erosion and earth-building are going on and vegetation is largely absent—in volcanic landscapes, on fire-ravaged slopes, along cutbanks, and in fault zones. BARRY LOPEZ

muskeg

The colloquial term muskeg is Algonquian in origin and refers to open peatlands or bogs interspersed with ponds and streams and dotted with stunted trees. Muskegs are widespread in subarctic regions of Alaska and Canada, often breaking up stretches of forest. Their hummocky terrain occupies poorly drained land layered with ancient organic peat at least a foot deep. Water-saturated sphagnum mosses play a critical role in muskegs. These mosses not only keep the water table high, but also release caustic acidic compounds that inhibit organic decomposition, leaving nutrient-poor groundwater. Since other muskeg plants can't make use of this acidic water, they trap what rainwater they can and have other features, such as waxy or fuzzy leaves, that help minimize water loss. Forest trees bordering muskegs struggle with the waterlogged soils and often die, allowing the bog to expand. This has sparked a debate about whether muskegs figure significantly in forest decline.   CAROLYN SERVID

muskrat house   M

A muskrat house might be said to be the sign determinative of a wetland—a land feature, often recognizable from a distance by the sight of humped muskrat houses on the horizon. A muskrat house is shaped like a miniature beaver lodge, but the muskrat builds its house not of sticks and wood from nearby dry land, as the beaver does, but from the stems of reeds and other soft water plants, densely packed together with mud. It is against the law throughout the United States for a trapper to break into a muskrat house to lay a trap in winter without closing the house up again and sealing it shut, for it is so well constructed that even a small breakage in its wall would cause all the animals inside to freeze to death. Muskrat are widely regarded as the easiest animal to trap, and many trappers learned their trade as children by trapping them. Until the collapse of the fur industry in the 1980s, a million muskrat were trapped annually in the United States. A trapping manual from the 1920s reports that the perceived value of wetland preservation fluctuated with the monetary value of muskrat pelts. Abandoned muskrat houses are used as nesting sites by the great variety of animals that inhabit wetlands, from snapping turtles to wood ducks and trumpeter swans. When Mole first sees Ratty's house in *The Wind and the Willows*, "dreamily he fell to considering what a nice snug dwelling-place it would make." SUSAN BRIND MORROW

narrows

Narrows is frequently used as a place-name to denote a constriction in a river, strait, valley, or pass. For example, The Narrows, between Staten Island and Brooklyn on the western tip of Long Island, has been spanned by the Verrazano-Narrows Bridge since 1964. From this lofty perch, the motorist has a magnificent panorama of the Lower and Upper Bays of New York Harbor. Narrows suggests, often strongly, a great turbulence and swiftness of waters. In the case of canyons, narrows are a downcutting slash, a thread of drainage, a dark-bluish passageway knifing through precipitous rock walls. A dramatic narrows on the Virgin River in Zion National Park, Utah, was brought to the world's attention by John Wesley Powell. Once a hiker enters this Narrows—unless he turns back—it will be sixteen miles downstream before escape from its depths is possible. In some places the vertical walls are more than a thousand feet high, but only twenty to fifty feet apart. A stream in flood moves with extreme rapidity through narrows, pushing any debris encountered before it, scouring the channel, cleansing it of all but the smallest pieces of gravel.   JOY WILLIAMS

natural bridge

Described by geologists as a "temporary and insecure" landform, an imposing natural bridge is a paradox in stone. Unlike arches, natural bridges always span water or an abandoned waterway and are created by flowing, not seeping, water. The water first breaches a rock wall where it's been worn wafer thin. Over time, the flow of water widens this portal. Further, finer sculpting and shaping of the opening may be the work of other erosional forces, including sand-laden winds. Natural bridges age and eventually collapse, but in their lifetime they are sometimes strong enough—and flat enough on top—to accommodate vehicular traffic. The grand example of the form is at Rainbow Bridge National Monument in Utah. A sandstone structure 290 feet tall with an opening 275 feet wide, it's a sacred site for Diné (Navajo) and other Native people. Man-made Lake Powell, when it began to back up behind Glen Canyon Dam in 1964, provided waterborne access to this once remote site. The Diné Nation fought unsuccessfully to prevent oil slicks from motorboats and windblown camping trash from befouling the place, and boat wakes from hastening erosion in the area. Navajo elders say that today this holy site, to which they still journey to evoke rain and to call upon the deep curative powers of the Earth, has lost much of its power. Another well-known natural bridge, a Monacan sacred site located near Richmond, Virginia, was purchased by Thomas Jefferson from George III of England in 1774 for the edification of the curious. It eventually found its way into Melville's imagination and a description of Moby Dick: "Soon the fore part of him rose from the water; for an instant his whole marbleized body formed a high arch, like Virginia's Natural Bridge, and warningly waving his battered flukes in the air, the grand god revealed himself, sounded, and went out of sight." TERRY TEMPEST WILLIAMS

natural levee

A river spreading over its banks slows and releases some of its burden of sediment. Flooding repeatedly, the river will coat its banks with sediment in the slower, lower reaches. Year after year the layer of alluvial soil is laid down as varve and dries, and over the centuries the banks get higher, keeping the river in its channel except when floods break through the barriers called natural levees. Rivers are dynamic and meandering, an ongoing process. Stream channels are always shifting across their floodplains, and sedimentation occurs along point bars and erosion tears at cutbanks. Along clearer, faster upland streams natural levees are made by seasonal floods in low ridges of sandy floodplain deposits, parallel or adjacent to the stream. Raised shoulders of loam and sand, they confine the normal stream in its channel, in the stretches where the current slows and the floods dump gravel, sand, and soil year after year. The banks may shift, crumble, or erode, but they are raised again by repeated floods and sweeping flash tides from the slopes above. ROBERT MORGAN

neck

Of the anatomical terms we have transferred to landscape—head, foot, arm, elbow, finger, mouth, tongue, tooth, nose, spine, teat—neck may be the most versatile. Early colonists brought the Old World sense of the term as isthmus or peninsula (Great Neck on Long Island), then extended it to mean a narrow stretch of land between tidal creeks. As George R. Stewart writes in *Names on the Land*, "Any land between two arms of water was a neck," with or without a prominent head, or headland. This usage gave rise to "neck of the woods," a forest settlement. A narrow stretch of water, too—a tight strait or inlet—is sometimes called a neck. In volcanic landscapes, a neck is a mass of lava solidified in a volcanic pipe and exposed by erosion, such as the summit pinnacles of Mount Washington and Three Fingered Jack in the Oregon Cascades. Shiprock Peak—in Navajo, *Tsé Bit 'A'í*, or "The Rock with Wings," is a dramatic volcanic neck in northwestern New Mexico. JOHN DANIEL

needle ice

Needle ice is also known as pipkrake, a word derived from the Swedish words *pip*, a musical tube, and *krake*, frozen ground. A musical tube in the frozen ground. The small, intricate, needle-like spicules form in moist, heavy soils in fall, winter, and spring, and act as agents of erosion. Water drawn toward the surface freezes into thin, tiny slivers that loosen the surrounding ground into ice flakes and chunks. Needle ice is a type of ground ice, but the term is sometimes used as a synonym for candle ice, especially when the "candles" are relatively short and narrow. Some also apply the term to random concentrations of small, sharp spicules that occasionally form on the surface of sea ice, creating a painful bed of nails for sled dogs.   GRETCHEN LEGLER

névé

Névé is the French term for snow that has accumulated on a glacier, has remained through one or more melt seasons, and has begun the recrystallizing process that will eventually turn it to glacial ice. The more common term is the German word firn. Firn's crystals have lost the delicate pointed edges of the original snowflakes and are somewhat compacted but have yet to become ice. Aerial views or photographs of glaciers can clearly reveal areas of firn where the newer snow appears fresh and white compared to the denser grayish ice. The lower edge of the firn area—the firn line—distinguishes the accumulation zone, where snow is amassing near the head of the glacier, from the ablation zone, where more of the glacier's snow and ice is lost than gained.
CAROLYN SERVID

niche glacier

Geography decides a glacier's shape: valley, cirque, piedmont, or niche. On precipitous north-facing mountain slopes, a niche glacier (also known as a pocket glacier) forms when snow fills a cup-shaped depression in a mountainside. Over years, this snow resists melting, compacts to glacial ice, spills over the lip of its rock niche, and begins to move. This smallest glacier type takes up only the space of a gully or hollow on a steep slope and resembles a large snowfield. Rarely, niche glaciers are natal forms of larger glaciers, evolving into a cirque (or corrie) glacier, which in turn may evolve into a valley glacier. More often, however, niche glaciers are remnants of cirque glaciers that have shrunk, a phenomenon more common in recent decades as a result of global warming. EVA SAULITIS

nickpoint

A stream flowing along on its way may encounter a broken gradient that drops gradually or abruptly—if gradually, the stream flows faster and creates rapids; if abruptly, the stream changes its flow drastically, falling over the edge of the break and becoming a waterfall. The spot at which this sudden change in stream elevation occurs is called a nickpoint, sometimes spelled knickpoint. Over time, the force of falling water gradually erodes a nickpoint, causing it to retreat. The nickpoint of the Horseshoe Falls at Niagara Falls is retreating at a rate of about 4.3 feet a year. This is "knickpoint retreat on a grand scale" and further evidence that the surface of the Earth is volatile, surging and shifting, changing in many ways constantly, all the time, even at this moment. PATTIANN ROGERS

N

nilas

One of the first phases in the life cycle of sea ice is nilas, a thin elastic crust that forms on calm water. It has a matte surface and is easily bent by waves. The word nilas comes from the Russian language in which it is pronounced "knee-lass." Related to nilas is grease ice, a soupy layer of crystals that forms on the water's surface after frazil ice, the first small spicules of sea ice to take shape, begins to consolidate. Like nilas, grease ice reflects little light, giving the sea an oily appearance. Both types are viscous and fluid, not yet constituting hard pieces of floating ice. As nilas moves before the wind or with the current it may turn to pancake ice—loose, mostly circular, pancake-shaped pieces whose outer rims are raised slightly, due to their rotating and bumping into one another. Pancake ice is sometimes called lily-pad ice, because of its resemblance to the green pads of these water plants. Fields of pancake ice may eventually grow large enough to become floes, and then consolidated pack ice—floes that have joined together in a massive, floating plain.   GRETCHEN LEGLER

nivation hollow

In *A Walk in the Woods: Rediscovering America on the Appalachian Trail*, Bill Bryson wrote: "I never met a hiker with a good word to say about the trail in Pennsylvania. It is, as someone told a *National Geographic* reporter in 1987, the place 'where boots go to die.' . . . Mile upon mile of ragged, oddly angled slabs of stone strewn about in wobbly piles. . . . These require constant attentiveness if you are not to twist an ankle or sprawl on your face—not a pleasant experience with fifty pounds of momentum on your back." Such a hiker on the Appalachian Trail in Pennsylvania might just as well have been complaining about nivation hollows. A bowl-shaped depression in the ground, a nivation hollow begins to take shape when ice forms over a shallow rock basin beneath a snow bank. The ice freezes and thaws over time. During the warm period, melted snow seeps into the bottom of the hollow. During the cooler period, the seep water freezes. The rock breaks up, weathers, and erodes. Meltwater carries away the finer rock particles and the hollow becomes larger and deeper.   MARY SWANDER

nook

Once a precise term of English land measurement for a small field ("Two Fardells of Land make a Nooke, and two Nookes make halfe a Yard of Land"), nook is now a more elastic term applied lyrically and affectionately to a small, secluded place somewhat closed in by trees or rocks, offering peace and retreat. The connection between a sylvan nook and the interior corner space also called nook (the inglenook by a fireplace, for example) seems to be that the original scrap of farm field called a nook was often triangular in shape. The triangular shape may also explain a now almost obsolete meaning of nook—as a promontory of land jutting into the sea and terminating in a point. (Note that such a promontory is now sometimes called a hook.) While the sheltered nook in a given landscape is a small, even tiny, spot, the word nook can also be used to refer to any place on the planet that is deemed remote, even if it is a very large area; thus Cotton Mather could once say of some visitors that they were "as genteel persons as most that ever visited these nooks of America." EMILY HIESTAND

N

nose

An isolated, buttresslike projection of rock, often from a cliff wall, flaring as it descends and ending abruptly, suggesting the human nose. Anthony's Nose, a classic example, juts prominently from a cliff face above the Hudson River at the east end of the Bear Mountain Bridge, near Westchester County's boundary with Putnam County in New York. Like the mouth of a stream, finger lakes, an arm of the sea, the crotch of a rock, the brow of a ridge, rock nipples, elbow canyons, a neck of land, and *les grands tetons* of Wyoming, another reminder of how we see ourselves in the places we inhabit. The Nose is a famous climbing route up the granite cliffs of El Capitan in Yosemite National Park. Another type of nose is the downwind part of a parabolic dune, which trails twin upwind arms as it advances. TERRY TEMPEST WILLIAMS

notch

A narrow passage between two elevations is called a
notch. Also a depression or dent, an opening or defile, a
cut in the surface of anything. In landscape, especially,
a mountain pass. This is the location in a mountain
range where a geological formation is lower than the
surrounding peaks, thus allowing passage. Notch can
simply indicate an opening through rough terrain. Also
a term in hybridization, where a notch is a slit made in
the ground to receive the roots of a seedling tree, or an
incision made in a twig to stimulate growth of a bud
lower down on the twig. Notch is also used to denote an
opening extending above water level in a surface placed
across a stream, like a weir. Finally, notch can be used
freely to mean any narrow opening, a break or breach.
Dozens of mountainous locations in the United States are
known simply as "The Notch." For instance, as Isabella
Bird writes in *A Lady's Life in the Rocky Mountains*: "On
arriving at the 'Notch' (a literal gate of rock), we found
ourselves absolutely on the knife-like ridge or backbone
of Longs Peak, only a few feet wide, covered with
colossal boulders and fragments, and on the other side
shelving in one precipitous, snow-patched sweep of three
thousand feet to a picturesque hollow, containing a lake
of pure green water." PATRICIA HAMPL

nubble

Off the coast of Maine, the surface of the ocean is
broken here and there by cone-shaped islands or piles
of rock referred to as nubbles, sometimes shortened to
nubs. These forms do not always stand alone in water;
in places the term is applied to the odd cliff or point of
land that ends in a dribbling of stone. The Cape Ned-
dick or Nubble Lighthouse in southeast Maine was built
on a low pile of rock separated from the mainland by a
treacherous channel. Although the word is uncommon

outside Maine, in Sonoma County, California, a naked, rocky peak bears the name The Nubble. JAN DEBLIEU

nunatak

Nunatak is from an Inuktitut (Inuit Eskimo) word, *nuna-taq,* meaning "something prominent standing alone" or, more prosaically, "lonely peak." (In the Iñupiaq language of the Iñupiat, who live on the Alaska coastal plain far from mountainous terrain, nunataq refers primarily to a cache of meat in the ground.) In its Anglicized form, the word refers to an isolated island of bedrock jutting out from a sea of glacial snow and ice. Nunataks are landforms that existed before glaciation, and within North America they are scattered in Alaska and Canada, and throughout the high-altitude, glacier-bound landscapes of the Rocky Mountains. One might think that these rock outcroppings sequestered in ice would be barren of life, but they have been found to be refuges for a diversity of species. Researchers studying nunataks in Canada's Yukon Territory have found miniature meadows and gardens of sedges, moss campion, mountain heather, tiny poppies, saxifrages, daisies, and other plants that host rare insects and a species of wolf spider and attract occasional butterflies. The collared pika, a tough little mammal, has also found its way to these nunataks and made them home. All too often, nunataks are the final resting place for straying migratory birds seeking an oasis in vast stretches of snow. CAROLYN SERVID

oasis

The word oasis is apparently of Egyptian origin and
refers to a place in the desert where water is present. An
oasis means life and fertility: permanent plant growth
and the possibility for human settlement, drinking
water, and enough moisture to grow plants and trees. An
oasis can vary in size, from an ooze in cracked mud to a
gurgling spring, to a pond or spring system so large it can
hold whole cities. Natural oases occur in artesian basins
or in deflation hollows, where dunes and sediments have
been removed by wind, thus exposing an area that is at
groundwater level. Nearly one hundred places in the
United States are named Oasis, including the town of
Oasis, California, the Oasis Reservoir in Colorado, Oasis
Pond in Montana, and Oasis Lake in Texas. Another sort
of oasis can be found in polar deserts—an ice-free area
in an icebound landscape. Pearyland at the top of Greenland is one. Historically, the word oasis has been used to
refer to the dark spots occurring on Mars. But most often
an oasis is an island of aquatic relief. It is the place where
lives are saved, and, figuratively speaking, refers to any
calm center. The piece of foam that holds flower stems in
a floral arrangement is called an oasis; it too, represents
an island of security, but one that sits just under the
water's surface. As a topographic feature, an oasis is life;
it is a gathering point, a sanctuary, and a feeding station.
It is the desert's umbilical.   GRETEL EHRLICH

ogive

Some valley glaciers carry on their surface a regular
pattern of thin dark lines, a series of concentric semi-
circles or arcs all pointing downhill. Unlike the single
dark trace of a medial moraine, the streaks of these
chevronlike marks are perpendicular to the flow of the
ice, and a set of them might consist of dozens of evenly
spaced lines. The dark lines are called ogives, after

ogee, an architectural term for a type of curve well
known from pointed Gothic arches. Ogives—they bow
convexly downhill because the center of a valley glacier
is often flowing faster than its sides—frequently turn up
downstream from an icefall. The stretching and fracturing of a glacier that occurs at an icefall (where there is a
sudden change of elevation), together with the normal
seasonal pattern of ice flow—it flows faster in the summer and with less surface melting in the winter—leads
to a combination of conditions that actually creates two
ogive patterns. The dark ogives mark the heights in an
undulating sequence of transverse valleys and ridges,
some of which might be seventy-five feet high. The
dark/light pattern is called a band ogive, the ridge/
valley pattern is called a wave ogive. Alaska's glacial
landscapes are full of ogives. Its many rivers of ice let you
know, with these patterns, that despite its stolid appearance the ice is alive, carving its powerful way through
the land.   GRETCHEN LEGLER

old-growth forest

Forest as elder, where trees coexist in the full spectrum
of their development—from seedling to sapling to
ancient, to snag and generative nurse log: old-growth forest features include thick duff, trees hoary with age, and
certain indicator species that rely on the settled richness
of variety in plant, insect, lichen, and other life forms.
It seems to take about two centuries for these features
to develop, by which time a forest crosses a threshold
between a monoculture of trees of similar age—often
the result of catastrophic fire or clearcut—to a multiage
population of trees, with attendant opportunities for
broad range in plant and animal populations. What old
age gives the individual person, old growth conditions
give a forest: a life-library of survival wisdom, flexibility,

initiative, and a sustaining life process. Formerly called
virgin forest, as untouched wilderness, old-growth forest
has become controversial and precious. Besides the old-
growth forests dominated by Douglas fir in the Pacific
Northwest, old growth includes local stands of redwood
in California, ponderosa pine east of the Cascade Mountains, eastern hemlock in the Great Smoky Mountains, as
well as cedar, cypress, tulip tree, oak, and other species,
often in tiny forest remnants.   KIM STAFFORD

open book

Cliff faces tend to be topographically intricate amalgams
of bulges, slabs, and intersecting facets. Some varieties
of rock—basalt and Wingate Sandstone, in particular—
commonly form escarpments that are particularly rich
in cleanly angled corners, some of which may stand hundreds of feet tall. The aspects of such features that exist
as inside corners are known as open books or dihedrals.
JON KRAKAUER

orchard

O

We would more easily recognize the origins of this word
if we spelled it "hortyard," for orchard derives from
the twin roots that gave rise to horticulture and yard.
An orchard is a stand of trees, usually but not always
cultivated, bearing fruit, nuts, or sap. Orchards on the
high plateau of eastern Washington yield apples, those
in lower Michigan yield cherries, while those in Georgia
bear mouthwatering peaches. Although Oregon's filberts
may also be said to come from orchards, plantations of
nut-bearing trees are usually called groves, as are the
orange and grapefruit plantations of Florida, Texas, and
California. While a stand of sugar maples may also be
called an orchard, it is more commonly, and sweetly,
called a sugarbush.   SCOTT RUSSELL SANDERS

outcrop

An outcrop is a portion of bedrock or other rock stratum that appears at or protrudes above the surface of the surrounding land. Shale showing on a valley floor or a boulder rising out of a meadow, for example, might each be described as an outcrop, or an outcropping. In *Michael, Brother of Jerry,* Jack London describes "the one rocky outcrop, in the dense heart of the mountain forest, where a score of rattlesnakes denned through the winters and warmed themselves in the sun." A synonym is basset, which suggests that a portion or edge of a rock formation has emerged at or above the surface of the soil. Figuratively, an outcrop is a coming into outward manifestation of any hidden or inner quality or aspect.   PATRICIA HAMPL

outer bank

Along the sandy ocean shore an outer bank is a sliver of land that barely rises from the water and lies much farther out to sea than other dry ground. It is quite literally the edge of the earth, the front line of battle against maritime storms. The name is most frequently applied to the thin islands off the coast of North Carolina that stretch for roughly 150 miles and include the great arcs of Cape Hatteras and Cape Lookout. As Mark Richard writes in "Rolltop Mantra of the Outer Banks," "If you could time-lapse the natural nautical clock, you would see the whole of the Outer Banks, the mons of woods, the limbs of sand, the rump of Jockeys Ridge, turning away from the ocean like an unhappy lover rolling over beneath a blanket of development. Or maybe it really is God's Plan, and Satan really is buried beneath Jockeys Ridge, and the prevailing winds are merely making his resurrection more expedient by whisking the mountain of sand off his grave."   JAN DEBLIEU

outwash plain

An outwash plain is the extensive stretch of sediment carried by a meltwater stream away from a glacier's tip, hundreds of miles in reach. Outwash plains are composed of gravel, sand, and clay (clay, being the lightest, is borne the farthest), with a topography from nearly level to hilly, and moderate to negligible in its rise and fall. A pitted outwash plain occurs when ice blocks separate from a glacier's tip and are borne along with the outwash, ending up partly buried. When they melt, the surface around them collapses, and the outwash plain's otherwise smooth surface is now pitted, the pits often water-filled. These are commonly called kettle lakes. Examples of pitted outwash plains can be found in Vilas County, Wisconsin, and near Lansford, North Dakota.   LARRY WOIWODE

overbank deposit

The silt, sand, and gravel left by floodwaters on lands adjacent to a river are collectively called an overbank deposit. Also called floodplain deposits, they refresh valley soils and raise the lips of riverbanks. When dams prevent the natural passage of sediments downstream and their overbank deposition, as does the Aswan High Dam on the Nile River, agricultural bottomlands suffer soil depletion. The heavy silt load of a river also limits the useful life spans of reservoirs, such as may be the case at Glen Canyon Dam and Lake Powell on the Colorado River. Dam removal requires careful study as to how the release of silt will affect banks and other habitats downstream, as with the planned elimination of the dams on the Elwha River in Washington's Olympic Peninsula. Undammed rivers, too, can become clogged by silt and gravel when subject to steep-slope logging upstream. This excess effluvium may exacerbate annual floods and exaggerate overbank deposits, swamping instead of renewing pastures.   ROBERT MICHAEL PYLE

overhang

On steep mountain walls, sections of rock may bulge beyond vertical to form an overhang. If an overhang juts horizontally from the adjacent face, it is called a ceiling or roof—for example, the Great Roof on El Capitan, which casts a shadow across the monolith's south buttress like an immense granite awning that hangs two thousand feet above the meadows of Yosemite Valley.   JON KRAKAUER

oxbow lake

An oxbow lake, also called a horseshoe lake, is a crescent of still water in an abandoned loop of river channel, named for the curved piece of wood used to yoke oxen. An oxbow forms when a river cuts across the neck of a meander and shortens its course. The former channel then fills with river overflow or groundwater seepage to form the oxbow. Having no current and no outlet, the lake is doomed. Gradually it fills with silt and decaying vegetation. Marsh plants and swamp trees encroach its edges. In time, the open water disappears, and only a swale, known as a meander scar, is left behind. Oxbows are so common in the landscape that the Geographic Names Information System of the U.S. Geological Survey lists 169 place-names in the United States containing the word oxbow. Given the transitory nature of the landform, possibly a minority of the namesakes of those places still exist as lakes.   WILLIAM DEBUYS

pack ice

In winter, a quixotic carapace of drifting sea ice blankets
millions of square miles of the polar ocean. Iñupiaq
Eskimo call the permanent part of the polar pack,
consisting of both multiyear and annual pack ice, *aakanga
siku*, "mother ice." The English-language term is meant
to include, as well, the extensive fields of younger, mobile
ice-of-the-year, the seasonal or annual ice that may
stretch much farther to the south as winter settles in.
During storms, pack ice cries out: grinding, screeching.
Winds, tides, and currents mangle floes into pressure
ridges or rip them apart to form temporary open water
leads. When Ernest Shackleton's ship *Endurance* became
frozen in Antarctic pack in January 1915, the dynamic
nature of the ice was made manifest in a ship that was
first cemented, then splintered, and finally sunk in place,
all while the pack traveled 670 miles in ten months,
shuddering and groaning incessantly. In his famous
poem, Coleridge depicts the fearful aspects of pack ice
encountered by the Ancient Mariner: "The ice was here,
the ice was there/The ice was all around:/It cracked
and growled, and roared and howled,/Like noises in a
swound!" Ishmael, *Moby-Dick*'s narrator, calls pack ice
"a boundless church-yard grinning . . . with its lean ice
monuments and splintered crosses." Eskimos in Arctic
Alaska hold quite a different view. For these native people,
annual ice forming over the continental shelf equals life.
In summer, melting pack ice releases freshwater and nutrients, helping spin a food web: algae, flagellates, zooplank-
ton, fishes, mammals. Polar bears and many species of seal
and whale are entirely dependent on pack ice for survival.
When the pack drifts far to the north, Eskimo hunters
scan the seaward horizon expectantly for its reflection in
the sky—ice blink—a brightness in the clouds. In recent
years, summer pack ice, reduced by global warming,
remains farther offshore and less accessible to hunters. In

this century, if current projections of continuous climate warming are correct, the shrinking ice pack will transform the Northwest Passage from occasional adventure to commonplace reality.   EVA SAULITIS

pāhoehoe

Galway Kinnell captures the marked differences in the congealed flows of the two types of lava erupted by Hawaiian volcanoes in his poem "Lava": smooth, ropy pāhoehoe is "a clear brazened surface / one can cross barefooted," while jagged ʻaʻā resembles "a mass of rubble still / tumbling." These terms are now standard for Western geologists describing the highly fluid basalt erupted by shield volcanoes (though Icelanders have their own names: *helluhraun* for pāhoehoe and *apalhraun* for ʻaʻā). As it cools, a slow-moving pāhoehoe flow may solidify into fantastic forms: geologists speak of entrail, as well as filamented, corded, sharkskin, slab, and shelly pāhoehoe. What Hawaiʻi residents call blue rock is an unusually dense basalt sometimes encountered when cutting roads through old lava.   PAMELA FRIERSON

painted desert

Located east of Grand Canyon, the Painted Desert is bordered on the south by the Little Colorado River. A heavily eroded land of sandstone, mudstone, and volcanic ash, mesas, and buttes, this desert is multilayered with reds, oranges, and pinks (the result of the presence of oxides of iron and aluminum in the soil) and blues, grays, and lavenders (the result of oxygen depleted by flooding or rapid sediment buildup). This is part of the Colorado Plateau, and its characteristic painted rock layers are typical of the region. Everett Ruess, a writer, artist, and wanderer of wildlands, wrote of his "serene and tempestuous days" walking 170 miles alone across the Painted Desert. From a 1931 letter of his to a friend: "On the open desert . . . the world has seemed more beautiful to me than ever before. I have loved the red rocks, the twisted trees, the red sand blowing in the wind, the slow sunny clouds crossing the sky, the shafts of moonlight on my bed at night." In 1934, at age twenty, Ruess disappeared while roaming the canyonlands of Utah. PATTIANN ROGERS

painted hill

Badlands produce colorful heaps and mounds called painted hills in central Oregon. Striped horizontally in soft, interbled hues of red, green, and pale gold, with punctuations of black manganese, the Oregon Painted Hills embody volcanic ash worked by plants, animals, and groundwater into ancient soils, now compacted into claystone layers. At present a region of semiarid steppe, this "geological library of antiquated earth," in the phrase of geologist Ellen Morris Bishop, records more than thirty million years of climatic and biotic regimes ranging from subtropical swamp through temperate oak savanna. Except for brief skullcaps of bunchgrass, little vegetation can root in the dense weathered clay of the Painted Hills. Their life is in their colors, which can shift subtly before one's eyes as the clay takes on the moisture of rain and lets it go. The Painted Desert of Arizona contains similar formations, called *pintadas* by early Spanish Americans, and by the Navajo, "land of the sleeping rainbow." JOHN DANIEL

pali

The Hawaiian word *pali* refers to any steep slope or cliff, though Hawaiian geographers employ it as a term for either the verdant rain- and stream-eroded scarps or the wave-eroded sea cliffs found on the windward side of the main islands. The thousand-foot precipice called Nu'uanu Pali, in the Ko'olau Mountains, is famous as the site where Kamehameha defeated the defending warriors of O'ahu by driving them off the cliff. The water-carved ridges and sea cliffs of the Nāpali (literally, "the cliffs") coast of Kaua'i are renowned for their beauty, but the towering pali of eastern Moloka'i—highest sea cliffs in the world, reaching up to 3,300 feet—are better known to geologists, who've long puzzled how water alone could carve such features on a barely middle-aged volcanic island. Sonar scanning of sea floors off the east coast of both O'ahu and Moloka'i revealed landslide debris strewn for over a hundred miles, and it is now thought that catastrophic land slumps contributed to the formation of pali along the eastern flank of the Ko'olau range and the east coast of Moloka'i. Paul Theroux once wrote, in *Fresh Air Fiend,* that Moloka'i's pali were "a gothic wall, as soaring and complex as a green cathedral. . . . The high islands of the Marquesas," he went on, "the smoldering volcanoes of Vanuatu, and the glorious mossy and ferny cones of Tahiti and Moorea" are all justly praised. "But nothing can compare with these thirty miles of [Moloka'i's] green cliffs, the highest, the most beautiful I have seen in Oceania." PAMELA FRIERSON

palisade

Palisade is a fortification wall made of tall wooden stakes, or palings, and has its origins in the Latin word *palus.* Geologically, a palisade is a tall, inaccessible cliff of column-shaped basalt. Palisades are formed when a sill—a thick volcanic flow that has forced its way through two layers of sedimentary rock—becomes exposed by a combination of uplifting, faulting, and erosion. As a result particularly of water erosion, palisades are often found bordering a lake or river, such as the spectacular Hudson River Palisades across from New York City. Rising as much as five hundred feet and extending for fifty miles, these palisades are magisterial in their solidity. Their raw geometry and primitive power stand in stark contrast to the steel, glass, granite, and sandstone palings of Manhattan and are reminders of the enduring forces that shape the surface of the planet and the temporal quality of human edifices.   MICHAEL COLLIER

palouse

The Palouse is a landscape of rolling hills with deep, rich soil along the Snake River in western Idaho and eastern Washington. These hills began forming six million years ago as the wind deposited a blanket of fine-grained silt called loess over the entire landscape. Once grassland, most of the region is now devoted to agriculture. The undulating patterns of golden summer wheat and green fields of lentils against the blue plain of the sky can be beautiful and entrancing. French Canadian voyagers gave the Palouse its name, *pelouse* being French for grassland. The Nez Perce (Nimi'ipuu) were called Pelouse by Anglos, and the horses they bred Palouse horses, later Appaloosas. When the Lewis and Clark Expedition passed through, staying for a time with the Nez Perce, Lewis noted in his journal: "Their horses appear to be of an excellent race: they are lofty, elegantly formed, active and durable." These fine horses were bred on the rich grasses of the Palouse.   PATTIANN ROGERS

P

pan

Derived from its use as a descriptor of receptacles and containers, a pan is a hollow or depression in the ground, especially one in which water stands. It may contain a small or large body of water, but it is always shallow and through evaporation may allow deposition of mineral properties, for instance salt. Such pans are common in the Great Basin region of the American West. The word frequently appears as part of compound nouns in geologic language—salt pan, ice pan, and in a somewhat different application (not necessarily a depression), hardpan.   JOHN KEEBLE

panhandle

A narrow strip of territory projecting from a larger, broader politically defined area is called a panhandle. This narrow strip, when seen on a map, resembles the handle of a pan. Alaska, Idaho, Florida, Oklahoma, Maryland, Texas, and West Virginia have panhandles. Some people even call the small piece of Nebraska that sticks out to the west a panhandle. A panhandle may claim its own history and politics and its own character distinctive from the rest of its state. People residing in such regions routinely identify themselves as "living in the panhandle," and organizations and businesses name themselves after it: Panhandle Outfitters, Panhandle Bird Club, Panhandle Railroad Historical Society, Panhandle State Bank, Panhandle Windsurfers, White Sands Panhandle Band, Panhandle Powerwash, Panhandle Jam. Panhandles have become part of American speech and the American psyche, even though they are simply the creation of boundary lines drawn on a map. Carl Sandburg's poem "Boy and Father" contains this line: "Buffaloes, blizzards, way down in Texas, in the panhandle of Texas/snuggling close to New Mexico."

PATTIANN ROGERS

parabolic dune

A dune with the crescent swoop of a parabola whose tapering arms point into the wind, not away from it, as happens with the barchan dune. Parabolic dunes are more common near beaches and in areas with moderate accumulations of sand; barchan dunes, much less vegetated, are found in rockier environments. In their natural state, parabolic dunes advance more slowly than barchan dunes but overwhelm whatever is in their path; barchan dunes tend to lose their shape against an obstacle. In *Dune Country*, Janice Emily Bowers offers an explanation for the slower movement of a parabolic dune: "[They] are well anchored with plants: Mormon tea, rosemary mint, squawbush, soaptree yucca, fourwing saltbush, crucifixion thorn, Rio Grande cottonwood, rubber rabbitbrush, claret cups hedgehog, and plains prickly pear." Michigan's Sleeping Bear Dunes, on the eastern shore of Lake Michigan, harbors many parabolic dunes among its striking array of perched dunes.   D. J. WALDIE

paraje

Un paraje is a stopping place. A camp. It was a term that penetrated the American Southwest with Spanish conquistadors and friars, as they wended their ways north and west, seeking Cíbola and pathways to Santa Fe and California. A paraje nowadays denotes a small settlement, a watered spot for a layover, or a fortuitous place where travelers have traditionally settled for the night. Travel writers Phil Archuletta and Sharyl Holden tell a good story in *Traveling in New Mexico* about the term that would be welcome at any paraje. They are writing of the land between Las Cruces and Socorro: "The trail was first blazed by Oñate in 1598. His notes say the group suffered terribly for lack of water until someone's dog appeared with wet paws. The travelers followed the dog to temporary water where the animals and people relieved their thirst. Known from then on as Los Charcos del Perrillo, 'the puddles of the little dog,' it became a paraje, or camping place, where caravans prepared for the harsh trip ahead."   LUIS ALBERTO URREA

park

Originally, a park was a hunting ground owned by royalty, fenced in and closed off from the hoi polloi. From there, the meaning expanded to include any pleasure grounds, public or private, usually with lawns, trees, and amenities such as walkways and benches. By the seventeenth century there were plots in London known as parks set aside for all citizens to enjoy. By the nineteenth century, the term was applied in the United States to sporting grounds, as in ballpark. With the establishment of Yellowstone National Park in 1872, the term was expanded again, making room for such natural wonders as geysers and grizzlies. In the Rocky Mountains, forest openings, especially flat, grassy valley bottoms, are also known as parks. It was the latter meaning Mary Austin had in mind when she wrote in *The Land of Little Rain*: "They have a better name in the Rockies for these hill-fenced open glades of pleasantness; they call them parks."

SCOTT RUSSELL SANDERS

parna

Parna is an Australian term used in the United States for dunes made of clay and silt, which are commonly found in the Great Basin. The related term lunette refers to a crescent-shaped parna, which often forms on the downwind perimeter of rainwater, or playa, lakes in the Texas panhandle. These formations are created by the motion of the wind, but unlike sand dunes, they are a textured mass of material and, though fragile, give the appearance of solidity.   SUSAN BRIND MORROW

pass

A pass is a traversable route through rough country, often a range of mountains. "Going over the pass" is a metaphoric phrase commonly used to suggest seeking adventure, new lands, wildness, and refreshed identities. In Glacier National Park, more than two thousand miles of hiking trails are maintained, mostly over passes, so hikers may at least imagine such exploits. The availability of passes for human use has had a great deal to do with settlement, land use, and economic patterns. Marias Pass, on the southern border of Glacier National Park, for instance, is the only feasible route for a railroad in a three-hundred-mile north-south reach of the Rockies, and that rail line has had an enormous effect on life along the thousand-mile U.S.-Canadian borderland. Going to the Sun Highway crosses Logan Pass, inside the park; utterly unsuitable for a railway, it's driven each year by thousands of tourists, many on their way to hike other passes, to profound effect on the social and economic life of northwestern Montana. South Pass in Wyoming is a gentle ramp connecting the valleys of the Platte River system with those of the Green River, and was an important passage on the Oregon Trail.

WILLIAM KITTREDGE

passage

The word passage evokes images of hallways, secret tunnels, openings between here and there; a sense of moving through, going between, crossing over. Passages allow movement. In the landscape they provide routes to get from one open area to another. Mariners look for passages such as Knight Island Passage in Prince William Sound or Saratoga Passage in Puget Sound—protected waterways between two larger bodies of water. Spelunkers crawl or inch their way through underground passages that link open rooms of a cave. Passage is related to the word pass, a way through the mountains. Perhaps no geographical passage has been more evocative or historically significant than the imagined Northwest Passage, a coveted route between the Atlantic and Pacific Oceans through the far northern ice-bound waters above North America.   CAROLYN SERVID

pasture

Pasture can be used as both a verb and noun, though "to pasture" is considered regional, meaning to graze or browse, allowing animals to forage and feed in a field or meadow of growing grasses, as in "That land will easily

P

pasture thirty cows." As a noun, pasture refers to an area of land covered with grasses or herbage suitable for grazing livestock. Alternatively, it can mean the provender itself—grasses or flowers. Related terms are pasturage and pastureland, used synonymously. The etymology of pasture, coming from Latin through Middle French into English, is straightforward, and refers to attending to the feeding of beasts. Beyond this, pasture has a figurative association with spirituality and rest: it is the root of the word pastor, connecting a spiritual leader to the role of the shepherd who assures his flock of good grazing land. One of the best-known Psalms, the Twenty-third, relies on this poetic association: "The Lord is my Shepherd. He maketh me to lie down in green pastures." In a wholly secular but also figurative use of the term, a worker who has retired has either "gone out to pasture" or "been sent out to pasture."

PATRICIA HAMPL

patch

Any small area of undefined shape may be called a patch, as in an area of floating pieces of ice, joining and overlapping one another. Patch can also refer to a collection of drift or bay ice where no single piece of ice is more than fifty yards across. A mountlike reef that is part of a larger complex is a patch reef. As a landscape ecology term, patch refers to a relatively uniform or concentrated area, such as a briar patch or weed patch or, agriculturally, a bean patch. A concentration of oil and gas wells is an oil patch. Patch cutting refers to the practice of clearing trees in an area in staggered blocks, the uncut blocks acting as a source of seeds for the clear-cut blocks, and the clearcuts providing fire protection for the uncut patches. In "Crossing Brooklyn Ferry," Walt Whitman interprets the patch emotionally when he writes, "It is not upon you alone the dark patches fall."   ARTHUR SZE

paternoster lake

Circular lakes found in a linear chain within a glaciated, U-shaped valley and created by the damming
action of morainal ridges or rock bars are called pater-
noster lakes. The name—*pater noster* is Latin for "our
father"—is derived from the chain's resemblance to a
string of rosary beads. The sequence of lakes is also
known as a glacial stairway, the result of a mountain
glacier pushing down a valley, scouring at various
intervals a series of watery basins connected by rapids
and waterfalls.   CONGER BEASLEY, JR.

patterned ground

Patterned ground is a geologist's term of art for the
conspicuously symmetrical distribution of stones on the
surface of areas subject to intensive frost. The patterns
formed can take the shape of circles, polygons, or stripes.
Circles and polygons form on relatively flat ground,
stripes on sloping ground. The term was coined by A. L.
Washburn, a geologist at the University of Washington
at Seattle. Several processes of freezing and thawing,
saturation and drying out, produce the patterns, and
there is a considerable literature on the subject. They
are frequent in periglacial regions, that is, areas where
a cold climate has contributed to the morphology of the
landscape.   ROBERT HASS

P

peak

A peak is a high, sharp point. (By comparison, a summit
is an extremity, but not necessarily a sharp point, on a hill
or mountain. While peaks are often rocky horns and/or
pinnacles, summits can be found at the quite unspectacu-
lar highest point on a loaf of a mountain. Thus, although a
mountain often has only one summit, which may resemble a peak, a mountain may also have multiple peaks
and summits, even while having only one highest point.)

There are a large number of peaks in the Teton Range, but the "Grand" Teton is the summit. "Going for the summit" can be a metaphor for human aspirations, particularly among mountaineers, Japanese climbers on Mount Fuji, and Native Americans seeking visions, all seeming to involve a testing of self and discovery of its essence in connection with a sight of the Altogether. Hopi Indians call the San Francisco Peaks a "cloud house" where gods live. The Navajos revere the wisdom of mountain gods. Taos Pueblo is oriented to sacred mountains. Ancient Greeks understood Mount Olympus as the home of the gods, and Tibetan Buddhists regard peaks and summits as centers of sacred energy.   WILLIAM KITTREDGE

peatland

In the United States, peatland is a less common, more technical name for a specific kind of wetland, the peat bog. Sixty percent of the wetlands on Earth are made of peat. Peatlands are generally in higher latitudes—the upper Midwest, upstate New York, and Canada, for instance—the result of glacial melt at the end of the last ice age. Peat is predominantly plant matter (much of which is sphagnum moss, but peat also contains trees, grass, and the insects and animals that lived in them) that has failed to decompose due to moist conditions, most often because of the high acidity created by waterlogging. In North America peat is found in remnant glacial areas like the Finger Lakes of New York State. Referring to the notorious fact that a peat bog is a trap for anything that walks, one text from the New York State Museum described how scientists "have frequently found wooly mammoth and mastodon skeletons in peat bogs at the bottom of these meltwater channels" near Syracuse. A peatland is the first stage in the formation of coal, hence ultimately diamond. In 2004, the uncontrolled burning of peatland in Indonesia was believed by some in the scientific community to be a significant factor in the dramatic rise of carbon dioxide in the atmosphere. There is also recent concern about the imminent release of high levels of carbon into the atmosphere by the rapid thawing of permafrost into peatland now taking place in the Arctic.

SUSAN BRIND MORROW

pebble beach

A pebble is a stone between the size of a corn kernel and a baseball, larger than a kernel of wheat, smaller than a cobble, or between 0.08 and 2.52 inches. By abrasion, through the action of passing water and wind, the stone fragments that make pebbles have become worn and rounded. A pebble beach, therefore, is a margin of land where loose pebbles have accumulated, bounding a sea, lake, pond, or stream, and is distinguished from sand beach or cobble beach. There is the well-known Pebble Beach on California's Monterey Peninsula, and pebble beaches in Del Norte, Marin, San Mateo, and Sonoma Counties, California, as well as one in Waldo, Minnesota, one in Nantucket, Massachusetts, and a small island off the coast of Washington called Pebble Beach.

JOHN KEEBLE

P

pediment

An architectural term, pediment refers to a low gable, typically triangular with a horizontal cornice, surmounting a colonnade or otherwise signaling a significant division in a façade. In geology, the angularity of architectural pediments has been taken up to refer to a gently sloping rock platform at the foot of an abrupt rise or face. Pediments are sometimes triangular in shape. They often extend over a considerable area, and typically they cut across geologic formations. Such phenomena are found in all climatic zones, but are most visible in arid and semi-arid regions. The pediment's surface has been eroded over a long period, and is mantled with a discontinuous veneer of alluvium fallen from above and in a state of transport across the pediment's grade.   JOHN KEEBLE

Pele's tears

Fragments of molten rock falling from a lava fountain may congeal in the air, forming solid drops of volcanic glass, broad at one end and tapering at the other. Hawaiians call the beautiful black fragments *waimaka-o-Pele*, or Pele's tears (in reference to the volcano goddess). Fountaining may also produce glass filaments as long as three feet, gold in color and as fine as human hair, either spun out from the tear-shaped ends of these drops or forming on their own. The delicate strands of *lauoho-o-Pele*, or Pele's hair, drift downwind, and collect in rock crevices on the leeward side of Kīlauea Volcano, gleaming with the mysterious presence of the deity for which they are named.   PAMELA FRIERSON

peña

Peña and *peñasco* are Spanish for boulder or large rock. The word peñasco is sometimes used when referring to a rocky promontory. People in the southwestern United States and throughout Mexico use the words to indicate landmarks when giving directions to travelers. Settlements were frequently named for the peñas or peñascos nearby, as in the New Mexico towns of Peña Blanca and Peñasco. In his book *Big Bend: A Homesteader's Story*, J. O. Langford writes: "That night we camped at old Fort Peña, where in 1881 a band of Apaches had made a last fierce and fatal effort to slaughter the United States soldiers there."   ARTURO LONGORIA

peninsula

Etymologically, a peninsula is almost an island. The word is broadly applied to various landmasses that are largely surrounded by water. A peninsula's connection to the mainland can be a narrow isthmus or a broader reach of land. Four peninsulas mark the corners of the United States and illustrate the variety of peninsular landforms. Baja California and Florida are long narrow extensions off the southern perimeter on opposite sides of the continent. Washington's boxy Olympic Peninsula forms the northwest corner, and the Canadian province of Nova Scotia dangles from an isthmus out into the Atlantic Ocean off the northeast coast of Maine.   CAROLYN SERVID

perched water table

When a lens of groundwater hovers in isolation above the general water table and is entirely separate from it, it's viewed as being perched there. The lens is created when surface water, percolating through the ground, encounters an isolated layer of bedrock or impermeable soil, a mass of limited extent. Perched water tables most often occur in areas with level topography, high rainfall, and poor drainage. Well diggers eagerly seek them out because they're closer to the surface than the main water table. Occasionally, a perched water table forms at such a shallow depth it intersects the ground surface and produces a flowing spring.   TERRY TEMPEST WILLIAMS

P

perennial stream

A stream or reach of a stream that flows year-round in a well-defined channel is known as a perennial stream, also called a permanent spring. The Army Corps of Engineers defines a perennial stream as one that flows 365 days in a typical year. The stream flows when it receives significant amounts of water during wet periods; when it receives groundwater discharge from below, reaching the surface through springs or seeps; or when it receives long-term water from melting snow and ice. Perennial streams can dry up, though, particularly during extended periods of drought, damaging the life within them that depends on constant flow. The distinction between perennial and intermittent streams is often a subject of controversy in localities, as specific conservation ordinances often set exact guidelines for a property with a designated perennial stream.   JEFFERY RENARD ALLEN

petrified forest

Petrification occurs when minerals, usually silica, replace the cellulose of a tree. The result is a mineral log that preserves many details of the original log, even the rings. Postglacial petrified forests are common in the estuaries of the American Southwest. The largest known petrified forest is to be found in (and the term in North America almost always brings to mind) Petrified Forest National Park in Arizona, adjoining the Navajo Indian Reservation. In over ninety-five acres, six separate "forests" display jasper and agate logs lying on the ground surrounded by variegated colors of ancient chips and fragments. These "stone trees" died and fell by natural processes, such as fire or fungus or even insect infestation. Buried in mud and sand that contained substances such as silica-rich volcanic ash or salts rich in uranium, groundwater carried minerals into the logs, replacing the wood cells and eventually resulting in striking statuary forms. Prehistoric North American peoples lived among these trees, and ruins of their dwellings remain. The adjective petrified means changed into stone or a stony substance. Figuratively, petrified suggests being startled or terrified, or being paralyzed with fear.   PATRICIA HAMPL

picacho

Picacho and pico both denote a landscape feature that rises and tapers to a peak. Picacho has the added sense of a pico that's out of the ordinary; it's a really imposing summit. It would be Pikes Picacho in an alternate history, not Pikes Peak. Other high, isolated landforms in the Southwest, although less grand than Pikes Peak, are sometimes given the descriptive title of picacho, perhaps because even a moderately tall butte is awe-inspiring enough to a born flatlander. Pico means "beak" or "snout" in conversational Spanish, and other things when the language gets vulgar. Place-names are often duplications when two language communities are in prolonged contact. Mount Picacho in New Mexico and Picacho Peak in Arizona, for example, are redundant. The most significant Civil War battle in Arizona took place near Picacho Peak in 1862, when a detachment of Union soldiers from California encountered a Confederate scouting party. The ashes of Mary Austin, author of *The Land of Little Rain*, were interred in 1934 on Mount Picacho above Santa Fe.   D. J. WALDIE

piedmont

A combination of the Italian *piemonte* and the French *pied*, piedmont describes a plain, terrace, slope, or expanse of hills at the base of mountains. In North America the term is largely synonymous with the wide band of rolling hills and farmland just east of the Appalachian range. (There is also a Colorado Piedmont along the eastern slope of the Rockies.) The clay soils and agrarian cultures of the eastern Piedmont stretch far beyond the shadow of the Appalachians. The region reaches from New Jersey to Alabama, bounded on the eastern edge by the fall line that drops to the sandy soils of the coastal plain. It forms a wide intermediary between the Atlantic coast and the mountains, a half step between sea level and the highest elevations the eastern half of the continent has to offer. The Piedmont was settled early and heavily in post-Columbian times and is now home to some of the most fragmented natural habitat on the continent.

JAN DEBLIEU

P

pimple mound

Tens if not hundreds of thousands of pimple mounds
dot the low, flat coastal country of southwest Louisiana and east Texas. Circular ones have diameters of
seventy-five feet or less; elliptical ones may be as long
as three hundred feet. They range in height from three
to six feet. Their soil, a coarse, sandy loam, differs
markedly from the heavy silt of the surrounding plain.
In aerial photographs, a pimple plain can resemble
densely granulated tapioca or heavily freckled skin.
Alphabetically, they have been attributed to everything
from ants and burrowing squirrels to whirlwinds and
wild cucumbers. Current speculation favors erosional
activity, but several scientists have presented evidence
of agradational, rather than erosional, origin.

FRANKLIN BURROUGHS

pingo

Pingo comes from the Iñupiaq word *piŋu*, which means
an individual round hill or a swelling. Pingos, then, are
swollen ice hills. They form most notably on Canadian
and Alaskan Arctic coastal lowlands, where they offer
one of the few prominent features in an otherwise flat
landscape. A type of ground ice, pingos most often
emerge on top of drained lakebeds where the underlying
permafrost has thawed. As the once insulating lake water
disappears, foundational soils below the old lakebed
freeze, squeezing out residual water. Arctic ground
temperatures freeze this free water, and hydrostatic pressure forces it upward, creating an ice dome covered with
the lakebed's soils. Pingos can grow to 150 feet in height
and be a thousand or more feet in diameter. They may,
however, have short lives. Pingo domes often rupture,
giving them a volcanolike appearance and exposing the
ice core, which can melt, causing the structure to gradually collapse.　CAROLYN SERVID

pit

A pit is a naturally formed or human-made hole in the ground. Sinkholes and pitted outwash plains are types of natural pits; borrow pits are work places from which soil has been "borrowed" for a building project. Large-scale pits are developed when land is mined to extract minerals or other materials, such as coal. The term can also refer to a surface formation containing prehistoric animal fossils. That is, the formation is a "pit" only in the sense that animal remains are forever trapped there. As fossil sites, tar pits deserve special mention, since in actuality they are not composed of tar but of a natural accumulation of tarlike bitumen at the surface of the Earth in which animal bones are preserved. Bitumen is a viscous or solid mixture of hydrocarbons and other substances distilled from petroleum that form asphalt, coal, and other materials. (Tar, narrowly, is residue created from the distillation of coal.) The La Brea Tar Pits in Hancock Park, Los Angeles, have produced one of the most extraordinary fossil collections in the world, containing the remains of thousands of animals from the Early Pleistocene epoch, some 2.5 million years ago, and even a more recent human fossil, the "La Brea woman." Brea means "tar" in Spanish, so "The La Brea Tar Pits" literally means "The The Tar Tar Pits." The pits actually contain a thick deposit of asphalt, the heaviest grade of petroleum, which is an excellent preservative as it saturates the bones and preserves the original organic matter.   JEFFERY RENARD ALLEN

pitch

A word with manifold meanings as a noun alone—in music and song, in printing and mechanical engineering, in baseball and golf, not to mention retailing—pitch usually has a bucolic cast as a landscape term. A section of grand lawn stretching down and away from a mansion might be characterized as a pitch. Essentially, it is a strip of land bounded in some way—by forests, by fields, or hills, or water—that rises upward or downward from the viewer's point of view. Like a reach of river water, a pitch of land has no strict measurement, but it is almost always loosely bound, the way a British playing field is or the Sheep Meadow in New York's Central Park, where people sunbathe and play catch. A climber, of course, who might refer to the severity of a wall's angle as its pitch, will also demarcate the section of the wall to be climbed as a pitch. And, haunted by the thought of a fall, recall one of the word's older, and now obsolete, meanings—the highest point, a geometry that prompted Milton's line in *Paradise Lost,* "Down they fell Driv'n headlong from the Pitch of Heaven, down into this Deep." BARRY LOPEZ

placer deposit

Their name derived from the Spanish term for a sand bank, placer deposits contain gravel or rocks rich in a valuable mineral—usually gold, platinum, diamonds, or tin. These materials have been washed out of ore veins, carried, and laid down as alluvial deposits at places in a river where the current slows, such as below a rapids. Placer deposits—the word rhymes with "sass her" not "place her"—are usually the first to be mined after a strike. They're at or near the surface, and the running water that laid the deposits down initially is often close at hand, a ready source for hydraulically sorting this (already) loosened material. It's placer mining that gave rise to the enduring image of a lone prospector panning for gold along a western stream. BARBARA KINGSOLVER

plain

The American Great Plains, an immense sweep of land that stretches east of the Rocky Mountains in the

United States, covers part or all of New Mexico, Texas, Oklahoma, Colorado, Kansas, Nebraska, Wyoming, Montana, South Dakota, North Dakota, and the Canadian provinces of Saskatchewan and Alberta. A plain, or a broad, flat, level expanse of land, supports prairie, or grasses, flowers, herbs, and a few trees. Euro-Americans referred to the prairie as a sea of grass, a treeless wasteland, a place where one could easily become lost, without landmarks or bearings. Native Americans—Lakota, Arapahoe, Crow, Cheyenne, Kiowa, and Comanche—knew it as a lush grazing land for the bison that provided bountiful food, clothing, and shelter. Robert Louis Stevenson, in *Across the Plains*, described the Great Plains as "a world almost without feature; an empty sky, an empty earth, front and back." Willa Cather, in *Death Comes for the Archbishop*, offers a strikingly different portrait of the plains sky: "The plain was there, under one's feet, but what one saw when one looked about was that brilliant blue world of stinging air and moving cloud. . . . Elsewhere the sky is the roof of the world; but here the earth was the floor of the sky. The landscape one longed for when one was far away, the thing all about one, the world one actually lived in, was the sky, the sky!" In more current times, crops such as wheat have replaced the prairie grasses and cattle have replaced the bison in the semiarid environment, which generally lies 1,000 to 6,000 feet above sea level.   MARY SWANDER

P

plateau

An extensive area of nearly level land that rises abruptly above a surrounding landscape on at least one side, known also as tableland, is called a plateau. Canyons often encroach on or dissect the plateau's flat surface, and it is distinguished from similar formations by its breadth—the Columbia lava plateau of eastern Washington and Oregon, for instance, is different from the isolated prominence of a mesa, is larger than a butte, is flat, and presents a dramatic vertical fall on all sides. Plateau also designates the American Indians who inhabited the plateau country between the Cascades and Rockies, and the food-gathering culture there.   LARRY WOIWODE

platin

Platin is a French Canadian term, used also in New England, for a flat, or floodplain—for example, the Green River in New Brunswick where it joins the St. John and forms the Platin de la Rivière-Verte.

SUSAN BRIND MORROW

playa

The Spanish word *playa* means "beach," "shore," or "seacoast." However, throughout the Spanish-speaking world—and in the United States along the Texas Gulf coast, Florida's Gulf and Atlantic coasts, and southern California's Pacific coast—the word usually refers more specifically to a sandy beach. Playa is also used when describing the sandy bank along a river bend, or at the edge of a lake or pond. In a curious appropriation of the word (perhaps as a result of a mistranslation), geologists and geographers have developed an elaborately esoteric definition of the word. Accordingly, playa refers to shallow, gravel-bottomed, recharge wetlands in semiarid and arid prairies, or dry nonvegetated flat areas at the lowest sections of undrained desert basins. One might speculate that while viewing a wetland, a scientist inquired of a Spanish speaker, "What do you call this?" The Spanish speaker—referring to the sandy edges around the wetland—said, *"Es una playa."* Unable to fully understand the foreign tongue, the scientist wrote dutifully that a "shallow, gravel-bottomed etc." is called a playa. What we are seeing then is language evolving. Perhaps in two hundred years playa will mean universally more than merely a sandy beach. For now, however, millions of Spanish speakers know the word playa only as beach.   ARTURO LONGORIA

playree

A Cajun version of the English prairie, playree is used by many French-speaking Louisianans to describe the vast coastal marsh whose reach resembles a great open grassland.   MIKE TIDWELL

plunge pool

A plunge basin is a cavity at the base of a falls formed by a stream or river as it pours over a nickpoint; the plunge pool is the water in that basin. Ethnobotanist Gary Nabhan, overlooking La Cascada de Basaseachic in Mexico, relates in his article "Mother Mountains" how he watched "water fall for close to 1,000 feet, atomizing into mist before it hit a large plunge pool on the canyon floor." Whether a large falls or a small one, most people are mesmerized by the sound and sight of falling water; pieces of broken rainbows created by sun and mist hanging midair, swallows circling, veering above the plunge pool, flying in and out, sometimes behind and around the falls, dippers in the rapids below. If the pool is calm, clear, and deep, and the weather mild or warm, a person might step in, enter, bodily and over the head, the rare country of a plunge pool.   PATTIANN ROGERS

pocket

Pocket derives from *pockete*, an Anglo-French word that means "bag" and is related to the French *poche* and its diminutive *pochette*. As a landscape term it refers to a recess, cavity, crevice, hole, depression, pit, hollow, or glen. Miners describe small veins or lodes of ore as pockets. And there is pocket ice as well as pocket valleys, pocket beaches, and water pockets. The hidden,

P

secluded, and secretive qualities attached to pocket make it seem a rare, intimate, and mysterious feature of the land or sea. MICHAEL COLLIER

pocket beach

A small gem, a pocket beach is a crescent of well-sorted sand tucked into a niche along a coastline. Where it occurs between headlands, it is generally hidden from view, and so all the more appealing. Pocket beaches are found along the coasts of Maine and Oregon and in other places where the land falls precipitously into the sea. Jennifer Hahn, in *Spirited Waters: Soloing South through the Inside Passage,* writes: "I'd seen only three possible campsites all afternoon. A new spot looked promising, but, eyeing the forest that lay behind a mattress-size beach of broken shells, I was disheartened. Telltale kelp fronds hung like Christmas garlands from the trees' lowest branches. By midnight this lovely pocket beach would be an aquarium." The term is synonymous with bayhead beach and cove beach. JAN DEBLIEU

pocosin

Pocosin (also anglicized as pocoson, poquosin, percoarson, perkoson) derives from the extensive Algonquian family of languages. The word apparently differed in pronunciation and signification from tribe to tribe. As appropriated by settlers in eastern Maryland and the tidewater country of Virginia and the Carolinas, it refers to swamps, bays, bogs, and marshy savannas. In his *History of the Carolinas* of 1799, John Lawson describes the land along the lower Santee as "scarce anything but swamp and percoarson," and unhelpfully defines the latter as a "sort of low land." Washington Caruthers Kerr, in *Report of the Geological Survey of N.C., 1895,* defines a pocosin or dismal as an isolated wetland.

FRANKLIN BURROUGHS

It should not surprise that so elemental a word as point
has several geographic meanings. Wherever land meets
water, from Point Barrow, Alaska, to Point Pleasant,
Florida, point describes the projection of dry ground into
the surrounding sea, bay, lake, or river. In Appalachia,
point may refer to the termination of a mountain ridge
projecting into a confluence of valleys. Even on prairies,
points abound. Several places called Point of Rock
were important landmarks along the Santa Fe Trail.
The most famous of these, located a few miles west of
Dodge City, Kansas, demarcated a low hill that ended in
a rocky escarpment. Unfortunately, this Point of Rocks
was destroyed by highway construction in 1981. In river
morphology, a point is the inside or convex curve of a
meander, where sediment tends to aggrade. The condition of vegetation on a stream's meander point is a useful
indicator of its ecological health: if vegetation is colonizing the point, the health trend is likely positive. The state
of the meander point is usually a better indicator of the
stream's overall condition than the presence or absence
of erosion on the concave or outer curve of the channel.
Erosion and consequent bank collapse on the outside of a
bend can be a natural feature of the stream's morphologi-
cal dynamic.   WILLIAM DEBUYS

P

point of rock

Travelers tend to identify a point of rock as that place
where they encounter an elemental difficulty. For the
mariner, a point of rock extends into the sea, and may
threaten shipwreck or offer desperate refuge after the
boat goes down. Climbers refer to the point of rock
as that place where the approach up a grade or talus
slope becomes the start of the ascent on the solid face.
Horse packers in mountain country sometimes refer to
the point of rock as that place where footing becomes

treacherous on exposed bedrock, or where passage is
tight at a precipitous turn in the trail. At such places,
the underlying rock addresses the traveler, becomes a
landmark, handhold, threat. There are two significant
points of rock on the Santa Fe Trail, one in New Mexico
and the other in Kansas. They served as both landmarks
and lookouts.   KIM STAFFORD

pokelogan

In the northeastern United States, lumbermen called
the stagnant backwaters of lakes and rivers pokelogans.
The word appears to be cognate with pocosin. The root
sense may have meant something like "land covered with
shallow water," but whereas a pokelogan is always part of
a larger body of water, a pocosin is landlocked. Thoreau
heard the term on his first trip to Maine from George
McCauslin, a log driver on the Penobscot River: "Now
and then we passed what McCauslin called a pokelogan,
an Indian term for what the drivers might have reason
to call a poke-log-in, an inlet that leads nowhere." Such
places as Pocasset, a village on Cape Cod, are etymological cousins, at a greater or a lesser remove, of pocosin
and pokelogan, according to William Tooker, writing in
an 1899 edition of *American Anthropologist*. Did the Euro-
American settlers realize that they were naming their
community something like Backwater or Large Puddle?
FRANKLIN BURROUGHS

pole road

A road of logs, poles, or planks was commonly laid down
on the roadbed in the nineteenth century to traverse an
area of wet ground or thick mud in spring, to make the
road passable. In states such as Kentucky, Pennsylvania,
and Tennessee travelers can still find valleys and streams
named for these old roads—Pole Road Hollow, Pole Road
Run, Pole Road Gulch. The folklorist Mary Hufford at

the University of Pennsylvania mentions the related corduroy roads in the cedar swamps in South Jersey, which were used to bring cedar out of the swamps. Corduroy suggests the construction of the road: poles laid horizontally together. A similar construction is sometimes used in national parks today to protect the fragile ecology of a wetland or seaside.   SUSAN BRIND MORROW

pond

Pond is one of the most flexible words for describing a small body of freshwater. Uplift, landslides, volcanoes, and glaciers can create ponds, as can human beings and animals. Beavers are great ponders, and so are farmers and ranchers who dig them for irrigation and livestock. Glacial kettle-hole ponds such as Thoreau's Walden and Cape Cod's freshwater ponds are important features of the New England landscape. George Stewart tells us in *Names on the Land* that "native peoples" of the Northeast called ponds *paugs* and that this has resulted in felicitous redundancies such as Mashapaug Pond in Massachusetts. At least since 1641, the English have referred jocularly to the Atlantic Ocean as the "great pond." And there is no end to the compound forms of the word: sagpond, millpond, fishpond, duckpond, pond life, pond lily, and pond yard to name a few. Regardless of size, location, or purpose, any pond can become the radiant and beguiling point of a landscape, even a muddy or algae-covered farm pond that's nothing more than an isolated earthen water tank. Thoreau thought of Walden and nearby North Ponds as "Lakes of Light" in "which the beholder measures the depth of his own nature."   MICHAEL COLLIER

pool and riffle

Few things assert the dynamism of nature better than the development of pools and riffles in a stream. Even if a channel is straight and the bed uniform, flowing water will generate turbulence. Depending on the resistance of the streambed, this turbulence may scour pools in certain places, which alternate with shallow bars called riffles or drops, where the excavated material is deposited. Generally the distance from one pool to the next is five to seven times the width of the stream, and successive pools will tend to develop on opposite sides of the channel, precursors to the formation of meanders. Very steep streams have step-pool sequences with similar cyclicity. Experienced anglers tend to be attentive to the patterns of pools and riffles, as fish like to wait in the slow water of a pool while watching for food to arrive from the faster flow of an upstream riffle. WILLIAM DEBUYS

portage

A portage is a path or passageway along which canoes or other small boats and goods are carried around obstructions in a stream or between navigable bodies of water. A portage is also a place where such a land route begins or ends, and it refers, too, to the act of carrying or transporting canoes and goods overland, usually to skirt unmanageable rapids or waterfalls. So established a fact of transportation were portages, there existed a portage collar, a strap that passed around the forehead and attached at each end to the burden being carried, which was then supported on the back. A portage was no picnic, but it made traversing the wilderness possible—eventually there were even portage railroads. Most portages were only known locally, but one became famous: the Chicago Portage, which made possible the crucial water route from the Great Lakes to the mighty Mississippi. DONNA SEAMAN

postpile

Postpile is a compound word. Think post, then pile—a pile of vertical posts. Only here, instead of wood, the posts are hundreds of columns of cooled basalt lava. Perhaps the best example is in Devils Postpile National Monument in California (on early maps, it still shows up as Devils Woodpile, the name the U.S. Cavalry buffalo soldiers patrolling Yosemite gave it, as had the Basque sheepherders before them), where the cooling conditions for a four-hundred-foot-deep lava flow were ideal enough that the cracks on the surface—the columnar jointing resulting from stresses of cooling—were able to branch down, forming long, delicate columns, or posts, each one having from three to seven sides. While all lava flows cool and crack, not much cools so regularly from top to bottom as the flow that became Devils Postpile. Seen from the side, where the formation was sheared off by a glacier and the columns revealed, the terms postpile and woodpile make sense. Standing on top of it, however, Devils Postpile looks like nothing so much as a polished tile floor. STEPHEN GRAHAM JONES

pothole

A pothole in a streambed, often surprising for its perfect roundness, was formed and enlarged by the grinding effect of pebbles and cobbles swirled around by the water's circular current. Scour hole is a regional variant. Prairie pothole refers to a large depressions in the hummocky terrain of a glaciated plain. As a general term pothole may be most familiar to people living in the pothole country of the northern Plains, a landscape of natural ponds scattered far and wide, habitat upon which migratory waterfowl, especially, are dependent. It's these potholes that gave rise to Minnesota's moniker, "The Land of Ten Thousand Lakes." But hikers and river runners from Georgia to Oregon know potholes as characteristic of stream flows over certain types of substrates—basalt, for example. And that during low water or after a flood these dry scour holes often contain small treasures neither wind nor water has swept away, like polished rocks and the delicate exoskeletons of insects. When speleologists talk of potholing they are using the term metaphorically to describe vertical cave systems.

BARBARA KINGSOLVER

pouroff

It's an easy hike to Burro Mesa Pouroff at the head of a narrow box canyon in Big Bend National Park, located in west Texas. Water from rainstorms has cut a channel into the cliff at the head of the canyon and thus has created a pouroff. Pouroff is also a term used by ranchers in the central Colorado Plateau to indicate a rock nickpoint where occasional runoff pours over the edge into a plunge pool below. Water falling over a pouroff can be sporadic, from none to little to torrents, depending on the amount of rainfall or meltwater in the area.

PATTIANN ROGERS

prado

Prado comes from the more common word, found in the work of Latin American poets like Pablo Neruda and nostalgic Argentine folk singers, *pradera*: meadow, or watered field. El Prado, of course, is the famous Spanish museum—and prado is currently used to define a park, a great lawn, a promenade, even a garden. Hence, the word covers a lot of ground—from alfalfa fields for grazing cattle, to urban promenades. From the lower forty to Central Park. You could even say, if you were feeling pretentious, that your yard is your prado.   LUIS ALBERTO URREA

prairie

In his poem "The Prairies," William Cullen Bryant wrote: "These are the Gardens of the Desert, these / The unshorn fields, boundless and beautiful, / For which the speech of England has no name." The French named them prairie (meadow or grassland) from glimpses of the phenomenon in their central and southwest regions. The herbaceous makeup of the prairie was so diverse, each species extending roots as deep as its height, that even the frightful fires from lightning strikes, with flames forming tearing twisters a hundred feet high, couldn't destroy it. Then plows came. An early passenger on a buckboard said, "As I looked about me I felt the grass was the country, as water is the sea" (Willa Cather, *My Ántonia*). This sea was later divided: tallgrass prairie, mixed prairie, and shortgrass prairie, all of which now exist only in tracts preserved by ranchers and farmers and bureaus of the government—although the lay of the land remains: as Tim O'Brien writes in *The Things They Carried*, "All around us the Minnesota prairies reached out in long, repetitive waves of corn and soybeans, everything flat, everything the same." LARRY WOIWODE

pressure ice

A general term for ice whose surface has been deformed by stress generated by wind and currents, pressure ice includes pieces of ice squeezed against the shore, or thrust up against one another—ice that is forced upward or downward. Pressure ice may be rafted, hummocked, or tented, commonly to heights (or depths) of thirty feet or more. (The underside of a mound or hillock of pressure ice is called a bummock.) Norwegian explorer Fritjof Nansen, in his narrative of travels in the Arctic, *Farthest North*, writes of his ship, the *Fram*, amid ice floes under the strain of pressure: "The ice is restless, and has pressed a good deal to-day again. It begins with a gentle crack and moan along the side of the ship, which gradually sounds louder in every key. Now it is a high plaintive tone, now it is a grumble, now it is a snarl, and the ship gives a start up. The noise steadily grows till it is like all the pipes of an organ; the ship trembles and

shakes, and rises by fits and starts, or is sometimes gently lifted." Nansen called these episodes "squeezings," and the ridges that resulted from them as "ugly sights," one particularly menacing one "like a high frozen wave."
GRETCHEN LEGLER

promontory

A promontory is a point of high land that juts out into the sea or some other body of water; a headland. It comes from a Latin word, *promontorium*, meaning a mountain ridge. It's usually a maritime term. Here is Czeslaw Milosz in *Visions from San Francisco Bay*, writing in English about Robinson Jeffers: "I even reproached Jeffers for his descriptive passages, too much those of an amateur painter who sets up his easel on a wild promontory." But the term also refers to freshwater topography. Here is Henry David Thoreau in *Walden*: "Already, by the first of September, I had seen two or three small maples turned scarlet across the pond, beneath where the white stems of three aspens diverged, at the point of a promontory, next to the water." And from the West, here is Isabella Bird's *A Lady's Life in the Rocky Mountains*: "This mountain-girdled lake lay before me, with its margin broken up into bays and promontories, most picturesquely clothed by huge sugar pines." Another instance is Promontory Point on Great Salt Lake.   ROBERT HASS

protalus rampart

Talus, or scree, is the broken rock lying at an angle of repose at the foot of a cliff or fracturing wall. This angular debris dislodges from rimrock or the face of a headwall through frost-weathering, exfoliation, or chip-spalling under impact. When this broken rock slides across the surface of a glacier or perennial snow patch at the base of the wall before coming to rest, it is known more specifically as protalus. Protalus ramparts are prominent mounds and ridges formed where these stones collect on or beyond the ice or snow. Accumulating in a line parallel to the headwall, they resemble moraines. Cirque walls on many a mountain in the West, having been scooped out by alpine glaciers, generate protalus ramparts, especially in winter when their basal tarns are frozen. Though forbidding, these ramparts and the rockslides that spawn them support a specialized fauna, including pikas, marmots, and arctic alpine butterflies perfectly cryptic against rock and lichen.   ROBERT MICHAEL PYLE

punchbowl

Punchbowl is a descriptive term frequently applied to broad-bottomed depressions in the landscape, often to steep-walled features that suggest this serving vessel on a superhuman scale: the work of gods or, more often in the American West, the doing of the Devil. Landscape features bearing the name Devils Punchbowl include a collapsed and flooded sea cave on the coast of Oregon and a shallow basin in Devils Punchbowl County Park outside Los Angeles, created by slippage of the San Andreas Fault. Punchbowl also describes a type of volcanic crater: a broad cone with a saucer-shaped interior, built of ash that has weathered and cemented together into a rocky material known as tuff. Punchbowl Crater above Honolulu, the prototype, was formed about 250,000 years ago, during a late stage of vulcanism after several hundred thousand years of dormancy had allowed the island to erode into ridges and valleys. Magma pushing up through a low region encountered groundwater and erupted in explosions of ash and steam. The Hawaiian name for the crater is Pāowaina, "Hill of Placing," and it once served as a burial site for chiefs. Now Punchbowl National Cemetery fills its broad interior.   PAMELA FRIERSON

pushcover

Pushcover is a regional term used in the eastern United States, specifically Appalachia, for thick brush into which an animal in a hunt, such as a foxhunt, is pursued. The word represents a kind of nominal compounding typical of German, but unusual in American English—in which, here, a verb is bluntly smooshed into a noun to create a more vivid or more specific descriptive image.   SUSAN BRIND MORROW

quagmire

Quagmire is a compound onomatopoeic word comprising quag, marshy land that quakes and trembles when walked upon, and mire, an impassable swamp or morass. Related meanings for quag are soft and fleshy; for mire they are mucky, muddy, slimy, oozy, sloppy, and slushy. A quagmire can describe any bog or wetland, but it primarily refers to one that shakes and moves under weight. Among the earliest uses of quagmire is the one most common still: a predicament or situation from which it is difficult to extricate oneself. When the U.S.S.R. invaded Afghanistan in the 1980s, the Soviets quickly found they were stuck in a quagmire, albeit an arid or semiarid one. Similarly, the rice paddies and swamps of the Mekong Delta of Vietnam trapped first the French and then the U.S. armies for three decades in its quagmires. Quagmires are common features of the marshy ground along the banks of the creeks and rivers that thread through the low land of the Chesapeake Bay.   MICHAEL COLLIER

quaking bog

The quaking bog is one of the most novel features of forests of the northern United States, especially those in New England and Wisconsin. It's an area of sphagnum moss, rushes, sedges, and decaying vegetation, the whole mass of which is floating on a pool of water. The surface appears solid and stable, until trusted with the weight of a step. What seems to be firm ground then shivers, sinks, and rises, like a natural trampoline or waterbed. If the first shimmy of this rich root mass underfoot is not heeded, one might easily break through the entangled mat into water and loose mud below, as if one had stepped into quicksand. The quaking bog suggests in perceptible human time the larger ripple, rise and fall, and shifting of the Earth's surface in geologic time.
ROBERT MORGAN

quarry

A quarry is a large depression where stone has been mined from the earth, or is still being mined. A quarry is generally created by human activity, although glaciers are said to be "quarrying" when they pluck off and carry along pieces of jointed rock. The name is also given to rock formations capable of being quarried, or to formations that in their natural state resemble a dug-out quarry. Occasionally diggers extract so much rock from the Earth in a human-made quarry that an underground spring is tapped. The space fills with water, forming a swimming hole of unsurpassed beauty, freshness, and depth. JAN DEBLIEU

quebrada

The Missouri Breaks could have been called the Missouri Quebradas. A quebrada is something broken. Literally, a break (from the verb *quebrar*). It implies the breaking up of the ground; a shattering of passes and horizons into a rougher country beyond. (A narrow pass between mountains, a deep depression in the land.) It can be used to refer to rugged canyons, a fissurelike ravine, broken and/or uneven ground, or the course of a stream. In the United States, it is most often taken to mean "a mountain stream" (derived either from the way it breaks out of canyons and gullies, or for the kind of country it breaks from). Trivia note: for Spanglish fans, it is worth noting that quebrada is the best slang some Chicanos can come up with for "getting a break" in life. *"Órale, vato— dame una quebrada."* LUIS ALBERTO URREA

quicksand

Quicksand is an ordinary bed of sand so saturated with water that it has become soupy and unstable. Most commonly found along beaches, riverbanks, lakeshores, and marshes, or near underground springs, quicksand can be triggered by earthquakes, which intensify the pressure of existing groundwater. As water flows in and fills the voids between sand particles, the friction between the particles diminishes, the bonds of the silicon molecules loosen, and a formerly solid bed of sand can suddenly become a viscous, incoherent mixture. The *quick* in quicksand suggests the speed with which sand in this condition moves, and also "quickness" in the sense of something that seems endowed with life. A cliché of B-movie adventures, quicksand has also been invoked by literary masters to vivify other engulfing forces, such as deceit and greed. Being caught in actual quicksand need not be fatal, however; the beds are usually only several feet deep, and although quicksands vary in buoyancy, it is usually easier to float in quicksand than in water. Struggling too much can indeed cause a person in quicksand to sink, but by relaxing, lying on the back, and slowly moving the arms, it is possible to float gradually to the shore and safety.

EMILY HIESTAND

Q

race

A race is a current of water flowing quickly through a
narrow or restricted channel. Such currents can occur
in nature or they can be man-made. A tidal race flows
with the changing tides, typically through a channel
from one end of a sand or mud flat to another. A human-
made millrace, on the other hand, takes advantage of
the steady flow of a river or stream. A channel is dug
into or raised above the ground, allowing a strong,
controlled current of water to move away from the river
in order to power a mill wheel. The head race leads water
toward the wheel (sometimes from a gather pond or
reservoir), while the tail race channels it away, typically
back to the river. Cedar Falls, Iowa, was once the site
of a notable millrace; constructed in 1848, it provided
much of the city with hydropower until the installa-
tion of electrical power made it obsolete. As Edgar Lee
Masters writes in *The Sangamon*, "At last I wanted to
take a shortcut from the dam to the shore. The millrace
was between me and the dam, but I did not know it was
the millrace, or for that matter what a millrace was.
It was a still body of water boarded in, and not more
than six feet across, but it was very deep, twenty feet
or more." LAN SAMANTHA CHANG

racetrack valley

The racetrack valley within Death Valley is called
Racetrack Playa, a dry lakebed with a very fine clay
surface. The term racetrack comes from the trails or
tracks the lakebed's rocks leave behind them when they
"race"—that is, mysteriously slide along the floor of
the lakebed. (Though the prevailing theory is that this
movement is due to a combination of strong wind gusts
and deceptively slick clay, so far no one's managed to
actually document a rock in motion.) In South Dakota,
however, the designation racetrack valley has nothing to

do with lakebeds or moving rocks. There, the feature is an oval valley of red shale and sandstone that rings the Black Hills. Sacred to the Lakota, this Racetrack Valley is the result of a great race run long ago by all the world's creatures. On American maps, it shows up as Red Valley, just between the Black Hills and the Dakota Hogback to the east of the hills. Yet another Racetrack Valley can be found on the western slope of the Rocky Mountains in Granite County, Montana. There, the name comes from association with Racetrack Lake and Racetrack Creek, which in turn get their names from Indians who camped around the warm springs in the area for long enough periods of time that horse racing became a regular occurrence.   STEPHEN GRAHAM JONES

raft

A floating assemblage of tree trunks, branches, bark, leaves, root wads, and litter that comes together in a river's flow goes under the collective name raft. Rafts ride the current until they break up, waterlog, and sink, or until they make landfall. For a mass of driftwood in the water, such as the great rafts that come down the Yukon after spring breakup, Koyukon Athabaskan say *neetohudaaneeltzaakk*. When a river undercuts its banks, sweeping tangled masses of vegetation out to sea, animals may go along for the ride. Rafts can bridge oceanic barriers, explaining cases of species disjuncture, whereby plants or animals occur in locations isolated from their main range. Log booms are the human-assembled, commercial equivalent. Benson rafts (or cigar rafts) were huge, elliptical booms up to fifty-five feet wide, thirty-five feet high, and a thousand feet long, cabled tight for towing downcoast to San Francisco. Flat booms are still pulled by tugs on the Columbia River, whose dams prevent rafts of natural debris from reaching the Pacific, depriving pelagic fish and their ecosystem of a vital source of nutrients and shelter.   ROBERT MICHAEL PYLE

railroad bed

In the settlement of the Midwest and the Great Plains, railway companies made an early push to link both coasts of the United States, laying thousands of miles of track. In *Across the Plains,* Robert Louis Stevenson wrote that "the line of the railroad stretched from horizon to horizon like a cue across a billiard board." To generate trade and income along their routes, railway companies recruited settlers from other parts of the country and from as far away as Europe to the American "Garden of Eden." The landscape outside the railroad rights of way soon filled with cultivated farms and developing towns and cities, their populations displacing Native Americans. Much of the rail laid back then on midcountry prairie, though it remains in place, is rarely used today for train travel. Unexpectedly, despite the century and more of human disturbance around them and their near abandonment, these rights of way served to preserve some of the last intact native plant communities on the prairies. In recent years, many hundreds of miles of these old railroad beds have been converted into trails where people enjoy hiking, biking, cross-country skiing, and going on nature walks. One of them is the Root River State Trail System, stretching over sixty miles, with the city of Lanesboro, Minnesota, at its hub. One of the most popular recreation trails in the nation, its rail bed was originally laid out in 1860, when the Southern Minnesota Railway Company cut its right-of-way through river bluffs in southeastern Minnesota.   MARY SWANDER

rain shadow

When prevailing winds encounter a large-scale topographic obstacle, usually a mountain range, the lee side

R

of the obstacle is voided of significant precipitation,
becoming a territory where moisture merely shadows the
other side. The cooling effect of high elevation causes
precipitation on windward slopes, thereby reducing
the amount of moisture available to the lee. The White
Mountains in east-central California are in the rain
shadow of the Sierra Nevada, and the semiarid interior
regions of Washington and Oregon are in the rain
shadow of the Cascade Mountains.   JOHN KEEBLE

raised beach

A beach raised above the present waterline and wave
action of a lake, river, or ocean, consisting of an accumulation of water-worn stones, gravel, sand, and other shore
material, is called, naturally, a raised beach. The raised
shore may be formed by the elevation of the coast or left
by receding waters, as in many lake and river regions.
A raised beach in a boreal forest is a sometimes called
a stranded lakeshore. Such shores exist in significant
numbers, particularly since boreal forests make up more
than one-third of northern hemisphere forests. In the
southeastern United States, raised beaches, regionally
called beach ridges, were formed by higher sea levels
that occurred during interglacial periods of the Pleistocene. They are often many miles from the present-day
coastline, and may be marked by the existence of dune
systems.   JEFFERY RENARD ALLEN

ramadero

The word ramadero comes from the Spanish *ramada*,
which means a place or shelter with interlaced branches
overhead. Ramaderos are heavily vegetated drainage
routes coursing between the low hills of Starr and Zapata
Counties in deep south Texas. From above they appear
like sinuous emerald ribbons winding through the
dry brushlands. Choked with tall mesquites, huisache,

and ebony, they are only a few yards wide and can be many miles long. They serve as migrating corridors for monarch butterflies and other insect and mammal species. A unique feature of a ramadero is that water diffuses beneath its sandy and clayey soils and does not begin to flow on top until the ramadero merges with an arroyo. The ramadero's expansive shade drops summer temperatures by as much as ten degrees. Extensive brush clearing has reduced ramaderos to less than ten percent of their historic acreage. What few existed in western Hidalgo County have been bulldozed out.   ARTURO LONGORIA

range

A term with numerous applications, including a legal one in the United States (as designated by the U.S. Public Land Survey system), range in its strictest, yet most abstract, sense means the outer demarcations between which variation is possible, or the difference between the highest and lowest values in any series. Hence, a mountain range is defined by its location, geologic character, and origin, and anything that occurs within that compass, however varied, is a part of the range. More than one distinct range may occur in close proximity to another, as with the Rocky and Big Horn Mountains, and the Wind River Range in Wyoming. A second, equally important application of the term is to the territory within which a creature, such as a cougar, or a species, or a group within a species, may reside, journey, and find sustenance. Domestic livestock, such as cattle, have ranges assigned to them. The ranges of all animals—and of flora, as well—interface in complex, mutually dependent ways, as suggested by John McPhee in *Basin and Range*: "The range of the cougar is the cougar's natural state, overlying tens of thousands of other states." There is also Annie Proulx's playful title *Close Range*.   JOHN KEEBLE

R

rapid

If a riffle is a murmur and a cataract a roar, rapids are all
the river voices in between. Rapids begin at a nickpoint,
a place where the gradient of a river tips more steeply
downward and the current becomes swift, turbulent, and
broken. Whitewater rafters learn to look for rapids where
side canyons debouch into the main channel, for these
are likely places for floods to have washed heavy debris
into the river, damming it slightly and creating a nickpoint. The intensity and character of rapids vary greatly
with water level. Some rapids become more dangerous as
flows increase; others flood out and become calmer. Anyone who has experienced the thrill and fear of shooting
powerful rapids will feel the anticipation in these words
of John Wesley Powell: "At last we find ourselves above
a long, broken fall, with ledges and pinnacles of rocks
obstructing the river. . . . The rushing waters break into
great waves on the rocks, and lash themselves into a mad,
white foam." Powell was describing a run of rapids in the
Grand Canyon that he and his men appropriately named
Sockdolager. In the vernacular of his day, a sockdolager
was a roundhouse, knockout punch.   WILLIAM DEBUYS

ravine

Ravine is French for mountain torrent, and comes from
the Old French *rapine,* or "violent rush." Larger than
a gully or a cleft but smaller than a canyon or gorge,
a ravine is a small, steep-sided valley or depression,
usually carved by running water. The word is most
often associated with the narrow excavated valley of a
mountain stream. A rarer usage denotes a stream with
a slight fall between rapids. In *A Lady's Life in the Rocky
Mountains,* Isabella Bird writes: "After descending about
two thousand feet to avoid the ice, we got into a deep
ravine with inaccessible sides, partly filled with ice and
snow and partly with large and small fragments of rock,

which were constantly giving way, rendering the footing very insecure." KIM BARNES

reach

The term probably derives from sailing—a reach is an extended run on one tack. In inland water—lakes or rivers—it is a comparatively long, straight stretch between two bends. In *Life on the Mississippi*, Mark Twain informs us that Fort Adam's Reach "is five miles long. A reach is a piece of straight river, and of course the current drives through such a place in a pretty lively way." In coastal waters, reach is more or less synonymous with sound. It is an arm of the sea that extends inland, or a passageway between islands. Unlike a fjord, it does not end in a glacier; unlike an estuary, it is not the entry to a river. It is generally narrower than a bay. Long Reach, adjacent to Harpswell Sound, off the Maine coast, is an example. FRANKLIN BURROUGHS

redd

Female salmon and steelhead (sea-run trout) returning upstream from the ocean to spawn construct several nests in which they deposit their eggs. Each nest is called a redd. A redd can also refer to nests constructed by the same female in a contiguous area. Maya Khosla, in *Web of Water*, writes: "The female salmon chooses an area of clean gravel and cobble, usually found at the tails of pools where water picks up speed and turns into a riffle. . . . Fanning the nest with her whole body, she slaps at the creek bottom to clean the gravel of silt and sediment," which are carried away by the current. In "Song for the Bones of the Salmon," poet David Wagoner addresses the salmon, asking that his song "be the scales lost/On the hard stones/Where you strained at nesting." Khosla again: "The female lays about 3,500 eggs, almost all of which are fertilized by an attendant male." Ah,

R

yes, the attendant male and salmon sex beneath clear,
moving waters.   PATTIANN ROGERS

redrock

Go to Morrison, Colorado, just west of Denver. There,
as you take in the Moody Blues concert at Red Rocks
Amphitheater, you can study the spectacular formations
that jut from the Front Range of the Rockies. Not only
is their color astounding, against the tamer colors of
the Rockies, but the angle of the formations lends them
a kind of intimidating presence—they are tilted at a
45-degree angle to the bedrock. If you drive south, to
Colorado Springs, this same redrock formation erupts
into Garden of the Gods, the nearly surreal pocket park
of hoodoos and huérfanos. Technically speaking, redrock
is predominantly granophyric rock of a red color. The
red is usually due to iron oxides—the cliffs are rusting.
Drillers on rock-blasting teams call all reddish sedimentary rocks of shale, sandstone, or limestone origin
"redrock." Redrock country is widely used as a synonym for all or parts of the Colorado Plateau.

LUIS ALBERTO URREA

reef

Few words have stoked the fears of ancient mariners or
tickled the imagination of modern tourists quite like reef.
These underwater structures, ridgelike or moundlike
in shape, are most commonly associated with corals and
composed mostly of those sea creatures' skeletons. But
electronic navigational gear aboard ships the world over
also probes shallow waters for other sorts of reefs: those
thrown up by powerful currents and composed of bottom
sediments, gravel, and seashells; and artificial reefs,
communities of living creatures that have established
themselves on bottom debris—railroad cars, automobiles, abandoned drilling equipment, sunk boats, and the

like. In U.S. waters (outside those of its commonwealth and territories), coral reefs are found off the coasts of Hawai'i and Florida. On land in the American West, the term reef is also occasionally applied to a cliff rising above level land, suggesting a marine reef rising from the seabed—for instance, The Reef near Salida, Colorado; Castle Reef in Lewis and Clark County, Montana; and Utah's Capitol Reef, a national park near the Fremont River and part of the hundred-mile-long Waterpocket Fold. This latter scenic region is well known for its white domes of Navajo Sandstone, reminiscent of a massive coral reef barrier and just as much a navigational impediment to travelers.   MIKE TIDWELL

refugium

Refugium is a technical term for a biological refuge, a place where occupants are secure from a range of threats, often lethal. Sailors in a storm seek the refuge of a harbor, a child the refuge of his mother, the patriot refuge from tyrannical government. While refugium carries all of these connotations, it primarily designates a landscape where animals and plants pursue lives protected from exploitation and pursuit. Some important refugia pass virtually unnoticed: undisturbed land along railroad rights of way and the unmanicured reaches of country cemeteries have long provided rare and endangered plants with a refuge from real estate development, agriculture, and invasions of exotic plants. Similarly, highly secured military compounds, such as the vast Marine Corps base at Twenty-Nine Palms, California, provide unintentional refuge for native flora and fauna. While the United States' national system of wildlife refuges formalizes the commonsense effort to protect the biodiversity of the country's native flora and fauna, it is in this realm of the unintended, the hidden, the inadvertent pocket of protection, that species large and small often find their

R

lives least disturbed. One of the most confounding questions in modern field biology concerns the whereabouts of animals once they are lost to our senses. To put the question another way, when animals long absent from a region suddenly turn up, where, precisely, is the "somewhere" from which they came? The myths and folklore of traditional people the world over are replete with descriptions and even geographic designations of refugia, the inviolable strongholds of animals and plants of which the storyteller and her people steer clear, places very like Western society's Eden, missing only the human, and holding out the promise of a less tumultuous future.

BARRY LOPEZ

relief

If you drive west across Iowa's farm plain toward its Missouri River border, suddenly you will encounter the Loess Hills, windblown silt rising up from the flat prairie to dominate the horizon. The Loess Hills are a relief in the landscape, or an irregularity of the Earth's surface. Vertical relief provides a change in one's view of the setting, and it is often the focal point of a visitor's first impression of a place. Specifically, relief means the difference between high and low points in the landscape—the variations in elevation and horizontal spacing that exist among landforms. Relief can be considered at a variety of spatial scales. For example, one might speak of the local relief—the difference between the hills versus the valley bottoms in an area. Or one might speak of the relief that exists across a continent—the difference between Death Valley and Denali National Park and Preserve. Still further, one might speak of relief across the globe, including the ocean depths—the difference between the Mariana Trench (the lowest point below sea level) and Mount Everest (the highest point above sea level): 65,236 feet.

MARY SWANDER

reserve

In his *Ornithological Biography,* John James Audubon quotes a letter from his friend, the South Carolina clergyman and naturalist John Bachman, who had paid a visit to Chisholm Pond, about seven miles outside Charleston, South Carolina, to seek nesting anhingas. The pond, Bachman noted, was artificial, and was a sort peculiar to the rice-growing regions of the Carolina low country. Such an impoundment, he wrote, "in this country is called a 'Reserve.' It is situated at the upper part of ricefields, and is intended to preserve water sufficient, when needed, to irrigate and overflow the rice." The definition cannot be improved upon. As nineteenth-century rice planters increasingly relied on diked fields and tides, reserves, no longer useful for irrigation, became permanently flooded swamps. Many survive, and several, made into bird sanctuaries, were crucial to the restoration of species threatened by the millinery trade. And so these particular impoundments have come to combine, quite by coincidence, two distinct senses of the word reserve: on the one hand, a reservoir, that is, a place where water is stored; on the other hand, a reservation, that is, land set apart for a special purpose. FRANKLIN BURROUGHS

reservoir

R

The term reservoir commonly refers to a body of water intentionally stored behind a dam for purposes of irrigation, power generation, flood control, or recreation, or to supply communal drinking water; but it is also used as a synonym for an underground aquifer or a natural lake that serves such purposes. The Army Corps of Engineers has documented more than eighty thousand dams in the United States, but not all of them have created appreciable reservoirs. Historically, small reservoirs were often created in or near traditional villages. Massive reservoirs would include Fort Peck Lake and Lake Oahe on the Missouri River; Franklin D. Roosevelt Lake on the Columbia; Kentucky and Wheeler Lakes on the Tennessee; and Clarks Hill and Hartwell Lakes on the Savannah River. Man-made reservoirs have become common enough features now to be widely imagined as natural lakes. Another sort of reservoir exists in porous and permeable rock where oil and gas have accumulated, often under pressure. As Rick Bass describes the process in *Oil Notes*, "Suppose you have a gas reservoir or, say, one with gas and water, the gas floating and bobbing up and down above the water. You perforate a little too far down in your well bore and one day the water can't resist: the gas above it is [already] flowing to the surface, [being] pushed out into the pipeline, sold to the companies and shot out to the nation." The Uintah Basin of eastern Utah, near Dinosaur National Monument, is an example of such a hydrocarbon reservoir, its oil and gas reserves being aggressively prospected by extractive industries. Most of these reservoirs, located as they are on the Uintah and Ouray Indian Reservation, could create a strong economic base for the resident Ute tribe. The physical invasiveness and the potential for social disruption generated by extraction technologies, however, have also stimulated requests from the Ute people for discussion and negotiation so that traditional tribal values will be taken into account in the planning process.

TERRY TEMPEST WILLIAMS

resurgence

The point of emergence for a stream that has been flowing underground—or that once disappeared underground to flow through a cavern, perhaps—and that regains the surface is called a resurgence. Often the resurgence occurs where an underground stream flowing through permeable rock strata encounters an impermeable rock layer. If the latter intersects the surface, it can guide the stream back above ground. One notable example is the spot where the Echo River in Kentucky emerges from the Mammoth Cave system. Another is on the Metolius, which begins abruptly northwest of Black Butte, Oregon.   DONNA SEAMAN

revetment

A revetment, or facing, protects an embankment against erosion. Revetment materials range from stone, concrete, and mixed rubble to dead trees and specialty fabrics known as revetment mattresses. Shoreline revetments may be used to check erosion on lakes and along coastlines. Stream revetments, also called riprap revetments, stabilize banks by reducing slumping and deflecting the channel away from the bank or slowing the stream's velocity against it. On small streams, tree revetments—cut trees laid against the bank—offer a biological alternative to the once common D-Day–style rubble pile of broken concrete.   ELLEN MELOY

ribbon fall

The name says it all. A ribbon fall is a tall, thin waterfall. Ribbonlike. The analogy was irresistible to settlers looking for words to fit the landscape, and so Ribbon—along with Bridal Veil and Rainbow—is among the most common names for waterfalls in North America. Falls called Ribbon can be found in Grand Canyon, Yosemite, and Rocky Mountain National Parks. Yosemite's Ribbon Falls is the highest single-drop waterfall in North America at 1,612 feet.   CHARLES FRAZIER

R

ribbon lake

As a glacier carves its way down a valley, differential rates of movement or areas of less dense rock may cause some sections of the valley floor to be cut deeper than others. As the glacier retreats, a long, thin depression remains behind, perhaps further dammed by deposited material. When these gouged troughs are filled by meltwater, streams, and rain, the result is a ribbon lake.   CHARLES FRAZIER

ridge

A ridge is best thought of as a spine traversing the top of mountains, hills, or any raised or upward-projecting landform. It is one of the most ubiquitous features of the Earth. Ridges are crossed, surveyed, cut through by roads, gained, climbed, walked, taken, and lost. Our eye measures and records their shapes: shoulder, spur, reef, rib, couch, neck, roostercomb, and hogback, to name a few. Developers use such terms as Ridgecrest, Ridgefield, Ridgemanor, and Ridgehaven to suggest a place of superior view, where in fact no ridge may exist. The Flatirons of Boulder, Colorado, are a dramatic example of a hogback ridge created by uplifting; the ridge and valley system of the Appalachian Mountains was formed by folding, and is also a superb example of ridges formed by erosion. The dominant feature of the Earth is the midocean ridge, a thirty-thousand-mile-long system of underwater fault ridges stitching the planet.   MICHAEL COLLIER

riffle

A riffle is the little brother of a rapid. It is a shallow section of stream where sediment has been deposited, often in response to the upstream scouring of a pool. As water flows over the obstruction, the current becomes more turbulent and breaks into a succession of small waves. Riffles produce some of the happiest voices of a river, murmuring and chattering, never roaring or growling with argument.   WILLIAM DEBUYS

rift valley

The Rocky Mountain Trench runs northwest-southeast through the western Rockies in British Columbia and connects to the Flathead and Bitterroot Valleys of Montana. Its fault zone bears some similarity to a rift valley, whereas the course of the Rio Grande in New Mexico actually follows a rift, the Rio Grande Rift. A rift valley is a trough between parallel faults which often forms a long, steep-sided valley, or sequence of valleys, with occasional side-faults. The causes are arguable, but they likely result from (1) a stretching tension in the Earth's surface, which pulls the sides apart, leaving the center to subside; (2) compression from the sides, which thrusts outside masses higher than a central block, forcing it down; or (3) the rising of an elongated domed stratum, which eventually cracks down its length, allowing the central block to subside and form the valley floor. The most spectacular example of a rift valley is the one that runs from the floor of the Dead Sea through the Red Sea and Horn of Africa to the Zambezi River. In the United States, the run of the north-south–connected valleys North Warner and South Warner in southeastern Oregon and Surprise Valley in northeastern California, all lying on the western edge of the Great Basin, can be thought of as forming a minor rift valley.   WILLIAM KITTREDGE

rill

R

The flowing consonants of rill affirm its traditional English meaning of "small brook," but the term also denotes a still smaller, shiftier, and more transient stream. Rainwater flowing as sheetwash down an erodable slope, as steepness and its accumulating depth enable it to move material, will often break midslope into incipient channels. These closely spaced, roughly parallel rills, or shoestring rills, an inch or two wide and deep, may enlarge and interjoin to form gullies lower on the slope. A primary sculptor of badlands and many desert landscapes, rilling is also the initial conduit system by which the soil of sloping farmland is lost to river drainages.

Wave or tidal backwash on beaches makes rilled patterns on saturated sand, and the term has been extended by astronomers—usually as rille—to denote long, narrow trenches on the surface of the moon.   JOHN DANIEL

rimland

Rimlands are found in the American Southwest, where the weathering effect of wind and water has sculpted the land into fantastic figures and shapes. The main rimland region in the United States is the Colorado Plateau—especially along the Mogollon Rim in northern Arizona, part of the southern edge of the plateau—where the horizontal rock strata have been dramatically uplifted, then subsequently eroded by streams. Rimlands are the stony epidermis of the Earth's upper crust, exposed for the eye to savor and enjoy. They form a stark vertical world, cut into immense chunks and sections that stand on their own in isolated splendor. Motoring along a highway, hiking inside a canyon, drifting along a river, you are confronted on all sides by towering cliffs composed of a bewildering variety of sedimentary strata. At the stupendous edge the Earth falls away, and you seem to fall with it into a world channeled and grooved by a labyrinth of secret passages. These massive layers of resistant rock overlooking a canyon or valley draw your spirit out of the husk it inhabits and enable you to observe the land from the perspective of a passing bird.   CONGER BEASLEY, JR.

rincón

Rincón is Spanish for corner. In the southwestern United States and throughout Mexico the word often refers to land or properties that are "at the end of the road" or "on the south end of *el rancho*." It can also mean the corner of a pasture, or "my little piece of land." *Rinconada* means "the corner place." Hamlets located at the end of a road

or at the far side of a ranch are sometimes named Rincón, as in Rincón, Texas, in the lower Rio Grande valley.
ARTURO LONGORIA

rip

A rip is created by crosscurrents, or by current flowing through an obstructed or constricted channel or over an uneven bottom. In salt water, rips appear, intensify, diminish, and disappear on a daily basis, as the tides ebb and flow. In rivers and streams, they are constant, their force varying with the level of the water. When named, a rip, like a waterfall, is normally in the plural: Niagara Falls; Stand-Up Rips. In *Maine Lingo,* John Gould says that a rip "is less than a rapid but more than a riffle," but this is erroneous, at least in Maine. Canoeists rate both Big Black Rapid, on the St. John River, and Spenser Rips, on the Dead, as class III whitewater. Rip(s) is preferable to rapid(s), being kinetic rather than merely descriptive. No canoeist, plunging down a steep and turbulent pitch, whoops out, "Let 'er rapid!"   FRANKLIN BURROUGHS

ripple

A wind of about ten and a half miles per hour will start to move dry sand, and ripples are the tiny, more or less parallel ridges of migrating sand that result. A ripple is to sand what a wave is to water, and just as a series of nearly identical waves may move across the surface of the sea, so a series of nearly identical ripples may crawl across the windward face of a dune. Reaching the crest, the ripples spill their contents down the leeward side, or slip face, of the dune, feeding its downwind migration. Stream currents or wave action on a shore may also cause bottom sand to ripple. Water, of course, also ripples. Born from wind, eddying current, tossed stones, or a thousand other varieties of disturbance, ripples radiate across otherwise still surfaces of lakes, ponds, and rivers. They also radiate across the surface of our thoughts, where they abide as the metaphor and epitome of lingering effect and continuing implication.   WILLIAM DEBUYS

riprap

In 1973, broken rocks, large pieces of cement, and concrete rubble tumbled and crashed down from the dump truck with banging thunders and billows of dust to begin the building of a dike along Green Bay, Wisconsin. This dike was typical of those composed of riprap to prevent future erosion and flooding. Riprap is human-made and used in many places to protect roads, bluffs, bridges, and shorelines from the erosion caused by wave action and to bolster structures threatened in other ways. Riprap also refers to rocks laid down on a smooth stone path to provide traction for horses on the slippery surface. "Lay down these words/Before your mind like rocks," Gary Snyder suggests in his poem "Riprap," comparing the granite words of a poem to the bolstering aggregation of riprap.   PATTIANN ROGERS

rising dune

The force of the wind can blow enough sand to the base of a cliff to push a dune partway up the cliff face, forming a rising dune. Similarly, wind can blow a dune at the edge of a cliff over the side to pile up a falling dune at the base. The best examples of rising dunes are on the Navajo Indian Reservation of northwestern New Mexico, northeastern Arizona, and southwestern Utah.
D. J. WALDIE

river capture

When a river or stream from one drainage system erodes through a land divide and acquires the flow from another drainage system, the first is said to have captured the second in an act of stream piracy. The headwaters of the captured river are diverted to the captor, and at this juncture, the two become one. For example, the Rio Grande once flowed into a closed basin called Lake Cabeza de Vaca; after it was captured it flowed into the Gulf of Mexico. A related term, elbow of capture, is the bend where the pirated channel is forced to change direction and flow into the waters of the aggressor. Wind gaps are the result of dry valleys left behind when the captured river departs. The most common form of capture, or river piracy, is called abstraction. It occurs when the stream that flows at a lower level cuts through the land dividing it from another stream flowing at a higher level, causing that higher-level stream to rechannel itself. This is how, in geography, the low takes the high. GRETEL EHRLICH

rock

In literature, a stone is a rock with gravitas. A rock is workmanlike, quotidian. ("Upon this rock I will build my church . . ."). A stone is fraught with anthropomorphized depth, a rock seen with metaphoric eyes. ("He rolled away the stone . . ."). In nature, however, a rock is a naturally formed aggregate or compact mass of mineral materials; these may or may not be "coherent"—in other words, a rock can be a small anthology of geological matter. A stone, in contrast, is a concentrated piece of earthy or mineral material, often defined as a section of a rock. If you get a piece of the rock, you have a stone in your pocket. Large masses of stone are called rocks. These can be quite large—promontories and cliffs, peaks and boulders, are all rocks. (Uluru—Ayers Rock—is a mega-example.) Stones achieve true gravitas when they are gems—it is not just slang that makes diamonds "precious stones." We elevate the stone in our culture: corner stone, gravestone, etched in stone. (Trivia note: The Rocky Mountains used to be known as the Stony

R

Mountains.) A rock is solid and stolid, forever depend-
able as an essential part of the Earth's crust; a stone is a
mineral metaphor, forever turning in the human mind,
bearing "meaning" on its facets. Perhaps this is what
moved Mexican poet Octavio Paz to write, "What is not
stone/is light." LUIS ALBERTO URREA

rock flour

If you walk up on a mountain stream, crystal clear but
for a mysterious streak of milky blue threaded through
its flow, you've likely found the telltale sign of a rock
flour deposit, a collection of silt-sized particles generated
by glacial erosion and swept along by glacial meltwater,
sometimes over very great distances. When the rock-
studded base of a glacier scrapes its way across a valley
floor, pieces of the ice-embedded rock are ground to a
fine powder. These tiny particles are mostly quartz, a
mineral that stays suspended in water long after other,
heavier material has dropped out, and it's this suspended
quartz powder that creates the milky blue tint and gives
rise to the term glacial milk. A simple test to determine
whether what you're seeing is rock flour is to dip a con-
tainer in the flow, shake it up, and look for light sparkling
in the swirling dust. Dried rock flour is sometimes
carried great distances by the wind, and then it may be
deposited as one of the components of a layer of fine, rich
soil called loess. The parts of western Idaho and eastern
Washington called the Palouse, as well as parts of Iowa,
are known for their fertile, gently undulating loess hills.
TERRY TEMPEST WILLIAMS

rock glacier

In high mountain country, one may stumble upon a
bulging, glacierlike mass of rock rubble spreading out
from a steep, perpetually frozen amphitheater: a rock
glacier. Around 1900, geologists first described—and

hotly debated the origins of—rock glaciers. Three types are now recognized: lobate, tongue-shaped, and spatulate. Unlike scree slopes, landslides, or rock avalanches, rock glaciers slide downhill at three to six feet per year by means of ice creep. Some contain interstitial ice a few feet or so below their surfaces; others simply ride on top of ice glaciers. Standing on a rock glacier, the surface appears to be a chaotic jumble of boulders. Viewed from high above, patterns emerge: furrows, parallel ridges, pits, crevasses, lobes. Actively moving rock glaciers, free of vegetation, can be 150 feet thick. Dormant or fossil rock glaciers are thinner, and lichens and other scruffy plants grow on their faces. Other names: chrystocrene, *coulée de bloc* (French), talus glacier, rock river. Rock glaciers are most common in polar or subpolar regions, or in the high mountains of the midlatitudes. A dramatic rock glacier shaped like a lava flow oozes down the forested slopes of Sourdough Mountain, near McCarthy, Alaska. The genesis of rock glaciers continues to provoke controversy among geologists. Some argue that true glaciers are essential precursors of rock glaciers. Others point to rock glaciers found in the southwestern United States, a region with no evidence of glacial history. Most concede that lobate rock glaciers, as evidenced by their shape, almost certainly derive from true glaciers. Geologist Dale Ritter's final pronouncement on the topic is that "enough disagreement exists . . . to refrain from sweeping conclusions at this time." EVA SAULITIS

rock stream

A rock stream, or block stream, is an accumulation of boulders or angular blocks, fragments that have fallen from cliffs or ledges above. Rock streams are usually found at the head of a ravine or on a slope below a summit, where they may extend into a forest or fill a valley floor. One well-known site can be found in the

Blue Ridge Mountains of central Virginia, downslope
from Black Rock Summit in Shenandoah National
Park. The quartzite-block fields on the northeast and
western slopes of the summit are randomly displayed,
suggesting that they were scattered by rockfall. Arthur
Bloom, in his book *Geomorphology*, describes the rock
streams in the Appalachians as relict features—that is,
formed in the past under much colder conditions, when
glaciers were nearby. In a less common usage of the term,
rock streams are distributed along with the mass of soil
that slides over a summer-melted layer of permafrost, a
process called solifluction.   LAN SAMANTHA CHANG

ronde

Rich, black loam, a legacy of the prairies across southern
Michigan and northern Indiana, came to be known
in the region as ronde. The term—French for round
or circular—may derive from Prairie Ronde, which
at several thousand acres is the largest of eight prairies
in Kalamazoo County, in the southwestern corner of
Michigan. (French Canadian trappers bestowed similar
names on places as far west as the Grande Ronde Valley
of Oregon.) In plowed fields, the prairie soils often appear
as dark disks, in contrast with the surrounding lighter
soils, and these circular shapes may also help account for
their being called rondes.   SCOTT RUSSELL SANDERS

rookery

Rookery today enjoys a healthy outdoor connotation and
pertains to natural places where birds and animals gather
to perform elaborate rituals involved in reproducing
their kind. But rookery has been part of the language
since 1792, when it was used as a slang term for "a cluster
of mean tenements densely populated by people of
the lowest class." Charles Dickens, in *Sketches by Boz*,
described this grim nineteenth-century London habitat

as "wretched houses with broken windows patched with rags and paper . . . filth everywhere . . . men and women in every variety of scanty and dirty apparel." The slang term "to rook"—to cheat or steal—evolved from the degrading experience of the slums. *Webster's Dictionary* (1913) defined the word as both a breeding place for birds and "a dilapidated building with many rooms and occupants." With the gradual disappearance of squalid slums in Great Britain, the word became associated almost exclusively with the crowded breeding places of gregarious birds and animals such as herons, penguins, and seals.   CONGER BEASLEY, JR.

root wad

Root wads are the root systems of upended trees. When the tree falls, its Medusa-like tangle appears with clumps of dirt and rock stuck among the separate roots, suspended now above a hole called a tip pit. Root wads that fall in wetlands or waterways such as streams and rivers are microhabitats for fish and aquatic invertebrates, which in turn provide food for fish, birds, and amphibians. The fallen tree also serves as a bridge between terrestrial and aquatic habitats, and young fingerling salmon, hatched in inland rivers, have been known to ride within root wads all the way to the ocean. Anthropologists and archeologists scrutinize root wads for evidence of shell middens, bones, and tools. An Alaskan ornithologist once used root wads of trees that had drifted ashore around Barrow to provide nest sites for black guillemots. Root wads have also been used by bioengineers in stream restoration projects. The roots act as sieves for debris, and help clean the streams. They are also used along the banks to reduce erosion. Sometimes several root wads are combined and buried into a streambank with the root fans exposed to the current, thus slowing the stream, and slowing the erosion of cutbanks.   GRETEL EHRLICH

R

rugosity

Rugosities are minuscule, ridgelike corrugations on a rock surface—generally having an inch or less of relief—which bring to mind wrinkled skin. Climbers sometimes grip rugosities with their fingertips to ascend vertical terrain, and refer to such features as crimps or crimpers. If a rugosity exists as a discrete bump rather than a tiny elongated ridge, it is called a nubbin.   JON KRAKAUER

run

A word with nearly inexhaustible applications but always denoting movement, run can refer to any small stream, brook, creek, rivulet, channel, overflow, or swiftly flow-ing watercourse. Also defined as a small stream and its valley (Bull Run, Virginia), run is often associated with defile and ravine. How it is differentiated from runnel, rundle, and runlet seems to be a matter of local prefer-ence. As for river, creek, and run, early Virginians came to think of the river as being the largest, the creek as smaller, and the run as the smallest of the three bodies of water. Run can also refer to an exposed branchlike body of ore or igneous rock. In mining, a run is a flow of sand; a slip, slide, or sudden fall of earth. In logging: any path followed in skidding logs (also called a skid road or gutter board); a run-around is that portion of the river where the water has changed its course, often because of a logjam; a tiered tower of hewn logs built into the bank at the curve of a driving river to keep logs from jamming is a run dam. Also, an extensive range of pasture or graz-ing land; a regular track made by certain animals, as in a rabbit run.   KIM BARNES

run-around

A crude handmade dike, commonly constructed of sacks of sand or earth, used alone to shunt water past a spot, or sometimes in the repair of a leak in a larger dam or levee, is called a run-around. In the *Dictionary of American Regional English,* a Mississippi man named Percy Lanterns uses the term like this: "What you do, if you have the gumption of a catfish, is build with sacks of earth a little 'run-around'—that is a small levee around the geyser to the height of its jet. That stabilizes the pressure, and the boil is safe."   SUSAN BRIND MORROW

runnel

Runnel, rundle, rindle, runlet, streamlet, brooklet, tricklet, rivulet, rill—the mostly archaic names for small-channeled flowings of water abound, and they all contain the phonemes /l/ and /r/, known linguistically as "liquids," which flow over and along the tongue like water on a smooth stone. All these terms can mean a little or tiny brook. Rivulet, which once meant "small river," now sometimes denotes the slightly larger erosional channels formed by rills merging on a steep slope. Runnel can suggest the same—a small natural gutter— and has a specific geomorphic meaning: a trough, formed by wave action on the lower portion of a beach, which is submerged by the incoming tide and drains the beach as the tide ebbs.   JOHN DANIEL

R

saddle

A saddle is a smooth, swaybacked ridge connecting the summits of two higher elevations; also known as a col. A saddle marks the low point on the crest of a divide between two watersheds that trickle down in opposite directions. It can also be described as a broad, flat gap or pass, sloping gently on both sides, the shape of a saddle sitting on the back of a horse. A well-defined saddle stretches between the twin summits of the Spanish Peaks, located in south-central Colorado southwest of the town of Walsenburg. Ute Indians call the peaks *Wah-to-yah*, "Breasts of the World," because of their resemblance to the torso of a headless woman with prominent breasts lying on her back at the foot of the Sangre de Cristo Mountains. The saddle between the peaks is known colloquially by locals as "the cleavage."

CONGER BEASLEY, JR.

saddle dam

Strictly speaking, a saddle dam is a dike or a wall built at the edge of a lake or reservoir to protect nearby land from flooding. The name derives from the low dip in the landscape—or saddle—across which the dam is constructed. All four dams at Horsetooth Reservoir in Colorado are saddle dams.   ANTONYA NELSON

sag

A sag is a depression caused by the uneven settling of the ground. The saddles and gaps of a ridge or mountain range, as well as the shallow dips in flat or mildly sloping terrain, are called sags. In cowboy jargon, the slope of a hill or mountain is sometimes called a sag. Sags frequently appear along major faults such as the San Andreas. When water collects in these fault depressions, sag ponds are formed. Lost Lake, Soda Lake, Jackson

Lake, and many others strung out along the San Andreas are all sag ponds. The Illinois and Michigan basins contain sags, and the till sheets of the Midwest often give way to an undulating topography called sag-and-swell. Oddly, Sag Harbor takes its name not from the marshy depression it occupies at the end of Long Island but from the nearby town of Sagaponack, which is a transliteration of the Algonquian *weg-wag-onuch* ("land at the end of the hill"). MICHAEL COLLIER

salt dome

A plug-shaped body of salt that has intruded into a sedimentary rock overlay, a salt dome is formed when salt, which is relatively buoyant, is forced upward through a fault in overlying sedimentary strata by subterranean pressure. A typical salt dome is roughly circular in shape and has a one- to two-mile diameter. There are over five hundred known salt domes in the Gulf Coast region alone, stretching from Mexico to the Florida Panhandle. The tops of most domes are commercially mined; they are an excellent source of nearly pure salt and often have oil and gas reserves along the flanks. In the West, subsequent erosion of the upthrust layers of a salt dome can produce dramatic fracturing along its edges, ultimately resulting in steep hogbacks. ARTHUR SZE

salt flat

When salt lakes dry up, whether permanently or temporarily, their beds become salt or alkali flats, glistening stretches of level, pale ground encrusted with saline minerals such as potassium, magnesium lithium, and sodium chloride. The evaporation of winter rains deposits salty materials—originally in solution—onto the floor of the lake basin, already smooth and flat because of its silt and clay base. Such is the case with the vast Bonneville Salt

Flats west of Salt Lake City, Utah. Its more than thirty thousand acres are so buffed that for decades it has been the site for attempts on the world land speed record. Rogers Dry Lake on Edwards Air Force Base in California is firm and flat enough that it is used as a landing area for spacecraft. In the Southeast, the term salt flat is used quite differently. There it denotes low-lying, grassy coastal land, sometimes flooded with salt water but not as continuously wet as a salt marsh.   CHARLES FRAZIER

salt-grass estuary

At the mouths of rivers where freshwater and seawater mingle, the effects of tides are evident and often dramatic. In shallow stretches alternately flooded at high tide and drained at low tide, salt grass thrives. In the low tide pools where water always stands, cordgrass *(Spartina)* grows in the changing salinity, temperature, and water level. But salt grass *(Distichlis)* tends to prefer the higher, radically filling and emptying stretches of the estuary. In a salt-grass estuary the grass holds only some of the fine particles of clay and silt laid down by the shifting currents, its roots and stems lacing the soft mud. The salt grass protects the shore by buffering the force of wind and tides. The dying grass also provides for the inhabitants of the estuary such as snails and periwinkles, oysters and fiddler crabs, which in turn feed many birds and animals. Salt-grass estuaries are primarily features of the eastern United States. North Carolina has more square miles of estuary than any other state. Different water levels, tidal patterns, salinity, temperature, and variations in sediment make each basin and salt grass meadow different. Early immigrants to New England sometimes settled near estuaries hoping to harvest salt grass for hay, but were disappointed when cows and horses did not care for the salty fodder.   ROBERT MORGAN

S

A large body of water with a high salt content, situated in a sere landscape, with no outlet to the sea, is known as a salt lake. Utah's Great Salt Lake, the shrunken remnant of Pleistocene Lake Bonneville, is so salty a swimmer can float on its surface without effort. In her poem "Salt Air," Sharon Bryan writes: "You cannot sink into this 25 percent solution,/it hosts no life but the microscopic/brine shrimp's, which must trace a narrow path/through blazing crystal knives." In his essay "The World's Strangest Sea," Wallace Stegner described Great Salt Lake as a thin horizon line "of quicksilver, of lead, of improbable turquoise, of deep-sea cobalt, or of molten metals, depending on the conditions of the day." Because it's part of a closed system (the Great Basin), Great Salt Lake rises if rainfall exceeds the rate of evaporation and recedes if evaporation exceeds rainfall. This shifting shoreline plays havoc with local roads. The Salton Sea, created in 1905–1907 when the Colorado River burst through poorly constructed and maintained irrigation controls south of Yuma, Arizona, and flooded an ancient lake depression in the Sonoran Desert in California, is another inland salt sea or saline lake. Mono Lake, near Lee Vining, California, on the rain shadow side of the Sierra Nevada, is an alkaline lake. Here, evaporation concentrates naturally occurring alkali salts that form a thin crust on the surface of the water. Nevada's Carson Lake, whose waters contain a high concentration of sodium sulfate and lesser amounts of the carbonates and chlorides found in all briny lakes, is the archetype of a bitter lake. Many mineral lakes, strangely to some, teem with bird life. In *Salt Dreams*, William deBuys's finely observed account of the Salton Sea, he describes the mismanagement of water, the response to cycles of drought, and the population and development pressures that are a part of the social history of the West's mineral lakes. TERRY TEMPEST WILLIAMS

sand

The sandy expanses of beaches, deserts, and dune fields
are loose aggregations of mineral grains, mostly quartz,
created by geological forces that include plate tectonics
and erosion. Wind and water sort this hard detritus so
efficiently into masses of like-sized particles that we are
able to speak of a sandbar (as distinct from a gravel
bar) and other discrete forms, such as a mudflat, which
is made up of same-sized particles of clay or silt. The
smallest fragments of the earth's pulverized rocks are
called clay (each one measuring less than .004 mm—or
forty microns—in diameter); the next largest are silt
particles (.004–.065 mm); grains of sand, finally, measure
between .065 and 2 mm. The word sand also refers to the
loose aggregation itself, just as silt commonly refers to
an infusion of fine earth suspended in the flow of moving
water. On the continuum from the coarsest silt to the finest clay, the earthy substance gets progressively stickier.

BARRY LOPEZ

sandhill

Landlocked and located far from existing coastlines,
some sandhills are the remains of dune fields and beaches
once amassed along the shores of ancient oceans; others
are the windblown products of erosion. Like present-day
coastal dunes, sandhills are eolian landforms, shaped
by winds acting on plentiful supplies of sand. Their
various locations—southwest from the Texas Panhandle;
miles inland from the Carolina and Georgia coasts; in
the heartland of Nebraska—are a geological timepiece,
marking these notably dry regions as former marine and
riverine habitats. The Carolina Sandhills, for instance,
indicate that the Atlantic Ocean was once much higher
than today, its waves anciently crashing near the present-
day Piedmont fall line. The extensive 24,000-square-
mile sandhill region of Nebraska has a more complex his-

S

tory: blown sand from ancient river deposits eroded from the sandstones of the Rocky Mountains, which were, in turn, the former seabed of an ancient inland sea that vanished as the North American continent and mountains were uplifted. In time the sandstone of the newly formed mountains began to erode; the resulting sand (along with silt and gravel) was transported across the plains by braided rivers, blanketing the plains east of the mountains. Then, over the last several million years, new rivers dissected the mass of sand, carrying some away, and exposing some to wind. Through differential wind-generated erosion, the finest particles were blown eastward to form loess deposits in Iowa; the heavier sand-sized particles remained behind and were moved only a short distance, forming the Nebraska Sandhills. Vast and undulating, ranging up to six hundred feet high, sand-hills are majestic, serene, and elemental places. For many of the Plains Indians, they were sacred, the final home for departed spirits. The term has been applied to towns (Sandhill, Texas); entertainment facilities (Sandhills Drive-In Theater, Box Butte, Nebraska); a magnificent bird (the sandhill crane); and historically, to inhabitants of the pinelands of South Carolina and Georgia, who were known as sand-hillers.   EMILY HIESTAND

sand prairie

Folklorist Mary Hufford describes the sand prairie country along the upper Mississippi River as a place once "bursting with goat's rue, fragrant sumac, horsemint, and the charming pink fruiting bodies of wolf milk's slime mold." With the arrival of early settlers, this habitat was significantly degraded, and the bursting quality abrogated. Sand prairies—small but growing over defined sheets of sand and found most famously in the sand counties of Wisconsin, but also along the Mississippi and Illinois Rivers in northwest Illinois—were founded on glacial outwash. This outwash is almost pure sand, deposited by streams carrying sediment and meltwater away from a deteriorating glacier. Sand prairie soils are droughty and support vegetation that tends to burn easily—the repeated fires keep out woody vegetation such as shrubs and trees. One rare Iowa ecosystem, the Cedar Hills Sand Prairie, has growing in its drier sites bluestem, switchgrass, sand dropseed, and purple lovegrass, while its wet areas are dominated by sedges. This prairie also supports hundreds of species of native plants, over fifty species of birds and butterflies, and over ninety species of indigenous leafhoppers. Willa Cather, in *My Ántonia,* describes such a landscape in the Midwest: "More than anything else I felt emotion in the landscape; in the fresh, easy blowing morning wind, and in the earth itself, as if the shaggy grass were a sort of loose hide, and underneath it herds of buffalo were galloping, galloping." In *Wisconsin,* Aldo Leopold, author of *A Sand County Almanac,* describes a life of restoration at his Wisconsin farm, caring for the precious swamps, savannas, and sand prairies there. Eloquent pleas have been made recently in the service of protecting similar regions still in existence—urging that steps be taken to help the sand prairie and its system of plants and animals heal itself. ELIZABETH COX

S

sand waves

Float a serene river, all attention on the bank, on indigo buntings in emerald willows. Suddenly, the river lifts into a long, silken comb that ripples, falls, then rises and falls all over again. The tawny transverse waves migrate upstream, defying the downstream flow, passing with the rushing sound of the river breathing. Sand waves are creatures of transient, underwater dunes. They are seen on high-volume, rapid-flow, sand-laden waters, whose currents shape their load sediments into dunes on the channel bottom. As the dunes shift, grow taller, and move upstream, waves build above them, some with eight-foot-high crests. The sand waves reach a climax, then, as the dunes collapse, drop into a smooth sheet of river again. From flatwater to full-amplitude waves to washout, the cycle lasts minutes. Sand waves are uncommon on most rivers, but renowned on the San Juan, Dirty Devil, and other southwestern rivers.   ELLEN MELOY

sassat

An entrapment of animals, especially narwhals or beluga whales, in pack ice or sometimes in a lead at the mouth of bays or fjords is called a sassat, a word derived from the Greenlandic *suagssat*. When the wind shifts direction in extremely cold weather, closing off most of a lead where whales have been feeding, the animals' increasingly frantic movements can be all that keeps a shrinking patch of water open. Animals caught in such a development find themselves unable, in a single breath, to swim far enough beneath the ice to reach another lead or the open sea. For Iñupiaq Eskimo hunters, who call the event *imayguaraat*, sassats are blessings. They travel across the sea ice to harvest meat where the whales, crowded tightly together, are lunging across each other's bodies to get a breath, before being forced under by others desperate for air. Sassats are audible events. In *Arctic Dreams,* Barry Lopez describes the noise: "[The whales'] bellowing and gurgling, their bovinelike moans and the explosive screech of their breathing, can sometimes be heard at great distances." Danish scientist Christian Vibe once described an attempt by trapped whales to grab their last bit of air in a sassat: "With a hollow whistling sound they inhaled the air as if sucking it through long iron tubes." And anthropologist Richard Nelson recounts a sassat near Wainwright, Alaska, when hunters were "guided to it by the frantic hissing and blowing of hundreds of [beluga] whales at holes along the edge of a closing lead." This sassat eventually opened, freeing the whales; others don't. During the brutal winter of 1914–15, over a thousand narwhals died at Disko Bay, Greenland. For the Inuit, the whales' misfortune was an unexpected source of life that very cold Arctic winter.   EVA SAULITIS

sastrugi

That wind is a powerful shaper of landscape is evident in sastrugi—the irregular ridges, corrugations, hills, peaks, and valleys that windblown snow makes. Sastrugi vary in height—from a few inches to many feet—and can be soft or rock hard. "Lilliputian canyonlands," writer Stephen J. Pyne calls them in his book *The Ice.* These sometimes spooky, whimsical shapes are often aligned parallel to the prevailing wind, with steep, concave, or overhanging ends facing the wind. A snowfield covered with sastrugi can look like the top of a lemon meringue pie, or like a desert sandscape, sculpted by wind into curvaceous dunes. The word comes from the Russian *zastrugi*, meaning a small ridge or furrow in the snow. In his last journal, British explorer Robert Falcon Scott defines them in the singular: "Sastrugus: an irregularity formed by the wind on a snowplain. 'Snow wave' is not completely descriptive, as the sastrugus often has a fantastic shape unlike the conception of an ordinary wave" (*Scott's Last Expedition*).   GRETCHEN LEGLER

S

savanna

The word savanna entered New World English in the sixteenth century by way of the Spanish, who had taken it from a Caribe term for meadow. And the diverse savannas of North America—whether pine savannas of the Southeast, oak savannas of the Midwest, ponderosa savannas of the Rockies, or juniper-piñón savannas of the Southwest—are all grassy, meadowlike landscapes, intermediate between treeless plains and closed-canopy woodlands. The savanna overstory is broken, patchy. Trees cover only about a third of the land and grow singly or in copses. The understory is composed largely of tall grasses, sedges, and wildflowers. Historically, North American savannas were maintained by frequent fires, either naturally occurring or set by Native Americans to control undergrowth and encourage grassy openings to improve habitat for the grazing animals they hunted. But savanna ecosystems have become increasingly threatened and rare as a result of fire suppression and clearing for commercial pine plantations, agriculture, and development. In the Southeast, for example, almost nothing remains of the old-growth longleaf pine savannas that once dominated the landscape of the coastal plain.

CHARLES FRAZIER

sawtooth

Sawtooth is an adjective used to describe a range of mountains or a single ridge in a series of peaks that resemble the jagged edge of a saw. "The best place I have found to glimpse the western land as it was in the last [the nineteenth] century, without squinting too much, is in the Sawtooth-Stanley country in south central Idaho," writes Harlan Hague in his article "The Sawtooth-Stanley Basin Country." In addition to this classic range of sawtooth mountains, other examples include the ancient Sawtooth Mountain Range that anchors the coast of Lake Superior along the north shore, and Sawtooth Mountain, found in the Indian Peaks Wilderness Area south of Rocky Mountain National Park in Colorado. In his poem "Steel Mountain," from *Sawtooth Country*, David Beisly-Guiotto writes of standing atop this mountain in Idaho: "sheer sky, blue air chipped by white peaks/far as we can see." Those jagged sawtooth peaks.   PATTIANN ROGERS

scarland

Barren rocky plains of the West with little or no soil cover are called scablands. Biscuit scablands are mounded prairie lands with rocky, shallow clay soils. Bluebunch wheatgrass, parsnipflower, buckwheat, milkvetch, and other grasses may grow between the scabrock on deeper-soiled mounds. In "The Great Scablands Debate," Stephen Jay Gould writes: "In the area between Spokane and the Snake and Columbia rivers to the south and west, many spectacular, elongate, subparallel channel ways are gouged through the loess and deeply into the hard basalt itself." These channeled scablands were formed near the close of the Ice Age fourteen to sixteen thousand years ago when Lake Missoula, two thousand feet deep and covering three thousand square miles, repeatedly broke through its ice dam. The powerful waters of these floods—as many as a hundred of them over two thousand years—created massively deep channels in the Earth. Gould writes that such floods "could have moved 36-foot boulders." The efforts of geomorphologists to discover the cause of these channeled scablands is an exciting story of controversy and brilliant detective work.   PATTIANN ROGERS

scarp

While scarp can serve as a synonym for escarpment, it's more commonly used to refer to discrete, relatively short sections of the larger landform, often with a modifying adjective of some sort. The traveler headed south from Tucumcari, New Mexico, will soon raise the Bluffs of the Llano Estacado, a particularly striking part of the serpentine, bare rock palisade that forms the western elevation of this extensive plateau. The rimrock along the escarpment here, near the town of Quay, is set off by a dark, narrow line of junipers—an eyebrow scarp. Elsewhere, these last few feet at the top of a similar wall

S

might carry a slight projection, or overhang, of caprock—
a hognose scarp. Typically, an escarpment is too massive
in scale—like the Adirondack Mountains or Okefenokee
Swamp—to imagine all at once. A virtually unscalable escarpment on the eastern side of the Kaiparowits
Plateau in southern Utah is called Fifty-Mile Mountain.
The Balcones Escarpment, the southeastern scarp of the
Llano Estacado, is another wall that can't be gathered in
one look, though it figures prominently, like a smaller-
scale object, in the agrarian history of East Texas.
Even the Niagara Escarpment, over whose nickpoint
the Niagara River cascades, is impossible to point out to
a viewer in its entirety. It is, rather, by the subdivision of
a continuous landscape that eyebrow and hognose scarps
are singled out along the general trend of an escarpment;
that pencil ridges—short, straight, thin—are separated
from the grander ridges of a range of granite mountains,
and reaches, bends, and falls are brought together to
comprise a river.   BARRY LOPEZ

scarpfoot spring

An escarpment is a line of steep, eroded slopes or cliffs.
Springs that emerge at the bottom of these slopes are
called scarpfoot springs. They are usually the result of
permeable rocks overlying impermeable layers: sandstone atop clay, for example. Water seeping downward
through that permeable layer is held up by the impermeable and moves laterally, emerging at the scarpfoot
spring.   CHARLES FRAZIER

scoria

Scoria is an igneous rock (igneous meaning hardened
molten magma), a variety of basalt that is "extrusive" in
nature. That is, it may have been squeezed or extruded
above ground near the site of a volcano or spewed
straight up from the volcano's core. In either case, the

magma's contact with air forms gas bubbles that remain inside when it hardens. These create scoria's identifying characteristics: airy, spongelike holes that cause it to feel lighter than it should for a rock its size. (Pumice is lighter, less crystalline.) Gardeners buy it in bags under the rubric of crater or lava stone, in shades of black or gray or red. In a regional variation, in the western Great Plains, scoria is clay that has been baked above a burning vein of lignite (one underground seam, for instance, smoldered for decades near Amidon, North Dakota), red-orange in color, with the density of heavy pottery. This scoria is dug from shallow pits and used as surfacing for rural roads and drives, creating the "pink" roads of western regions, such as Wyoming's Powder River Basin.

LARRY WOIWODE

scour hole

Scouring, in geologic terms, is concentrated erosive action, especially by high-energy stream water, often at a bend in a waterway. Similar phenomena occur on beaches and the ocean floor, as a result of strong tides and tidal currents. Such scouring may result in scour flats, scour ways, scour flutes, and scour holes, the latter of which is a relatively deep depression in mud or sand. However, scour holes also occur in bedrock as a result of rock particles entrained in swirling water that erode in a ballmill action. Many New England streams exhibit such a feature, at times also called potholes.   JOHN KEEBLE

scree

Rock loosened from cliff or mountain buttresses falls around the base in a scree slope. The fallen debris cones against its parent mass in a sloping bed, a process as slow as weathering, as sure as gravity: a rockfall in edgy stasis. (The Norse root word is *skritha*, a landslide.) In the sense that both compose landforms, scree and talus are synonymous. However, mountaineers are more likely to use scree to describe the loose gravel spread across thin-air slopes above timberline—an altitude, in John Muir's words, of "storm-beaten desolation."   ELLEN MELOY

scroll

Surging river current erodes the outer bank of each meander, while along the inner bank the current slows, sometimes separating into an eddy, and deposits sediment. This deposition forms a point bar, extending the tongue of land enclosed by each meander, and over time the meanders migrate outward and downstream like transient bends in a hose whipped side to side. A point bar's topography tends to be scalloped with a series of crescent-shaped ridges of sand or gravel separated by shallow troughs, all mimicking, more or less, the curvature of the migrating meander. These ridges with their attendant depressions are called—no doubt for their scalloped form—scrolls, or meander scrolls. They are tracks left by the living river.   JOHN DANIEL

scrub

The origin of the word scrub reaches back into Middle English as a variant of shrub, which was often considered a kind of failed tree. In nineteenth-century American usage, the word always implies this sense of the inferior, a kind of mongrel or deficient quality. Not just scrub-oaks and scrub-pines, but scrub horses (the exact opposites of purebreds) and scrub baseball players (far below the first string). Scrublands, then, are tracts considered to have little commercial value, overgrown with low, stunted trees, brushwood, underbrush. In the wetter climates of the East, scrub is often a temporary, intermediate stage in the process of plant succession, as denuded land heals itself back to forest. In drier climates, where there is a deficit of water, it is a more permanent plant community, for example the sage scrub of the West, or the upland sand-pine and palmetto scrub of Florida.

CHARLES FRAZIER

sea arch

The erosive action of water plays a key role in forming sea arches, just as with their terrestrial cousins, the spectacular rock arches of the Colorado Plateau. In both cases, the minerals in the water act to dissolve the rock, though for sea arches the sculpting process begins with the brute force of waves carving away weaker sections along a coastal promontory or headland. A sea cave formed by such action on one or both sides of a headland, its development aided by weathering, eventually wears through, creating a sea arch. Erosion and gravity then work on the opening until the arch collapses, leaving behind an islanded portion of headland called a sea stack. Sea arches are common along the coast of Hawai'i Island below active Kīlauea Volcano, where lava tubes are sculpted by wave action into sea caves and arches, such as ninety-foot-high Hōlei Sea Arch.   PAMELA FRIERSON

sea cave

Sea caves are usually hollowed at the base of sea cliffs by the erosive force of water. Under the onslaught of waves, weaker sections of rock in a sea cliff erode more quickly than neighboring harder rock, and wave-cut nips and notches begin to form. Crashing waves may bear rocks or sediment, augmenting their scouring power. Wave action can also force open any dikes, faults, or fractures in sea cliffs, speeding up the erosive process. Sea caves are also found in headlands, as waves, refracted when they encounter the coast, sweep parallel to the land, and converge on prominent coastal features. Oregon's Sea Lion Caves are among the Pacific coast's most popular destinations. Painted Cave, a 1,227-foot-long sea cave on

S

Santa Cruz Island off the coast of California near Santa Barbara, is one of the world's largest. Its name comes from the colorful lichens and algae that grow on the cave's walls.   PAMELA FRIERSON

sea stack

A tall island in the sea, a geologic bone, the sea stack represents rock harder than what once surrounded it and has been eroded away. In some instances, this harder material was originally a volcanic intrusion into sedimentary strata. The sea stack which in desert country might be called a chimney, pinnacle, needle, knob, horn, or pillar rises in the ocean, and is often favored by cormorants, puffins, and gulls for nesting and whitewashing with clamorous possession. The stack has been whittled by waves in a cycle that may begin as a cliff cave at sea level, cut away to be an arch at sea, and then twin stacks, then one, before weathering to a stump that subsides in time to be a reef below the waves. Sea stacks that abound on the West Coast (Oregon's Haystack Rock is technically a sea stack) shouldn't be confused with another resistant geologic remnant, the haystack, which is found in karst terrain more common in the East.

KIM STAFFORD

section

In Thomas Jefferson's imperial imagination, the trans-Appalachian West would be made American by geometry. The West's conquest (and conversion into real estate) was begun when Congress adopted Jefferson's scheme to lay over the disorderly wilderness his rigidly orthogonal grid of township and range. The Land Ordinance of 1785 called for subdividing federal land into square townships consisting of thirty-six one-square-mile sections, later defined by Congress as 640 acres each. The Homestead Act of 1862 extended the logic of this system to thousands of immigrant farmers west of the Mississippi by granting each head of household a quarter section (one-quarter of 640 acres, or 160 acres). A "forty" is forty acres, or one-sixteenth of a section. Sections in a township are numbered from east to west and then from west to east, turning back at the end of each row of six sections. This pattern is called boustrophedonic, meaning "turning like oxen in plowing." Roads, city and county limits, and private property lines in the West often follow the Jeffersonian grid. These section and township lines cross mountain ranges and deserts, blind to history and natural features. A geometric mindset on the part of eastern lawmakers is why so many western states have sharp corners.   D. J. WALDIE

section-line road

In most of the United States west of the Appalachian Mountains (Texas being the largest exception), the grid of section-line roads, running north-south or east-west at intervals of a mile, imposes a tidy scheme on an unruly landscape. In farm country, more often than not, such roads are gravel or dirt, so they signal the passage of cars or trucks by plumes of dust. The ninety-degree turns imposed by the grid often stymie drivers, especially those whose judgment is impaired by alcohol or testosterone, as Norman Maclean illustrates in *A River Runs Through It*: "My brother said, 'I don't know how to explain what happened next, but there was a right-angle turn in the section-line road, and the rabbit saw it, and I didn't.'"
SCOTT RUSSELL SANDERS

S

seep

Places where groundwater percolates to the surface too slowly to be considered a spring are seeps. Water oozes out of the ground rather than flows. The soil around the seep is seasonally or perpetually wet, and enough water may collect to form a pool or an area of wetland. This term also applies to places where petroleum rises naturally to the surface, such as the asphalt seeps in Los Angeles known as the La Brea Tar Pits. Material collected from oil seeps in various parts of the continent were used by Native Americans to waterproof baskets and canoes and as medicine.   CHARLES FRAZIER

seif dune

There are four major dune shapes: crescent, linear, star, and parabolic. The shapes are determined by the direction and variability of the wind and by the supply of sand. A seif dune is a linear, or longitudinal, dune (*sayf* is "sword" in Arabic); seif dunes form in ridges, parallel to one another and to the direction of the wind, so that the prevailing wind sweeps through the troughs between them. They are narrow dunes with steep crests and slip faces on either side. The origin of seif dunes is a matter still under study, but it is generally agreed that they are formed where the wind comes strongly and perhaps seasonally from at least two different directions. The Algodones Dunes in the Imperial and Coachella Valleys contain the largest stretch of linear dunes in California. They are under more or less regular assault from the off-road vehicle lobby. A spectacular pair of seif dunes can be seen at Sand Mountain in Nevada, off Highway 50, sixteen miles southeast of Fallon.   ROBERT HASS

sendero

A sendero is a cleared pathway (always in a straight line) through the woods or brushlands of south Texas and Mexico, often several miles long. Not until bulldoz-ers were used for oil and gas exploration did senderos become commonplace. Most senderos are from twenty to fifty feet wide, though some are as much as fifty yards across. Hunters often set up blinds (shooting towers) along senderos to harvest deer as the animals cross. In the book *A Vaquero of the Brush Country*, John D. Young and J. Frank Dobie write: "I have sought to open a sendero, as we say on the border—a clearing—that will allow people to behold some of the secrets that the brush has hidden." ARTURO LONGORIA

sérac

When the slope beneath a glacier becomes sufficiently steep, the overlying body of ice will fracture into a jumble of hulking, unstable shards that can stand more than one hundred feet tall. The ice blocks that collectively comprise an icefall are known, individually, as séracs—a term coined in 1787 by the Swiss scientist Horace Bénédict de Saussure (who also takes credit for inventing the sport of alpinism). Icefalls on Mont Blanc reminded him of sérac, the ricotta-like white cheese that is a dietary staple in the French Haute-Savoie, and Saussure's usage was widely adopted. In his book *The Shameless Diary of an Explorer*, which recounts an unsuccessful ascent of Alaska's Mount McKinley in 1903, the journalist Robert Dunn described "an enormous sérac, the whole breadth of the glacier, massing into a white Niagara, hinting of the world's end, the unknown range, and the hidden deserts of the moon." JON KRAKAUER

shallows

In a strict sense, shallows occur anywhere a body of water decreases in depth, whether near the shore or miles from land where shoals and sandbars rise. More generally taken to mean the rim of quiet water along the edges of a creek, river, lake, or ocean, the shallows is an area where children can safely play. Shallows may extend far into the water or may drop abruptly away from dry ground. The word is associated more with areas of slow water and backwash than with swift-flowing currents. "The oarsman pulls precisely," writes John R. Stilgoe in *Shallow Water Diction-ary*, "for in the shallows a wrong stroke or two, a slight falling off before the wind, means a gentle grounding in clean white sand or grayish-black mud." JAN DEBLIEU

sheepback rock

Gray humps of rock poking up through the soil are a common sight in northern New England, where the soil covering is typically less than thirty feet deep. The formation is known as a sheep rock, sheepback rock, whaleback, boulderback, or roche moutonnée. The latter French term means "fleecy rock," a rock that looks like a sheep lying prone. Properly defined, these knobs are erosion-resistant outcroppings of bedrock, all of them shaped by glacial movement in a characteristic way—a smooth, gentle slope on the upstream side, and "plucked" or left ragged on the steeper, downstream side. (Sheep-back rocks are always found with their long axes parallel to the direction of the glacier's movement.) Sheepbacks are not random rocks lying loose atop the soil but expo-sures of the bedrock below; that is, not rocks dropped by retreating glaciers but features cut in place by the grind and push of glacial ice, moving over the uneven surface of a rock that stood fast before such forces. In the many places where these rock forms appear across New Eng-land, you may also find obvious scratch marks and gouges in the parent bedrock. Called striations, these lines were etched by bits of harder rock, embedded like styluses on the underside of a passing glacier. GRETCHEN LEGLER

shelf

A shelf is solid rock, or bedrock, found beneath alluvial soil or deposits, a flat-surfaced stratum. A shelf can also be a flat ledge of rock or a projecting rock layer, as on a slope. The term is most commonly used to refer to a continental shelf, a gently sloping, nearly horizontal

marine platform that was dry land during the last ice age
and is now beneath the waves, projecting gradually away
from the present-day shoreline to a depth of between 60
and 1,800 feet.   DONNA SEAMAN

shelterbelt

A shelterbelt provides a more intense, thicker protection
for man-made structures, livestock, crops, and pasture
than a windbreak. While windbreaks are usually long
and narrow, a shelterbelt has multiple rows of trees
(four or more). They are planted along the edges of a
farmstead or around groups of farm buildings to provide
a small but intense zone of protection. A shelterbelt
usually begins with the lowest-growing species on the
side with the most wind exposure; the plantings then
increase in size. After the tallest species, the plantings
again diminish in size. Because a shelterbelt is wider than
a windbreak, it offers an increased area of protection for
indigenous species and also provides a wildlife corridor
and habitat for other creatures.   ARTHUR SZE

shield volcano

A shield volcano is so named for its broad dome shape,
reminiscent of the convex bulge of ancient Teutonic war
shields. Oceanic volcanoes, built up from innumerable
highly fluid lava flows, take this form, eventually rising
from the seafloor to create islands, including those in the
Hawaiian and Galápagos archipelagoes. Mauna Loa, on
Hawai'i Island, is the largest shield volcano, and in fact
the largest mountain on Earth. Measured from the ocean
floor, where its footprint is over 180 miles in diameter, it
rises over six miles. Its massive dome shape dominates
the skyline from the south end of the island, giving the
odd impression of a huge moon partly risen over the
horizon. Indeed, shield volcanoes are interplanetary
features, found on the moon, Mars, and possibly Venus.

S

The moon's Olympus Mons, over 370 miles in diameter, currently holds the title of largest shield volcano in the solar system.   PAMELA FRIERSON

shingle

The word shingle is of obscure origin. It is used most often to describe a gravelly shore of loose waterworn pebbles. Ralph Waldo Emerson, in *English Traits/Ability,* speaks of "the enchantments of barren shingle and rough weather." Although some shingles can support lichens and grasses, the term most often connotes a beach that is rough, dreary, and inhospitable. When Brown, the heroically deceiving and self-destructive sailor in Robert Stone's *Outerbridge Reach,* steps "ashore on a shingle of flint that shifted beneath his boots," he is about to experience a landscape decidedly unwholesome and hallucinatory.
JOY WILLIAMS

shinnery

A type of low brush thicket, the shinnery takes its name from the shin oak *(Quercus havardii),* but nothing is simple here. American English deploys a wide range of words to designate landscapes difficult to impossible to cross on foot or horseback. Thickets of switch cane, sugarcane, and other woody grasses (canebrakes), of heathlike plants (briar patches), of blackberry and other entwined, thorny wands (brambles), and of manzanita, ceanothus, chamise, and similar stiff-branched, leather-leaved scrub (chaparral) all qualify. The term shinnery is used in eastern New Mexico and panhandle Texas for brush thickets where shin oak, sometimes called Havard oak; a variety of the sandpaper oak *(Q. pungens)* called Vassey oak; and Mohr oak *(Q. mohriana)* grow in close ranks. Where a single shin oak develops a massive root system over hundreds of years, sending up numerous stems (which look like separate plants) over a wide area, it creates a thicket called a motte. The oaks in a shinnery vary in height according to the soils they take root in, but much of the brush is only waist high. To cut through a shinnery on foot means to get cracked repeatedly across the shins by the stout limbs of this shrub. Thus the shin oak, and thus is a shinnery any thicket of scrubby oaks that so marks the trespasser. By a very different line of reckoning, the shinnery takes its name from *chênière,* Cajun French for a hummock in a swamp with a dense growth of any of several species of oak (*chêne* in French).   BARRY LOPEZ

ship rock

Situated in northwestern New Mexico, Shiprock Peak is an ancient volcanic neck, exposed by erosion, which looms almost 1,400 feet above the surrounding land. The rock itself is composed almost entirely of volcanic mate- rial, while the nearby land consists of nearly horizontal sedimentary layers. In Navajo, the peak is called *Tsé Bit 'A'í,* "The Rock with Wings." In a creation story, Navajos relate that this rock brought their ancestors through the air from the north and landed on the site, which there- after marked their land. Near the end of Willa Cather's novel *Death Comes for the Archbishop,* it is described as "the figure of a one-masted fishing-boat under full sail, and the white man named it accordingly."   ARTHUR SZE

S

shoals

If streambeds and river bottoms were smooth, water would slide through with barely a riffle. But the bed rises toward the surface in some places, disturbing the flow. These shallow-water areas are known as shoals, as are the underwater sandbars, rock ledges, or debris that compose them, and which are often hazards to navigation. Shoals also occur at sea. Off Cape Hatteras, North Carolina, the collision of the Gulf Stream and the Labrador Current causes sediment to settle to the bottom, forming the

treacherous Diamond Shoals. In *The Outermost House,*
Henry Beston writes of a "wall of ocean dunes" on the
forearm of Cape Cod: "Five miles long, this wall ends at
a channel over whose entrance shoals the ocean sweeps
daily into a great inlet or lagoon." A large school of fish
breaking the surface is also referred to as a shoal; the
movement causes the water to shiver as it would running
across a gravel bar.   JAN DEBLIEU

shore

"The common margin of the land and a body of water"
(*Dictionary of Geological Terms*). Shore can be parsed
further into the subsets of beach and coast. One could
say that shore is the more formal-sounding and "elegant"
of the three—as evidenced by real estate developers and
bad poets. Beach: a gently sloping shore made of sand or
pebbles, washed by waves and tides. (Louisiana has few
beaches, but lots of shore.) A shore can be more abrupt
than a beach—it can be muddy, or rocky, or swampy.
Coast: a segment of land that contains the territory
between the shore and the first major change in terrain
features (such as sea cliffs). A shore can contain those
terrain features. (See California's Route 1, or the Oregon
Coast.) A shore, then, is the ultimate boundary between
two worlds. If you're not at sea, you're on the shore. And
if you're a gospel singer, you're rowing for the far shores
of Heaven. A shore is all-encompassing, and a beach is a
part of that shore: every year, millions of people go to the
beach at the Jersey shore.   LUIS ALBERTO URREA

shore lead

The journals kept by explorers in the polar regions are
thick with tales of sought-after passages through the
frozen landscape. It makes sense then that these passages,
or leads, have a taxonomy of their own. Hence the term
shore lead as a type of lead, like an open lead (any very

wide crack in pack ice) or a flaw lead (the variable strip of open water between landfast ice and mobile pack ice). Shore leads occur when a stretch of open water forms between landfast ice and the shore or between the mobile pack and shore. Shore leads are most often created by offshore winds, often aided by tidal currents. They may be narrow enough to leap over or several miles wide.   GRETCHEN LEGLER

shortgrass prairie

Carpeting the western Great Plains, the shortgrass prairie is composed of grasses that thrive in poor soil over a short growing season, such as buffalo and blue grama grass, neither of which reaches a height of two feet. In the fall of the year, with the near-continual winds of the plains, "The red of the grass made all the great prairie the color of wine-stains, or of certain seaweeds, when they are first washed up. And there was so much motion in it; the whole country seemed, somehow, to be running," writes Willa Cather in *My Ántonia*. The image of motion and running seems meant to recapture a glimpse of the shortgrass prairie's most common early species, the American bison, as here, from Alexander Henry's *Journals*: "I had seen almost incredible numbers of buffalo in the fall. . . . The ground was covered at every point of the compass, as far as the eye could reach, and every animal was in motion."   LARRY WOIWODE

S

shoulder

A bench running along a slope, parallel to a valley below, is called a shoulder, as is a short, rounded spur on a mountainside. The term is also used to designate the crease in a glaciated valley where its steeply eroded lower slopes meet the gentler angle of its upper slopes, land that remained above the ice flow. The margins of a road are also called shoulders, if they're flat enough and wide enough for a vehicle to pull over safely.   WILLIAM KITTREDGE

shrub carr

Visitors to a shrub carr are likely to find themselves hopping between raised hummocks to avoid the damp depressions between. This type of wetland is usually found along the edges of streams, lakes, ponds, and other drainages, and often serves as a transition zone between forest and open water or swamp. Various willows, red osier dogwood, and scrub birch often dominate the hummocks; grasses and sedges, the dips.   BILL MCKIBBEN

sidehill

A sidehill is the side or slope of a hill—the sloping ground or descent. In *The Meadow*, James Galvin writes of the feature this way: "As he drove past the sidehill where the winter road attacks the ridge he just glared; he had fought that hill for forty winters. Every winter it rose white against him and he fought it, sidling down the sidehill into deeper drifts, digging out, grinding in again."   MARY SWANDER

sierra

In Spanish, sierra originally meant "saw," and still does—as in *sierra de mano* (handsaw)—though it's a term also used in a broader sense in both English and Spanish to describe mountains with serrated (sawtoothlike) peaks or ridges, leading to names like Sierra Madre in Mexico and Sierra Nevada in North America. In regional use, either of these ranges (and all the others with Sierra in their names) is often shortened to either la Sierra or the Sierra. Sierra is oftentimes used simply to mean mountains, as in *Conquest*, by Hugh Thomas: "The Castilians were able to see, from the top of the sierra, much of the valley of Mexico."   STEPHEN GRAHAM JONES

singing sand

Sand falling from the crest of a dune can produce sounds that have haunted desert travelers for millennia. In the past, the sound was likened to the strumming of a lute, the muttering of immensely deep voices, or the crashing of waves on an invisible shore. Later, the sound was compared to cannon fire or armies in battle. Today, the loudest booming is said to sound like the passage overhead of a squadron of propeller-driven aircraft. All of these sounds are caused by an incompletely understood interaction of wind, humidity, and the geometry of individual grains when a sheet of sand with the right properties slumps from a dune's crest. Booming sands, a type of singing sand, are relatively uncommon, but they can be heard at Sand Mountain near Fallon and Big Dune near Beatty, both in Nevada; and at the Kelso Dunes near Kelso, California. Unique barking sands can be found on the west coast of Kaua'i, Hawai'i. Unlike booming sands, which produce a range of low-frequency sounds, some sands produce a single tone that has been variously described as squeaking or whistling. Walking on or shifting these musical sands produces a very short, high-frequency sound. Squeaking sand can be found at many beaches, lakeshores, and riverbanks around the United States.   D. J. WALDIE

sink

S

In *Close Range: Wyoming Stories*, Annie Proulx writes: "It was impossible to run cows in such tough country where they fell off cliffs, disappeared into sinkholes." A sink, or sinkhole, is a closed depression that is dry or through which water seeps or flows, resembling in shape a basin, funnel, or cylinder. Sinkholes develop by solutional processes or from collapse into subsurface voids. On the Mitchell Plain in southern Indiana, most trees that remain in the fields are in sinkholes whose slopes are too steep for clearing and plowing. The Big

Lost River of Idaho comes out of the mountains and sinks into the porous basalt flows of the Snake River Plain. The December Giant Sinkhole, 400 feet wide and 150 feet deep, formed in 1972 near Montebello, Alabama, was most likely a collapse of surface material into an underlying limestone cavern. At least fifty synonyms have been recorded, including doline, shakehole, swallet, swallow pit, leach hole, interior basin, and sotch. A desert sink, such as the Carson Sink in Nevada, is a depression where a desert stream ends or disappears by evaporation. Glacial sink is an obsolete term for a depression in a terminal moraine. A volcanic sink, or pit crater, is a circular depression on the flank of a volcano, formed by collapse. Not all sinks are naturally occurring, however. In Pittsburgh in the 1960s, underground mines caused surface land to sink, destroying neighborhoods. Less spectacular but more widespread is the surface shrinkage in the arid West caused by excessive pumping of underground water for overland irrigation, as has happened in Antelope Valley, California. KIM BARNES

sinter mound

Sinter mounds are one of the impressive forms in which sinter—deposits of minerals precipitated out of water—accumulates around geysers and hot springs. Sinter mounds develop slowly, increasing by only about an inch per century, but can grow very large; the vast sinter mound surrounding White Dome Geyser at Yellowstone National Park, Wyoming, is an example. (Such a large deposit might eventually close off a geyser vent entirely.) In addition to mounds, sinter also forms as scalloped edges on hot pools, as ornate cones around geysers, and as sheets or terraces. Sheets of sinter, such as the broad sinter plain around Old Faithful Geyser at Yellowstone, occur when mineral deposits are carried across a geyser basin by flowing water. Silica-rich, or siliceous, sinter, the kind that emerges around geysers, is more common than calcium rich, or calcareous, sinter. The former originates underground as the hot alkaline waters that feed a geyser dissolve silica from the surrounding volcanic rock. When the silica-enriched water gushes to the surface and begins to cool, silica precipitates out as siliceous sinter, a porous material commonly referred to as geyserite. (Siliceous sinter—technically, hydrous silicon dioxide—is chemically similar to, and sometimes resembles, opal.) Chemically different, calcareous sinter precipitates from calcium-rich waters, most often in limestone caves, where it accumulates in the form of calcite formations, rising from the cave's floor (as stalagmites) or hanging from its ceiling (stalactites). Calcareous sinter also forms the beautiful sedimentary limestone called travertine. Sinter is the umbrella word that encompasses both the several types of material (travertine, geyserite, calcite) and the variety of forms these materials take (mounds, terraces, spikes, ribbons, tubes, drip curtains). The word comes from the Old German, and is an etymological cousin to the English cinder.   EMILY HIESTAND

slab

A scarp of vertical rock is usually known as a cliff, crag, precipice, or wall. But when the terrain in question lies at an angle that's no steeper than, say, sixty degrees, mountaineers will refer to it as a slab—for example, Satans Slab, a massive, tilted plane of red sandstone among the Flatirons above Boulder, Colorado. If polished by glaciation or water, a slab can be mirror-smooth and very challenging to ascend, in which case it may be called a friction slab.   JON KRAKAUER

slackwater

The term slackwater refers to a stillness, or even stagnancy, in a body of water that usually sees regular flow or movement. In the ocean, slackwater occurs when the tide is neither ebbing out nor flowing in, that moment when the current or tension of tidal flow is absent, or "slacked." Slack-water can also be found in the stillest sections of a river, or otherwise outside the current's sway—in eddies or behind objects such as dams—where it's been known to confuse fish accustomed to the river's flow. The Columbia River's slackwater lakes are what allow barges to navigate the river downstream all the way to Portland, Oregon. Whether in the ocean or on a river, these calm stretches of water often provide a brief stopping point for boats seeking easier navigation and rest.   LAN SAMANTHA CHANG

slash

In low, coastal regions, wet or swampy ground overgrown with brush and various canes, or slash-pine, loblolly, or shortleafed pines, is called slash. In highland mountain forests, slash is an open tract strewn with the debris and fallen trees from logging, windstorms, fire, or slash-and-burn agriculture. Slash debris left behind after logging, often overgrown with thickets, can be seen in most North American forests, and vividly in the former cedar forests on the Queen Charlotte Islands off British Columbia.   WILLIAM KITTREDGE

slickrock

Found in the canyon country of Utah and Arizona, and also in the canyon country of western Colorado and northwestern New Mexico, slickrock, buffed smooth by water and wind, undulates for miles in rounded waves of varying size. Slickrock plateaus were formed when the desiccation of vast oceans once covering the region left miles of bare sand dunes and seabeds to petrify. Although it is not truly slick or slippery (except perhaps when wet), it was named for the challenges it posed to the metal-shod livestock of early settlers. Later hikers, too, found treacherous passages along the slickrock, including several characters in Edward Abbey's *The Monkey Wrench Gang*: "They reach the rim of another incipient canyon, a typical slickrock-country gash in the stone, with overhanging walls and inaccessible floor—a cleft too wide to leap, too deep and too precipitous to descend." Today, particularly near Moab, Utah, thrill-seeking mountain bikers put their faith in the friction their rubber tires create with the red Navajo Sandstone, traversing the miles of free-flowing trails threading the slickrock plateau between Moab and the Colorado River. LAN SAMANTHA CHANG

slip face

The gradual, inexorable movement of dunes occurs when winds from one direction blow unceasingly upon mounds of uniform sand. Individual grains move up along the windward side of the dune, eventually reaching its crest. There they cascade down its steeper, leeward side, known as the slip face, before resting at an angle of repose at its foot. This process causes the dune itself to advance, as many as several dozen feet per year, often covering roads, farms, and most other objects in its path. LAN SAMANTHA CHANG

slip-off slope

As the lateral erosion of a river meander advances, the cutbank on the outside of the curve recedes, and the slip-off slope on the inside steadily grows, fed by deposition as the current slows against it. The sediments stranded on this gently sloping bank are called point-bar deposits. WILLIAM DEBUYS

slot canyon

Slot, or slit, canyons are rare formations, the result of the combined forces of wind and water on sandstone. The narrow crevice sliced through a mesa by rushing water evolves from a hairline crack into a series of convoluted hollows, in some instances stacked many stories high. Little light enters, but its quality, as filtered, refracted, reflected, and observed from below, illuminates incandescent striations of the sandstone as it has been etched over centuries by the flow of subterranean rivers. In 1931, a twelve-year-old girl was herding sheep in what is now the Navajo Indian Reservation in the Four Corners region when she discovered the country's best-known slot canyon. It's most often called Antelope Canyon, but is also referred to as Corkscrew, Upper Antelope, Wind Cave, or the Crack. A slot canyon that looks as if it has been cut out of the sandstone with a saw is called a saw-cut canyon. Most U.S. examples of this feature are found in Arizona's Glen Canyon, and include Labyrinth Canyon, which is about three miles of a twisting, turning passage that's no more than two or three feet wide at the bottom and hundreds of feet high. ANTONYA NELSON

slough

A slough—also slow, slew, sloo, slue—is a narrow stretch of sluggish water in a river channel, inlet, or pond. A slough can also be a marsh, swamp, bayou, or any soft, muddy, or waterlogged ground. The great, flat city of Chicago is built on filled sloughs, or swampy bottomlands. Slough is also a verb, meaning to mire in a slough or swamp, and "to be sloughed" can mean "lost in a swamp." Used as slang, "to slough in," or "slough up," is to arrest or imprison, to be inhibited, or bogged down. Nineteenth-century travelers reported horses sinking up to their necks in sloughs that looked no deeper than a puddle. Prairies, especially those radiating from the Mississippi, are (or were) riddled with sloughs, and sloughs run along the St. Paul, Pacific, and Sioux City Railroad tracks and other elevated rights-of-way, providing ideal homes for muskrats. DONNA SEAMAN

snow bridge

A common feature in glacial landscapes—for travelers
sometimes a blessing and sometimes a hazard—a snow
bridge spans a crevasse in a glacier. Snow bridges form
first as cornices, arms of wind-sculpted snow that reach
out to each other, like the branches of trees reaching high
across a street, sidewalk, or forest path. Eventually the
cornices meet and become covered with snow to form a
bridge. Robert Falcon Scott, making his way across Antarctica's Ross Ice Shelf toward the South Pole, like many
other polar explorers, suffered losses—dogs, equipment,
men—due to collapsed snow bridges: "Suddenly Wilson
shouted 'Hold onto the sledge,' and I saw him slip a leg
into a crevasse. . . . We had been actually traveling along
the bridge [over] a crevasse, the sledge had stopped on it,
whilst the dogs hung in their traces in the abyss. . . . Why
the sledge and ourselves didn't follow the dogs we shall
never know." GRETCHEN LEGLER

snow line

The border between winter and summer expressed in
altitudinal terms, rather than seasonal terms, the snow
line resides at sea level toward the poles, and climbs
higher as one moves toward the equator. The snow line
fluctuates up and down a mountain between continuous snow cover and perennial open ground. Some older
references use the phrase permanent snow line, but with
changing climatic conditions the term has become more
dynamic. A high snow line in the mountains speaks to
drought below, so a city dweller in the West can often
gauge the coming predicament with a glance toward
bare summer peaks. South-facing and very steep slopes
may be free of snow above the general regional snow
line, because such slopes receive more solar radiation
than surfaces facing other directions or with less steep
slopes, while snow might persist in gullies or on north

S

slopes throughout the summer. So the snow line is rarely simple, existing in a dance with season and aspect—the direction a slope faces—and shade at the working boundary.　KIM STAFFORD

sod

Sod is the surface layer of ground containing a mat of grass and some nongrass herbaceous plants and roots. In contemporary U.S. lawn maintenance, sod is farmed in fields, cut, rolled up, transported to building sites, and laid down on bare earth. In landscapes with little wood, sod has been used as both fuel and building material. In pioneer days on the American Great Plains, settlers often lived in sod houses. The densely tangled deep prairie roots of grasses, forbs, and topsoil made a tough and freely available building material. Settlers cut two-foot-square sod bricks and stacked them up into sturdy, thick walls. Heavily insulated, the houses helped keep families warm in winter and cool in summer. Wood was used sparingly—for doors and perhaps a window or two. Pioneers whitewashed the inside sod walls and stuffed the cracks with newspaper to hold out the wind whipping across the prairie. Grasses often continued to grow on the roof of the soddie, where the family goat might find a meal. In *Little House on the Prairie,* Laura Ingalls Wilder writes: "Pa had a new plow, a breaking plow. It was wonderful for breaking the prairie sod. It had a sharp-edged wheel, called a rolling coulter, that ran rolling and cutting through the sod ahead of the plowshare ... the strip of sod was exactly twelve inches wide, and as straight as if it had been cut by hand."　MARY SWANDER

soil

Erosion, volcanic eruption, earthquakes, floods, tectonic grinding, landslides, and other natural forces act continuously on the Earth's crustal rock, creating various types of debris: gravel deposits, mudflats in the tidal estuaries of creeks, cobble terraces, and beaches of black lava sand. When chemical agents such as phosphorus and nitrogen infuse this debris, and biological entities including microbes and earthworms work material into it organic enough to support plants, it becomes soil. A soil that is chemically or organically exhausted, that's been pulverized or become deeply parched, that has been invaded by decomposing rock, or that's been fouled by sewage or industrial pollution to the point where it cannot support plant life is called dirt.   BARRY LOPEZ

solfatara

Associated with Solfatara Volcanic Crater west-southwest of Naples, Italy, a solfatara, which is Italian for sulfur mine, is a fumarole, or vent, emitting predominantly sulfurous gases. Most often found in areas of diminishing volcanic activity, solfataras are nonexplosive, and their gentle vapors, when cooled, may result in a rimming deposit of minerals. A solfatara is also known as a soffione, suffione, or soffoni. The solfataric stage of volcanic activity is often used in a wider sense to include all fumaroles. A solfatara field, a group of solfataras, is also called a fumarole field.   KIM BARNES

sound

Sound, referring to a feature of coastlines, comes from the Middle and Old English *sund*, "to swim." The word in its modern guise evokes both this watery root, as well as the idea of soundings—measurements of depth, quests, or probings, downward and inward. A sound is a waterway connecting two larger bodies of water or two parts of the same body, though the term can also refer to an arm of the sea forming a channel between a mainland and an island. Examples of sounds include Puget Sound on the northwest coast of the United States, and Long Island

Sound on the east. Prince William Sound in Alaska is also a classic example. It was here that in 1989 the *Exxon Valdez* spilled more than 10.9 million gallons of crude oil into the ocean, creating an environmental catastrophe of unimaginable magnitude. American writer Marybeth Holleman, in her book *The Heart of the Sound: An Alaskan Paradise Found and Nearly Lost*, writes of Prince William Sound that it "is a world unto itself. It is delineated not just by the coastline, the way it indents at Cape Puget and at the Copper River Delta into what, upon his visit in 1899, John Burroughs called 'the enchanted circle.' It is contained by a string of mountain peaks, among them the highest coastal mountains in the world, some of them nunataks, jagged spires that jut through an ice field. These mountains enclose the Sound, hold clouds and rain in. They encircle it like sentries. The mountains, the water, the ice fields—it seemed to me they were all protecting this place, guarding it from harm."

GRETCHEN LEGLER

spatter cone

A spatter cone forms when a limited amount of basaltic lava erupts from an active volcanic vent. The molten rock falls back to the ground in liquid gobs that agglutinate, or weld together. The result is a steep-sided cone up to a few dozen feet high that resembles the sand-drip forms children squeeze from their fists at the beach. If the lava erupts along a fissure, the molten gobs may adhere in a long, narrow heap known as a spatter rampart. Spatter zones sometimes include fragments so molten that they flatten when they hit the ground, called cow pie bombs by geologists. Spatter mounds formed not by active venting but when lava pushes up through an opening in the roof of a lava tube have an equally colorful name: hornito—a diminutive of the Spanish word for oven.

The latter sometimes solidify into fantastic globular heaps and spires.   PAMELA FRIERSON

spit

Sand is never stationary, constantly moving with the wind-driven water along the seashore, piling up as sandbars, hooks, necks, fingers, and points. Currents that stream parallel to the shore build up land by carrying their sediments along the coast. When the outline of the coast changes abruptly, the current cannot change quickly enough to accommodate it; through the force of its inertia, the current continues in a straight line, depositing sand into deeper water, creating a spit. Spits cannot grow indefinitely. Their creating currents are eventually overpowered by swifter currents. Provincetown, Massachusetts, is at the end of a long, dramatically curved spit—Cape Cod.   JOY WILLIAMS

spoil bank

A mound of earth beside a mining tunnel, road cut, or quarry is called a spoil bank, though the term is most often used to describe the material piled on the edges of canals and harbors after dredging. The connotative ring of "spoils of war," or "spoiling," cannot be shed when one utters the words spoil or spoil bank. The mounded leavings of the miner, the quarry maker, the road cutter, the canal dredger, a spoil bank reveals the human perception that a place in its natural state has "overburden," obstructing access to something of greater value. Like a cutbank opened by erosion, a spoil bank becomes a place for scavenging, where builders find stone or geologists pick up orphaned specimens without the work of digging into native earth. Often the chemical content in a spoil prevents revegetation, but sometimes a spoil bank can represent latent transformation. Spoil bank:

S

seed bank. Plant life colonizing a spoil bank parallels the recovery of life following a receding glacier, gouging flood, landslide, or other catastrophe. At such a place, each green tendril is heroic by its pioneering impulse on barren ground.   KIM STAFFORD

spread

In common usage, spread simply means "distributed over a wide area," be that area gambling, toast, a dining table, or ranching. Inherent to the term—and very important—is the idea not just of extension, but of covering. Thus in ranching, where spread is in all likelihood a shortened version of cow spread, it doesn't refer just to the land the ranch encompasses, but also to the buildings, fences, cattle, horses, equipment, and hands scattered, or "spread," over the place, holding it together and making it work. However, as the term has been imported back into urban areas, where "wide area" is something of a relative idea, spread is seeing use again on a much more limited scale, as in Carl Hiaasen's *Sick Puppy*, set in South Florida: "Nice spread the guy had: old two-story Spanish stucco with barrel-tile shingles and vines crawling the walls."   STEPHEN GRAHAM JONES

spring

A spring—or its Spanish equivalent, *ojo*, widely used in the southwestern United States—is a natural flow of freshwater from the Earth's surface, generally issuing strongly under its own pressure onto land or into a body of water. (Where the flow is not distinct but dispersed, it is more correctly termed a seep.) Springs are characterized by temperature, prevalence, and mineral content (as well as taste and smell), and their presence often informs place-names: Hot Springs, Arkansas; Thousand Springs, Idaho; Altamonte Springs, Florida. In his memoir *This House of Sky: Landscapes of a Western Mind,* Ivan Doig recalls his childhood spent near White Sulphur Springs, Montana, and describes springs both potable—"across our entire empire of pasture, there was a single tiny spurt of fresh water for us at a trickling spring near the ridge base"—and sulfur-tainted—"the spring always was coated with this sickly whitish curd, as if something poisonous had just died there." KIM BARNES

spur

A finger of elevated land that juts out from a mountain or ridge into lower ground but doesn't outdo its parent mountain or ridge in size is called a spur. A single spur trailing out into a plain or other open area often functions as a funnel for game, animals looking to stay covered as long as possible. STEPHEN GRAHAM JONES

stair-step canyon

When erosional forces break down the rims and sidewalls of a canyon, disintegration proceeds more quickly in the softer layers of rock. Where the softer layers alternate in some regular fashion with harder layers, erosion creates a pattern of scree slopes (the softer rocks) and vertical cliff walls (the harder rock), suggesting a staircase of risers and (tilted) treads. Without this sidewall erosion, geological uplifting and downcutting by the canyon's streamflow system would produce a narrow, U-shaped cut in the earth. It's erosion of the sidewalls that creates the classic V-shape of a canyon. The higher one points on the canyon wall, the longer, at that spot, erosion has been going on. The rock is eroded directly by wind and rain, by cycles of freezing and thawing that spall rock and force open cracks, and by the pull of gravity. The process goes all the faster, oddly, in landscapes with little rainfall, which lack a deflecting cover of vegetation. The orderly stacking of extended sheets of sedimentary rock, all laid down parallel to one another, like a pile of thick

S

blankets of different weaves on a slightly rumpled bed,
is what makes stair-step erosion so stark and readable.
TERRY TEMPEST WILLIAMS

staked plain

A dry, southern extension of the Great Plains, stretching south from the Canadian River all the way down to
the Pecos, the staked plains, home of the Kiowa and the
Kwahadi Comanche, are usually referred to by Coronado's term from 1541, *llano estacado*. According to legend,
he called them "staked" because they were so vast and
featureless that his men had to mark their trails with
stakes so they could find their way back. Another possible
explanation is that, because there was nothing to tie the
horses to at night, Coronado's men had to use stakes for
this purpose. Either way, he was right: the Llano Estacado
is both vast (forty thousand square miles) and without
landmark—the largest, flattest tableland in North America. Natives to the areas around Amarillo and Lubbock—
the respective centers of the north and south plains of the
Llano Estacado—often feel cramped in the mountains of
the Northwest or the dense tree cover of the Southeast,
simply because the sky, in comparison to the Llano
Estacado's, is so small. STEPHEN GRAHAM JONES

stalactite

Mineral formations that look like icicles and grow slowly
down from the ceilings of caves are called stalactites.
They occur when rainwater and snowmelt seep through
cracks in limestone. The slow, steady drip of water from
a cave ceiling, enriched now with calcium carbonate,
creates a small, tapering deposit of calcite. The stalactite
begins as a hollow tube, conical in shape but sometimes
straight (a "soda straw"). Eventually, after millions—
countless—drops of water have slid down its flanks and
fallen to the cave floor, the tube closes, though it contin-

ues to grow. This creative force is secreted, hidden, in the darkness of the cave. Where the lime-rich drops hit the cave floor, a stalagmite can start to grow, building up, rising toward the stalactite above. If they come together, the formation they make is called a column. These creations have an inviting beauty and strangeness that compel humans to enter the cave's darkness. At the same time, there is a sense that this is a world closing itself up, teeth, a cage, as if to say keep out, stay away, do not enter, do not leave, we are closing Earth.   LINDA HOGAN

stand

There's a utilitarian bias wrapped up in this term, stand, which refers to a standing growth of trees, corn, alfalfa, or other plants awaiting harvest. Farmers walk their fields to assess how good a stand of hay or wheat they have. A timber stand is not a woods, but a crop that's sooner or later to be felled. When foresters speak of stand density, they mean trees per acre, and when they speak of stand age, they mean the average age of the harvestable trees.
SCOTT RUSSELL SANDERS

standing wave

Whitewater rapids break a river's smooth flow into descent and chaos, then restore a civilized flow line again. Waves express the energy of motion through each stage of this passage. From silken tongue to runout, you can follow this sequence through a rapid: lateral, or diagonal waves, when the river constricts and its energy is poised between slow and swift flow; a roiling, erratic turbulence in the rapid's frothing heart; then stationary, standing waves formed as the river's current slows over deep water. A rollercoaster series of standing waves is known as a wave train. Elongated standing waves, with spray peeling off their crests, are called rooster-tails. Large, symmetrical standing waves are haystacks. In big

S

water their slopes can rise steeply enough to block out the downriver view and your boat will slide right off their face.   ELLEN MELOY

star dune

A dune with a central mound and many ridges radiating from it (think of a starfish) is called a star dune. Each ridge is produced by winds that blow alternately from different directions at different times of the year.
D. J. WALDIE

starved basin

A sedimentary basin in which the rate of subsidence exceeds the rate of sedimentation is called a starved basin. Basins can be dynamic for hundreds of millions of years as depositories of water-borne sediment. Starved of water, they quickly (in geological time, a few million years) become stranded and lose their sediments to wind and erosion. Marathon Basin in west Texas exhibits the exposed rock belt of a starved basin system. During the Eocene Era—some fifty million years ago—the area of Fossil Butte in southwest Wyoming harbored palm-fringed lakes teeming with fish, crocodiles, turtles, and other animals. Changing salinity levels and variations in the amount of water flowing from the Uinta Mountains caused dead plants and animals on the deep lake bottoms to be covered with fine sediment. When the lakes dried up, subsidence thrust up rich worlds of fossilized sediment. These starved basins of Wyoming are unique in that they have also disclosed fossilized birds and bats.
JOY WILLIAMS

steephead

A word both functional and vivid, employing a kind of yeoman poetry, steephead is the nearly vertical wall at the head of certain stream valleys. The wall typically bends in semicircular fashion to form what's called a pocket valley or blind valley. At the base of the wall a stream is born, springing from underground pools that spill forth a headwater flow from seemingly secret beginnings. Steepheads are especially common in the sandy terrain of northwest Florida and extreme south Alabama and Georgia. Because of their distinct microclimatic conditions, steephead forests support an unusually large number of plants and animals.   MIKE TIDWELL

stillwater

Stillwater is a term that describes a curious phenomenon of quiet water. In the United States over two hundred places are named Stillwater—including rivers, canyons, streams, ponds, even flats and towns. In the late seventeenth century one such town, bordered by the Hudson River near Saratoga, New York, was chronicled as a place where "the water passes so slowly as not to be discovered, while above and below it is disturbed, and rageth as in a great sea, occasioned by rocks and falls therein." In the late 1800s the best-known city by this name, Stillwater, Oklahoma, formed near a back-eddied place on a creek. Lesser-known Stillwater towns in Nevada, Montana, and elsewhere also grew up around pools of tranquil water. Such cities, because of their names, are often presented as stereotypically tranquil places to live, as depicted in Richard and Florence Atwater's *Mr. Popper's Penguins*: "It was an afternoon in late September. In the pleasant city of Stillwater, Mr. Popper, the house painter, was going home from work." Stillwater is a term also used by meteorologists in predicting storm surges. In deep water they look for the midpoint of the wave crest before it reels down; in shallow water they look for the trough and crest of the wave. The stillwater level is the highest water level measured if wave action were completely smoothed out.   ELIZABETH COX

storm beach

A storm beach is a paradoxical feature of the coast, a barrier of gravel, rocks, shingle, even boulders, piled up by extreme storm waves behind the normal margin of the beach and acting as a shield or curtain wall against all but the most violent later storms. In the protection of the storm beach many kinds of vegetation thrive that otherwise might not survive the force of prevailing winds and storm waves. The low rounded ridge nurtures a unique coastal habitat in its wind and wave shadow, a flourishing, diverse culture of plants and birds and other wildlife. Perhaps we might think of an analogy with Offa's Dyke, a ditch and wall thrown up in the eighth century to protect the Saxons from the Welsh, but which also served to keep Wales lush and wild behind the rough, excluding boundary. Left by the fiercest gales, the storm beach provides sanctuary to a community otherwise unlikely to flourish so close to the battered shore.   ROBERT MORGAN

strait

A strait is a narrow passage or corridor of water connecting two larger bodies of water. Straits are often turbulent, deep, current-vexed, and dangerous. They are transition zones that test the psyche of sailors, for, entering a strait, one is often returning from the vastness of the ocean, while leaving one is saying goodbye to the firm earth and the community of the land. For the ancient Mediterranean people, the Hellespont, Bosporus, and Straits of Gibraltar signaled the end of the civilized world and were gateways to oblivion and barbarity. The periods of early and late European exploration left many straits named for mariners such as Magellan, Cook, Bering, and Juan de Fuca. Since the 1960s, the Straits of Florida have become the main crossing point for thousands of Haitians and Cubans fleeing economic and political hardships.
MICHAEL COLLIER

strand

The sandy stretch that lies between the lapping waves of an ocean and the grasses of the dunes, where sunbathers lounge and children build sand castles, is known as the strand. But the term has also been applied indiscriminately to different features of inland and coastal beaches: the narrow strip that lies between the high and low tide lines, the sandy spits and crescents sometimes found along lakes and rivers, even the entire width and length of barrier islands. The sixty-mile stretch of coast between Little River and Georgetown, South Carolina, is known locally as the Grand Strand. In Florida, the term takes on a completely different meaning. There a strand is a depression in karst or limestone terrain, caused by a fault or an underground stream. The cypress strands of south Florida are among the most haunting of landscapes. JAN DEBLIEU

strata

Strata are layers of sedimentary rock that form beds or bands of colored or textured material. From smooth black shale to rough white limestone, rock strata are most easily identified in cliffs, canyons, quarries, road cuts, or the exposed banks of rivers. Strata vary in thickness from a centimeter to a kilometer or more. Each bed contains fossils set down in a specific sequence with a definite mode of deposition—river silt, beach sand, coal swamp, sand dune, or lava. When John Price explored Badlands National Park in his book *Not Just Any Land*, he "followed a bison trail up to a high, hot place" and viewed "the impressive, serrated edge of the distant Pinnacles, their strata bleached white in the sun." Hikers elsewhere might have a view of many strata from above. For example, at the Grand Canyon, erosion has exposed rock strata ranging from the 1.7-billion-year-old Vishnu Schist at the bottom of the inner gorge, through brilliantly colored limestone,

S

shale, and sandstone formations, to one-million-year-old
black lava flows in the western canyon.   MARY SWANDER

stratovolcano

Stratovolcanoes, also called composite or cone volcanoes,
are known for their stature as mountains and for their
variety of utterance. Venting at times pyroclastic—"fire-
broken"—particulates, as Mount St. Helens did in 1980,
and at other times exuding lava, a stratovolcano develops
a layered composition as it grows (hence the name).
The steeply bedded ash and cinders of its pyroclastic
explosions tend to give it a conical form, while its gentler
expressions of lava provide structural stability. All the
major Pacific Rim volcanoes are stratovolcanoes. By present measurements, it takes anywhere from roughly twenty
thousand (St. Helens) to more than half a million years
(Hood and Rainier) to build a stratovolcano of respectable
size. Some erupt so exuberantly that they self-destruct.
Mount Mazama, a twelve-thousand-foot peak in the
southern Oregon Cascades composed of several overlapping volcanoes, emptied its magma chamber and blew
off its upper four thousand feet—twelve cubic miles of
rock—in a single day some 6,800 years ago, collapsing
into a caldera we call Crater Lake.   JOHN DANIEL

stream

A stream is an expression of its watershed; that is, liquid
is literally "expressed" from an ecological matrix, the
green breast of Earth, to form a flow confined by discernible banks. A stream's water originates in snow, spring,
and rain. At its head, it may ooze from a muddy slope;
at its mouth, it spreads wide and gives itself to another
body of water—a lake, a river, an ocean, or even another
stream. Its velocities are various: it can flow in ribbons,
braids, or as flat as a scarf. Sometimes a stream runs
underground or deep in the Earth's surface, as in *Typee,*

where Herman Melville writes: "Starting to my feet, the sight of those dank rocks, oozing forth moisture at every crevice, and the dark stream shooting along its dismal channel, sent fresh chills through my shivering frame, and I felt as uncontrollable a desire to climb up towards the genial sunlight as I before had to descend the ravine." A stream can also, eventually, cut through rock like a blade. A stream always moves under the spell of gravity. It is a medium for transport—silt, pollen, pine needles, and leaves float its rapids and riffles and are deposited in its bed. Under the water is that streambed, all rock-and-roll, a home for sediment and rock and a nesting ground for fish. Steelhead, trout, and salmon lay their eggs one to three feet deep in a gravel redd, while benthic invertebrates such as stoneflies, mayflies, blackflies, and caddis flies hide in a stream's cobbles. A stream is dynamic—and it receives, and thus reflects, the abuses that have taken place on the land.   GRETEL EHRLICH

stream sink

Sinking creeks lose their water to underground routes, usually through an observable stream sink, or swallow-hole. Where the substrate is porous, entire streams drop underground to flow through caves and interstitial spaces in the rock. The streams' reemergence, called a rise or resurgence, often produces substantial artesian springs, such as those in the Ozarks and Florida. Stream sinks abound in karst topography, where limestone solutions carve underground caverns. Lost River, Indiana, flows eight miles from sink to rise. Creeks may also sink into lava tubes and other holes in basalt. Another Lost River disappears into the Snake River Plain near Arco, Idaho, contributing to the dramatic Thousand Springs in the Snake River Canyon, hundreds of miles (and years) away. One of the most dramatic swallowholes is the Sinks of the Popo Agie River near Lander, Wyoming, and

a magnificent resurgence is the Rise of Metolius near
Sisters, Oregon.   ROBERT MICHAEL PYLE

strike valley

When a stratum of rock is tipped by tectonic forces,
earth scientists characterize its orientation to the surface
of the Earth—imagining the surface as a horizontal
line—in terms of its dip and strike. If a layer of rock is
tipped forty degrees below the horizontal, it would have
a dip of forty degrees. If the slope faced south, its strike
would be east-west, the orientation of a line perpendicular to the line of its dip. If a person were characterizing,
in this instance, a particular sandstone outcrop, he'd say,
"This layer of sandstone has a dip of forty degrees to the
south and its strike is east-west." If an uplifted layer of
rock buckles, creating a ridge parallel to its strike, that
would be a strike ridge. If a river eroded a valley in a
line parallel to the strike of the rock it was eroding, that
would be a strike valley. If a layer of rock fractures into
two blocks and one slides past the other horizontally,
it's a strike fault. The word strike has nearly eight dozen
meanings. There's little reason to believe that the
straight path of a strike valley, its determined direction,
gave rise by itself to the expression "to strike out on one's
own," but a strike valley beckons in a way a tortuous
valley does not.   BARRY LOPEZ

strip mine

The term strip mine describes a controversial method
of mining, usually for coal. During these operations,
whole mountaintops are blasted away, the vegetation,
animals, and topsoil "stripped" so coal seams can be
exposed and the mineral extracted. Strip mining has had
a significant impact on the environment. Acid runoff and
seepage have changed the nature of groundwater. Toxic
substances have been brought to the surface of the land.

Geologies have been upended, landscapes transformed, Earth scarred, and there is, in the wake of all this, the absence of a once-majestic world. In West Virginia, hundreds of miles of streams have been buried and large areas of the state toppled as strip mining has turned peaks and valleys into flatlands. Plans to strip-mine part of the Overland Trail in South Dakota to get at limestone deposits would destroy what remains of an eight-thousand-year-old settlement site, including Native artifacts and teepee rings. The practice here would also destroy the habitat of endangered species that still dwell in the prairie. LINDA HOGAN

submarine canyon

A submarine canyon is a deeply incised, steep-sided underwater gorge or canyon that winds along or cuts across the continental shelf, sometimes continuing the line of a major river. These V-shaped canyons, whose tributaries resemble those of a river-cut land canyon, may have been formed by fluctuation of sea level, uplift and faulting of landmasses, and cutting and shaping by ancient rivers. Avalanches of sand and mud in suspension scoured the canyon walls and enlarged them as sediment was carried to deep-sea basins. Off the coast of California, the numerous submarine canyons include the Mattole, Delgada, Mendocino, Carmel, Redondo, Newport, and Scripps, but none can compare in scale to the one located off the center of Monterey Bay. Monterey Canyon is as large as the Grand Canyon; it extends more than ninety miles from the coastline and plunges to a depth of thirteen thousand feet. ARTHUR SZE

submerged coast

Ice ages tie up immense quantities of the planet's water in continental glaciers, lowering the sea level precipitously. In interglacial periods like our own, the ice melts

S

and raises the oceans by hundreds of feet, resulting in submerged coasts. Tops of hills become islands, and old valleys turn into bays or fjords. In the short moment of our industrial civilization, as we warm the climate by burning fossil fuels, scientists predict this inundation will continue, probably with catastrophic results for hundreds of millions of people living on flat ground near the ocean's edge.   BILL MCKIBBEN

sugarloaf

In the seventeenth century, American settlers purchased their sugar (when they could find and afford it) in the form of a rounded cake that rose to a point at the top. As New England was colonized, bowl-shaped hills and small mountains, usually sparsely covered with timber, began to be named for this sugarloaf. Many such peaks were granite, a rock that tends to erode into humped forms. The appealing name spread throughout the continent, even as the sugar served at table changed to the more petite, cubed form and the loose powder sold in bags. There are Sugarloaf Mountains in California, Maine, Maryland, Massachusetts, Michigan, Pennsylvania, and Nevada, and a Sugarloaf Island in North Carolina.   JAN DEBLIEU

sunk fence

The sunk fence is a divider dug into the earth rather than one erected upon it, a ditch with one sloped side and a single retaining wall. This inverted concept allows for separation—between mown ground and grazed grass, for instance, between lawn and field—without the use of vertical fixtures or usual fencing materials such as wood, stone, or metal. Imported from landscaped parks in England by Frederick Law Olmsted in the mid–nineteenth century, the sunk fence was adapted to suit peculiarly American needs. In Olmsted's design of Central Park, sunken roadways perform the same function as the sunk fence, entrenching what otherwise would interrupt the clean, aesthetic expanse of park or garden. Sunk fences are also called ha-has—a name suggesting both the startled exclamation of the person who stumbles into one, and the amusement of the witness to such antics.   ANTONYA NELSON

swag

A shallow subsidence in the ground that collects water, a swag can be a natural formation or one generated by a mining excavation. Swags occur in flat or slightly rolling terrain, and may also be called sag ponds. Many older references, alas, involve accidents, such as the one in which two nineteenth-century brothers drowned while "bathing in the old colliery swag." In mountainous regions of North Carolina, the term is applied to landforms more generally; for example, an inn located atop the Cataloochee Divide takes its name from a ridge that locals call The Swag because it overlooks a dip in the ridge. From the inn's brochure: "Think of swag draperies, swag lamps, or a sway-back horse, and you will see in your mind's eye the gentle curve of our landscape." These meanings all derive from swag in the sense of something heavy and loose that sways or sags under its own weight. In addition, swag is an Australian term for a tramp's bundle (thus, swagman), and widespread slang for a thief's loot, a meaning revived, playfully, for the copious giveaways at modern-day conventions and conferences. Place-names derived from swag include Swag Gulch, a valley in Colorado, and Swag Fork, a stream in Wyoming.   EMILY HIESTAND

swale

In *The Land of Little Rain*, Mary Austin describes a typical Paiute encampment as being "near the watercourse, but never in the swale." In constructing his "campoodie,"

Austin goes on to say, "the Paiute seeks rising ground, depending on air and sun for purification of his dwelling, and when it becomes wholly untenable, moves." The swale avoided by the Paiute—and every other knowledgeable camper—is a marshy or moist depression (sometimes mimicking a stream course) in a gently rolling landscape. These elongated hollows were likely created by fingers of glacial ice that melted more slowly than the rest of an ice sheet, depressing the ground beneath them as they did so. (At the same time, the ground between the swales absorbed some of this meltwater and rose.) In Florida, poorly drained swales alternate with beach ridges to form dune-and-swale topography. In the midwestern prairies, a series of swales in an area of little vertical relief, and with only slight rises above the general horizontal line of the glacial plain, is called swale-and-rise topography. Hoosier Prairie, on the southeastern shore of Lake Michigan, is a typical example. With less than a ten-foot change in elevation across its 430 acres, the nearly treeless plain is equal parts dry and wet, its swales harboring ecosystems of great biological diversity. Rich plant communities, including bracken and sweet ferns, originally established thousands of years ago on sand dunes above the prairie, survive today in the protection of the damp swales. Another example of extensive swale-and-swell topography, which disappeared almost completely with agriculture in the late 1880s, is the area around Dallas and Guthrie Counties, Iowa, which was carved during the Wisconsin glaciation. Once a mosaic of wetlands and rolling savanna bordering the Mississippi River, the area must have been a hush of relief to migrating waterfowl. TERRY TEMPEST WILLIAMS

swamp

Our common word swamp comes from a rustic dialect of English, and only became widely used in North America in the seventeenth century. Swamp is a truly popular word, with a broad range of meanings, referring to wet spongy ground and often used interchangeably with bog, marsh, mire, and fen. But in precise usage, swamp refers to land with more trees than a marsh, better drained than a bog. A swamp has stretches of low-lying ground often interspersed with pools and hammocks of raised soil. Swamp water steeps roots and rotting vegetation, and is often colored like tea. Large swamps are found in saturated, low-lying flat terrain, but small upland swamps are common where the soil is clay and underground seepage abundant, for example in the Finger Lakes region of central New York. Most swamps have little peat accumulation, and no floating mats of vegetation typical of bogs. Swamps are Noah's Arks of species, where scores of birds, insects, spiders, and amphibians live in the recesses. A paradise of alligators, muskrats, sometimes bears and panthers, swamps are a significant refuge for wildlife partly because they are of little commercial use unless drained. The Great Dismal Swamp in Virginia and the Okefenokee Swamp in Georgia are two of the largest and best known. Swamps are places of overwhelming diversity of life, of primeval, melancholic gloom and ecological subtlety, haunted by poisonous insects, spiders, reptiles, and rare flowers, and sheltering great beauty.   ROBERT MORGAN

S

swash

On the fretted seam between water and land, ocean breakers send a rushing sheet of seawater—a swash—up the beach. The swash receding, pulling seaward with a drag force that takes the sand right out from under your bare feet, every particle felt, is backwash. In *The Edge of the Sea*, Rachel Carson called the swash zone "a world of force and change and constant motion, where even the sand acquires some of the fluidity of water."   ELLEN MELOY

swell

Though many first picture a swell as a feature of the ocean's surface, the term is also used to identify a long, roundly arched, often isolated elevation on the surface of the Earth, created where soil absorbs a great deal of water. Used in this way, the term usually includes an adjective, such as broad, bulging, undulating, protruding, round, or oval. Isolated swells are sometimes called domes or arches, though these terms are technically inaccurate. Swells are correctly called rises when found on extensive plains in combination with the depressions known as swales, the rises being part of an undulating, wet-and-dry, swale-and-rise topography, formed by the differential melting of glacial ice, which once stretched for hundreds of miles across the Midwest. Perhaps the best-known swell in North America is the domal San Rafael Swell in southeastern Utah. From the air, its eastern front resembles a fifty-mile-long wave advancing across the desert, even to its seeming to break in a sea of froth over a spectacular "reef" of white Navajo Sandstone along its eastern perimeter. Formed forty to sixty million years ago, this two-thousand-foot-high swell bowed up so slowly that three rivers in the area—the San Rafael, the Muddy, and the Price—were able to maintain their courses across the uplifted land. They continue to cross the swell today.   TERRY TEMPEST WILLIAMS

swimming hole

An Americanism, a swimming hole is designated as such by the choice and use of people, especially young ones, and in its literary appearances carries pastoral, idyllic, and melancholy associations. James Whitcomb Riley captures this in his poem "The Old Swimmin' Hole": "Oh! The old swimmin' hole! In the happy days of yore / When I ust to lean above it on the old sickamore." Swimming holes often have suitably evocative names—for example,

Peekamoose Blue Hole in the Catskills, Cave Hole on the Potomac in West Virginia, and Grover Blue Hole on the Edisto River in South Carolina. These are places deep enough for swimming, and for dropping into from ropes suspended from tree limbs, and for diving from favorable positions on rock overhangs or the bank, and are customarily located on moving freshwater in the protected vicinity of a crook or bend. In "big water" and swift streams, the bounds of a swimming hole may be clearly marked by the eddy line, which is a surface expression of the eddy fence that separates the two circulation systems in three dimensions. On the far side of the eddy line, trouble awaits.   JOHN KEEBLE

switchback

Most understandings of switchback have to do with human interventions—road cuts with their hairpin turns or hiking trails that reverse direction as they ascend and descend the sides of a steep canyon. The switchback trails of the Grand Canyon, for example, or Colorado's San Juan Mountains, described by Rick Bass in *Lost Grizzlies*: "We're climbing out of the valley, packs creaking as we switchback through giant ponderosa pines, moving from patches of warm sun to cool shade, brightness to shadow, hiking quickly up the mountains." The term switchback also alludes to places where the flow of magma turns back on itself, and to the bends and crooks where streams and rivers meander, zigzag, through a valley. It's also used as a mining term, to describe the appearance of certain compressed layers of rock, particularly where a seam of coal, bedded between other rock layers, has been folded back on itself, serpentine. The curves and turns of the past world.   LINDA HOGAN

S

tableland

A tableland is a broad, relatively flat, and steep-sided plateau that rises high and abruptly above the surrounding region. One of the basic topographical landforms, tablelands are essentially youthful plains, and are most commonly found on the American continents. Tablelands can be localized—a relatively small, isolated, cliff-edged version is called a mesa—but the term is most often applied to an extensive region, such as the area Willa Cather describes in her novel *One of Ours*: "The tableland, from horizon to horizon, was brilliant for the mass of purple vapours rolling in the west, with bright edges, like new-cut lead." Two prominent North American tablelands are the Colorado Plateau and the Llano Estacado of the southern Great Plains. Place-names derived from this landform include Tableland, California; Tableland Reservoir in Oregon; and Table Mountain in Butte County, California.   EMILY HIESTAND

taiga

In his book *Wild Harmony*, naturalist William Pruitt recalls boyhood dreams of living as a misfit trapper in a mythical "Great North Woods" teeming with wild game. As a man, he came to realize that his once-imagined landscape was real and called the taiga: the farthest-north circumpolar belt of conifer forest, an ecosystem of slow-growing plants, sparse animal populations, and weather extremes. Some ecologists consider taiga the very northern part of the boreal forest biome, the tree limit—sometimes called "land of little sticks"—that fringes the tundra. Most biologists, however, use taiga and boreal forest interchangeably. In *Coming into the Country*, John McPhee aptly observed that in this land of little sticks, most of the spruce trees "looked like pipe cleaners. The better ones look like bottle washers."

In the taiga, a tree an inch in diameter might be fifty years old. Yet on a journey from the Arctic Ocean inland, the sight of the first tree inspired the explorer Roald Amundsen to exclaim: "A very diminutive, battered little Christmas tree, hanging out of a crevice . . . produced a wonderful sensation, reminding me that we were now out of the Polar regions and on more homely human ground." The original Yakut word *taiga* (literally, "clumps of woodland") connotes the Siberian landscape of open, rocky ground patchworked by stunted conifer stands. This description resonates in Sigurd Olsen's text, when he, like a caribou, "sought shelter in the islands of dwarf spruce known as the taiga." EVA SAULITIS

tailings pile

After a mineral ore has been mined, crushed, and stripped of all concentrates valuable enough to be smelted, the remaining pulverized rock debris is called tailings. Being of no economic use, these loose waste materials are dumped near an active mine into tall, barren tailings piles, whose sides slope according to the angle of repose. A large mining operation turns the Earth inside out as it buries surrounding landscapes under vast, pyramid-shaped mountains devoid of vegetation. A tailings pile is typically the most prominent physical evidence of a mine. BARBARA KINGSOLVER

tailings pond

Modern mining operations in the United States are required to contain and treat their waste piles because of the toxic cocktails they contain: zinc, copper, mercury, cadmium, lead, and other heavy metals are commonly present, along with the acids of cyanide and sulfur that are used in slurry extraction processes. The resulting dammed depressions are not ponds in any sense dreamed of by Thoreau at Walden, but rather, immense puddles of suspended pollutants. The hazards of holding volumes of poisonous fluids above ground are obvious: foundation seepage, seasonal flooding, or structural collapse will release the concentrated toxins into groundwater or the receiving watershed.   BARBARA KINGSOLVER

tailwater

Usually turbulent, like a tail wagging from the hindquarters of an animal, tailwater is the water downstream from a dam, mill, turbine, or other obstruction to the flow of a river. The channel that carries water away from the obstruction is a tailrace. On irrigated fields, the excess water that runs off into low spots or holding ponds is also called tailwater.   SCOTT RUSSELL SANDERS

tail wave

After a river plunges over the rocky debris of a rapid, it blasts out from the constriction and finishes in a series of high-momentum tail waves. The waves stand like glassy dunes, stationary in form even as the river flows through them toward stillness again. When their foamy crests roll over and slide partway down their face, like the archetypal wave in a Katsushika Hokusai woodblock print, they are sometimes known as curlers.   ELLEN MELOY

tallgrass prairie

The tallgrass prairie, extending from central Illinois through Iowa and Missouri into the eastern Dakotas, Nebraska, Kansas, and Oklahoma—and benefited with more rainfall than the shortgrass prairie—was named after its upright bluestem, which can reach heights of six feet (switch and other shorter grasses form an intermediate layer, grama its base), causing travelers even on horseback sometimes to get lost. The drama of immigrant entry into its oceanic expanse—thus "prairie schooners," a schooner a sailing ship—is suggested in *Giants in the*

T

Earth, by O.E. Rolvaag: "Bright, clear sky over a plain so wide that the rim of the heavens cut down on it around the entire horizon ... 'Tish-ah!' said the grass ... It bent resiliently under the trampling feet; it did not break, but complained aloud every time ... 'Tish-ah, tish-ah!' it cried, and rose up in surprise to look at this rough, hard thing that had crushed it to the ground so rudely, then moved on." LARRY WOIWODE

talus

Talus is the mantle of debris below cliff or outcrop, the sloping skirt of boulders and rock broken off by weathering and erosion, then carried downward by gravity, as described by Zane Grey in *Wanderer of the Wasteland*: "A broad belt of huge bowlders [*sic*] lay beyond the shack, the edge of the talus, the beginning of the base of a mountain-side, wearing down, weathering away, cracking into millions of pieces, every one of which had both smooth and sharp surfaces." Rock falling from the cliff, on its way to the talus, is a debris fall. The slow movement of rock debris down the angular slope is called talus creep. John C. Van Dyke, who on foot and horseback explored the Mojave and Colorado Deserts in the early twentieth century, often without the vaguest notion of where he was, describes the traversing of talus as a scramble "over splintered rock, stepping from stone to stone, creeping along the backbone of bowlders [*sic*], and worrying over rows of granite blocks." ELLEN MELOY

tank

Tank, when referring to either ranching or the land, tends to be a shortened version of stocktank, as used in Cormac McCarthy's *All the Pretty Horses*: "The water they found was at a stocktank and they dismounted and drank from the standpipe and watered the horses and sat in the bands of shade from the dead and twisted oaks at the tank and watched the open country below them." The aboveground type of tank McCarthy is talking about is man-made—stone here, though they're also formed from concrete or galvanized steel and fed by either a windmill or waterline. A second type of tank is simply a pond that livestock drink from. While the latter tend to be natural—as in a depression where water stands and has been standing—they can also be man-made, such as the one Lonnie stands at in Larry McMurtry's *Horseman, Pass By*, waiting for horses: "They weren't at the tank, but I stood on the dam and watched them coming out of the brush to the north." Aside from watering cattle, a tank is also a good place to beat the heat: just jump in. Although the water in aboveground tanks tends to be cooler (they're fed from underground) and cleaner (cattle can't stand in them) they're not as deep. Also, they're stringy with moss and rarely stocked with fish, as the one in McMurtry's *The Last Picture Show* was: "The corks bobbed undisturbed in the brown water of a large stock tank." That it's "the worst stocked fishing tank" in the whole county doesn't deter characters Sonny and Sam and Billy, as fishing a tank is less about the catch and more about "watching the rings in the water, the dragonflies skimming along the surface." STEPHEN GRAHAM JONES

tapestry wall

Sheets of darker colors seem to hang like curtains on the faces of many canyon walls in arid environments. The towering, buff-colored sandstone cliffs of Canyon de Chelly in northeastern Arizona, for example, which are famously revealed in the photographs of Edward Curtis and others, seem draped with umber hangings. The patterns of color on such tapestry walls record the patterns of water spills and seeps that periodically irrigate the walls with snowmelt and storm runoff. When the water evaporates, it leaves behind microscopic deposits of the minerals it once contained. These minerals gradually oxidize, perhaps as a result of the metabolic activity of bacteria that colonize the rock, and the buildup of oxides, rusty to brown where iron is dominant, accounts for the contrasting colors of the tapestry. Vegetation can also produce the impression of a tapestry hanging on the sheer face of a cliff or canyon wall. Vesey's Paradise in the Grand Canyon, for example, is fed by a spring that pours from a seam high on the side of the lower canyon. A jungle of green seems to hang from the mouth of the spring, and, notwithstanding that much of this vegetation consists of nettle and poison ivy, such a profusion of green in a sere and sun-blasted environment gives an impression of a kind of Eden.   WILLIAM DEBUYS

tarn

Tarn was once primarily used in northern England as a name for a small, deep, self-contained mountain lake, especially those of the Lake District. In fact, the tourist boats of Lake Windermere today are known as Tarn Taxis. Since the 1950s, geologists have used the term to refer to lakes that occupy erosional basins or cirques, and it is now a synonym for cirque lake. What ponds were to Thoreau, tarns were to Wordsworth, who described one as "round clear bright as heaven" and another as "solitary." But other poets, such as Edgar Allan Poe and A.E. (George William Russell), have found in the isolated depths of these glacial scours "dank" or "dark" qualities. Seamus Heaney, in his poem "Bogland," about a very different landscape, refreshed the word in the following lines: "Everywhere the eye concedes to/Encroaching horizon,//Is wooed into the cyclops' eye/Of a tarn." Glacial tarns such as Duck Lake, Lake Virginia, Big Bear Lake, and Desolation Lake, to name a very few, dot the John Muir Wilderness in California's Sierra Nevada.   MICHAEL COLLIER

teepee butte

A butte is an isolated eminence with steep slopes to its
sides, common to the plains and high plains—a mountainous upheaval in the midst of rolling or flat land. The
teepee butte is a variation identified by its shape: that of a
teepee or cone. Some teepee buttes are the residual mass
of an actual volcano tip isolated by erosion, as East Butte
in Shoshone County, Idaho.   LARRY WOIWODE

terrace

With almost carpenterlike precision, using water as
a favorite tool, nature frequently carves from sloping
terrain the benchlike surfaces known as terraces. A lake
terrace commonly occurs at the water's edge but may
sometimes be well above it, marking the height of an earlier lake level. In glacial terrain, wave action along a lake
coast frequently creates a steep-fronted breaker terrace
of heavy cobbles that will remain intact during severe
storms that destroy associated breaker terraces composed
of lighter gravels, built up by previous storms. Marine
terraces are found at the seaward edge of the land,
gently sloping terrains of water-sorted geological debris
eroded from sea cliffs and often uplifted by tectonic
forces. Hanging bog is a term often used to designate a
water-saturated terrace located partway up the lower
slopes of wooded hillsides. A river terrace might be part
of a former floodplain, a nearly level area of sand, clay,
gravel, and silt left behind when a river excavated its bed
through wet and dry climatic periods. Terrace flights are
the most dramatic examples of river terracing, a series
of platforms that resemble stairs and which are created
by the looping meanders of a stream steadily cutting its
bed. The flow of mineral-rich waters at a hot springs, on
the other hand, builds up terraces of opal-like travertine,
bringing an angular beauty to the landscape. Arresting

T

examples occur at Thermopolis, Wyoming, and along
Havasu Creek in Arizona.   MIKE TIDWELL

terracette

A small-scale terrace—usually a series of such formations occurring on hillsides with steep elevations, thus
creating a ribbed pattern of low ledges running parallel and at equal distance from each other—is called
a terracette. The geological occasion of this slippage
is uncertain, but terracettes are often thought to be
evidence of soil creep, of overgrazing by animals on the
slope, or perhaps the result of earthen or geologic material standing at an angle too great to sustain stability.
Terracettes are colloquially called sheep tracks in hilly
areas where the animals tend to use them as walkways.
PATRICIA HAMPL

thalweg

The thalweg (also spelled talweg), meaning "valley way"
in German, is the line on a topographic map that connects the lowest points in a river channel—an abstract
vector that predicts various features of the watercourse.
Water velocity will be greater in the thalweg, because
there is less friction where the bed is deepest. As Rebecca
Lawton writes in *Reading Water: Lessons from the River,*
"In flatwater the thalweg will carry a boat downstream
faster than rowing. In rapids, it will find a way between
boulders or through the deepest, safest channel nine
times out of ten." Where the river cuts into its bank, the
thalweg will be closer to the bank than to the middle
of the channel. Less commonly, the thalweg is the
subterranean portion of a stream. In law, the thalweg is
the invisible divide through the center of the deepest
channel of a border river, thus assuring the navigation
rights of both suspicious parties. When a boundary river
shifts, the boundary can remain in the thalweg of the

original channel, even though it's now dry, such as along portions of the Rio Grande between the United States and Mexico, and the Colorado River between California and Arizona.   D. J. WALDIE

thank-you-ma'am

A thank-you-ma'am is a bump or depression in a dirt or gravel road in the country, especially at an intersection. Etymologists disagree on the exact origins of the phrase, as it is ringed with folkloric and metaphoric associations. Some say the term comes from the ride itself: on an unpaved road when you hit a bump, your head nods forward as though in acknowledgment of a favor. "Thank-you-ma'am." Other folk sources point to the horse-and-buggy days. A young man and woman might be out for a Sunday afternoon ride. A bump in the road throws the man toward the woman, where he steals a kiss. "Thanky-ma'am." Such Sunday buggy drivers were said to seek roads full of potholes. Franklin Roosevelt spoke of "thank-you-ma'ams" as bumps in the road to recovery from the Depression. Today, some thank-you-ma'ams are put into roads intentionally to drain off excess water, and sometimes private landowners add them to slow down drivers. In *The Guardian Angel* by Oliver Wendell Holmes, one woman used the term this way: "'We all have our troubles. It isn't everybody that can ride to heaven in a C-spring shay, as my poor husband used to say; and life's a road that's got a good many thank-you-ma'ams to go bumpin' over, says he.'"   MARY SWANDER

thaw hole

A melt hole in sea ice, formed at the site of an *allu* (a seal's breathing hole) where surface water flows through an underlying universe of dark seawater, is called a thaw hole. As Gretel Ehrlich writes, "This is the eye into the universe/that has gone past seeing." When large volumes of surface water from melting snow begin draining through an allu, the swirling current scours out a basin centered on the cone-shaped shaft a seal has gnawed through from below. Depending on the volume of water involved, some of these roaring whirlpools can be dangerous to anyone who approaches. Once the surface water has largely drained away, the basin fills with sea-water, creating a calm, transparent eye with a dark pupil. EVA SAULITIS

thicket

The word thicket is ancient, little changed in sound or spelling from the Old English *thiccet*, meaning "thick place." So, thicket is a dense growth of vines, canes, succulents, shrubbery, small trees, impenetrably tangled, almost impassable. Thicket is often a transitional phase of plant succession, between scrub and woodland. It can also be a more permanent feature, such as the Big Thicket National Preserve in east Texas. CHARLES FRAZIER

tidal bore

A term coined by seamen around 1600, tidal bore describes a violent wall of water rushing up a shallow, narrowing river, estuary, or bay. Bores (also called bore tides) form when an incoming tide meets a particular geography, a resistance—sand, silt bars, narrowing channels—and heaps water up to fifteen feet high, moving inland at ten to fifteen miles per hour. Most bores build after low water of a spring tide—the year's biggest tidal flux. Famous bore tides occur in the Truro River in Canada's Bay of Fundy, and in Turnagain Arm in Alaska's Cook Inlet, the latter driven by a tidal rise of thirty feet in six hours. In summer, travelers driving along Turnagain Arm can witness windsurfers bundled in drysuits dancing along the wave's face, their brightly colored sails a dramatic contrast to the gray, silty inlet.

When it surges up the lower Amazon, the bore—*pororoca*—can shave forests and destroy homes. It is greatly feared by locals, yet ridden by elite surfers from around the world.   EVA SAULITIS

tideland

Tides are the oceans' slosh, long-period waves caused by the tug of the moon and the sun, affected by the Earth's rotation and the moon's orbit. Incoming and outgoing tides spread estuarine silt across the intertidal zone, sands near the low tide line, and mud nearer the high tide line. At the ebb, tideflats stretch in bare, shining expanses for miles in big shallow estuaries such as Willapa Bay, Washington. A tidal flat's flatness depends on its fauna of clams, oysters, shrimp, crabs, and worms, and its flora of eelgrass, cordgrass, and algae. Atlantic cordgrass *(Spartina alterniflora)* valuably anchors tideflats in the East, where it is indigenous; as an introduced alien in the West, it makes dense meadows hostile to oysters and shorebirds. Through the tideflats run sinuous, brackish sloughs and channels. Tidal inlets push seawater into outflow, stirring salinity into freshwater as it goes. The Columbia River is tidal more than a hundred miles upstream, beyond the city of Portland to Bonneville Dam.   ROBERT MICHAEL PYLE

tide pool

When the tide retreats, it leaves seawater in intertidal rock hollows. Deeper bowls remain filled until high tide returns; leaky crevices, fissures, and shallow basins are temporary. Tide pools owe their ephemerality, pH, temperature, salinity, and species complement to depth, distance from low tide, height of tides and waves, wind and storms, and air temperature. Tide pools harbor high diversity and an abundance of plants and animals immune to dunking and drying, such as sea stars,

T

anemones, urchins, limpets, barnacles, mussels, sponges, hydroids, and many algae. Animals that must remain wet, such as nudibranchs (sea slugs) and sculpins, use lower pools or go in and out with the tide. Few habitats more richly reward the careful watcher with color and riveting activity. In *The Edge of the Sea*, Rachel Carson writes: "Tide pools contain mysterious worlds within their depths, where all the beauty of the sea is subtly suggested and portrayed in miniature." ROBERT MICHAEL PYLE

till

When used as a verb, till means to work the soil for farming, as by plowing or harrowing. When used as a noun, till is the geologists' name for the sediment left behind by a glacier—a mixture of clay, sand, gravel, and boulders. Unlike sediment dropped by moving water, these materials were not sorted by size and weight, which is why those mining the sand-and-gravel pits dotted across the northern Midwest in deposits of glacial till must do the sorting mechanically. Wherever the lobe of a glacier broke off from the main ice sheet and slowly released its sediment over an extensive area, as across central Illinois and Indiana, it formed a till plain. If farmers don't actually till the till, they do cultivate the rich soil formed on top of it by windblown loess (another gift of the glaciers) and humus (a gift of the prairies and forests that succeeded the glaciers). SCOTT RUSSELL SANDERS

tillage

If you see a plow, disk plow, chisel plow, subsoiler, sweep plow, rotary hoe, rodweeder, or a cultivator in a farm field, chances are you're also seeing tillage. Tillage is the disturbance of the soil in an agricultural seedbed. The term can also refer to land that is tilled. Primary tillage loosens the dirt and incorporates plant residues and fertilizers, creating a rough, textured soil. Secondary tillage disrupts and kills weeds and prepares the ground for seed, producing a finer soil. Primary tillage often occurs right after harvest, while secondary tillage often occurs before planting another crop. In the pioneer days in the United States, stones lying above or below ground were the biggest obstacle for tillage and often broke a homesteader's plow. For all its beneficial properties, tillage also contributes to erosion. If ground is tilled, left bare and uncovered, it can wash away in rain, melting snow, or floods. Or ground can blow away in the wind, as it did on a large scale in the 1930s Dust Bowl. Modern agriculture has moved toward the use of herbicides and no-till farming methods in answer to these kinds of erosion problems.   MARY SWANDER

timberline

Often used interchangeably with tree line when referring to an altitudinal or latitudinal line or zone above or below which trees do not grow, timberline can also refer to the upper limit of continuous forest, or a line, given to change due to economics and the development of logging technology, above or below which trees large enough for lumbering do not grow.   WILLIAM KITTREDGE

toe slope

When soil and rock move downslope and come to rest, they form a toe slope, named for its similarity to the human form. The movement may result from the slow, downhill migration of sediment or from the cataclysm of a landslide. In the latter instance, the rearranged topography embraces the metaphor of the entire human form: it runs from headwall to toe slope.   WILLIAM DEBUYS

tombolo

A tombolo is a bar of sand or other sediment that connects the mainland to an island—indeed, the island often plays a part in its creation as incoming waves refracted around the island deposit sand behind it. As a result, tombolos are especially common on relatively youthful coastlines where the offshore islands have not yet eroded away. Perhaps the longest tombolo on Earth was the so-called Rama's Bridge, which once connected Sri Lanka across eighteen miles of the Palk Strait to the coast of India. Built, according to Hindu legend, so that Rama could rescue his wife from the demon king Ravana, it was breached by a violent storm in the fifteenth century and now survives as a chain of shoals that menace mariners. Closer to home, a tombolo connects the tied island at Marblehead to the Massachusetts mainland. Another noted tombolo, perhaps the longest in the Great Lakes, connects the major part of Grand Island on Michigan's Lake Superior coast to the portion of itself now known as The Thumb. On the West Coast, what rises up from a flat beach today as Point Sur was formerly a detached coastal island. BILL MCKIBBEN

tool mark

A tool mark is an impression, cut, scratch, gouge, or abrasion made by an instrument in contact with an object. In forensic science, detectives look for a gouge in the windowsill made by a burglar's crowbar or the scratch of a key on a car door. Earth scientists look for an erosion impression or gouge made in sedimentary rock by a solid object such as a mudstone fragment, a shell, or bits of water-logged plant material—twigs or branches. Tool mark also refers to the traces of abrasion made by an object dragged across a rock layer during glaciation or sedimentation. These marks include grooves and prod, skip, and bounce marks, each deriving its shape from the indentation of the object on the surface. At a crime scene, detectives rarely find the crowbar—just the impression left in the windowsill wood or on the car door. Likewise, earth scientists rarely find the tools on the bed surface—only their imprint or trace on the rock.   MARY SWANDER

tooth

Tooth is applied to mountains (or their satellite summits) that resemble incisors, canines, or—in the case of the Mooses Tooth, a well-known 10,300-foot mountain in the Alaska Range—bicuspids. Other pieces of anatomy widely used to describe precipitous topography include head (Lizard Head in Colorado and Cabezon in New Mexico), finger (the Fuhrer Finger is a narrow couloir on Mount Rainer), and thumb (Devils Thumb is a 9,077-foot prong of ice-encrusted diorite on the Alaska–British Columbia border; Zumies Thumb is a distinctive spike of granite in Colorado's Rocky Mountain National Park).

JON KRAKAUER

topsoil

Soil is composed of mineral and organic matter, water, and air. The actions of wind, rain, ice, and sunlight break down rock into smaller particles ranging in size and texture from clay and silt to sand and gravel. Air and water fill the gaps between the larger particles. Plant roots bind particles together and raise minerals from deep in the ground. Plants and their remains form food for burrowing insects and earthworms. When bacteria and fungi decompose the dead plants, animal droppings, and dead animals, the end product is dark, fertile humus. This top layer of earth, dark and rich in organic matter, is called topsoil. It varies in depth and is tilled in the cultivation of gardens and farm fields. Iowa has some of the best topsoil in the United States and in the world. The root systems and organisms of the region's past vegetation— prairies, marshes, bogs, and fens—transformed the raw mineral deposits into an invaluable natural resource.

MARY SWANDER

tornado alley

Tornado Alley is the area of the United States in which tornadoes most frequently occur. It encompasses the great lowland region of the Mississippi, Ohio, and lower Missouri River valleys. While no state is entirely free of tornadoes, these storms occur most frequently in the prairie and plains region between the Appalachians and the Rocky Mountains, particularly in Alabama, Mississippi, Arkansas, Florida, Oklahoma, Texas, Kansas, Nebraska, Iowa, and Missouri. The absence of mountains in the middle part of the continent enables masses of warm, moist air to drift northward from the Gulf of Mexico. This air is buoyant and lifts easily as a result of daytime heating of surfaces underneath or along frontal zones associated with the cooler jet stream. Large, active thunderstorms develop, with complex up-and-down drafts. Sometimes circulating wind systems within the thunderstorm clouds result in tornados. Tornadoes are characterized by extremely low air pressure at their vortex—that's what generates the tremendously high wind speeds. They aren't very big, measuring on average a hundred yards in diameter, but with winds reaching as high as three hundred miles per hour, their intensity is greater than that of any other type of storm.

CONGER BEASLEY, JR.

tower

North American climbing guides identify any number of spires, columns, arêtes, peaks, and high ridges, named usually by their first ascenders, as towers. The term is related to tor, a Celtic-rooted British word for a high rock or rocky hill. A prominent feature of this kind is Devils Tower in Wyoming, an 865-foot volcanic neck scored by closely spaced vertical cracks. Its name conforms to a Euro-American habit of identifying dramatic landforms with the underworld. The Kiowa people, according to

N. Scott Momaday in *The Way to Rainy Mountain*, have a more heavenly view of this tower's origin. Seven young sisters, chased by a bear who had been their brother, took refuge on a great tree stump that called to them and bore them into the sky, the bear scratching futilely at its sides. The stump became the tower the Kiowa call *Tso-aa*, the sisters became the seven stars of the Big Dipper, "and so long as the legend lives," writes Momaday, "the Kiowas have kinsmen in the night sky." JOHN DANIEL

township and range

In keeping with the Land Ordinance of 1785, most of the United States west of the Appalachians was surveyed into a grid of mile-square sections, each of 640 acres. A block of thirty-six sections, six miles to a side, formed a township, and a series of townships stretching north and south along the meridian, like a string of boxy beads, was named a range. Hence, township and range describes this rectangular system for carving up, numbering, and naming the public lands. A township is more likely to serve as a unit of government in the densely settled eastern regions, as in Ohio or Michigan, than in the sparsely settled West, as in Wyoming or Nevada. Between eastern Utah and California, the series of mountain ranges alternating with long valleys forms a physiographic region called Basin and Range. The unfenced grazing lands there, and elsewhere in the West, are known as rangeland or open range, inspiring the cowboy song "Home, Home on the Range." SCOTT RUSSELL SANDERS

T

trace

A trace is, simply, a line etched across a plane. A feature like the famous Natchez Trace (featured in Eudora Welty novels) is, then, a line in the dirt etched across the land. Boones Trace, Daniel Boone's famous hunting path through the Cumberland Gap, was similarly a line etched along the mountainous plain of the land. Traces are old game trails that have evolved into human footpaths. They are ancient thoroughfares first cut by hooves and claws, and followed by indigenous walkers. Only when white men "discover" them do they become "traces." The Natchez Trace, running from Natchez, Mississippi, to Nashville, Tennessee, is prehistoric in origin. It was used as a walking route by Chickasaws and Choctaws until explorers, traders, and boatmen made it the busiest highway in what was called the "Old Southwest." Mississippi boatmen would float their goods down the river, then walk from New Orleans to the Trace and head north. America's original serial killers, the Harp brothers, set up their bloody operation along the Trace; Andrew Jackson marched it; mailmen followed. For a time, outlaws attracted by trade made the Trace the most violent place in America. Meriwether Lewis committed suicide—or was murdered—at an isolated inn on the Natchez Trace. Perhaps the Natchez Trace can be called America's original exurban strip mall. Historians note that the boots of thousands of travelers cut a gap in the ground at the southern end twelve feet wide.

LUIS ALBERTO URREA

trail

A trail is a simple path worn by animals or people passing repeatedly through a remote or rugged territory. The many kinds of trails include cattle, deer, and mountain trails; historic trails of Native American origin; trails for skiing and hiking, and for walking through parks and nature sanctuaries. As a word for such routes, trail comes into use around 1800; the earlier word, still used in southern states, is trace. In American English, trail has taken on iconic status, suggesting a journey into wilderness or unknown territory. But not into the entirely unknown, of course, for the trail is itself a guide, embodying collective intelligence about the best way through a region. Indeed, many full-fledged roads now follow the route of former trails; the Yadkin Road, in Moore County, North Carolina, for example, grew from a Catawba trail, which in turn likely grew from a path first made by buffalo migrating between the Piedmont and coastal marshes. Named American trails include the Iditarod Trail (Anchorage to Nome, Alaska); the Oregon and Santa Fe Trails (used by settlers going west); the Appalachian Trail (Katahdin, Maine, to Springer Mountain, Georgia); and the Trail of Tears, the route of the forced Cherokee trek. Of that route, Edna Ferber writes, in *Cimarron*: "Tears came to his own eyes when he spoke of the Trail of Tears, in which the Cherokees, a peaceful and home-loving Indian tribe, were torn from the land which a government had given them by sworn treaty, to be sent far away on a march which, from cold, hunger, exposure, and heartbreak, was marked by bleaching bones from Georgia to Oklahoma." In recent decades the new occupation of trailbuilder has arisen, reflecting a contemporary American desire to spend more time in remote and wild places. Each summer now in the West thousands of young people make their living "digging trail" deep into the wilderness.   EMILY HIESTAND

trainasse

Trainasse is a Louisiana French word for the narrow ditch that bayou inhabitants dredge through the marsh for straight-line access to fishing holes, duck stands, and trapping camps. A typical trainasse is just wide enough for a pirogue (simple wooden canoe). By paddle or pole, the pirogue moves along this marsh "path" with a draft so shallow "she can travel on a dew," writes Harnett T. Kane in his classic *The Bayous of Louisiana*. Older trainasse channels often enlarge into bayous, becoming permanent features in the marsh-swamp complex. Geographers and hydrologists have found that the crisscross of artificial waterways has affected drainage patterns and has contributed to the deterioration of the region's marshes.

MIKE TIDWELL

transverse dune

A transverse dune is a ridge of sand (rather than a simple curved mound) that develops in areas where sand is abundant and wind direction constant. The windward slope of such a dune is comparatively gentle. As Janice Emily Bowers writes in *Dune Country,* "The transverse dunes are low, usually no more than forty feet tall, but they make up for their lack of height in breadth and depth: some are up to eight hundred feet long and four hundred feet across." Ranks of transverse dunes look like immense ripples lapping on a desert shore.

D. J. WALDIE

traprock

A dark, finely grained rock that has crumbled from natural processes and lies scattered across the ground is known as traprock, especially when it is composed of basalt, dolerite, or another igneous material. Naturally formed traprock often paves the surface of canyons and valleys. The term is also applied, however, to rock crushed into stones an inch to several inches in size and sold as a building material; this is carefully placed beneath downspouts and in other key positions in "French drains" to absorb the flow of water. The word derives from *trapp,* Swedish for stair step. Basalt is an extrusive rock that often forms large flows; trap or trapp refers to the steplike structure occasionally seen at the end of such flows. Some of the most impressive examples are found in southeast India at the Deccan Traps, an area of crumbled lava that covers two hundred thousand square miles. Smaller-scale examples are found in the American

Southwest. In Cormac McCarthy's *All the Pretty Horses*, two characters crossing a basalt landscape in Cook County, Texas, ride "through broken hills dotted with cedar where the ground was cobbled with traprock." JAN DEBLIEU

travertine

Crusty, porous, like pale plaster, travertine forms when dissolved limestone (calcium carbonate) settles out of flowing water and becomes solid again. Around hot springs, travertine creates rinds, mounds, cones, and terraces like those veiled beneath the hot-spot vapors of Yellowstone. Off the silty main stem of the Colorado River in the Grand Canyon, Havasu Creek flows in a necklace of milky turquoise pools over terra-cotta rock, terraced by scalloped ledges of travertine. The travertine forms when the creek's calcareous precipitate coats roots, branches, and other trapped matter, then builds on itself even as the organics rot away. Smoothing the lip of each apron of travertine, the creek cascades into pools, its downstream energy checked by stair step rather than by meander. Severe flash floods have periodically flushed out Havasu's travertine. Then the encrustation begins again—though it takes time for the turquoise to come back. ELLEN MELOY

tree farm

Unlike forests, which provide their own nutrients, capture and filter their own water, and harbor high levels of biodiversity, tree farms are usually plantations of one or a few species grown in large stands of uniform age and cut down well before they reach the maturity character-istic of old growth. Such farms might produce Christmas trees, but more commonly they produce lumber or pulp, as in the pine plantations of the southeastern United States. Concerned about the replacement of mixed forests with industrial monocultures, several organizations now

certify management plans for tree farms aimed at pre-
serving biodiversity, water quality, and wildlife habitat.
The Menominee Indians of Wisconsin have shown what
sustainable practices might accomplish, by harvesting,
over the past century and a half, more than two billion
board feet from their tribal lands while improving the
health of their forest and increasing the amount of standing timber.   SCOTT RUSSELL SANDERS

tree island

More commonly known as hammocks in South Florida,
these slight elevations in the slim grassy waters of the
Everglades host palms and hardwood trees. Peter Matthiessen in *Lost Man's River* compares these "tear shaped
islands in the slow, sparkling sheet of grassy river" to a
"green armada sailing north against the sky." Water once
flowed more strongly through the Everglades—*Pahayokee*
to the Seminoles—than it does today, and those currents
molded the islands to their distinctive elongate shape.
Cool, green, and dry, hundreds of tree islands now dot
the sawgrass plain. One of the largest is Paradise Key,
measuring a mile by a mile and a half; it lies along
the western edge of Taylor Slough, near the national
park's headquarters. The term tree island is used in
other contexts as well—for example, near tree line in
alpine terrain, where islands of stunted trees may clump
together within a matrix of herbaceous vegetation.
JOY WILLIAMS

tree line

A line above or below which trees of any dimension
do not grow, governed by temperature, solar energy,
water supply, soil conditions, and exposure. The upper
elevation of tree growth is called the cold tree line, to
distinguish it from a lower tree line or dry tree line,
below which the moisture supply in certain regions

doesn't facilitate growth. In northern New Mexico and southern Colorado, the cold tree line is around 12,000 feet in elevation, while in northern Colorado it is around 11,000 feet. (The lower line here happens to be at 5,600 feet.) The upper limit drops progressively to the north, as growing seasons become shorter, the line descending to 8,000 feet in Montana's Glacier National Park, and to sea level at the edge of the Arctic lowlands north of the Mackenzie Mountains in the Canadian Yukon.
WILLIAM KITTREDGE

tree tip pit

When a tree falls, its upended root ball leaves a depression as well as a mound of earth made of the displaced material. In the Pacific Northwest, tree tip pits are common sights, as the ubiquitous Douglas fir has a shallow root system (owing to the abundance of water falling on the ground) and is prone to fall over more easily than other large trees. Both pits and mounds are microhabitats for all kinds of forest inhabitants. In wet seasons, the pits act as small catchment ponds for birds or animals that need a drink. Squirrels and other rodents use the soft mounds as a cache for their collected nuts and food. At the end of winter in the Tongass National Forest, a black bear may take refuge in the pit, pushing over the log to look for grubs while her two cubs play on the mound—or she might take a nap under the prow of the tree's trunk. Perhaps that is why the tree tip pit is also referred to as a cradle and knoll. In general, tree tip sites can be indicators of old-growth forests, since slim young trees with tap roots usually resist the kinds of winds that blow the heavy old trees down.   GRETEL EHRLICH

trembling prairie

A prairie is by nature trembling, being made of grass. The phrase seems to describe an interesting quality of optical illusion, that rising shimmer over a vast expanse of disparate entities, which, in the tumbling liquid motion of the wind, gives a panorama the appearance of a single living thing. A couple of lines from Paul Hoover's "At the Desiring Vine" capture the term's primary meaning: "We're decaying gracefully, thank you,/as shaky as a 'trembling prairie.'" The reference here is to instability beneath the apparent ground, as with the Seminole word *okefenokee,* meaning "land of the trembling earth" and the given name of a peat bog region on the Georgia coast. The term is commonly used around freshwater and brackish coastal marshes on the lower Mississippi. Experts at the Center for Environmental Communications at Louisiana University explain that these are a special form of marsh, called *flotant* by the locals and often referred to as *la prairie tremblante,* a floating marsh not anchored to the ground beneath. It consists of tightly entangled plants and their roots, mixed with peat; typically, there is water flowing below it, over a layer of clay covered with oozing soil. In 1899, George W. Cable wrote in *Strong Hearts* of "a maze of marsh islands—huddling along that narrow, half-drowned mainland of cypress swamp and trembling prairie, which follows the Mississippi out to sea." SUSAN BRIND MORROW

truncated spur

A periglacial spur whose tip or leading edge has been planed off by glacial erosion is known as a truncated spur. Due to the depth of the valley formed by the spur's parent mountains, the glacier was forced to go through, rather than over or around, the spur, summarily "truncating" it. The consequent bluff or blunt slope can be both visually stunning and quite dangerous. Striking examples of truncated spurs are found in Yosemite and Glacier National Parks. STEPHEN GRAHAM JONES

tseghiizi

The Navajo word for a rock fissure, seen from above, is *tseghiizi*. The English near-equivalent is slot, or slit, canyon. You can easily touch both sidewalls when passing through a tseghiizi, and you might be able to see only a few feet ahead or behind you—it's like walking in the belly of a snake. Antelope Canyon, near Page, Arizona, is a tseghiizi well known for a translucent light that causes sections of its walls to take on the appearance of draped silk or satin. The tortuous passage of a tseghiizi has sometimes been the site of a flash flood fatal to hikers— neither handholds nor shelves are available to those who suddenly need to get to higher ground. The tseghiizi's narrows are seductive, suggestive of secrets. To those who seek the close intimacy of these places, the land's interior is revealed.   TERRY TEMPEST WILLIAMS

tsegi

In Navajo, *tse* means "rock," and *-gi* means "at" or "in"; as a word, *tsegi* means "canyon" or "rock canyon." The word is a close approximation of *Tséyi*, the Navajo name for the place others call Canyon de Chelly. When people use the name Canyon de Chelly (chelly being a French corruption of tsegi) or Tsegi Canyon, they are speaking redundantly. But perhaps "canyon canyon" is fitting at Canyon de Chelly. Located a few miles east of Chinle, Arizona, in the heart of Navajo country, it's one part of a Y-shaped labyrinth of canyons. In addition to Canyon de Chelly, which is twenty-seven miles long, the labyrinth includes Canyon del Muerto (in Navajo, *'Ane'é Tséyi*, or "Behind Canyon de Chelly"). This complex of redrock cliffs contains Anasazi ruins and pictographs, meandering streambeds that provide irrigation for farming and water for Navajo sheepherders, as well as Spider Rock, a rock tower central to Navajo mythology. Near the mouth

T

of the canyons, one can attain a glimpse of all this from
Tsegi Overlook.   ARTHUR SZE

tuckamore

Tuckamore is a Newfoundland term for gnarled and
tangled stands of stunted spruce and balsam fir. Individual trees are dwarfed and weathered into swept-back,
sculptural shapes by harsh coastal growing conditions.
Most of the growth occurs on the lee sides, the windward
branches having been nipped and wrenched by wind,
salt air, and cold. Tuckamore forests are tight and prickly
places, very difficult to penetrate.   CHARLES FRAZIER

tule

Tule derives from the Aztec *tullin* or *tollin,* meaning
any of several wetland plants, specifically bulrushes.
The tules are marshy, swampy wilderness regions in
California where these grasslike perennial herbs, cattails,
bulrushes, and sedges are prevalent and may reach
heights of fifteen to twenty feet. Tule has given its name
to the small California elk, the tule elk, once nearly
extinct, and to a population of the California marsh
wren, the tule wren. Because of the thick, harsh wildness
of the tule areas, "to be deep in the tules" means to be in
trouble. "To pull freight for the tules" means to run from
the law. In *An Apostle of the Tules,* Bret Harte describes the
tules in Tassajara Valley, California, this way: "A more
barren, dreary, monotonous and uninviting landscape
never stretched before human eye . . . the breath of the
ague-haunted tules in the outlying Stockton marshes
swept through the valley." Tulare Lake in California's
Central Valley, named for its expanses of tules and once
one of the largest freshwater lakes in the West, is today
a dry lake, virtually all the water in its major feeder
streams—the Kings, Kaweah, and Tule Rivers—having
been diverted for irrigation.   PATTIANN ROGERS

tule land

Tule land is a term recorded as early as 1856, just after the California gold rush. It usually refers to the flats of bulrushes and other reeds along the rivers of the West Coast. In the muddy shallows along the Sacramento, for example, as the river takes its time joining the San Joaquin and approaching the San Pablo and San Francisco Bays, there are vast thickets of reeds, home to waterfowl and fur-bearing animals. Tule lands are especially common at the junctures of rivers, where the slightest breeze will set the rushes whispering and rasping over the mud and standing water. The Wintu Indians called tule land "the storehouse of instant tools" because the rushes could be used to make so many things: mats, clothes, baskets, lodges, boats, and cradles, sandals, brooms, fish traps, and talismanic images.   ROBERT MORGAN

tundra

Diminutive and slow-growing, tundra vegetation is found in cold, dry alpine and arctic regions where trees cannot fully develop. Alpine tundra circumscribes high mountain slopes in many parts of the world, while arctic tundra circles the Earth at high northern latitudes, edged by the Arctic Ocean to the north and boreal forests to the south. Here, the tundra's vast plain of distinctive vegetation is underlain by a thick layer of permafrost. Arctic tundra is frozen and snow-covered much of the year, but is brimming with life during brief northern summers. Barry Lopez notes, "Arctic tundra can open suddenly . . . when any intimacy with it is sought." Witness the detail of sedges, mosses, lichens, and miniature flowers. The infestations of summer insects. The dozens of bird species that migrate to the tundra for nesting season. Caribou, polar bear, wolverine, muskox, grizzly. Cairns, graves, tent rings, carved wood: isolated and subtle signs that humans have moved across its reach.   CAROLYN SERVID

turbulent flow

In contrast to laminar flow, in turbulent flow any particle of a body may move in any direction with respect to any other particle. Hydrologists and river scientists, as well as the curious, beginning with Leonardo da Vinci, have studied turbulence in the Earth's water and atmosphere, and all have found such movement difficult, if not impossible, to predict. Turbulence in a river occurs when rocks, holes, or sudden changes in the river channel obstruct the flow of the water. River rafters characterize turbulent flow by its irregular velocity and movement, reserving the term chaotic flow to describe the most dangerous parts of a whitewater river, where the river's movement cannot be anticipated. LAN SAMANTHA CHANG

U-shaped valley

The cross section of an ice-carved valley is U-shaped.
U-shaped valleys, also called parabolic valleys, often
began their histories as V-shaped river valleys whose
sloping sides were steepened and whose narrow floors
were broadened by glaciers that bored out their contours.
As valley glaciers advance down a river valley, they blade
the bottom flat, destroying and polishing rock walls
as they do so and pushing the debris into high fenders
called moraines. Gradually, the vertical walls and wide,
slightly rounded bottom of a U-shaped valley are formed.
When a valley glacier meets the sea, and then melts back
during an interglacial period, rising waters can fill the
valley, creating a fjord. U-shaped valleys are also called
glaciated valleys, and classic examples exist in Glacier
National Park in Montana and throughout the Rocky
Mountains. GRETEL EHRLICH

uinta structure

The technical term anticline describes a structure—
such as a mountain range—in which layers of bedded
rock fall down on either side of an axis. This is the case
in the Uinta Mountains in northeastern Utah, "a classic example of subsidence and uplift on a stupendous
scale," according to geographer Dudley Stamp. The
Uintas offer geology students a textbook landscape for
the study of a type of warping of the Earth's crust that
results in a uinta structure, where, writes Stamp, you
see "a flattened flexure from which the strata descend
sharply on either flank and then run horizontal again."
A series of faults (which once relieved pressure in the
bending layers of uplifted rock) marks both the crest
of the range and its base. The Uintas—the name is
from *uintats*, a Ute word for pine lands—are one of the
few east-west–trending ranges in the Rocky Mountain
chain. TERRY TEMPEST WILLIAMS

unaka

The Unaka Mountains, which form a boundary between
Tennessee and North Carolina, get their name from
the Cherokee word *unega*, which roughly translates as
"white," perhaps referring to the foggy haze that distinguishes the Great Smoky Mountains, of which the Unaka
Mountains are a part, or to the Unaka's domes of exposed
white granite, quite striking and very white against the
dark green forest background. Like the Baraboo Hills in
Wisconsin, the Unaka Moutains, called at various times
the Iron Mountains and the Iron and Yellow Mountains,
were formed when hard, erosion-resistant rock stayed
put, as it were, while softer rock around the group of
hills was worn away by weather, water, and time. In the
lexicon of geography, unaka has been a generic term
denoting an erosion-resistant range of hills, but the term,
used in this way, is regarded as out-of-date. Properly
used, Unaka is now a place-name only. Unakite, a
pinkish-green granite gemstone, gets its name from these
mountains.   GRETCHEN LEGLER

unconformity

A stratum of amnesia in the geologic record, where
overlying rock, significantly younger than what lies
below, represents some break in an otherwise continuous
story of formation. Often, the original strata have been
established, then lifted, tilted, folded, or severely eroded
before being topped with new deposits by vulcanism
or sedimentation. This unconformity represents the
place in deposition when time passed without leaving a local record. As the rings in a tree indicate a
steady counting of seasons from the pith of origin to
the living cambium of the present moment, the lithic
record in bedrock may show an unbroken stratigraphic
succession of events, materials, and processes. The
unconformity in this succession represents a time when

the recorded sequence of geologic progress was broken before the next stage in development began to leave a new record.   KIM STAFFORD

undercliff

The undercliff is that mass of rock jumbled at the base of a standing cliff, or it can be a subsidiary cliff formed by fallen material and then trimmed to a vertical profile by waves or other action: a slump of mud, or the collapse of eroded gullies on a cliff face. The action of waves against a sea cliff, or a soft lower stratum being eroded by wind or water faster than what lies above, can also lead to collapse. The undercliff is often an area of jumbled, tilted, slumped, and highly unstable material that protects the remaining cliff from further erosion.   KIM STAFFORD

upland

Elevated land or higher ground found inland, away from coastal areas, and from which rivers collect drainage is called upland. Like plateaus, uplands stand above floodplains. They are often of subdued relief with relatively even terrain, although some are designated "channeled" or "grooved" uplands—eroded areas that often contain small, round lakes. Mountainous areas are also uplands. Depending on the region, some uplands remain always covered in ice or snow; others, like the uplands of Monroe County, Illinois, are fertile and much loved by farmers. Illinoisan poet Carl Sandburg often praised these parts of his native state, as he does in "Uplands in May": "Lush in the lowlands grasses rise / And upland beckons upland. / The great strong hills are humble."   DONNA SEAMAN

U

upland forest

Upland seems to have been a nautical term, referring in general to the country lying away from the sea, or to the interior and higher part of a landmass, perhaps far from the coast. The gradient from coastline to upland may be sudden, as it is with the Chugach Range and its spruce forests of south-central Alaska, or gradual in the extreme, as in localities along the Gulf Coast. Within the interior region, however, upland also refers to ground that is higher than surrounding plains and valleys. Differing weather and soil conditions, and differing levels of exposure to the "elements," produce upland forest growth distinct from that of the lowlands. In the Florida Panhandle, for example—and generally speaking—the palmetto gives way to the (threatened) longleaf pine, and farther northward in Alabama and Georgia, to the loblolly pine and hardwoods of the Piedmont Plateau at the southern reach of the Appalachians. But of course, the Piedmont has its own detail of uplands, where pine, oak, and hickory are most common, and its riparian lowlands, where cottonwood, sycamore, river birch, and alder hold sway.   JOHN KEEBLE

upwind

Upwind means toward the wind's source; moving in the direction from which the wind is blowing; moving or positioned toward the wind or in the direction from which the wind is blowing; or a specific wind that blows against one's course or up a slope. The term suggests success, progress, optimism, and good fortune. So an "upwind" person lives a life of achievement and triumph. And someone "traveling upwind" looks fully ahead to the future. Said person desires to be in the vanguard, keeping fully abreast of and fully in tune with the most significant forces and trends emerging in business, industry, technology, or lifestyle.   JEFFERY RENARD ALLEN

V-shaped valley

Valleys made by water are, in cross section, shaped like
a giant V. Water, depending on its velocity, cuts down
into rock, engorges itself in rock, and keeps cutting.
The Grand Canyon of the Yellowstone is an example of
a V-shaped valley. There, water spills out, tumbles, pools
in rock basins, spills again, eventually carving more
depressions into rock. When these basins overflow, the
cutting through earth and rock begins again; water coils
in a sinuous braid, drops again, and cuts deeper. Some
rivers tend to flow in a straight line; thus the sediments
they carry quickly erode the rocks below and carve a
classic V-shape. (This pattern is, however, sometimes
interrupted by climate change or tectonic activity.) Other
rivers flow more slowly, cutting from side to side, creating the common S-curves characteristic of these rivers.
GRETEL EHRLICH

vale

Vale is an archaic, poeticized term for valley, a word
that likely has its origins in the Greek *oasis,* taken by the
Greeks from the Arabic word *wadi,* meaning a low-lying
area or depression—one often, as a landscape feature, hidden and a well-kept secret, of great significance because
this is where water can be found. In English we have "vale
of tears" for life itself. There is a kind of visible onomato-
poeia in the word, as though it contains within itself the
visual shape of its meaning. V is a declivity, the shape of
the land rising on either side. The rest of the word is fluid,
the flow of the vowels through the V like the river flowing
through the valley.   SUSAN BRIND MORROW

valle

Valle is Spanish for valley. The word *vallecito* is simply the diminutive form of valle, and means "small
or little valley." The word valle is occasionally

applied to delta regions, as in *el valle del Río Grande* in south Texas. ARTURO LONGORIA

valley glacier

Smaller than continental glaciers or ice caps, valley glaciers (also called mountain or alpine glaciers or ice streams) originate high in the mountains and, moving a foot or less per day, crawl down valleys, sometimes to the sea. When they retreat, these glaciers leave behind characteristically U-shaped valleys with extremely steep sides. In some valley glaciers, the ice is thousands of feet thick. Outlet valley glaciers, such as the Jakobshavn Isbrae in west Greenland and the Hubbard in Yakutat Bay, Alaska, formed when tongues of ice sheets or ice caps extruded through gaps in mountain ridgelines, then descended into valleys. Alpine valley glaciers, such as the Schwan Glacier in Alaska's Chugach Mountains, are born in mountain cirques where old snow compacts to firn, then glacial ice, and slides down a valley. Snow avalanching from steep slopes is the chief nourishment of alpine valley glaciers. On a cruise with missionaries in the Chilkat country of southeastern Alaska, John Muir was awed by mountains carved by valley glaciers: "Gloriously arrayed in snow and ice, some of the largest and most river-like of the glaciers [flowed] through wide, high-walled valleys like Yosemite, their sources far back and concealed, others in plain sight, from their highest fountains to the level of the sea" (*Travels in Alaska*). Not all valley glaciers are riverlike in appearance. Muir describes the glacier named after him, in the east arm of Glacier Bay, Alaska, as "a broad undulating prairie streaked with medial moraines and gashed with crevasses." EVA SAULITIS

varve

Deriving from the Swedish word for layer, a varve is a pair of two thin, adjoining sheets of sedimentary clay and silt. The word was originally used to refer exclusively to the layered, annual sediments that were deposited (as long as eighteen thousand years ago) in ancient glacial lakes and other still water pools formed from glacial meltwater. However, varves continue to form today, and have been found to form in lakes (even tropical lakes) as well as artificial reservoirs. They can be expected in any part of the country where seasonal sedimentation in lake basins occurs. The thicker and coarser band of sediment deposited in summer (by rapid streams fed by melting ice) is lighter in color and often includes iron oxides. The thinner band of fine clay and other organic material that settles out in winter (from grains suspended in still pools) is darker in color. Because successive layers of glacial varves were deposited annually, they can be counted and compared in thickness and used to calculate the age of the deposits, to track the retreats and advances of glaciers, and to establish data about climate change— much the way tree rings can be used to identify age and varying growth conditions. Such use of varves, developed in 1878 by the Swedish geologist Gerard de Geer, is called varve chronology (or geochronology) and is one of the main techniques that confirmed the Ice Age as not merely a hypothesis, but a fact of prehistory. Contemplating the abundance of varved clays around the Baltic Sea, de Geer wrote that "nature must have conserved all the years that have passed in these sediments." Recently, as scientists have learned that varves occur in marine habitats as well as in lakes, an alternative term, rhythmite (from the seasonal nature of the deposits), has come into favor.   EMILY HIESTAND

V

vega

Throughout the American West the word vega suggests meadow. Las Vegas, Nevada, takes its name from an entry in John Frémont's 1848 diary, in which he refers to Spanish words used to signify marshy plains. The Spanish meaning of vega is fairly general: "flat bottomland." But in Cuba it means, more specifically, a tobacco plantation or any fertile low area. In Chile, vega refers to a swamp. In south Texas and northern Mexico, the term often means the first bench above the river, usually filled with river cane. In *The Man Who Killed the Deer*, Frank Waters writes: "At a stream a mile ahead, he turned off upon a narrow trail. The wild plum thickets gave way to grassy vegas, tawny pastures, brittle corn fields." ARTURO LONGORIA

vein

When hot, mineral-rich waters surge into the faults and cracks of a host rock, depositing crystalline and metallic minerals in relatively pure, complex sheets and ganglia-like structures, geologists refer to the threads, ropes, and tabular forms as veins. The vein pattern may incorporate, as well, large, irregular nodes of the mineral. When economically valuable deposits occur in relatively close proximity to each other, the vein is sometimes referred to as a mother lode. Quartz, a mineral of little commercial value, is the ore most commonly found between layers of rock, and it's possible to see striking examples—ribbons of such vein quartz—gleaming in the dark, metamorphic rock of Ruby Canyon on the Colorado River west of Grand Junction in Colorado Canyons National Conservation Area. Miners, of course, are more interested in vein deposits when the ores are of higher economic value, such as native metals—silver, copper, and gold—and sulphides of zinc, mercury, and lead. Iron-rich solutions of some of these latter minerals might migrate great distances underground before streaming upward and hardening in rocks closer to the surface. Well-known and storied mineral lodes would include the Comstock silver lode in Nevada; the copper lodes of Michigan's Keweenaw Peninsula;

the Homestake gold deposits in South Dakota's Black Hills; and silver, lead, zinc, and nickel deposits around Coeur d'Alene, Idaho. Related terms include ore shoot, a ribbonlike column of ore within the ore-bearing rock; ore body, the well-defined mass of a mineral deposit; and bonanza, an especially rich vein of a precious ore.   TERRY TEMPEST WILLIAMS

vent

Vent is a general term for an opening in the surface of the Earth's crust, such as a mofette or solfatara (each a kind of fumarole), through which molten material or gas is forced during volcanic activity. Vents may consist of a single circular-shaped structure, a large elongate fissure and fracture, or a tiny ground crack. A vent can also be the conduit or channel through which material is extruded. The term also applies to an opening that releases gas during the burning of underground coal seams. Burning Hills in Grand Staircase–Escalante National Monument offers stunning examples of dark red and black surfaces pitted with vents from the burning of underground coal seams ignited by lightning strikes.   KIM BARNES

ventifact

Ventifact, linguistically derived from the Latin *ventus* (wind) plus *factus* (a form of the verb "to make"), is a stone shaped, altered, or faceted by windblown sand or other particles. At first, wind will wear away the upwind side so that a facet or bevel is formed. As the wind changes direction, or if the stone is overturned, other bevels may form. Shifting wind may be the explanation for a dreikanter (a three-faceted ventifact). Large numbers of ventifacts can be found east of Afton Canyon in the east-central Mojave Desert, and in the area locally known as Ventifact Ridge in Death Valley.   ARTHUR SZE

V

vernal pond

The site of a vernal pond (vernal means "spring") is an arena of change. Also known as ephemeral wetlands, vernal ponds form wherever water stands for a minimum of two months, the period needed to form their ecosystem: varieties of frogs, salamanders, and fairy shrimp, all protected from their usual predators, fish (none in a vernal pond), feed on smaller creatures such as phantom midges, copepods, mayflies, and water striders. In the poem "Vernal Sentiment," Theodore Roethke includes a vernal pond in a lighthearted celebration: "Though the crocuses poke up their heads in the usual places,/The frog scum appears on the pond with the same froth of green,/And boys moon at girls with last year's fatuous faces,/I never am bored, however familiar the scene." So should none be at a vernal pond.   LARRY WOIWODE

viewshed

A viewshed designates a field of vision witnessed by onlookers. It can be forest, grassland, ocean, or desert, and represents a biotic community within a cultural context. To have a viewshed, there must be a viewer, and a reason for this spot or area to be scrutinized. Like the word landscape, viewshed implies a witness, often for aesthetic reasons, or with an eye toward conservation because of the natural beauty of the place. On the other hand, a viewshed can hide what its creator doesn't want the eye to see: for example, clearcuts in old-growth forests are often obscured by a viewshed of trees that mask the devastation behind.   GRETEL EHRLICH

vly

A small swampy area was first called a vly by early Dutch colonists in what is now New York, perhaps the earliest occasion being on Long Island, but also in the Hudson Valley. This Dutch word, usually indicating the marshy headwaters of a brook or stream, where the water table first surfaces, is little used anymore, though many New York place-names retain it, including Vly Mountain in Greene County, Vly Lake in Hamilton County, and Vly Brook in Herkimer County. It can connote low ground, sometimes under water, a marsh or creek. One plausible etymology, proposed by lexicographers with some uncertainty, suggests that the old Dutch name for "market," *vly*—which also meant "valley," and which was pronounced "flea"—may have occasioned the name of New York's rowdy Fly Market, which was a fixture of Lower Manhattan from before the Revolution until about 1816. But this may be fanciful.   PATRICIA HAMPL

volcanic bomb

The volcanic bomb is a specimen of igneous rock uniquely formed by flight. Molten stone—a pyroclast—flung from a volcanic vent during eruption may adopt in flight a spherical, disc, teardrop, radial, spindle, or other shape as it cools, falling toward Earth. Like yeasty dough, the lump may form a crusted exterior before the bubbly interior hardens, hence the alternate term breadcrust bomb. A network of cracks on the surface may indicate the continued expansion of the interior after the crust began to harden.   KIM STAFFORD

volcanic neck

Technically, a volcanic neck is the open tunnel through which an active volcano releases molten rock, ash, and gases from deep in the Earth. In common usage, however, neck is sometimes used (as is volcanic plug) to describe the column of solidified lava that hardens in this opening once the eruption is over—a stone column that may be exposed by subsequent erosion. In the stricter definition, one might say that a volcanic neck is a filled volcanic pipe, a pipe an active neck. Notable volcanic

V

necks include Huérfano Butte in Colorado, Agathla Peak in northeastern Arizona, and Cabezon Peak in north-western New Mexico.   KIM STAFFORD

volcanic plug

A volcanic plug is the stopper in the genie bottle of volcanic extrusion, left as a record of gravity reversed from below. A volcanic vent may spew ash and build a cinder cone, the vent pipe being filled last by a denser column of molten rock. If this hardens as a vertical core, the ash cone may be eroded in time to leave the core plug as a standing spire. Well-known examples are Smith Rock, Oregon; Ship Rock, New Mexico; and the Boar's Tusk in Wyoming's Jack Morrow Hills.   KIM STAFFORD

walled lake

When water freezes, it swells, expands. What this means on the scale of a lake is that when the water turns to ice, it takes up more space than it did when liquid. The result is a gradual pushing up of shore sediment, a yearly "shove" by the ice as it makes room for itself. Let this happen for enough years in a row—centuries, in the case of the Great Lakes—and the result is a series of ridges along the shore of the lake. These ridges are called lake ramparts (a rampart being a mound of earth fortifying a position). A lake that has surrounded itself with lake ramparts is, thus, a walled lake.   STEPHEN GRAHAM JONES

wallow

A depression in the landscape formed where large animals habitually roll in the dirt, taking dust baths to combat biting flies and parasites on their hides, is called a wallow. Some blowouts begin as wallows, then are further scooped out by wind. Wallows may be dry, seasonally wet, boggy, or even persistent pools. Waterholes and wallows are not mutually exclusive. Some animals indulge in mud wallows, or even swim if pools are deep enough. The best-known North American wallows, some of them still visible, were excavated by bison. Wallows of various kinds have left their names on the land, such as Buffalo Wallow, Iowa; Bear Wallow, Arkansas; and Hog Wallow Hollow, Kentucky. Elk wallows on lands of the Quinault Indian Nation in Washington are known as important habitats for aquatic organisms such as amphibians. The Skookum Cast, one of the more intriguing recent pieces of evidence for Bigfoot, involves possible hand, buttock, heel, and thigh impressions recovered and cast from an elk wallow southeast of Mount St. Helens.   ROBERT MICHAEL PYLE

wash

The word wash is used to describe areas where subtle contours allow water to flow, or "wash," from elevated sites to lower zones, like the bottoms of canyons or along gullies or next to ponds. Carrizo Wash in Arizona and Hunters Wash in New Mexico are examples of washes that run for many miles. A dry streambed or creek is often called a dry wash. In some areas of the American Southwest the words arroyo and arroyo seco are used interchangeably with wash and dry wash. In *Desert Solitaire*, Edward Abbey writes: "Streambeds are usually dry. The dry wash, dry gulch, arroyo seco. Only after a storm do they carry water and then briefly—a few minutes, a couple of hours." ARTURO LONGORIA

washboard

Travel down an unpaved road can turn into a teeth-rattling, bumpy ride that might send a car spinning into the bar ditch. Narrow ridges that spring up from the surface of the road in a wavelike pattern, resembling the metal ribs of a washboard, are usually to blame. Until the early 1960s, the washboard effect was thought to be the result of "peculiar" soil, wind from passing vehicles, car exhaust, or impulses from car engines. Then geophysicist Keith Mather set up a homespun experiment to determine the cause. He attached a small wheel to the end of a strut and then set the strut in motion, like the hour hand of a clock, to mark a circular path in a bed of sand. Regular corrugations appeared. The faster he spun the wheel, the faster the washboard texture developed. The prerequisite was merely a dry, rough surface. When a tire hits a bump, dip, or rock in the road, it hops into the air and crashes down, spraying sand and gravel forward and sideways to form valleys. The moving tire hits the valley and hops again, repeating the process. The next car on the road only makes matters worse. Route 66, commissioned in 1926, was one long, dusty washboard road, crossing the country from Chicago to Santa Monica, until it was paved. Today, washboard roads are still found throughout the country, on every kind of bare ground.

MARY SWANDER

waterfall

At certain points in the course of many rivers, water descends vertically; these waterfalls may come where the river leaves a plateau, where it crosses bands of resistant rock, or where it encounters a fault scarp. On rivers, waterfalls are often wider than they are tall; in mountain streams, they tend to be higher than they are wide. In almost every case the sound and sight of glassy water turning into froth and fury is an irresistible lure to humans. Niagara Falls, the continent's highest-volume cataract, was one of the first headquarters of the sublime for American painters, writers, and other travelers. Waterfalls are in constant motion in more ways than one—they migrate slowly upstream as the lip erodes and the wall is undercut in the plunge pool at the base.

BILL MCKIBBEN

water gap

The places where water has cut a deep pass through a cuesta or high ridge are called water (or wet) gaps. They have persistent flow, even if it is ephemeral. Dry gaps occur where water has ceased to communicate across such a cutting. Water gaps channel streams through low-lying valleys or narrow gorges across ranges of hills, contrary to the common impression that watercourses flow out of mountains but do not cross them. When a once-blocked river regains its former course and keeps it by eroding the land as fast as uplift raises it, a water gap is said to arise through antecedent drainage, and its agent is called an antecedent stream. The Delaware Water

W

Gap, a tall and verdant slot where the Delaware River cuts through Kittatinny Mountain near Stroudsburg, Pennsylvania, is the definitive example of this landform. Gap towns are settlements built near, and commanding, strategic water gaps. ROBERT MICHAEL PYLE

waterpocket

Waterpockets are small erosional basins formed in layers of sedimentary rock. They resemble tidal pools, and with their ripple effects of wind and water they can seem like vestiges of the great sea that once covered the American Southwest, where they are apt to be found. During monsoon season, they act as porous cisterns for birds and animals, and often knobs of grass and chevrons of rushes grow at their verge. Waterpocket Fold, a vast monocline populated with spectacular canyons, cliffs, spires, domes, and monoliths, and which lies within Capitol Reef National Park, is named for the many waterpockets that exist along this stunning and isolated part of southern Utah. MICHAEL COLLIER

watershed

A term coined to refer to the higher ground—the line, ridge, or summit—that separates two drainage basins, watershed has since come to mean the region drained by such a divide, and an area through which water is drained into a particular watercourse or body of water. Watershed also refers to a turning point, or dividing line, that precipitates significant change. Due to this multiplicity of meanings, some scientists consider watershed "undesirable" as a scientific designation, yet it remains a standard term more or less synonymous with drainage basin. In thinking about life in the watershed of the Kentucky River, Wendell Berry writes: "Pondering on the facts of gravity and the fluidity of water shows us that the golden rule speaks to a condition of absolute interdependency and obligation. People who live on rivers—or, in fact, anywhere in a watershed—might rephrase the rule in this way: do unto those downstream as you would have those upstream do unto you." DONNA SEAMAN

wave-cut platform

As an erosive force, water rules the Earth, surpassing junior partners wind and ice. Hour by hour, eon by eon, the oceans and rivers turn great mountains into mere grains of sand. This handiwork is on full display at the base of rocky coastal cliffs the world over, where daily tides burrow into the Earth's stony foundations. The burrowing gradually undermines the cliff at a place called the wave-cut notch. Eventually, whole sections collapse. The cliff face slowly retreats as a result, extending landward the edge of a gently sloping underwater platform of wave-cut debris whose seaward edge, which might lie far beyond the breaker zone, marks the point where ocean waves first started eroding the cliffs. Sublime examples of wave-cut platforms can be found in western Newfoundland and at Pebble Beach near Arcata, California. MIKE TIDWELL

waxing slope

The component parts of a hillside are (1) the convex waxing slope at the top, eroding from top down; (2) the extensive downward free face, or constant slope; and (3) gentler concave waning slopes at the foot, where fine materials collect after being brought down from erosion on higher slopes. Waning slopes can come to dominate landscapes as erosion erases differences in elevation, and are sometimes used as a metaphor for failing or diminished human expectations. WILLIAM KITTREDGE

W

weathering pit

A depression on a flat surface in rocky terrain, varying in shape and ranging in size from a few inches to several yards in width, is known as a weathering pit. As the name suggests, weathering and erosion enlarge these pits, which are a common feature of granite terrain. They are found in many parts of the Southwest, including sites at Glen Canyon on the Colorado River and Enchanted Rock State Natural Area in Texas. A giant sandstone pit can be found near Red Breaks, Utah. JEFFERY RENARD ALLEN

well

In its commonest use, a well is a vertical shaft that people bore into the saturated zone of substrate in order to draw up groundwater. In literature and old maps, especially of the desert Southwest, Well appears often as a place-name where no wells have been dug, but where naturally occurring springs are reliable enough to be well-known for human use. A splendid example is Montezuma Well in Arizona, where a warm spring emerges from the bed-rock and a travertine rim around the spring has created a pool. BARBARA KINGSOLVER

wetland

Wetland covers a constellation of names and traits, but all generally refer to an ecosystem, land covered by shallow water and dependent on constant or recurrent inunda-tion. A short string of wetland forms: swamp, ciénega, marsh, fen, tulare, pocosin, vernal pool, sponge bog, quaking bog. A wetland may be freshwater, saltwater, or brackish. Found over the full swath of the continent, from Alaska's muskegs to the South's cypress swamps, with the inland marshes of the Great Basin in between. Found along lakes and rivers, or in isolation, a pothole on a prairie, restless with skeins of birds. In *A Sand County Almanac*, Aldo Leopold frames an image of wetland diversity: "Out on the bog a crane, gulping some luckless frog, springs his ungainly bulk into the air and flails the morning sun with mighty wings." ELLEN MELOY

The Old English version of wharf was *hweorf.* It referred to any substantial structure of wood or stone built along the water's edge so that ships could pull up alongside, and it was in use as early as 1067. Pier, quay, mole, breakwater, and seawall are all historically linked. Originally, a pier extended out into the water, as opposed to a wharf, which didn't. Its purpose was also to facilitate the loading and unloading of ships, and also perhaps partly to form or protect a harbor. The word pier was in use by 1390. By the nineteenth century, it tended to refer to raised structures built on columns, still for the purposes of docking, but also for promenading and for fishing. A mole—the word derives from the Latin *moles,* or "mass"—is a much larger structure, usually of stone, built out into the water, often in a circular or enclosing shape. One could load or unload ships on moles, but their essential function was to serve as a breakwater, which created an artificial harbor. The word came into use, probably from France, in the sixteenth century, and it came to mean not only the breakwater but also the harbor it enclosed. A quay, from the French *quai,* originally referred to an artificial bank or landing place that either lay parallel to or projected into navigable waters for the loading and unloading of ships. A definition of 1696 describes a quay (pronounced "key") as "a broad, paved space upon the shore of a river, a haven or port for the unloading of goods," which would seem to make it a synonym for wharf, and it is. Breakwater, though a thoroughly Anglo-Saxon combination, does not show up in the written record until the eighteenth century, where it is treated as a synonym for jetty and seems to mean distinctly a maritime structure built to protect land from the action of waves. Seawall in its earliest Old English use referred to a sea cliff; by the fifteenth century it had come to mean a breakwater.

ROBERT HASS

W

whirlpool

A downward-sucking, circular eddy in the sea, produced
by a tidal current flowing through a tight, irregular
underwater channel, or at the point where two or more
strong currents meet in a river, is called a whirlpool. The
effect is similar to the swirling action of waters circling
and recircling in a basin at the foot of a major waterfall,
such as the one at Niagara Falls, or to the turning of
waters in a rocky gorge, as in the one downstream from
Niagara. Whirlpools have occasionally been literary
metaphors for disorder, famously in *The Odyssey*, where
Homer personified a deadly whirlpool called Charybdis,
caused by a formation of rock on the Italian side of the
Strait of Messina, opposite a sea cliff on the Sicilian side,
as a female sea monster given to devouring sailors.

WILLIAM KITTREDGE

wilderness

Wilderness is a cultural, not an ecological, concept. While
its meaning and the values that attach to it have shifted
through the ages, it stands essentially for the land and
space where culture is not, or at least where the impacts of
human culture are minimal: the desert wilderness of the
Old Testament; the Adirondack wilderness of the Hudson River painters; the comparatively prosaic concepts
of backcountry, bush, or the "high lonesome"; and the
administrative designation conceived by Aldo Leopold as
"a continuous stretch of country preserved in its natural
state . . . big enough to absorb a two weeks' pack trip, and
kept devoid of . . . works of man." The most powerful of all
definitions of wilderness is to be found in the 1964 Wilderness Act: "A wilderness, in contrast with those areas where
man and his own works dominate the landscape, is hereby
recognized as an area where the earth and its community
of life are untrammeled by man, where man himself is a

visitor who does not remain." The National Wilderness Preservation System, which the act established, now includes over 105 million acres of federal land, more than half of which is in Alaska. Irony necessarily abides in so protean a term: land that westering white Americans in the nineteenth century judged to be wilderness was home ground from the point of view of native tribes, and the birth of the wilderness preservation movement in the twentieth century occurred only after the lands on which it focused had been substantially tamed by the removal of the natives who inhabited them. Today wilderness remains one of the most evocative concepts in American culture. It might be said to describe any place on land (or sea) where the powers of nature are paramount and where the call of the wild might be heard. Ed Abbey, among many others, has meditated on its meaning: "Wilderness. The word itself is music. Wilderness, wilderness.... We scarcely know what we mean by the term, though the sound of it draws all whose nerves and emotions have not yet been irreparably stunned, deadened, numbed by the caterwauling of commerce, the sweating scramble for profit and domination." WILLIAM DEBUYS

windbreak

A windbreak is a linear arrangement of trees, shrubs, and even plants in one or more closely spaced rows that are oriented across the direction of the prevailing wind to provide shelter for dwellings, soil, crops, or animals. By influencing wind speed, temperature, and humidity, windbreaks reduce wind chill and damage, control snow drift, reduce soil erosion, and also enable buildings to be heated with less fuel. As windbreaks, conifers are far more effective than deciduous trees. Windbreaks have been a part of midwestern farmlands since white settlement. ARTHUR SZE

W

wind gap

Wind gaps exist where the topography funnels airflow through a notch in a ridge. The persistent winds further incise such traces. Many wind gaps began as water gaps that were later left high and dry. This can happen through stream piracy, where the river that cut the gap is later captured by another river more vigorously extending its channel upstream through headward erosion. Wind gaps do not always indicate former stream courses, however, and often lie at a higher level than neighboring water gaps. Cols, passes, and saddles are all forms of wind gaps, as is the cleft formed when back-to-back cirques meet and their arête fails. The Keyhole on Longs Peak in Rocky Mountain National Park, Colorado, forms a memorable wind gap, especially for climbers passing through it in a gale.   ROBERT MICHAEL PYLE

window rock

Window Rock, its entire shape and form magnificent, the blue sky seen through its opening, is a part of a larger landform standing on the Navajo Reservation in northeastern Arizona at *Ni'Alníi'gi* ("Earth's Center"). Navajos call it *Tséghâhoodzáni,* "Rock with a Perforation." Tséghâhoodzáni is one of four places where Navajo singers (healers) collect water for use in the Waterway ceremony. Created by chemical weathering and freeze-thaw cycles in minute cracks in the rocks, the window is a 47-foot-wide opening in a 200-foot-high wall of red Entrada Sandstone. According to Navajo mythology, it was created by a giant snake passing through the formation. While most visitors talk about the "hole," most tribal people talk about the rock itself, perhaps because they recognize the life in land. Native people, then, often refer to the feature as a rock bridge or a rock rainbow, not a "pothole natural arch" as some geomorphologists have it. Another window rock, Grandfather Mountain, exists in the Blue Ridge Mountains near Boone, North Carolina. While its archway is not completely open, another formation called Denim Rock is visible through the opening.   LINDA HOGAN

witness tree

In land surveying, a property corner sometimes cannot be marked because the true point lies on a cliff or in a swamp, stream, or lakebed. A substitute may be established on any one of the surveyed lines leading to the true corner and within a distance of ten chains (660 feet) from it. Such a stand-in is known as a witness corner, and the monument placed there is the witness mark, witness post, or witness stake. A witness tree is a large tree so situated that it can serve as the reference point. The Umbrella Tree, a huge Douglas fir near Deep River, Washington, was a famous witness tree saved from logging for that purpose. In his book *A Witness Tree* (1942), Robert Frost describes one in a poem called "Beech": the title tree, having been "impressed as Witness Tree," allows truth to be "established and borne out,/though circumstanced with dark and doubt."   ROBERT MICHAEL PYLE

wood

"I went to the woods because I wished to live deliberately, to front only the essential facts of life, and see if I could not learn what it had to teach, and not, when I come to die, discover that I had not lived." So wrote Henry David Thoreau in his famous book about living on Walden Pond, originally titled *Walden; or, Life in the Woods.* A forested area or region is called a wood or woods. A small wood is often referred to as a grove. A wood is filled with trees, or woody plants reaching a mature height of at least twenty feet with a single stem or trunk and a more or less crown shape. A wood may contain either hardwoods, including broad-leafed trees like oak, sugar maple, and hickory, or softwoods, including pines, spruces, and poplars. When people live on the edge or make frequent forays into a forest, they often speak of this thick collection of trees as a woods, as in, "We hunted morels in the woods." Throughout literature, woods have taken on metaphorical and mythological connotations as both places of refuge and places of danger. While Thoreau found solitude in the woods, Hansel and Gretel found themselves alone and lost. Little Red Riding Hood had to brave her way through the woods to get to her grandmother's house. In Robert Frost's poem "Stopping by Woods on a Snowy Evening," the features become a mixture of both sanctuary and peril: "The woods are lovely, dark and deep." MARY SWANDER

woodland

An apparently rather straightforward word, woodland is in fact a richly ambiguous landscape term that is used both as an overarching term for all wooded lands (forests, timberlands, plantations, even orchards) and to indicate a subcategory of forest—a subcategory itself quite ambiguous, but perhaps most simply described as sparsely wooded land with an open canopy in which the crowns of trees do not touch. (The full extent of the variations of the term woodland may be enjoyed in the numerous pages devoted to the term in a report generated by a United Nations conference convened to "harmonize forest-related terms.") Attempting to distinguish woodlands from forests, forest professionals use several gauges, including crown cover, projective foliage, and the richness of life on the floor. Very generally, a woodland is not less than ten acres, with a vibrant carpet of herbs, grasses, mosses, ferns, and shrubs, and a canopy of between ten to thirty percent projective foliage cover. (An open forest has thirty to seventy percent; a closed forest more than seventy percent.) Woodlands can be broadleaf or coniferous, and are further identified by the dominant tree species. Taken together, the spacing of trees and the principal type of tree determine the amount of sunlight that penetrates the canopy, which in turn influences the richness of plant, animal, and insect life within a particular woodland. Thousands of American places are named after woodlands. Some, like The Woodlands in Houston and Woodland Pond Park in Bend, Oregon, refer to actual wooded surroundings. Many more places—including schools, churches, subdivisions, cemeteries, shopping malls, and whole towns—are given the name Woodland for a sylvan quality more longed for than real.

EMILY HIESTAND

woodlot

Historically, a woodlot was a parcel of private forest that could be managed to provide a landowner with firewood, building materials, and timber for sale. Owning and managing a working woodlot used to be a necessity of farm life, especially in northern forested regions; it was part of a self-sustaining style of existence, and income for farmers during the winter. Timber harvesting still occurs in modern woodlots, but more commonly these small wooded tracts are maintained for nature lovers and wild animals to enjoy. Woodlots can be small or large, from ten to one thousand acres, and typically include a variety of different kinds of trees, distinguishing them from monoculture plantations. A healthy woodlot is a forest ecosystem. Henry David Thoreau comments in *The Maine Woods* that in the mid–nineteenth century the tamed woodlots of Massachusetts were a far cry from the wild forests of Maine. In Maine, he writes, "you are never reminded that the wilderness in which you are threading is, after all, some villager's familiar wood-lot, some widow's thirds, from which her ancestors have

W

sledded fuel for generations, minutely described in some old deed which is recorded, of which the owner has got a plan, too, and old bound-marks may be found every forty rods, if you will search."   GRETCHEN LEGLER

wrack line

The line of dried seaweed, marine vegetation, and other organic debris and detritus left on the beach by the action of the tides is called the wrack line. Tides strand the remains of marine creatures and sea grasses on the beach, including small invertebrates and bits of eelgrass. The wrack line may also contain man-made litter and refuse and is easily identifiable to the naked eye on that area of the beach where no plant life grows. Although there may be viable seeds hidden in the organic detritus of the wrack line, germination and seedling growth will typically occur only when a storm tide has left the debris at the highest and most landward edge of the beach, far out of reach of the daily high tides and waves. The wrack line serves as a prime feeding ground for birds and other animals that hunt here for food then defecate in the sand, providing organic matter essential to a strong ecosystem.   JEFFERY RENARD ALLEN

yard

You can hear in yard its resemblance to garden and girdle. All three words arise from a root meaning "to enclose, surround." The most familiar sort of yard is the plot of ground surrounding a house, often planted in grass, flowers, and bushes—hence the ubiquitous yard sales and laborious yard work. Nearly as familiar, and probably older, is the use of yard to describe a plot of ground that is itself enclosed by a fence or wall and devoted to a specific purpose, as in a farmyard, churchyard, or shipyard. When loggers haul felled trees to a landing, they are said to be yarding. By analogy to the pen where poultry and livestock are kept, yard also means a place where deer or moose gather to feed in winter.   SCOTT RUSSELL SANDERS

yardang

Derived from the Turkish word *yar*, meaning a "steep bank" or "precipice," yardangs are a desert landform: they are narrow, steep-sided ridges carved from bedrock or any consolidated or semiconsolidated material formed by wind abrasion (by sand and dust) and deflation. Yardangs usually occur in groups, with the ridges running parallel to each other and in the direction of the prevailing wind. Yardangs are typically three or more times longer than wide, and they are highest and broadest at the blunt end that faces into the wind. Yardangs may be found in the Mojave Desert as well as in Oregon coastal sand dunes.   ARTHUR SZE

yazoo

Named after the Yazoo River, which flows along the eastern bank of the Mississippi River for miles before joining it above Vicksburg, a yazoo is a tributary that, deferred from joining the mainstream by a natural levee formation, parallels the larger channel for some significant distance, until at last an opening in the bank or levee allows it to empty into the trunk stream. Alternative terms are yazoo stream and deferred tributary. The word yazoo itself was originally the name of a small, now vanished Native American tribe that once inhabited central Mississippi. Historians still debate the meaning of the tribe's name; their educated guesses include widely varying possibilities—grass, river of death, hunting ground, as well as a verb meaning "to blow on an instrument." Contemporary place-names derived from yazoo include the Yazoo Cutoff, in Madison, Louisiana; the Yazoo Backwater Levee, in Sharkey, Mississippi; and Yazoo County, the storied region where the Mississippi hills descend into the Delta.   EMILY HIESTAND

zanja

When Spanish conquerors moved into southern California, they established encomienda, hacienda, and mission systems that required much larger volumes of water for growing food and raising domestic animals than the indigenous people, with their much smaller scale irrigated plots, were accustomed to using. To channel a steady flow of water from wetlands to agricultural fields, stock tanks, and settlements, Indian people were coerced into helping develop systems of ditches—*zanjas*—for the distribution of water. The zanja complexes eventually passed into disuse, but not before large wetland areas had been drained and destroyed. Some abandoned zanjas have since been reclaimed by Chumash people. They're slowly replanting native vegetation, including willows and reeds, to bring back the precontact, small-scale, zanja habitat—the life in and at the edges of the zanjas, which has been missing for so long. Today, the word zanja refers to a dry as well as a wet ditch, and the expression zanja madre, the mother or main ditch, carries with it the idea of an agriculture more suited to the landscape of southern California than the one envisioned several centuries ago by European immigrants.   LINDA HOGAN

zigzag rocks

Used only in the plural, zigzag rocks refers to one or to a series of low chevron-shaped dams, open at their apex and reaching, usually, from bank to bank across a river or stream. They were built by Native Americans, notably in the Northwest and on rivers along the fall line of the Appalachian Mountains. Constructed on hard river bottoms swept free of soft sediments, the converging lines of boulders and cobbles were designed to funnel fish toward weirs—traps—constructed at the apexes. Some structures were laid out in the shape of a W, to trap both anadromous fish swimming upstream to spawn and

497

catadromous fish swimming downstream. A staggered sequence of such separate weirs might extend a half mile or more downriver, as was once the case on a stretch of the Susquehanna near Harrisburg, Pennsylvania. Long-abandoned zigzag rocks, one of the most distinctive marks of human interaction with the Earth, can still be seen in some places.   SUSAN BRIND MORROW

BIBLIOGRAPHIC NOTE

OUR GENERAL INTENTION IN DEVELOPING *HOME GROUND* was to bring an interesting group of writers together, people with divergent backgrounds, whom we would ask to say something useful and memorable about "place." For us, this would mean their researching the words Americans use to describe the specific features of the landscapes they occupy, and then having them provide those words with texture and substance.

We had a sense when we began that "geography" was beginning to emerge as a key concept in political and economic conversation in the United States, a geography not of recalling state capitals or the names of rivers but a geography that dealt with the idea of place. What was it that turned raw space into an actual place? Did one actually benefit from being connected to a specific place, as opposed to occupying generic space? Yi-Fu Tuan had written clearly and eloquently about these questions in *Space and Place: The Perspective of Experience* (1977). John McPhee's books on the geology of America, beginning with *Basin and Range* (1980) and continuing through *Assembling California* (1993), had drawn curious readers from far outside the world of formal geology and geography. A series of contemporary popular novels—Cormac McCarthy's *All the Pretty Horses* (1992), Charles Frazier's *Cold Mountain* (1997), Marilynne Robinson's *Housekeeping* (1981), and Peter Matthiessen's *Killing Mr. Watson* (1990)—had revitalized an awareness of how central American landscape is to the American story. The same could be said of several popular memoirs of the same period—Tobias Wolff's *This Boy's*

Life (1988), Annie Dillard's *An American Childhood* (1987), and Harry Crews's *Childhood: Biography of a Place* (1978).

Our contribution to this ongoing conversation, we determined, would be the vocabulary of place, what people called the things they saw in and on the land.

The broad range of landscape expression used in ordinary writing and everyday discourse in America today is only hinted at in *Home Ground*, for several reasons. Little of this kind of language, outside of technical terms, has been written down. What has been committed to paper has not, for the most part, been brought together in one place. And the scope of unrecorded folk terminology is staggering. No doubt this will soon change. Debate about the preservation, commercial exploitation, and public use of land has become more widespread and common in the United States. A need for specificity and clarity in finding solutions to disagreements over the fate of specific plots of land is felt by everyone involved.

Definitions for the most common technical and popular terms used to designate American landscape features have long been carefully set out in geographical dictionaries of different sorts, but books that deal with how and why we use this language are still relatively scarce. Perhaps the most widely known is John Stilgoe's *Shallow Water Dictionary: A Grounding in Estuary English* (1990). A handful of glossaries that focus on literary sources for landscape terms have recently come into existence, such as Scott Thybony's *Dry Rivers and Standing Rocks* (2000), each one organized with a different purpose in mind. Landscape terms drawn from regional American dialects in the United States, such as Gullah and Cajun, are scattered through the several volumes of *The Dictionary of American Regional English* (1985 et seqq.) but, again, they have not been brought together. Folklorists intent on indexing vernacular landscape expressions and explaining them have almost always focused on a restricted geographical area, partly because, even on this scale, the vocabularies are so challenging. Mary Hufford's *One Space, Many Places: Folklife and Land Use in New Jersey's Pinelands National Reserve* (1986) is one such example.

We asked the *Home Ground* writers to begin their research by reviewing entries in the best standard reference works—*The Dictionary of Physical Geography* (2000), by David Thomas and Andrew Goudie, for example, or *Glossary of Geology* (1997), by Robert L. Bates and Julia Jackson. We asked them to look at May Watts's *Reading the Landscape of America* (1975); at the four volumes of Donald Meinig's landmark work on American history and geography, *The Shaping of America* (1986 et seqq.); at Grady Clay's *Real Places: An Unconventional Guide to America's Generic Landscapes* (1994); and at the writing of George Stewart, including his *Names on the Land* (1945). We urged them to reacquaint themselves with works of American literature in which landscape plays an important role, from Susan and James Fenimore Cooper's books up through Cather and Steinbeck. We suggested the novels of Wendell Berry, Annie Proulx, and William Eastlake. We directed them toward specialized indexes, including *Woods Words: A Comprehensive Dictionary of Loggers Terms* (1959), by Walter Fraser McCulloch, and *Illustrated Glossary of Snow and Ice* (1973), edited by Terence Armstrong, Brian Roberts, and Charles Swithinbank. We asked them to delve into works that considered the deeper meaning and importance of place, such as Keith Basso's *Wisdom Sits in Places: Landscape and Language Among the Western Apache* (1996) and *Patterned Ground: Entanglements of Nature and Culture* (2004), edited by Stephan Harrison, Steve Pile, and Nigel Thrift. We pointed them toward regional dictionaries, such as Rubén Cobos's *A Dictionary of New Mexico and Southern Colorado Spanish* (2003). And, having learned that geography is one of the fastest growing majors in U.S. universities, we asked them to look at the most representative textbooks, such as

Robert Christopherson's *Geosystems: An Introduction to Physical Geography* (2006).

In the course of developing *Home Ground*, we made several discoveries. One was the striking depth to which American fiction and poetry in general are informed by landscape. Another was that standard dictionaries and glossaries of landscape terminology sometimes disagreed about what certain terms meant, or simply remained vague about the meaning of a term. And, finally, we learned that landscapes are not only seen differently by different people (a flyfisher and a riverboat guide each use a markedly different set of terms to describe the sequence of features that comprise a rapid) but some parts of a given landscape are so minutely dissected by specialists that an uninitiated onlooker is unable to recognize the separate parts. Surfers, for example, use an elaborate vocabulary to distinguish the many features of a single breaking wave. Rock climbers do the same with the complicated face of an escarpment. The diversity of these vocabularies—regional, occupational, recreational, professional—suggests, of course, that the nature of whatever it is that is being addressed is, ultimately, unknowable.

An interested reader can easily track down most of the standard literature of landscape terminology (like the Bates and Jackson book mentioned above) and gain from it, as we did, some sense of how often these definitions become trailheads, the start of routes leading off into the unknown, the unexplored, and the uncatalogued. An indication of what hasn't been written down, on the other hand, the largely unrecorded nature of American landscape language, can be gotten from the experiences of one of our advisors on *Home Ground*, Enrique Lamadrid. For some years Enrique has collected and studied Spanish-language terms for landscape features, particularly in the Southwest. One of his ongoing interests is the vernacular of hand irrigators—people working with little more than a shovel, a few floodgates, and a series of ditches to draw water from a river, distribute it through a contiguous pattern of agricultural fields, and then funnel what remains back to the river. The larger distributary ditches are called *acequias* (the main ditch is the *acequia madre*), the smaller ones *sangrías*. Unabsorbed water—the tailwaters or *desagüe*—returns to the river through the "veinous" side of the irrigation system, where the sangrías empty into the acequias.

On a recent visit to a set of irrigated plots at Embudo, New Mexico, next to the Rio Grande, Enrique spent an afternoon with the "boss" of the acequia system, the *mayordomo*, who decides how much water will go into the fields, what the timing of that will be, and which fields at that moment are most in need of water. In a single afternoon with this mayordomo, Enrique told us, he heard half a dozen words that were new to him. *Las melgas*, it was explained to him, are irrigated plots not quite as saturated as *los ancones*, the plots lower down on the irrigated slope and closer to the river. (Different vegetables are planted accordingly, each with slightly different requirements for water.) And there was a new word for a particular kind of diversion structure that this mayordomo had engineered into his system of *acequias y sangrías*.

Enrique also heard the mayordomo refer to the structure he used to take water from the river—a headgate in English, *la presa* or *la toma* in Spanish—as *el azud*, an Arabic word. In northern New Mexico, with its strong strains of Iberian culture, and knowing the great impact that Arab irrigation technology had had on Spain up through the fifteenth century, it made sense to Enrique that the mayordomo would know this word. What surprised him was that he had never heard such an Arabic term before. What else unrecorded was waiting for him, uttered offhandedly by a man clearly *of* a place, not merely standing *in* it?

Once, in discussing the term *campo* with us, Enrique volunteered that in Spanish the expression *mi campo* can refer to one's professional pursuits or field of interest, as well as to a physical field or plot one might own. When we asked him about the origin of this metaphor, he characterized farming as the most basic of honorable professions and said it would be entirely natural to want to associate the dignity and essential importance of this kind of work with whatever you were doing as a professional person. Thus, he seemed to suggest, do myriad terms for the physical features of a place—the elementary, generic language a mayordomo might use to describe what he does with water and his shovel—evolve into expressions that make a human connection with a place comprehensible, deep, and elevating. The terms originate in an unquestioning belief that it is fitting for us to feel at home in a place. To feel that we belong.

Our intention is that *Home Ground* point the reader toward an emerging American literature about landscape and culture, and that it provide an impetus for the rediscovery of an extensive American language, used to establish and reaffirm intimacy with our home place.

THE EDITORS

To contribute landscape terms not defined in
Home Ground, *or to comment on the book's definitions,*
please go to www.ourhomeground.com.

INDEX OF TERMS

Words in SMALL CAPS are defined entries listed alphabetically in *Home Ground* and page numbers in *italics* indicate their location.

bottomland. *See* BOTTOM

boulder. *See* CHOCKSTONE;
   DOMER; ERRATIC

BOULDER GARDEN, *60*

BOULDER JAM, *60*

bowl. *See* CIRQUE

BOX CANYON, *60*

BRAIDED STREAM, *61–62*

BRAKE, *62*

branch. *See* FORK

brash ice. *See* FLOE

BRAZO, *63*

brazo muerto. *See* BRAZO

breadcrust bomb. *See* VOLCA-
   NIC BOMB

breaker terrace. *See* MARINE
   TERRACE

BREAKS, *63–64*

breakwater. *See* JETTY

BREATHING CAVE, *64*

BRECHA, *64–65*

BRIAR PATCH, *65*

BRIDAL VEIL FALL, *65–66*

bridge, natural. *See* NATURAL
   BRIDGE

BRINK, *66*

BROKEN GROUND, *66*

brooklet. *See* RUNNEL

brownfield. *See* BROWN LAND

BROWN LAND, *67*

BROWSE LINE, *67–68*

BRÛLÉ, xxiii, *68*

brushwood. *See* COPSE

BUCKBRUSH COULEE, *68–69*

BUFFALO JUMP, *69*

BULL PEN, *70*

bulrushes. *See* TULE

bummock. *See* PRESSURE ICE

BURIED SOIL, *70–71*

BURN, *71*

burnout soil. *See* GUMBO

BURN PILE, *71–72*

BURROW, *72–73*

BUTTE, *73*

BUTTRESS, *73–74*

C

CAIRN, *75*

calcareous sinter. *See* SINTER
   MOUND

CALDERA, *75–76*

caldera lake. *See* CRATER LAKE

caldero. *See* CALDERA

caliche. *See* HARDPAN

caliche flat, xx

CAMELBACK, *76*

campground. *See* GROUND;
   PARAJE

CAMPO, *76*

CAÑADA, *76–77*

CANAL, *77*

CANDLE ICE, *77–78*

canebrake. *See* BRAKE

cañón, xxv

cañoncito. *See* CAÑADA

canopy. *See* FOREST

CANYON, xix, xxii–xxv, *78*

CAPE, *78–79*

CAP ROCK, *79–80*

CAROLINA BAY, *80*

CASCADE, *80–81*

CASTLE ROCK, *81–82*

CATARACT, *82*

CATENA, *82–83*

CAT HOLE, *83–84*

cat line. *See* FIRE LINE

CATOCTIN, *84*

cat road. *See* DUGWAY

hard-bottom swamp. *See*
DRY-BOTTOM SWAMP
HARDPAN, *220–21*
HASSOCK, *221*
HAYSTACK, *221*
haystack wave. *See* STANDING
WAVE
head. *See* TOOTH
headgate, *503*
HEADLAND, *221–22*
HEADWALL, *222*
HEADWATERS, *222–23*
HEDGEROW, *223–24*
HEIGHTS, *224*
HELL, *225*
hiatus. *See* GORE
HIGH BANK, *225*
HIGH DESERT, *226*
HIGH PLAINS, *226–27*
HILL, XX, *227*. *See also* COLINA;
FELL FIELD; KNOLL
HILL COUNTRY, *227–28*
hillock. *See* KNOLL
hinterland. *See* BACKCOUNTRY;
BACKLAND
histic soil. *See* BOGHOLE
HOGBACK, *228*
hogback ridge, xxv
hognose scarp. *See* SCARP
hog wallow. *See* MIMA MOUND
HOLE, xxii, *228–29*. *See also*
CRANNY
HOLLOW, *229–30*. *See also*
DEFLATION HOLLOW; NIVA-
TION HOLLOW
HOMESTEAD, *230–31*
hommock. *See* HUMMOCK
HONDO, *231*
hondonada. *See* HONDO

HOODOO, *231–32*
HOOK, *232*
HORIZON, *232–33*
HORN, *233*
hornito. *See* SPATTER CONE
HORSEBACK, *233–34*
horseshoe bend. *See* BEND
horseshoe lake. *See* OXBOW
LAKE
hostile ice. *See* LEAD
hot deck. *See* COLD DECK
hot line. *See* FIRE LINE
HOT SPRING, *234*
HOURGLASS VALLEY, *234–35*
HUECO, *235–36*
HUÉRFANO, *236–37*
HUERTA, *237*
HUMMOCK, *237–38*. *See also*
HAMMOCK
humus. *See* TOPSOIL
HUNDREDTH MERIDIAN, *238*
hundred-year-flood plain. *See*
FLOOD PLAIN

I

ice. *See* ANCHOR ICE; CANDLE
ICE; DEAD ICE; FAST ICE;
FLOE; GLACIER; LEAD; MELT-
POND; NIVATION HOLLOW
ice blink. *See* PACK ICE
ice cake. *See* FLOE
ice crevasse. *See*
BERGSCHRUND
ICE DAM, *239*
ICEFALL, *239–40*
ice front. *See* FLAW LEAD
ice jam. *See* DEBACLE; ICE DAM
ice lens. *See* GROUND ICE
ice shelf. *See* FLAW LEAD

N

O

P

SWASH, *437*

swash channel. *See* GULCH

SWELL, *438*

SWIMMING HOLE, *438–39*

SWITCHBACK, *439*

synclinal ridge. *See* FOLD
    MOUNTAIN

syncline. *See* ARTESIAN BASIN;
    FOLD MOUNTAIN

T

TABLELAND, *441*. *See also*
    PLATEAU

TAIGA, *441–42*

TAILINGS PILE, *442*

TAILINGS POND, *442–43*

tailrace. *See* TAILWATER

TAILWATER, *443*

TAIL WAVE, *443*

TALLGRASS PRAIRIE, *443–44*

TALUS, *352–53*, *444*

talus glacier. *See* ROCK
    GLACIER

talweg. *See* THALWEG

TANK, XXVI, *444–45*

TAPESTRY WALL, *445–46*

TARN, XX, XXV, *446*

TEEPEE BUTTE, *447*

tejón. *See* HUÉRFANO

tension fault. *See* FAULT

tent ground. *See* GROUND

TERRACE, *447–48*. *See also*
    BENCH

terrace flight. *See* TERRACE

TERRACETTE, *448*

terrain vague, xxiii

THALWEG, *448–49*

THANK-YOU-MA'AM, *449*

THAW HOLE, *449–50*

thaw lake. *See* BEADED
    DRAINAGE

thermal spring. *See* HOT
    SPRING

thermokarst. *See* BEADED
    DRAINAGE

THICKET, *450*. *See also* CRIPPLE;
    SHINNERY

thrust fault. *See* FAULT

thumb. *See* TOOTH

thunder egg. *See* GEODE

TIDAL BORE, *450–51*

tidal flats, xxiii

tidal race. *See* RACE

tideflat. *See* TIDELAND

TIDELAND, *451*

TIDE POOL, *451–52*

tied island. *See* TOMBOLO

TILL, *452*

TILLAGE, *452–53*

till plain. *See* TILL

TIMBERLINE, *453*

timber stand. *See* STAND

tinaja. *See* CISTERN; KISS TANK

tip pit. *See* ROOT WAD

toe, xxv

TOE SLOPE, *453*

toma, *503*

TOMBOLO, *453–54*

tongue. *See* STANDING WAVE

TOOL MARK, *454–55*

TOOTH, *455*

TOPSOIL, *455*

TORNADO ALLEY, *456*

TOWER, *456–57*

tower karst. *See* HAYSTACK

TOWNSHIP AND RANGE, *457*

TRACE, *457–58*

tractor line. *See* FIRE LINE

INDEX OF NAMES

Names in **bold** indicate contributors to *Home Ground*. Page numbers in **bold** indicate pages on which their entries appear.

INDEX OF PLACES

THE WRITERS

JEFFERY RENARD ALLEN
An associate professor of English at Queens College of the City University of New York and an instructor in the MFA writing program at New School University, Jeffery Renard Allen is the author of *Harbors and Spirits,* a collection of poems. A second book of poems, *Stellar Places,* will be out in October 2006. His novel *Rails Under My Back* won the *Chicago Tribune*'s Heartland Prize for Fiction. Other prizes include a Whiting Writers Award and a John Farrar Fellowship in Fiction at Bread Loaf Writers' Conference. At present, he is at work on another novel.

KIM BARNES
Kim Barnes is the author of the novel *Finding Caruso* and two memoirs, *In the Wilderness: Coming of Age in Unknown Country,* winner of the PEN/Jerard Award and finalist for the 1997 Pulitzer Prize; and *Hungry for the World.* She is co-editor of *Circle of Women: An Anthology of Contemporary Western Women Writers* (with Mary Clearman Blew) and *Kiss Tomorrow Hello: Notes from the Midlife Underground by Twenty-Five Women over Forty* (with Claire Davis). She teaches at the University of Idaho and lives with the poet Robert Wrigley and their children on Moscow Mountain.

CONGER BEASLEY, JR.
Conger Beasley, Jr., has published two novels and three collections of short fiction. A nonfiction work, *We Are a People in This World: The Lakota Sioux and the Massacre at Wounded Knee,* won the Western Writers of America Spur Award for the best contemporary nonfiction book published in 1995. An earlier nonfiction work, *Sundancers and*

River Demons: Essays on Landscape and Ritual (1990), won the Thorpe Menn Award for the best book published by a Kansas City writer. In 1991 he was given the World Hunger Media Award for journalism for his three-part series "Of Pollution and Poverty" in the former *Buzzworm* magazine.

FRANKLIN BURROUGHS

Franklin Burroughs was born in Conway, South Carolina, and grew up there. In 1968, he took a job teaching at Bowdoin College, in Brunswick, Maine; upon completion of his thirty-third year of teaching, he promoted himself to the rank of professor emeritus. He is married and has three grown daughters. He and his wife continue to live in Maine. He has written a collection of essays, *Billy Watson's Croker Sack*, and *The River Home*, a book about Horry County and the Waccamaw River, in South Carolina. His essays have been published in a variety of quarterlies; two were reprinted in *Best American Essays*.

LAN SAMANTHA CHANG

Lan Samantha Chang was recently named director of the University of Iowa's Iowa Writers' Workshop. She is the first woman and first Asian American to head the preeminent writing program. Chang published her first story in the *Atlantic Monthly* at age twenty-eight and is the author of the novel *Inheritance* and the acclaimed fiction collection *Hunger*. Her work has been translated into nine languages.

MICHAEL COLLIER

Michael Collier is the author of five books of poems, *The Clasp and Other Poems, The Folded Heart, The Neighbor, The Ledge,* which was a finalist for the National Book Critics Circle Award and the Los Angeles Times Book Prize, and most recently *Dark Wild Realm*. He has received Guggenheim, National Endowment for the Arts, and Thomas Watson fellowships. Michael Collier has taught for many years at the University of Maryland. In 1994 he was appointed the sixth director of the Bread Loaf Writers' Conference and in 2001 poet laureate of Maryland.

ELIZABETH COX

Elizabeth Cox has completed three novels: *Familiar Ground, The Ragged Way People Fall Out of Love,* and *Night Talk.* She has also published a collection of short stories, *Bargains in the Real World.* One of these stories, "The Third of July," was chosen for the 1994 O. Henry Collection. Her next novel, *The Slow Moon,* is due out from Random House in fall 2006. She has taught creative writing at Duke University, MIT, Boston University, and Bennington College. She now shares the John Cobb Chair of Humanities with her husband at Wofford College in South Carolina.

JOHN DANIEL

John Daniel lives and writes in the Coast Range foothills west of Eugene, Oregon, and teaches regularly in writer-in-residence positions around the country. His most recent book is *Rogue River Journal: A Winter Alone*; others include *Looking After: A Son's Memoir, The Trail Home* (essays), *Common Ground* (poems), and *Winter Creek: One Writer's Natural History.* He has been the recipient of a Wallace Stegner Fellowship in Poetry at Stanford University, a grant from the National Endowment for the Arts, and two Oregon Book Awards in Literary Nonfiction.

JAN DEBLIEU

Jan DeBlieu is the author of four books and dozens of articles and essays about people and nature. Her first book, *Hatteras Journal* (1987), is considered a regional classic. *Meant to Be Wild* (1991) was followed by *Wind* (1998), which was awarded the John Burroughs Medal. In *Year of the Comets* (2005) she studies the unknown reaches of the universe and the inner cosmos of the human mind. Jan DeBlieu's writings explore the subtle ways we are shaped by the landscapes where we live and work.

WILLIAM DEBUYS
William deBuys is a writer, teacher, and conservationist based in Santa Fe, New Mexico. From 2001 through 2004 he served as chairman of the Valles Caldera Trust, which administers the 89,000-acre Valles Caldera National Preserve. He currently teaches in the Documentary Studies Program at the College of Santa Fe. His books include *The Walk*, *A Great Aridness*, *River of Traps*, *Salt Dreams*, and *Seeing Things Whole*.

GRETEL EHRLICH
Gretel Ehrlich is the author of *This Cold Heaven* and *The Solace of Open Spaces*, among other works of nonfiction, fiction, and poetry. Her most recent book is *The Future of Ice*. She divides her time between California and Wyoming.

CHARLES FRAZIER
Charles Frazier, American novelist, was born in 1950 in Asheville, North Carolina. His first novel, *Cold Mountain*, traces the journey of Inman, a deserter from the Confederate Army near the end of the Civil War. The novel won the 1997 National Book Award and was adapted as a film by Anthony Minghella. His new novel, *Thirteen Moons*, will be published in October 2006.

PAMELA FRIERSON
Pamela Frierson is the author of *The Burning Island: Myth and History in Volcano Country, Hawai'i*, *The Last Atoll: Exploring Hawai'i's Endangered Ecosystems*, and many articles and essays. Raised in Hawai'i, she lived for many years in the American West, was on the staff of the *Whole Earth Catalog*, and was one of the founding publishers of the innovative quarterly *Place Magazine*. She returned to the Islands fif-

teen years ago and now lives on the slopes of Mauna Kea Volcano, on Hawai'i Island, working as a freelance writer, photographer, and educator.

PATRICIA HAMPL

Patricia Hampl's latest book is *I Could Tell You Stories*. A recipient of the MacArthur Foundation Fellowship, she is Regents Professor at the University of Minnesota and is on the permanent faculty of the Prague Summer Program. A new nonfiction book, *Blue Arabesque: In Search of the Sublime*, is forthcoming in 2006, and a memoir, *The Florist's Daughter*, in 2007. She lives in Saint Paul, her hometown.

ROBERT HASS

Robert Hass's first book, *Field Guide*, won the Yale Series of Younger Poets Award in 1973. Three more collections followed: *Praise* (1979), *Human Wishes* (1989), and *Sun Under Wood* (1996), which won the National Book Critics Circle Award for Poetry. Hass served as poet laureate of the United States from 1995 to 1997 and is currently a chancellor in the Academy of American Poets. He won the National Book Critics Circle Award for Criticism for *Twentieth-Century Pleasures: Prose on Poetry* (1984). He collaborated for years with Nobel Prize–winning Polish poet Czeslaw Milosz to bring his major works into English. Hass is a professor at the University of California at Berkeley.

EMILY HIESTAND

Emily Hiestand is a writer and visual artist. Her books include *The Very Rich Hours: Travels in Orkney, Belize, the Everglades, and Greece*; *Angela the Upside-Down Girl*, true stories about identity and place; and *Green the Witch Hazel Wood*. Her writing has appeared in the *Atlantic Monthly*, the *Georgia Review*, the *New Yorker*, *The Nation*, and *Salon*, and in *Best American Poetry* and many other anthologies. Her awards include the Whiting Award, the Pushcart Prize, the National Poetry Series Award, and the National Magazine Award. She is married to the musician and writer Peter Niels Dunn.

LINDA HOGAN

Linda Hogan is a Chickasaw writer. She is the author of many books, including *Dwellings: A Spiritual History of the Natural World*; *Power*; *Mean Spirit*, finalist for a Pulitzer Prize; and New York Times Notable Book *Solar Storms*. *The Book of Medicines* was a finalist for the National Book Critics Circle Award for Poetry. Her most recent books are *The Woman Who Watches Over the World: A Native Memoir* and *Sightings: The Mysterious Journey of the Gray Whale*. Hogan has received a National Endowment for the Arts grant, a Guggenheim Fellowship, a Lannan Foundation award, and the Five Civilized Tribes Museum playwriting award, and in 1998 she received the Lifetime Achievement Award from the Native Writers Circle of the Americas.

STEPHEN GRAHAM JONES

Stephen Graham Jones is the author of *The Fast Red Road*, *All the Beautiful Sinners*, *The Bird Is Gone*, and *Bleed into Me: A Book of Stories*. His newest novel, *Demon Theory*, was published in spring 2006 by MacAdam/Cage.

JOHN KEEBLE

John Keeble is the author of four novels, including *Yellowfish* and *Broken Ground*, and a work of nonfiction, *Out of the Channel: The Exxon Valdez Oil Spill in Prince William Sound*. A collection of stories, *Nocturnal America*, is forthcoming from the University of Nebraska Press. His works have appeared in such periodicals as *Outside*, the *Village Voice*, *American Short Fiction*, *Zyzzyva*, the *Idaho Review*, and *Best American Short Stories*. He has held a Guggenheim Fellowship and has been a longstanding member of the MFA faculty at Eastern Washington University, where he is now professor emeritus. He has also served as the Distinguished Visiting Chair in Creative Writing at the University of Alabama.

BARBARA KINGSOLVER

Barbara Kingsolver's eleven books include novels, essay collections, short stories, poetry, an oral history, and most recently *Last Stand: America's Virgin Lands*. In 2000, Kingsolver received the National Humanities Medal, our nation's highest award for service through the arts. Kingsolver grew up in Kentucky but has lived and worked in many parts of the world. She received degrees in biology before becoming a full-time writer. With her husband, Steven Hopp, an ornithologist and guitarist, she co-writes articles on science and natural history, and performs in a jazz band. Barbara, Steven, and their two daughters grow most of their own food on a farm in southern Appalachia.

WILLIAM KITTREDGE

William Kittredge is the author of many books, as well as editor of *The Last Best Place* and *The Portable Western Reader*, anthologies of western literature. He was an associate producer of the film *A River Runs Through It*, and his magazine writing has appeared in *Harper's*, *Outside*, the *Atlantic*, and the *Paris Review*. In 1994 he won the Charles Frankel Prize, awarded by the National Endowment for the Humanities to citizens who through their scholarship, writing, and leadership have enriched the nation.

JON KRAKAUER

Jon Krakauer grew up in Corvallis, Oregon, where his father introduced him to mountaineering as an eight-year-old. The author of *Under the Banner of Heaven, Into Thin Air, Into the Wild*, and *Eiger Dreams*, he has earned a National Magazine Award, the American Geophysical Union's Walter Sullivan Award for Excellence in Science

Journalism, and an Academy Award in Literature from the American Academy of Arts and Letters. In 1998, Krakauer was one of three finalists for the Pulitzer Prize in general nonfiction. He lives in Colorado.

GRETCHEN LEGLER

Gretchen Legler is an associate professor in the Program in Creative Writing at the University of Maine at Farmington, specializing in nonfiction. Pieces from her first collection, *All the Powerful Invisible Things: A Sportswoman's Notebook* (1995), won two Pushcart Prizes and have been widely excerpted and anthologized. Her scholarly work on nature writing has appeared in numerous journals and anthologies. Her second book of nonfiction, *On the Ice: An Intimate Look at Life in McMurdo Station and Antarctica*, was recently published by Milkweed Editions.

ARTURO LONGORIA

Arturo Longoria lives in south Texas. He is the father of four sons. The eldest is a saxophonist in "The President's Own" in Washington, D.C.; the second eldest is a physician in Dallas; and the two youngest are in high school and middle school, and keep the old man entertained with their guitar playing and companionship. In other secondary accomplishments, Longoria has worked as a journalist and taught at the university level. He is the author of *Adios to the Brushlands* and *Keepers of the Wilderness*, both from Texas A&M University Press.

BILL MCKIBBEN

Bill McKibben is a former staff writer for the *New Yorker*. His books include *Hundred Dollar Holiday, Maybe One, The End of Nature, The Age of Missing Information,* and *Hope, Human and Wild*. McKibben is a frequent contributor to a wide variety of publications, including *Harper's,* the *Atlantic,* the *New York Review of Books, Outside,* and the *New York*

Times. McKibben lives with his wife and daughter in the mountains on either side of Lake Champlain, a territory he describes in his most recent book, *Wandering Home: A Long Walk through America's Most Hopeful Landscape.*

ELLEN MELOY

Ellen Meloy's *The Anthropology of Turquoise* was one of two finalists for the Pulitzer Prize in general nonfiction, a Los Angeles Times Book of the Year, and winner of the Utah Book Award and Banff Mountain Book Award. She is also the author of *The Last Cheater's Waltz* and the recipient of a Whiting Writers Award. *Raven's Exile,* her account of living on Utah's Green River, won the admiration of readers and river lovers everywhere. Meloy, who died suddenly in 2004, lived in southern Utah.

ROBERT MORGAN

Born in Hendersonville, North Carolina, in 1944, Robert Morgan grew up on a farm in the Blue Ridge Mountains. He began writing at North Carolina State University and later graduated from the University of North Carolina at Chapel Hill. He has published eleven books of poetry, most recently *The Strange Attractor: New and Selected Poems* (2004). He is also the author of three books of short fiction and five novels, including *Gap Creek* (1999), a *New York Times* best-seller, and *Brave Enemies: A Novel of the American Revolution* (2003). Since 1971 he has taught at Cornell University and has served as a visiting writer at Davidson College and Appalachian State, Furman, and Duke Universities.

SUSAN BRIND MORROW

Susan Brind Morrow, a 2006 Guggenheim Fellow, is the author of *The Names of Things: A Passage in the Egyptian Desert* and *Wolves and Honey: A Hidden History of the Natural World.* A naturalist, classicist, linguist, and poet, she is a lifelong resident of New York State.

ANTONYA NELSON

Antonya Nelson is the author of eight books of fiction, the most recent being a collection of stories, *Some Fun* (2006). She teaches at the University of Houston and in the Warren Wilson MFA Program, and lives in New Mexico, Colorado, and Texas.

ROBERT MICHAEL PYLE

Robert Michael Pyle is the author of fifteen books, including *Wintergreen*, winner of the John Burroughs Medal; *Where Bigfoot Walks*, which he researched while on a Guggenheim Fellowship; *The Thunder Tree*; and *The Butterflies of Cascadia*. He is also co-editor of *Nabokov's Butterflies*. His column "The Tangled Bank" appears in each issue of *Orion* magazine. Pyle has a Ph.D. in ecogeography from Yale University and lives along a tributary of the Lower Columbia River.

PATTIANN ROGERS

Pattiann Rogers has published numerous books, most recently *The Grand Array, Firekeeper: Selected Poems*, revised and expanded edition, and *Generations*. Rogers is the recipient of a Lannan Literary Award in Poetry, a Lannan Literary Fellowship, two National Endowment for the Arts Grants, and a Guggenheim Fellowship. Her poems have won three prizes from *Poetry*, two from *Prairie Schooner*, and five Pushcart Prizes, among other awards. Her papers are archived in the Sowell Collection at Texas Tech University. She is the mother of two sons, has three grandsons, and lives with her husband, a retired geophysicist, in Colorado.

SCOTT RUSSELL SANDERS

Born in 1945, Scott Russell Sanders is the author of nineteen books, including *Staying Put, Hunting for Hope*, and *A Private History of Awe*. For his work in nonfiction, he has won the Lannan Literary Award and the John Burroughs Essay Award. In all of his books he is concerned with our place in nature, the pursuit of social justice, and the search for a spiritual path. He is Distinguished Professor of English at Indiana University. He and his wife, Ruth, a biochemist, have reared two children in their hometown of Bloomington, in the hardwood hill country of the White River Valley.

EVA SAULITIS

Eva Saulitis is a writer, teacher, and marine biologist. She grew up on the southern tier of New York, on Lake Erie, but migrated to Alaska in 1986. She received her M.S. and M.F.A. from the University of Alaska, Fairbanks. For eighteen years, she has studied the behavior of killer whales in southern Alaska and has written and co-authored many scientific publications. Her poems and essays have been appeared in *Quarterly West*, *Alaska Quarterly Review*, *Ice-Floe*, *Prairie Schooner*, *Northwest Review*, *Connotations*, *Cimarron Review*, *Seattle Review*, *Crazyhorse*, and various anthologies. She lives in Homer, Alaska.

DONNA SEAMAN

Donna Seaman, an associate editor at *Booklist*, has recently compiled *Writers on the Air: Conversations about Books*, a collection of her author interviews. She is editor of the anthology *In Our Nature: Stories of Wildness* and host of the radio program *Open Books* on WLUW in Chicago; she regularly contributes reviews and essays to the *Chicago Tribune*, *Tri-Quarterly*, *Speakeasy*, and the *Atlanta Journal-Constitution*, and has written for *American Writers* and the *Oxford Encyclopedia of American Literature*. Seaman has received several Pushcart Prize Special Mentions, grants from the Illinois Arts Council, the James Friend Memorial Award for Literary Criticism, and the Writer Magazine Writers Who Make a Difference Award.

CAROLYN SERVID

Carolyn Servid is the author of the essay collection *Of Landscape and Longing*, a personal reflection on land, home, and community set in Sitka, Alaska, where she lives. She and her husband, Dorik Mechau, are co-directors of the Island Institute, an organization dedicated to fostering creative, collaborative thinking about vital communities—the web of human relationships and our connections to the greater natural world. She edited the award-winning anthology *From the Island's Edge: A Sitka Reader* and co-edited *The Book of the Tongass* and *Arctic Refuge: A Circle of Testimony*.

KIM STAFFORD

Kim Stafford is the founding director of the Northwest Writing Institute and the William Stafford Center at Lewis & Clark College. His recent books include *100 Tricks Every Boy Can Do, The Muses Among Us: Eloquent Listening and Other Pleasures of the Writer's Craft*, and *A Thousand Friends of Rain*. He considers the Columbia River watershed his home ground, and he lives in Portland, Oregon, with his wife and children.

MARY SWANDER

Mary Swander's latest book is a memoir, *The Desert Pilgrim: En Route to Mysticism and Miracles* (2004). She is a Distinguished Professor of Liberal Arts and Sciences at Iowa State University.

ARTHUR SZE

Arthur Sze is the editor of *Chinese Writers on Writing* and the author of numerous books of poetry, including *Quipu, The Redshifting Web: Poems 1970–1998*, and *The Silk Dragon: Translations from the Chinese*. He is the recipient of a Lannan Literary Award for Poetry, two National Endowment for the Arts Fellowships, a Guggenheim Fellowship, and an American Book Award. He has lived in Santa Fe, New Mexico, for over thirty years and is a professor emeritus at the Institute of American Indian Arts.

MIKE TIDWELL

Mike Tidwell is the author of five books, including *Bayou Farewell*, *In the Mountains of Heaven*, and *Amazon Stranger*. His work has appeared in *National Geographic Traveler*, *Reader's Digest*, and the *Washington Post*. He is the recipient of an National Endowment for the Arts Fellowship and two Lowell Thomas Awards for travel journalism. He was born in Tennessee, raised in Georgia, and now lives in the Washington, D.C., area.

LUIS ALBERTO URREA

Luis Alberto Urrea, a poet and a writer of fiction and nonfiction, was born in Tijuana, Mexico, in 1955 and grew up in San Diego. His nonfiction book *The Devil's Highway* was a finalist for the Pulitzer Prize, and *Across the Wire* was a New York Times Notable Book in 1993. The son of an Anglo-American mother and a Mexican father, he says: "Home isn't just a place, it is also a language."

LUIS VERANO

Luis Verano has been a faculty member in the Department of Romance Languages at the University of Oregon since 1971. His specialty is Spanish Golden Age literature, with a particular interest in Cervantes. He also teaches courses in Peninsular and Latin American poetry, advanced Spanish language, and pedagogy. He is the recipient of six teaching excellence awards, and his teaching interests have led to the publication of language texts, video programs, and many ancillary materials.

D. J. WALDIE

D.J. Waldie is the author *of Holy Land: A Suburban Memoir* and *Where We Are Now: Notes from Los Angeles.* He is a contributing writer at *Los Angeles* magazine.

JOY WILLIAMS

Joy Williams is the author of four novels (the most recent, *The Quick and the Dead*, was a finalist for the Pulitzer Prize in 2001), three collections of stories, and a book of essays, *Ill Nature*, which was a finalist for the National Book Critics Circle Award for Criticism. Among her many honors are the Rea Award for the Short Story and the Strauss Living Award from the American Academy of Arts and Letters. She lives in Key West, Florida, and Tucson, Arizona.

TERRY TEMPEST WILLIAMS

Terry Tempest Williams is known for her passionate voice regarding the wildlands of the American West and issues of social justice ranging from nuclear testing to women's health. She is a strong advocate for free speech and has been included in the artist Robert Shetterly's book of portraits, *Americans Who Tell the Truth.* Her books include *Refuge: An Unnatural History of Family and Place, An Unspoken Hunger: Stories from the Field, Leap, Red: Passion and Patience in the Desert,* and most recently *The Open Space of Democracy.* Williams is the recipient of a Lannan Literary Fellowship and a Guggenheim Fellowship in creative nonfiction. In 2005, she received the Wallace Stegner Award from the Center of the American West.

LARRY WOIWODE

Larry Woiwode's books include *What I'm Going to Do, I Think*; *Beyond the Bedroom Wall*; *Indian Affairs*; *Silent Passengers*; and the memoir *What I Think I Did.* He is a Guggenheim and Lannan Fellow, and his short fiction has been collected in four volumes of *Best American Short Stories.* He has received the Aga Khan Prize, the William Faulkner Foundation Award, the John Dos Passos Prize, and the Award of Merit Medal for "Distinction in the Art of the Short Story" from the National Institute of Arts and Letters, among other awards, and in 1995 he was named poet laureate of North Dakota. He has lived in southwestern North Dakota for twenty-seven years, where, with his wife, Carole, and their family, he raises registered quarter horses.

ABOUT THE EDITORS

BARRY LOPEZ
Upper McKenzie River, Oregon Cascades

Barry Lopez is the author of *Resistance, About This Life, Light Action in the Caribbean, Arctic Dreams,* for which he received the National Book Award, and nine other works of fiction and nonfiction. He has written for a wide range of magazines, including *Harper's, Granta,* the *Paris Review,* the *Georgia Review, National Geographic,* and *Outside,* and is a recipient of fellowships from the Guggenheim, Lannan, and National Science Foundations. For more information, please go to www.barrylopez.com.

DEBRA GWARTNEY
Salmon, Idaho

Debra Gwartney is the author of the memoir *Live Through This,* a finalist for the 2009 National Book Critics Circle Award and the Pacific Northwest Booksellers Award. Her work has appeared in the *American Scholar,* the *Kenyon Review, Prairie Schooner, TriQuarterly,* and *Salon,* and she has received fellowships from the Helene Wurlitzer Foundation, Hedgebrook, the Ucross Foundation, and the Oregon Arts Commission. She teaches in the low-residency MFA writing program at Pacific University in Oregon.

Designed and Typeset by
BookMatters, Berkeley

Cover design by Rebecca Lown

Typeset in 10/13 Janson with
Cheltenham and Buillion display